# *Skiing*
# COLORADO'S
# BACKCOUNTRY

I know no form of sport which so evenly develops the muscles, which renders the body so strong and elastic, which teaches so well the qualities of dexterity and resource, which in an equal degree calls for decision and resolution, and which gives the same vigor and exhilaration to mind and body alike. Where can one find a healthier and purer delight than on a brilliant winter day when one binds one's "ski" to one's feet and takes one's way out into the forest? Can there be anything more beautiful than the northern winter landscape when the snow lies foot-deep, spread as a soft white mantel over field and wood and hill?

Where will one find more freedom and excitement than when one glides swiftly down the hillside through the trees, one's cheek brushed by the sharp cold air and frosted pine branches, and one's eye, brain and muscles alert and prepared to meet every unknown obstacle and danger which the next instant may throw in one's path? Civilization is, as it were, washed clean from the mind and left far behind with the city atmosphere and city life; one's whole being is, so to speak, wrapped in one's "ski" and the surrounding nature.

*The First Crossing of Greenland, 1892*
Fridtjof Nansen

# *Skiing* COLORADO'S BACKCOUNTRY

## *Northern Mountains – Trails & Tours*

# Brian Litz & Kurt Lankford

FULCRUM, INC.
GOLDEN, COLORADO
1989

Copyright © 1989 Brian Litz and Kurt Lankford

Book Design by Chris Bierwirth

Cover Photograph by Brian Litz

Interior Photographs by Brian Litz and Kurt Lankford

Maps by Kurt Lankford and Karla Lankford

All Rights Reserved.

Library of Congress Cataloging-in-Publication Data

Litz, Brian, 1961–
     Skiing Colorado's backcountry : northern mountains, trails and
tours / Brian Litz, Kurt Lankford.
          p.     cm.
     Bibliography: p.
     ISBN 1-55591-044-0
     1. Cross-country skiing--Colorado--Guide-books. 2. Colorado-
-Description and travel--1981– --Guide-books. I. Lankford, Kurt,
1959–     . II. Title.
GV854.5.C6L58     1989                                        89-33451
796.93'2'09788--dc20                                              CIP

Printed in the United States

10  9  8  7  6  5  4  3  2  1

Fulcrum, Inc.
Golden, Colorado

# CONTENTS

# FOREWORD

## RICHARD D. LAMM
### FORMER GOVERNOR OF COLORADO

I came to Colorado not to be a politician but to be a skier. The outdoors is my recreation, my church, my psychiatrist, my doctor, my teacher. What can compare to a cross-country skiing trip to the quiet, magnificent backcountry cathedrals of Colorado?

But one must know where to go and how to be safe. *Skiing Colorado's Backcountry* is thus a ticket to unimagined adventures. It offers the practical and useful information of where to go and how to get home safely. This is a book that offers a lifetime of pleasure. It will likely be handed down, well worn, to your heirs.

# ACKNOWLEDGMENTS

Many people contributed their valuable time, knowledge and creative ideas to make this book a reality. The authors would specifically like to thank the following: Ken Morr and Judith Goater, without whom the project would never have gotten off the ground; Karla Caldwell, who helped extensively with preparation of the maps along with Ken Morr; Betsy and Richard Armstrong, who applied their valuable knowledge and expertise to the tasks of writing the avalanche section and recommending a format for the avalanche rating; Betsy also spent countless hours coordinating the many details that go along with publication; Gary Neptune and Dick Dumais, who supplied valuable advice; Jeff Cobb, for his computer advice and help; John Fielder, for his general support and advice; Patricia Scott, who donated the use of her computer and helped edit several chapters of the first draft; Doug Freed, Karla Caldwell, Polly Lankford, Alice Scott, Pat Fortino, Debra Taylor, Joe Burleson, Melissa Bronson and Laura Caruso, who edited sections of the first draft; and all of the people at Fulcrum Publishing.

We would also like to thank the following equipment manufacturers for their support: Lowe Alpine Systems/Lowe-Pro, Patagonia, North Face and Chouinard Equipment.

There are many others who offered advice and encouragement. We are grateful to all.

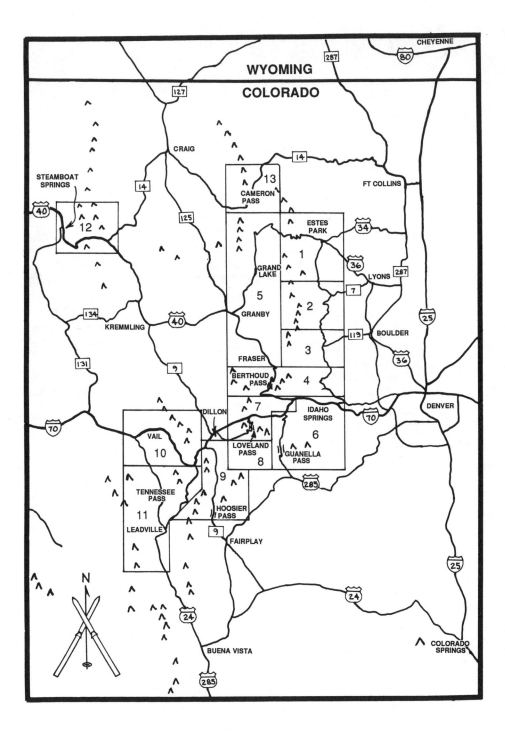

# INTRODUCTION

Each winter, in increasing numbers, outdoor sports enthusiasts take to Colorado's backcountry in search of recreation, exercise and solitude. Equipped with skis and a taste for adventure, backcountry skiers can explore the Rocky Mountains in a manner that few experience. The mountains, devoid of the massive summer crowds, take on an almost mystical quality. Jagged peaks seem higher and more precipitous, forests pristine, winds brisk. Few states rival Colorado in alpine diversity and sheer magnitude of wilderness environment.

In an area roughly bounded by Vail and Steamboat Springs to the west and the Front Range to the east is an unequalled mountain paradise lying in close proximity to major metropolitan areas. The rugged topography of Rocky Mountain National Park and the Indian Peaks, the history-packed Front Range and Clear Creek Mountains and the superb snows of the Tenmile and Southern Gore ranges form a spine of skiable terrain within two hours of Denver. Countless peaks towering into the rarefied air above 13,000 and 14,000 feet, long valleys choked with thick spruce and pine forests, beautiful alpine lakes laid silent by thick blankets of snow and ice await your silent passage.

Blending uniquely with the wilderness is Colorado's colorful history. The Centennial State's past has flavored the landscape with a seasoning of cantankerous men, flamboyant women and legendary tales of the near-Herculean efforts needed to settle the high alpine valleys and extract silver and gold from the very heart of the Rockies. The miners were the state's earliest skiers, strapping eight-foot-long strips of wood to their feet to travel to such settlements as Breckenridge and Georgetown to enjoy a Saturday night far from their Spartan existences in isolated mining camps. Many of the tours in *Skiing Colorado's Backcountry* follow the roads and trails to these historic tunnels, cabins and mining structures. One of the state's most famous men-of-the-cloth was Father Dyer, who traveled on skis to spread inspiration to the mountain inhabitants, many of whom were in need of a little salvation after a raucous night in the saloons. During the winters of the 1800s, ski travel was the primary method of mail delivery to the majority of tiny hamlets sprinkled throughout the Front Range.

In the 20th century all forms of skiing matured into actively pursued sports. Many individuals, however, yearn for the unrestricted freedom inherent in backcountry skiing. With a pair of skis, boots, poles, warm clothing and a healthy respect for the winter environment, you can escape into the soul-enriching experience of backcountry skiing. Those who leave the downhill ski areas and groomed trails to follow a map and compass rarely regret their decision, returning from their outings glowing with excitement, dreaming about their next adventure. Backcountry skiing is a varied sport possessing a wealth of challenge and reward. Lunch on a windswept mountain summit under blue Colorado skies, telemarking through powder-filled glades, exciting 2,000-foot descents on flawless spring snow, a game of Hearts with friends in a small mountain hut—all are experiences we will never forget, that draw us to return season after season.

This book provides a source of information for all aspects of backcountry skiing, from enjoyable romps along twisting trails to spring ski-mountaineering trips. Skiers of all abilities will find a vast selection of the finest tours in the northern mountains. Difficulty ranges from classic novice tours to spring mountaineering routes, the latter as classic as they are thrilling. The upper limit of difficulty was set by the rule that skiers would not need technical mountaineering gear to ski a route. In fact, every route in this guide was skied on standard metal-edged touring or telemark skis and boots. On a very small selection of routes, such as the northern gully of Torreys Peak, individuals may opt for alpine touring or downhill equipment to maintain that extra margin of safety. Each tour is rated for avalanche terrain encountered. Avalanche hazard assessment is the responsibility of the individual. We encourage conservative and careful decision-making. Many tours offer variations on the route, which provide excellent opportunities to tackle challenging backcountry downhill runs and powder skiing (which just happens to be one of our favorite pursuits).

This book was written by two friends whose lives have been enriched by the days spent skiing in the Rocky Mountains, deriving an appreciation for Colorado's environment. *Skiing Colorado's Backcountry* will help you enjoy and learn more about Colorado's northern mountains and the sport of backcountry skiing.

Good skiing. See you in the powder!

# HOW TO USE THIS GUIDE

This book will help you in your backcountry ski experience—not define it. From day to day, season to season, backcountry skiing conditions can be highly variable. The descriptions that follow are averages based on reasonably expected conditions. It is impossible to experience each tour under every possible combination of snow and weather conditions. Colorado winters are graced with many days of fine weather. Major storms rarely last more than a few days. However, within the span of a few hours the local environment where you are skiing can change dramatically. Consequently, you should approach the backcountry with respect and prudence, and expect the unexpected. Beginning skiers should seek out seasoned partners or ski clubs to help them gain experience in a safe and progressive manner; advanced skiers should leave their egos at home and choose less severe routes when avalanche danger is high, when a major storm is approaching or when they are paired with less experienced folks.

Each route description is broken down into three parts. First, a heading summarizes the most critical information concerning a tour's overall nature. This allows quick analysis as to whether a tour is appropriate for your party on that particular day. Second, a narrative section describes in detail the method of access, character of the trip and any special notes or safety tips. The third feature is a series of annotated maps which delineate the route on USGS topographic quadrangles. Additional trip notes are included on these maps. *Skiing Colorado's Backcountry* was designed to be used in conjunction with USGS 7.5 minute maps. It is essential that you have a basic understanding of these extremely useful tools. The ability to orient yourself with a map and compass is mandatory for safe backcountry travel. Within the narrative, prominent map features are mentioned (e.g., Point 12,251); these refer to elevation in feet.

The tours are grouped into chapters based upon geographic location; for example, Berthoud Pass. Each chapter begins with an introduction to the area: access, local weather peculiarities and brief history. Overview maps supplement these chapters and help give a feel for the regional topography, including peaks, towns, roads and tours.

Finally, the appendixes summarize the information in this book: a breakdown of tours based on difficulty, equipment list, emergency information, nonemergency information with important telephone numbers (avalanche information, road information, ski conditions, forest service information, hut and association information) and cross-country skiing centers.

The following describes the nomenclature used in the headings that preface each tour. Most are based upon terminology commonly used in ski touring guides but exact definitions may vary slightly.

## DESCRIPTION

This describes the season, whether a tour is commonly skied during the winter or spring and brief comments on length and other features. In general a winter tour can be skiable from early November to late spring, depending on such factors as elevation and exposure (north or south, etc.). Spring descents generally lie above treeline on steep slopes that are exposed to extreme weather conditions in winter. These slopes are often dangerous, if not impossible, to ski in winter. During spring, when the snowpack consolidates, the more sheltered slopes and gullies offer enjoyable skiing on soft, forgiving corn snow. Additionally, the description gives a brief taste of the route, including, for example, whether the tour follows easy roads or encounters difficult off-trail bushwhacking, whether it leads to a hut or high-country telemark area and how physically demanding the tour is if completed (e.g., gently graded or very steep, a short or long tour). Considering such factors as elevation gain and distance is extremely important in deciding whether a route is a safe choice for your day's objective. Finally, some tours end at a destination that is different from the starting point, hence a car shuttle will be required. This information is also listed.

## SKILL LEVEL

The skill level of a tour indicates the overall level of technical skiing ability and conditioning required to complete a tour in reasonable time without pushing yourself to extremes.

*Novice* tours may be skied by those with minimal skiing experience who understand the basics of double-poling, kick and glide and the simple snowplow.

*Intermediate* tours are aimed at skiers who have completed, for example, 10 to 15 novice tours and who desire greater distances and more challenging terrain. These individuals generally have not completely mastered the telemark turn and other techniques required for steeper off-trail skiing, but should be able to control their speed while tackling moderate off-trail terrain.

*Advanced* tours either are long enough to require most of a day to complete or, if shorter, demand strenuous technical skiing in varied conditions. Skiers who tackle these routes should have several seasons of experience. The few advanced "plus" routes in this guide require a mastery of downhill techniques such as the telemark and parallel turns. These routes are steep and temperamental but easily managed by those comfortable skiing at this level. Many of the advanced tours are not listed under the winter ski tour classification because these routes often lack adequate snow-cover or are winter avalanche paths that only become safe with spring consolidation. No spring descents carry a novice classification because all of these tours involve steep downhill runs at high elevations. Several spring routes are quite moderate, however, and are fine introductions to spring telemark touring. Always keep in mind that changing environmental conditions can greatly alter the difficulty of a tour.

## TIME

This is a relative indication of the time required to ski a route from start to finish. This does not include travel time to and from the trailhead. The time it takes to ski a route varies considerably with snow and weather conditions, fitness of the group and even type and weight of gear. Therefore, instead of strict hourly time estimates, each tour has been placed into one of four basic categories: *Quarter days* refers to very short tours that take two hours or less to complete (Loveland Pass north face, tour 85). *Half-day* trips require two to four hours to complete (Sally Barber Mine, tour 99 or Left Hand Reservoir, tour 30). *Full-day* ski tours normally require four to seven hours or more to complete (Shrine Pass, tour 127). *Possible overnight* indicates that the tour takes more than seven hours to complete and slower groups might consider carrying camping gear (Commando Run, tour 128 or the Skyline Traverse, tour 51). The times do take into account a conservative (leisurely, but efficient) pace with a half- to full-hour lunch (if full day) and several photo/refreshment stops of usually 5 to 15 minutes. One would expect advanced skiers to cover stated mileages more quickly. Hence novice tour times are weighted for newer and possibly slower parties to allow for an enjoyable outing. Again, these times are approximations. Know your ability and endurance level and take into account your past performances when planning a route.

## DISTANCE

Tour distances are figured by measuring the line of the tour on a USGS 7.5

minute map. Distances are listed as round-trip mileage in the tour headings. The tours that travel in one direction only (i.e., loops and tours ending at a different point than their beginning) give mileage measured in one-way distances.

## ELEVATION CHANGE

This is a measure of the cumulative elevation gain in a tour and can be one of the most important factors to consider when choosing a ski tour. A short trip can pack in a lot of climbing, making for a very strenuous outing. Elevation gain is calculated on USGS 7.5 minute series maps, where contour intervals are equal to 40 feet. If a tour ends *between* contour intervals or climbs above one contour without reaching the next higher line, this intracontour distance is calculated as one-half a contour interval or 20 feet. In many cases tours begin and end at features bearing specific elevations printed directly on the map (e.g., lakes, mountain summits, benchmarks). These elevations are used in arriving at total *elevation gain*. Of special note are the few tours that are descents from start to finish and will have a cumulative elevation loss figure.

## STARTING ELEVATION

This is the elevation at the point of departure for a tour. *Starting elevation* is used as opposed to *highest*, because while a party's final destination may vary, all tour variations begin at a common point. The highest elevation attained on a tour is a cogent measure of overall difficulty and is an important indicator of the environmental conditions that may be encountered: This statistic is easily calculated by adding accumulated elevation gain to the starting elevation.

## AVALANCHE TERRAIN

Avalanche conditions change continuously; hence in an effort to aid skiers in understanding the potential hazards of each tour, we have included a brief categorization of the terrain through which the intended trail travels. The terminology is self-explanatory and should be used in conjunction with the most recent Colorado avalanche hazard forecast to determine which routes are the safest for those particular days. The following avalanche terrain classifications are used throughout the book.

1. None
2. Some avalanche terrain encountered; easily avoided
3. Route crosses avalanche runout zones; can be dangerous during high-hazard periods
4. Route crosses avalanche slopes; prone to skier-triggered avalanches during high-hazard periods
5. Mostly avalanche terrain; wait for spring consolidation

Both categories 4 and 5 assume the knowledge, experience and ability to assess slope stability. This ability is essential before traveling these routes.

Spring ski descents should be skied only after the snow above treeline has consolidated and metamorphosed into stable spring "corn." This does not occur until at least late April—with best and safest conditions usually in late May and early June. It is dangerous to ski the steeper of these slopes during or after a snowfall, even during spring.

## USGS 7.5 MINUTE MAPS

This is a listing of the USGS 7.5 minute maps (including their most recent date of publication) necessary to complete a tour, given in order of use. Publication dates are important because many maps are out-of-date and in need of revision, so expect a few contradictions between the maps and reality. We have tried to make note of any critical inaccuracies or changes on these maps in the written tour descriptions. Fortunately, many of the maps covering northern Colorado have undergone photo-reinspection in recent years, which has highlighted the many changes that have altered the landscape (small changes such as I-70!). Paying careful attention to these dates and changes (especially for trailheads!) will save a great deal of time and confusion.

## MAP

This lists the page number of the annotated map for that particular tour. Some tours cross several of the book's maps; their page numbers are listed in sequence of usage.

## HIGHLIGHTS

These point out portions of tours that will be of special interest to novice, intermediate or advanced skiers. As an example, some advanced tours begin on gentle terrain that would provide enjoyable skiing for less proficient skiers. They are indicated in the skill-level heading with an asterisk. The description of the highlight precedes the narrative. Highlights are also used to call attention to slopes or areas that provide good backcountry telemark skiing but that are off the main route.

We have tried to avoid creating a ski-by-the-numbers tour guide, which eliminates any sense of adventure, trying instead to provide a useful information source. Remember that Colorado's mountains are a dynamic and often hazardous arena that rarely concedes a second chance. The opportunity to test yourself both mentally and physically in this complex environment is the unique essence of backcountry skiing. You must combine your experience, common sense and knowledge of backcountry survival, weather and snow dynamics to make wise decisions as to whether a trip should be attempted or left for another day. This book provides the fundamental information about the tours. The final decisions are left to you.

# EQUIPMENT

Backcountry ski equipment has evolved significantly in the past 10 years. In the past, the standard setup for ski touring was a pair of wooden skis, bamboo poles and leather low-cut ski boots. This combination worked fine for most skiing situations. Then in the mid-1970s came the marriage of downhill ski technology with traditional backcountry philosophy. The first "synthetic" touring skis were hybrids, wooden-cored skis sheathed in brightly colored, durable plastic. Soon, however, the entire touring ski was redesigned. Complex structures of blown foam and wood/metal laminates encased by high-visibility graphics began to replace the simpler wooden skis. The elimination of secondary camber and the addition of true offset metal edges with severe tip-to-tail sidecut made an incredible improvement in ski performance. While some resisted the inevitable, most backcountry advocates embraced the new gear with zeal. The days of pine tar and lignestone edges came to an end. The changes ushered in by this new application of technology had wide-ranging impact. Cross-country skis became lighter and stronger, allowing for greater confidence and personal performance. Whether on the untracked powder fields or the racing circuit (both telemark and track racing), no one could deny the vastly superior performances achieved by switching to modern gear. Improved ski design quickly demanded a rethinking of boot construction and pole construction too. Sleek new boots with hiking-boot-thick soles and strong extendable aluminum poles soon followed. Backcountry skiers now had the tools to truly redefine the limits of cross-country skiing. Amazing telemark descents have been recorded in the last 10 years: the 18,000-foot Mexican volcanoes, Longs Peak's Notch Couloir, the Liberty Ridge on Mount Rainier and, incredibly, the Grand Teton. At the same time, many downhill ski areas experienced an explosion of highly proficient telemark skiers—some nearly indistinguishable from their alpine-equipped cousins.

In Colorado's backcountry these advances have meant greater freedom and enjoyment for skiers of all abilities. People are able to ski trails more efficiently and can challenge downhill terrain with greater confidence, making for truly exciting outings. This has contributed to a steady increase in the sport's popularity. The rising cost of downhill skiing and the desire for increased personal fitness have further buttressed this trend. Today ski touring seems to have entered an "anything goes" era. The reemergence of cable bindings, increased interest in randonnée or alpine touring, downhill skis mounted with three-pin bindings, plastic reinforced telemark boots, backcountry skiers on super lightweight racing gear and even a few purists waxing nostalgically (so to speak) on their wooden Trysl-Knuts and Bonnas are all part of the modern "off-piste" adventure. Because of the diverse nature of the routes in *Skiing Colorado's Backcountry* and skiers' personal preferences, it is difficult to make definitive equipment recommendations. The following discussion, however, will briefly highlight the fundamental equipment that should accompany all skiers on a well-planned and safe tour.

# SKIS

The ski is obviously the essential piece of equipment and requires careful selection. Skis fall into several basic categories of construction materials and design. While some argue the benefits of foam skis versus wood skis versus metal skis, overall ski design is of far greater importance. Modern backcountry skis come in a variety of flex patterns (soft to stiff), different widths, possess single and double cambers (the overall arc of the ski when seen in profile while sitting unweighted on a flat surface), come equipped with or without metal edges and have radically different sidecuts (profile of the ski when looking down on it). Softer flexing skis "float" through variable backcountry snow conditions (powder snow, clumpy wet spring snow, wind-compacted crust), turn more gracefully and will compensate for the shortcomings of less proficient skiers. Stiff skis in comparison transmit the skier's energies much more rapidly, making for quicker turns and more temperamental performance. These skis are better suited for ice, groomed slopes and the feet of intermediate to advanced skiers.

Traditional touring skis are built on a double camber, which means that in addition to the primary sideview arc from tip to tail, they have a smaller secondary arc directly under the foot. The entire base of the ski gets a coating of glide wax while the smaller arch (the kicker or wax pocket) receives only the climbing wax. When weight is placed on the ski, the kicker comes into contact with the snow momentarily and the wax sticks (you hope!). When the ski is unweighted, the skier glides on the ski's tips and tails. The presence of this secondary camber detracts from downhill performance. When a ski is turned, it bends into a continuous curve; the smoother the arc, the quicker and more predictable the turn. Wax pockets in double-cambered skis are very stiff. They resist bending with the entire ski, interrupting the ski's overall flex and consequently inhibiting superior downhill performance. Double-cambered skis are designed primarily for general touring and are most efficient for forward motion over flat and rolling terrain. Single-cambered are the superior choice if telemark skiing (turning) is preferred since more of the ski's edge is used during a turn, which provides greater security. Sidecut also affects ski ability. The greater the difference between the width of a ski's shovel (widest section of the tip) and tail and the waist (the thinnest portion of the ski normally found directly under the foot), the more responsive the ski will be in turning.

Wider touring skis are becoming more popular. Traditional touring skis are about 55 to 60 millimeters wide. If you are enamored with ski mountaineering, powder skiing or telemark skiing at ski areas, you might opt for wider backcountry skis (up to 75 mm), which provide greater surface area and stability. They also approach alpine touring/downhill gear in performance and price.

For the majority of tours in *Skiing Colorado's Backcountry,* a safe bet would be a strong double- or single-cambered ski in a width close to or slightly wider than a traditional touring ski. They should have metal edges (which bite into ice and hard snow) and accept both wax and climbing skins. If you tend to remain on trails, then anything beefier than a skating/racing ski will be adequate and cost much less. Trail skis also should be purchased with a double camber (i.e., wax pocket). Finally we need to mention "waxless" skis. There are many forms of these skis, most of which utilize some form of "fish scale" pattern on their bases. In general these skis provide greater convenience for novice skiers while severely reducing the overall performance required and demanded by intermediate to advanced skiers.

## BOOTS

The next and equally important component is boots, which are critical to overall comfort as well as performance. Lighter boots or touring "shoes" will work adequately for trail skiing. However, the most popular boots today are similar to medium-weight leather hiking boots. Although heavier and less comfortable, this type of footwear, once broken in, is warmer and more durable, and greatly enhances control over the skis in advanced skiing conditions. Wear these boots with a combination of a thick wool or polypropylene sock and a thin liner sock to ensure the comfort and warmth of your feet. Skiers with perpetually cold feet might also look into double boots and/or insulated "supergaiters," which cover the entire boot from the welt up. Supergaiters have several advantages: They are relatively light in weight, they do not affect the boot's performance to a great degree and they can, in the insulated versions, add significant warmth.

## BINDINGS

To connect yourself to your "boards" you will need bindings. These seemingly simple devices have also been considerably improved recently. Touring bindings come in two primary varieties: traditional three-pin clamp-down types and cable bindings. The basic three-pin binding is still the "Nordic norm," but most models are much stronger now. While a basic lightweight aluminum binding will work fine on moderate trail tours, trips into rugged off-trail territory will demand a binding constructed out of a heavier alloy with slots on the sides to insert a strap if a bail should break. Broken bails are less common today, but the experience has been known to ruin a good day. Cable bindings have shown up again in vastly superior forms in the last few years. They are an excellent alternative to three-pin bindings, especially if you spend a lot of time turning. Their reliability is unmatched and they tend to cause less damage to your boots' pinholes and welts. Two handy binding accessories are the small plates that mount behind the binding under the ball of the foot, and a set of safety straps. The parallel rows of serrated teeth on the plates help grip the sole of the boot during a turn. Safety straps prevent skis from getting lost in deep powder or down the side of a steep mountain. They are also required if you visit a lift-accessed area.

During the last few years an almost revolutionary boot/binding system has become increasingly popular. Known as the New Nordic Norm (or NNN), this strong yet light high-tech system has been used primarily on groomed tracks for skating and diagonal stride. Now, several beefed-up versions of this binding system are available. With heavier construction and mid-weight boots, the NNN-BC (backcountry) provides skiers with an extremely versatile ski system designed to tackle a variety of terrain and conditions. Reports from individuals who have tested the NNN-BC indicate it to be an excellent system for all around general touring with an emphasis on trail touring on mid-weight skis, recreational telemark skiing and light hut touring. Most versions currently available will not yet replace heavier backcountry skis and boots for serious telemark skiing and overnight winter excursions with heavy packs. The NNN-BC boot/binding system seems to be a glimpse into the future and is worth some experimentation by recreational tourers as well as gear freaks.

## POLES

Ski poles seem like the least important piece of equipment, but they do add comfort and safety and can improve skiing performance. Poles are essential in propelling a skier forward and the correct length will make this process more efficient and infinitely less tiring. Most touring poles in use now are metal (aluminum), which has greatly reduced breakage, probably the single most common equipment failure plaguing skiers today. Avalanches can be a serious threat to backcountry skiers and ski poles that convert to avalanche probes are vital in the quick locating of buried victims. These models are costly but worth the added investment. Many skiers (especially spring skiers and powder-hounds) choose extendable poles which allow them to climb uphill easily, then once at a desired destination skiers can shorten the poles for the trip down the hill. Shorter poles create more stability and allow the skier to link faster repetitions of telemark and parallel turns. Other features to consider when selecting backcountry poles are self-arrest grips, breakaway straps and basket design.

## CLIMBING SKINS

Recently there has been a resurgence in the popularity of climbing skins. These fuzzy strips, when properly attached to the base of the skis, allow you to climb easily up very steep inclines. They are truly amazing and work well in spring and early summer when it is nearly impossible to wax correctly (aside from resorting to klister waxes . . . ugh!). There are many brands and models to choose from, with their difference being whether they are of a natural or man-made material, their method of attachment (reusable adhesives or straps) and price. Opinions abound as to which types offer superior performance but all work well.

## WAXING

During the winter months most skiers still rely primarily on waxes to create adhesion between their skis and the crystalline structure of the snow. Snow is a dynamic, constantly changing material, so different waxes are necessary for different conditions. Properly waxed skis will provide good traction when you weight the central kick section of the skis and, conversely, efficient forward motion when gliding on the tips and tails. They will both climb and glide well, saving time and energy (skins can freeze up and can be very time-consuming to put on and take off).

Waxing is really not as complicated as it may seem; a small selection of waxes will fill most of your needs during a typical Colorado winter. Green, blue and purple cover about 90 percent of Colorado's skiable winter days. Green wax is used on the coldest days, blue is the choice for average temperatures, while purple is for warmer winter skiing. Red wax is very soft and works well for late winter/early spring skiing when daily air temperatures climb above freezing (although if you are climbing, you may want skins). Recently, the color delineations have been further subdivided into "extra" and "special" classifications. These are slightly "warmer" and "colder," respectively, than the primary colors and allow more precise adjustment of your waxes. These waxes work quite well in Colorado and are worth a little experimentation. Finally, a good base wax of either "Polar Green" or a running wax will create a fast base for frictionless downhill glide. Learn to wax: It is as fundamental to ski touring as double-poling!

## PACKS

Another useful piece of equipment is a sturdy backpack, flexible enough to meet the varied demands of backcountry touring. Choose a comfortable one that has enough capacity to carry all of your warm clothes, food, shovel, and so on. For spring skiing a pack that will carry your skis is very handy as many spring tours require some hiking.

## SAFETY EQUIPMENT

Finally, don't neglect safety and first aid equipment. Avalanche transceivers (or beacons) are one of the most valuable safety items skiers can carry. Unfortunately these expensive (but worth it!) items have yet to become a standard piece of gear on most outings. A transceiver is the single most effective device for locating a buried avalanche victim. These small devices used in conjunction with a shovel and avalanche probes can make a life-and-death difference if someone is buried by an avalanche. Even when avalanche danger is not present, at least one person in each group should carry a repair kit and first aid kit. The repair kit should include items such as wire, replacement screws, epoxy, steel wool, wooden matches, screwdriver, duct tape, nylon cord and small metal plates which can be used to reinforce broken skis. Know how to use these tools before venturing into the backcountry.

## CLOTHING

Anyone who has spent even a small amount of time in the mountains is probably familiar with layering. Layering is the process of building a system of heat-trapping layers of long underwear, shirts and sweaters, culminating in a nonporous nylon shell to protect against bitter winter winds. Skiers adjust for comfort by removing or adding various layers of clothes. Modern materials such as polypropylene, pile, PolarPlus, Capilene and Thermax far outperform that old standby wool in terms of warmth, lightness and ability to transport moisture away from the exercising body. Wool, however, can come at a fraction of the cost of these "high-tech" (and more stylish) products and remains very popular with outdoors people. For the outer shell, garments of Gore-Tex-backed nylon and other modern laminate coatings strike a balance between waterproofness and breathability and are a superior choice for general winter mountain use. Once again, many other nylon types work well as shell materials and are much more economical. Durable gaiters, warm gloves and hats, a balaclava, sunglasses and a pair of goggles round out a versatile ski wardrobe (and don't forget sunscreen!).

Purchase well-made ski gear. It does not have to be the best or most expensive, but when your comfort and well-being are on the line, trying to cut costs usually proves to be a false economy. A good mountaineering equipment shop can provide information on the latest products and can rent many types of equipment, providing you with invaluable insight into gear selection. Surplus stores normally carry a wide selection of durable (and more bucolic) clothing and gear. In the backcountry you will see just about every possible combination of gear and style of clothing. Experience will quickly demonstrate that while the quality of your equipment can make a difference, it is familiarity with the gear and proper use within its limitations that can help to keep a memorable experience from turning into a miserable epic. (We have listed suggested equipment in Appendix 2.)

# Mountain Weather and Snow Conditions

## Early Season
Depending on the year and the location chosen, it is possible to ski Colorado's backcountry from mid-November clear through June. Indian summer, characterized by cool, dry, cloudless days, gives way to winter with the arrival of the first big snowfall. This can come as early as September or as late as mid-December. These early-season storms are short-lived: When they end, snow at the lower elevations quickly melts. But the high country remains locked in winter's icy grip until spring. Early-season skiing can be a nerve-racking, rock-strewn fiasco if you pick the wrong location. The snowpack has not yet had enough time to form a solid base. Even with two feet of fresh powder, you may find your skis submarining into an unseen rock or stump. Breaking trail can be equally frustrating: Wallowing in waist-deep powder, you can expend enormous amounts of energy while gaining only a few hundred feet.

If you ski early season, try to pick a tour that has already been packed down by snowmobiles or is high enough to have acquired a good solid base. Tours near the summit of Berthoud or Vail Pass, as well as the Jones Pass and Montezuma areas, are your best bet. Often the skiing above treeline is better in November than it is in midwinter because the high winds that normally rake the alpine tundra in winter have not yet arrived. If you do go above treeline in early season, be careful of the avalanche danger. Early-season avalanches are difficult to predict and quite common.

## MIDWINTER

Often by late December to early January (or later in drought years), the snowpack will have had a chance to consolidate. Six to 10 inches of Colorado's famous light, dry powder on top of a solid base becomes the rule rather than the exception. Skiing is consistently good from the lower elevations all the way to treeline. Snowfall increases with increased elevation. It is not uncommon for ski areas to get four times the amount of snowfall at the top of the area as they do at the bottom. Temperatures also vary with elevation, but not always in ways that you might expect. In general, temperatures decrease 3 to 5 degrees F. for every 1,000 feet of elevation gained. At night, however, cooler air often settles into the valleys, creating so-called temperature inversions, when the layer of air near the ground is colder than the layer above it. Dramatic examples of this are the inversions that occur in Grand County. Nighttime lows in Winter Park are usually 8 to 10 degrees F. warmer than they are in Fraser, located only a few miles down the valley. And while Fraser is commonly referred to as the icebox of the nation, Tabernash, four miles farther down the valley, is usually colder by another 8 to 10 degrees.

In midwinter above treeline, fierce winds continuously pound the high peaks, sweeping exposed slopes completely bare of snow. Where the snow does remain, it is usually hardpacked *sastrugi* (snow with a hard, intricately textured surface that has been sculpted by the wind), which is very difficult and unpleasant to ski. Rocky Mountain National Park and the Indian Peaks are susceptible to particularly strong winds. An exception occurs when an upslope storm backs against the Front Range from the east, often depositing large amounts of snow on the plains and the lower elevations, leaving the mountains relatively untouched. The winds that normally ravage the eastern side of the divide temporarily subside until the storm moves on.

## SPRING

As the arc of the sun climbs higher with each passing week, daytime temperatures increase accordingly and often go well above freezing in late March and April. Snow surfaces that are exposed to the sun melt during the day, then refreeze at night, causing a melt-freeze crust. Skiing these crusty slopes is at best challenging and at worst downright impossible. During this transition season it is best to stick to tours with a northern exposure. They can retain their powdery winter conditions clear through April and into May.

Not until the snowpack above treeline has changed into spring corn and stabilized and the danger from wet-snow avalanches had ended is it time for the spring ski descents. This takes many days of melting and refreezing of the snowpack and in most years doesn't occur until late May. The transition from good winter conditions to good spring conditions can take several weeks, during which most skiers become discouraged and put away their skis. This is a mistake. Some of the finest skiing is yet to come. All winter long the snow above treeline has been compacted by high winds. In spring these hardpacked slopes soften up and become perfect for carving telemark and parallel turns. Descents of 2,000 feet or more, down seemingly impossible slopes, become exhilarating dances of controlled flowing motion. If you're an advanced skier and have never tried skiing a mountain in good spring conditions, you are really missing something. It's like taking up a whole new sport.

# AVALANCHE AWARENESS

Avalanches are a very real danger. They represent the greatest single hazard to mountain backcountry travelers in winter. From 1950 through the 1988–1989 winter, avalanches have killed 346 people in the United States. Colorado leads the nation in this statistic, and the number of deaths per year continues to increase. In the 1970s an average of 12 people a year died by avalanche in the United States; thus far in the 1980s that number has increased to 17 per year. As more people venture into the high country, the number of fatalities will surely rise.

Limited space does not allow a full assessment of all the factors that go into avalanche prediction, avoidance and rescue. There are several good texts devoted entirely to this subject: A few of the best are listed in the Suggested Reading section. Anyone planning to spend time in the high country should study one or more of these books thoroughly, and attend one of the many avalanche classes or clinics available. Here, it is only possible to give a brief summary of the basics. Our goal is to create an awareness of avalanches so that skiers can recognize a potentially dangerous situation.

A little knowledge goes a long way toward evaluating avalanche hazard. However, avalanches are notoriously difficult to predict and those who simply do a bit of reading on the subject may get a false sense of security. We do not want to create the impression that by reading this section you will be able to safely and effectively evaluate the snow conditions. We merely want to provide enough knowledge for you to understand the risk.

An avalanche is a mass of snow sliding or flowing down a mountainside. Sometimes avalanches are called snowslides. The basic requirement for an avalanche is nothing more than a steep snow-covered slope. Years of observation have shown that the steepness of the slope, or slope angle, that produces the most avalanches is within 30 to 45 degrees. However, the snowcover types that produce avalanche conditions are not so easily defined. Because the winter's snowcover represents the interaction of a series of snowfalls and weather conditions, a complex layered structure results. Numerous combinations of snow type and layered structures can contribute to avalanche formation.

For example, if the surface layer of snow is cohesive, meaning the individual snow grains all stick together as a unit, and this cohesive layer is resting on a weaker layer, the upper layer may break loose and slide down the slope. First it will move as a cohesive blanket of snow, but then after traveling some distance, it will break up into blocks or lumps of snow. This is called a slab avalanche and represents the greatest danger because slabs may release large amounts of snow over large areas (several acres at once, for example), making escape extremely difficult. The slab avalanche may involve a layer of snow only a few inches in thickness, or it may release the entire winter's snowcover and be 6 to 12 feet or more thick. The second basic type of avalanche is the loose snow or point-release avalanche. This type occurs when the surface snow possesses a totally different character. It is cohesionless—the snow crystals rest on the slope as if they were dry sand with nothing holding the individual grains together. If one grain slips out of place and dislodges others as it moves down the slope, the moving snow will spread out into the characteristic inverted V-shape of the point-release. These avalanches typically do not involve nearly as much snow as the slab avalanche and are therefore less dangerous.

Although avalanches often release on large open slopes, along ridge crests, well above treeline, it is very important for the backcountry skier to note that avalanches may also occur on much smaller, shorter slopes at lower elevations such as gullies, road cuts and small openings in the trees. Avalanches can release and travel through light to moderately dense forests—so trees are not always an area of safety, especially during extreme avalanche conditions.

In the simplest of terms, avalanches occur when the stresses that exist in the snowcover equal the strength of the weakest layer. This critical condition may result from either the stress increasing or the strength decreasing. Stress, or load, on the potential avalanche slope can increase either by natural causes, such as snowfall or the redistribution of windblown snow, or by artificial loading, such as the weight of a skier. In both cases the final overload is called the trigger.

Most skiers caught in avalanches trigger the slide themselves. At some location within the snow layer beneath the skier, the structure is too weak to support the additional load. Failure occurs, and then because of the specific mechanical properties of a slab avalanche, a crack propagates over some distance, releasing a large area of the snowcover. Skiers have been caught in natural avalanches, but the odds of just passing by as a natural avalanche occurs above you are minimal.

The concept of natural and skier-released avalanches leads back to the discussion of avalanche slopes or avalanche terrain. The terrain, unlike the evolving snowcover, remains unchanged. Wise use of terrain in route finding can allow safe backcountry travel under a variety of hazardous conditions. One can avoid triggering an avalanche simply by avoiding avalanche terrain. However, even when travel is generally limited to gentle slopes, the possibility of being caught in a natural avalanche releasing from the slopes above you must always be considered. Obviously one should avoid traveling at or near the bottoms of narrow valleys, steep-sided ravines or gullies from which escape would be virtually impossible.

Most natural avalanches run during or shortly after a storm (within a few hours to a day or so). During this time the new snow either avalanches or begins to consolidate and become firmly attached to the layer below, thus decreasing the probability of a natural avalanche. However, strong winds can also increase the chances of natural releases, with or without new snowfall. Be alert to blue-sky days with strong winds, especially when you see blowing snow moving across the

*Brian Litz telemark skiing in Baldy Bowl,
Kurt Lankford photo.*

ridgetops. The deposition of snow by this process is rapid and avalanche hazard can increase in a very short time.

During periods of avalanche danger the snowcover often gives you clues. If you observe recent natural avalanche activity, you can be certain that the danger is high and skier-triggered avalanches are likely. All steep terrain should be avoided. If the snow beneath you collapses with a "whoompfing" sound, or cracks shoot out through the snow as you ski along, the conditions for dangerous slabs are present. Again, avoid steep terrain. Unfortunately, deep slab releases can occur when the slope is overloaded by one or more skiers and because the instability is deep within the snowcover, no surface clues are apparent prior to the release.

Some of the tours in this book involve steep terrain where avalanche hazard evaluation would be difficult during midwinter; therefore, these tours are recommended only during "spring conditions." However, this is not because avalanche hazard is absent in spring but rather because avalanche conditions are less frequent and easier to recognize. In the following discussion we will use the term "spring conditions" because they may occur through a broad range of time, developing as early as March or as late as May or June, depending on the specific weather patterns of the given year. The snow structure of a particular winter becomes more stable as spring conditions progress. This occurs because as the snow surface warms and meltwater moves downward through the snowcover, the complex layered stratigraphy of midwinter becomes more homogeneous. The snow grains of all the layers begin to melt and refreeze and the weaker layers settle and become more strongly connected to the stronger layers above and below. For complete or mature spring conditions to exist, the entire snow depth must have warmed to the melting point, followed by several additional days of melt conditions. It is in fact at just about this time that the conditions for natural wet-snow avalanches are present. These avalanches result from the loss of strength in the layers as the meltwater moves through them. They may occur as loose or slab avalanches, for basically the same reasons as were described above for dry-snow releases. Depending on the existing stratigraphy and the weather conditions, such as rate of warming of the snowcover, wet avalanches may or may not occur in a given year. When a wet avalanche cycle begins, it follows a generally predictable pattern in terms of elevation and slope aspect. Slopes with a southerly aspect (facing generally from southeast through southwest) at lower elevations will be first to produce wet-snow avalanches because the snow will be warmed to the melting point first at these sites. Slopes with a northerly aspect will take longer to warm, and wet-snow avalanche hazard may lag behind the south slopes by several days to several weeks if the north slopes are at much higher elevations. Unlike midwinter dry-snow avalanches that occur as a result of specific triggers and have no relationship with time of day, spring wet-snow avalanches show a pattern within the warming and cooling cycle of the day. The backcountry skier can put this pattern to use. At night the wet spring snow will often refreeze and become solid and stable. In the morning avalanche-prone slopes that face southeast will be the first to become dangerous. As the day progresses and sun angle changes, other exposures become dangerous.

If skiing a southeast exposure is your goal, you must be at the top of the slope well before the melt process begins. A thin layer of melting corn snow makes for the best skiing; deeper penetration of meltwater causes the quality of the skiing to diminish and the avalanche hazard to increase. If your goal for the morning is a west- or north-facing slope, you would not have to be in such a hurry, as these slopes will not be receiving as much direct solar heating during the morning and will be warmed more slowly by the warming air. Wet-snow hazard on west-facing slopes will come later in the day but will not disappear when the sun goes down. It will take several more hours for the snowcover to refreeze and stabilize. It should be noted that during unusually warm nights, often associated with overcast skies, the snowcover, even at high elevations, may not refreeze; with such conditions, the avalanche paths on all aspects may not be safe for travel the following morning.

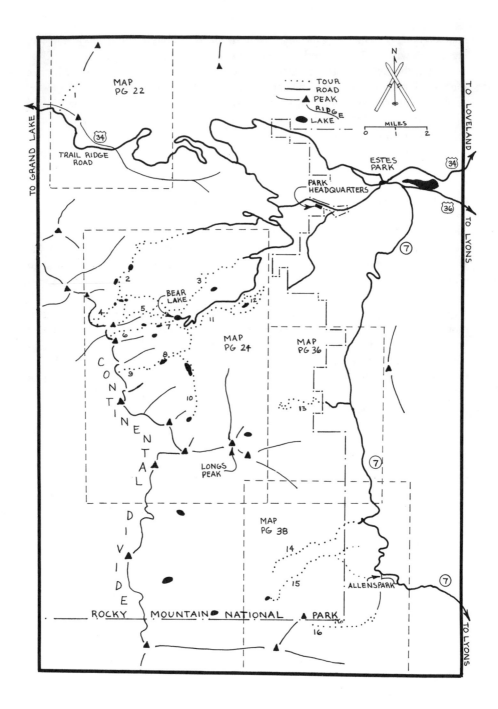

# CHAPTER ONE

# ROCKY MOUNTAIN NATIONAL PARK

## INTRODUCTION

Rocky Mountain National Park contains some of the most beautiful and rugged mountain scenery in the United States. It is well known for its glacier-carved valleys, pristine treeline lakes, jagged peaks and high alpine meadows, so well known that literally millions of visitors come each year to take in the majestic sights. Most visit during the summer months when the weather is mild and the wildflowers are in bloom. In winter, however, the park takes on a different character. The number of visitors drops to scarcely a trickle. Trail Ridge Road closes for the season. Elk come down from the high country, banding together in open fields and meadows where snow-laden grasses are easily uncovered. High winds sweep over the divide, raking the alpine tundra and depositing deep snowdrifts in the valleys. Visiting the park during winter can be a cold and miserable experience if you get caught above treeline in a whiteout. However, if you're prepared, a winter visit can be extremely enjoyable and far more rewarding than hiking a congested trail in summer.

In winter, Rocky Mountain National Park receives more than its fair share of high winds. Even on days when the plains are mild and sunny, the park is usually very windy, especially above treeline. This makes winter touring in the park somewhat of a dicey proposition. If you're counting on finding consistently good powder, some of the other areas would probably make a better choice. When spring arrives, and the winds die down, the park's glaciers and snowfields provide some of the best spring ski descents in the Front Range. The bowls above treeline are transformed into vast playgrounds of velvety corn snow, ideal for carving linked telemark turns. For diehard enthusiasts, this is when skiing in the park is at its best.

### HISTORY

Native Americans on hunting expeditions from the plains were the first to set foot in this area. Crafted Clovis and Folsom projectile points have been discovered on Trail Ridge Road dating back some 10,000 to 15,000 years. Called Paleo-Indians, these people coexisted with the now-extinct mammoth and super-bison. Later, Utes and Arapaho roamed this area to hunt and occasionally raid each others' camps. The Arapaho were steadily forced northward during the 1870s and eventually confined to the Wind River Reservation in Wyoming. The Utes, who preferred secluded mountain valleys to open plains, remained free until the 1880s when they too were confined to reservations. In 1914, the Colorado Mountain Club arranged for two elderly Arapaho to return to Estes Park so they could tell their tales and legends of Indian life during the time when the Arapaho roamed freely through the valleys of Rocky Mountain National Park. Gus Griswold, then 73, and Sherman Sage, 63, told an interesting legend about Griswold's father, Old Man Gun, a great warrior, medicine man and hunter who skillfully trapped eagles from the summit of Longs Peak. The eagles were prized for their feathers, which were used to make headdresses. Old Man Gun climbed Longs at night while the watchful eagles were in their nests. There he excavated a hovel just big enough to hide in without being seen. He carried a stuffed coyote for bait, tallow for scent and special herbs to appease the gods. When an eagle landed he would strike with lightning quickness, snatching the eagle by the talons, bare handed.

White men first explored the area when French fur trappers arrived in the 1800s looking for beaver. Major Stephen Long, for whom Longs Peak is named, scouted to the base of the mountains in 1820, but did not venture beyond the foothills. Gold was discovered in Colorado in the late 1850s, bringing a flood of prospectors to areas such as Central City and Idaho Springs. Virtually every major valley west of Denver saw mining activity of one form or another during this period. Farther north, however, the streams and hillsides of Rocky Mountain National Park contained little gold, and except for a few unsuccessful exploratory ventures, were left relatively untouched.

In 1860, Joel Estes brought his family from Denver to establish the area's first homestead. Others followed, including Mountain Jim Nugent, a colorful character torn from the pages of the Old West. The entire right side of Jim's face had been sliced off in a fight with a grizzly bear. Despite his nasty reputation and rugged appearance, he had a remarkable way with women. He was a captivating storyteller, able to spin tall tales of heroism and wit—a liar perhaps but with a charming flair. Mountain Jim was murdered in 1874 by Grif Evans, a Welsh immigrant and proprietor of the first dude ranch in Estes Park.

The first confirmed ascent of Longs Peak was in 1868 by a group of seven, men including John Wesley Powell, who later became famous for his exploration of the Colorado River. Soon after Powell's successful climb, Longs Peak became a fashionable goal for adventurous Colorado tourists. Reverend Elkana Lamb climbed the peak in 1871 and descended via the east face down a gully now called Lambs Slide. It was a harrowing experience. At one point Reverend Lamb lost his footing on the icy snowfield and would have slid to the bottom, had it not been for a large rock which he managed to grasp as he flew by at great speed. Today the lower portion of Lambs Slide is frequently climbed and occasionally descended on skis.

Toward the turn of the century Estes Park gained a national reputation for its pristine beauty and abundant fish and game. In 1909, Enos Mills, a naturalist, writer and conservationist, began to campaign for preservation of the area. Mills's campaign succeeded, and in 1915 Rocky Mountain National Park was created. Since that time the park has been administered by the Department of the Interior.

REGULATIONS

The U.S. Park Service has done an excellent job of preserving a magnificent natural resource, at the same time allowing several million visitors a year to enjoy it. This, of course, means that rules and regulations are strictly enforced year-round. In winter and spring, when the number of visitors is down, some of the regulations may leave you with the impression that Big Brother is again stepping on your toes. Please remember that these rules and regulations are there to protect a beautiful yet fragile ecosystem for you and future generations to enjoy. If you are in doubt about any of the park regulations, please contact a ranger or visit park headquarters.

# 1    SUNDANCE BOWL

**DESCRIPTION: Spring ski descent, very steep, car shuttle optional**
**SKILL LEVEL: Advanced +**
**TIME: Quarter to half day for one round-trip descent**
**DISTANCE: 1 mile descent plus return hike**
**ELEVATION CHANGE: 1,800 feet total loss**
**STARTING ELEVATION: 12,080 feet**
**AVALANCHE TERRAIN: Mostly avalanche terrain; wait for spring consolidation**
**USGS 7.5 MINUTE MAP: Trail Ridge, 1977-PR**
**MAP: page 22**

Descending Sundance Bowl on skis is not for the novice telemark skier or the faint of heart. This extreme tour is somewhat deceptive—which may be credited to the tour's profile, resembling a convex curve. It begins on the flat tundra surrounding Trail Ridge Road (Rocky Mountain National Park) and becomes progressively steeper as the descent continues. The lower half of this nearly 2,000-foot ski is quite steep and offers little respite to aching thigh muscles and dull metal edges. Sundance Bowl is not actually a bowl or cirque but rather a wide couloir or snowfield. This stupendous spring tour is one of the best choices for advanced telemark or alpine tourers who want to spend the day carving turns and elevating respiratory rates.

Sundance Bowl is reached by driving on Trail Ridge Road (normally not open until Memorial Day) to a small turnout found on the south side of the road, approximately 0.4 miles east of the easily discernible "rock cut" where the road passes through a spectacular outcrop of stone. Remember, during tourist season traffic can move very slowly.

From the parking area, cross the road (watch out for tourists watching everything but the road!), climb over the snow bank on the north side of the road and head due north, aiming for the very flat saddle which sits west of Sundance Mountain. No elevation is gained here.

From the saddle the descent begins in a very gradual style, allowing for numerous warm-up turns. Continue north as the gradient increases noticeably. The

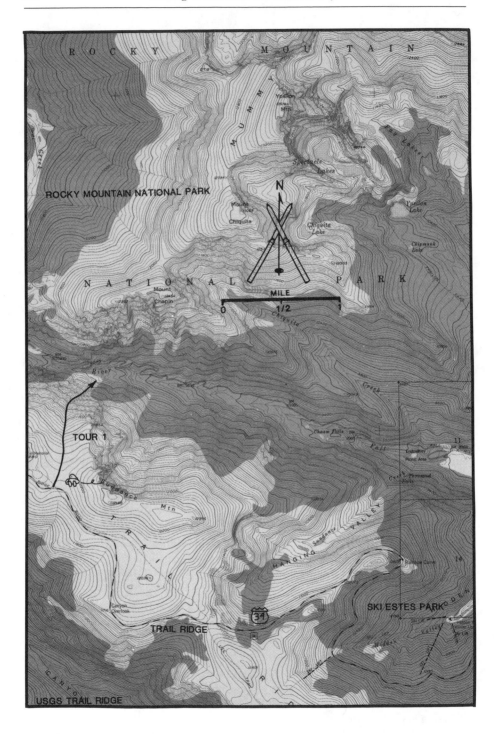

bowl in this zone fans out to the west and east; several choices for routes present themselves. To the east two larger tongues of snow provide the widest area for turning and the most gentle runout, while to the west small rock islands divide the run into many narrower chutes. These are all of about the same difficulty.

At the bottom there are two choices to get back to the start of the route. The first is to simply retrace your steps. The second is to walk out Fall River Road (located a short distance up on the north side of the creek). While the former involves regaining all of your lost elevation on foot, we prefer this route because the latter requires a long (nearly 6 miles) hike out to Endovalley picnic area where a car shuttle is required.

# 2    LAKE HELENE AND ODESSA LAKE

**DESCRIPTION: Winter backcountry tour, varied terrain, mostly trails, more down than up, car shuttle required**
**SKILL LEVEL: Advanced***
**TIME: Full day**
**DISTANCE: 10.5 miles**
**ELEVATION CHANGE: 1,200 feet total gain/1,480 feet total loss**
**STARTING ELEVATION: 9,460 feet**
**AVALANCHE TERRAIN: Route crosses avalanche slopes; prone to skier-triggered avalanches during high-hazard periods**
**USGS 7.5 MINUTE MAP: McHenrys Peak, 1957**
**MAP: page 24**

**\*INTERMEDIATE HIGHLIGHT: The first section up to Lake Helene is moderate trail skiing.**

When snow conditions are good, this is one of the finest tours in the Front Range. It covers a wide variety of terrain—from steep heavily wooded sections to flat-road and trail skiing, with everything in between. It is also a long tour. An early start is recommended to allow plenty of time to complete the route before dark. Snow conditions from one end of the route to the other can be extremely variable. Unfortunately, the lower section to Moraine Park often lacks adequate snowcover, so it is best to ski the route within a few weeks after a big storm, before the snow in the lower section has had a chance to melt or blow away.

The tour starts at Bear Lake and ends at Moraine Park, so return transportation must be arranged. From the Beaver Meadows entrance to Rocky Mountain National Park, take the Bear Lake road to the turnoff for Moraine Park. Follow this road for about a mile to its end at a plowed winter parking area. Leave one car here. Return with the other car to the Bear Lake road and follow it up to Bear Lake where the tour starts.

Ski around the right side of Bear Lake, following the bright orange trail

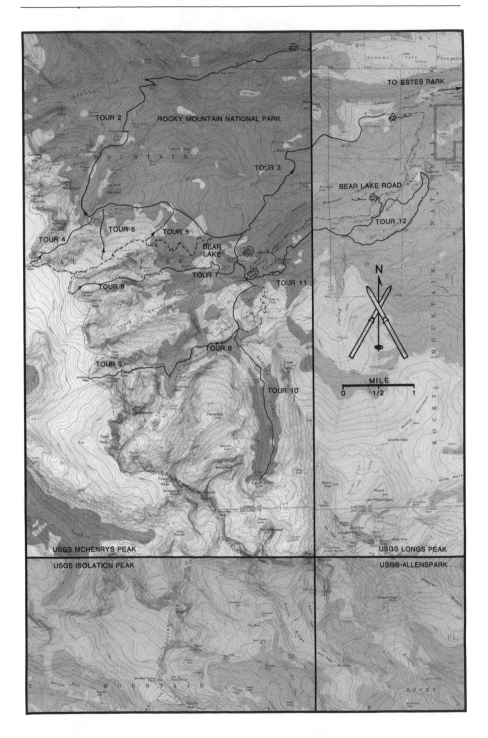

TO ESTES PARK

TOUR 2    ROCKY MOUNTAIN NATIONAL PARK

TOUR 3

BEAR LAKE ROAD

TOUR 5    TOUR 5

TOUR 4

TOUR 12

BEAR
LAKE

TOUR 6

TOUR 7

TOUR 11

N

TOUR 8

TOUR 9

TOUR 10

MILE
0    1/2    1

USGS MCHENRYS PEAK                                    USGS LONGS PEAK

USGS ISOLATION PEAK                                   USGS ALLENSPARK markers of the Flattop Trail as it begins a diagonal ascent up the hillside to the northeast of Bear Lake. Switchback sharply left at the trail junction for Bierstadt Lake and continue up the Flattop Trail. Once on the ridge you'll come to another trail junction. Go right here following the main trail which leads to Two Rivers Lake and Lake Helene. The other (left) fork switchbacks up Flattop Mountain. Lake Helene is reached after a 2-mile traverse around the base of Flattop Mountain. On a clear day you will get a spectacular view of the south face of Notchtop as you round the corner below Two Rivers Lake. From the north end of Lake Helene find a short steep gully between rock outcrops which enables you to drop down into the valley above Odessa Lake. Exercise caution here; this slope is steep enough to slide. Continue down the valley, cross Odessa Lake and begin to descend the narrow outlet drainage. The section from here down to Fern Lake is steep and heavily wooded. You can follow the creekbed, a tight, fast roller-coaster ride with numerous obstacles or stay up in the woods to the right, difficult but enjoyable timber-bashing.

Once down at Fern Lake the tour "mellows out" considerably. Pick up a trail at the east end of the lake near an old park service cabin and follow it on a continuous descent with several switchbacks down to the headwaters of the Big Thompson River. The remainder of the tour (several miles) follows the trail out to Moraine Park.

# 3     BEAR LAKE TO HALLOWELL PARK

**DESCRIPTION: Winter ski tour, backcountry forest trails, more down than up, car shuttle recommended**
**SKILL LEVEL: Intermediate**
**TIME: Half day**
**DISTANCE: 4 miles one way to car shuttle**
**ELEVATION CHANGE: 250 feet total gain/1,380 feet total loss**
**STARTING ELEVATION: 9,460 feet**
**AVALANCHE TERRAIN: None**
**USGS 7.5 MINUTE MAP: McHenrys Peak, 1957**
**MAP: page 24**

This is one of the best winter tours in Rocky Mountain National Park. Sheltered from the wind by dense forest, the route makes its way from Bear Lake over the Bierstadt Lake ridge and down into the Mill Creek drainage. It is an excellent choice for those times when you just want to get away from the daily rat race and experience the quiet solitude of winter. Snow conditions are generally very good, although you may encounter some thin rocky sections at the beginning and end of the tour.

The tour, as described, starts at Bear Lake and ends at Hallowell Park. You will need a car shuttle, unless you have time to reverse the route. From the Beaver Meadows entrance to Rocky Mountain National Park, take the Bear Lake road to the turnoff for Hallowell Park. A small parking area is available 0.2 miles up this road.

If you plan to do a car shuttle leave one car here, then return to the Bear Lake road and drive to the parking area for Bear Lake where the tour starts.

From the Bear Lake parking area take the marked trail that skirts around the east side of the lake and veers off, heading up the ridge to the northeast. This is the same trail that leads up to Flattop Mountain and Odessa Lake. At the first switchback, 0.25 miles above the lake, take a right fork and continue up to the top of the ridge. From here the trail goes through pleasant forested terrain, heading for Bierstadt Lake. You can either take the trail that heads straight north off the ridge and down into Mill Creek, or take a side trip to Bierstadt Lake and come back to intersect the direct route. The descent into Mill Creek is fun. It drops quickly along the wooded hillside, and has a few hairpin turns at the bottom to keep you on your toes. Once in the valley, the trail continues along the south side of Mill Creek. Eventually it crosses to the north side and continues down the valley and out to the wide Hallowell Park area.

Car shuttle back up to Bear Lake or reverse the route.

ALTERNATE ROUTE: If a car shuttle is out of the question, a round-trip tour from Bear Lake to Bierstadt Lake is highly recommended.


# 4    PTARMIGAN POINT SNOWFIELDS

**DESCRIPTION: Spring ski descent, hike to Continental Divide, ski steep cirque and spectacular glacial valley**
**SKILL LEVEL: Advanced**
**TIME: Full day**
**DISTANCE: 9 miles round trip**
**ELEVATION CHANGE: 3,000 feet total gain**
**STARTING ELEVATION: 9,460 feet**
**AVALANCHE TERRAIN: Mostly avalanche terrain; wait for spring consolidation**
**USGS 7.5 MINUTE MAP: McHenrys Peak, 1957**
**MAP: page 24**

Ptarmigan Point is located at the head of the valley between Flattop and Notchtop along the Continental Divide. The summit itself is little more than a high point on the ridge. A permanent snowfield that comes down from the ridge to the little lake below Notchtop, however, makes for a spectacular ski descent. Depending on when you ski the route, you should be able to ski all the way to the lake, and then catch intermittent snowfields the rest of the way down to Lake Helene.

The route is best done as a loop trip from Bear Lake. To reach Bear Lake drive west from Estes Park to the Beaver Meadows entrance to Rocky Mountain National Park. Once past the entrance booths, take the first left and proceed approximately 9 miles to the Bear Lake parking lot.

Ski (or hike) around the right side of Bear Lake, following the Flattop Trail on a diagonal ascent up a hillside to the northeast. Switchback sharply left at the trail junction for Bierstadt Lake and continue up the Flattop Trail. Once up on the ridge you'll come to another trail junction. Cut left here, following switchbacks up the east flank of Flattop Mountain. From the summit of Flattop Mountain angle northwest along the Continental Divide to the saddle between Flattop Mountain and Ptarmigan Point. Be sure to go all the way to the lowest point in the saddle before descending east down Ptarmigan Glacier. The slope is steepest near the top but never exceeds 35 degrees. Continue down the valley past a small lake and proceed out to Lake Helene. Find the Odessa Lake Trail at the east end of Lake Helene and follow it southeast back to Bear Lake.

# 5 FLATTOP MOUNTAIN SNOWFIELDS

**DESCRIPTION: Spring ski descent, approach hike, east- and north-facing snowfields, relatively quick access**
**SKILL LEVEL: Intermediate***
**TIME: Half to full day**
**DISTANCE: 2.5 miles or more round trip**
**ELEVATION CHANGE: 750 feet or more total gain**
**STARTING ELEVATION: 9,460 feet**
**AVALANCHE TERRAIN: Mostly avalanche terrain; wait for spring consolidation**
**USGS 7.5 MINUTE MAP: McHenrys Peak, 1957**
**MAP: page 24**

***ADVANCED HIGHLIGHT: The north snowfield is steeper and more advanced.**

This is a popular destination for spring ski mountaineers—and deservedly so. The access is relatively easy. You can take a run down the front (east) snowfield, and be back in the car in less than four hours. Or head to the top for a larger, more challenging run down the long north snowfield. Either way, you can count on Flattop for an enjoyable spring day.

The route starts from Bear Lake. To reach Bear Lake drive west from Estes Park to the Beaver Meadows entrance to Rocky Mountain National Park. Once past the entrance booths take the first left and proceed approximately 9 miles to Bear Lake. From the Bear Lake parking lot, begin the tour on the Flattop–Odessa Lake Trail. It starts on the east side of Bear Lake and makes one long switchback up the ridge to the north. If you go straight (right) at the first switchback, you'll end up at Bierstadt Lake (see tour 3). Instead, go left and continue up onto the ridge another 0.25 miles to a second fork. The main trail here (right fork) is the Lake Helene and Odessa Lake Trail, which traverses north along the east flank of Flattop Mountain to Two Rivers Lake and Lake Helene. The left fork (the one you want to take) is the Flattop Trail, which cuts off by itself and switchbacks up the east side of Flattop Mountain. The front (east) snowfield is in a glade just north of the switchbacks. If you go to the highest switchback you should be able to get a good run of 300 to 400 feet back down to intersect with the Odessa Lake Trail at the bottom.

To ski the longer, more challenging north snowfield, continue up the Flattop Trail to the very last hump below the summit. The north snowfield goes from here all the way down to Two Rivers Lake. You can't see the entire run until you're actually in the middle of it, because it's convex at the top. You shouldn't have any trouble finding it, if you start on the main snowfield just east of the summit, and then drop straight north heading for Two Rivers Lake. The Odessa Lake Trail runs along just east of Two Rivers Lake. Follow it 3 miles back out to Bear Lake.

# 6    TYNDALL GLACIER

**DESCRIPTION: Spring ski-mountaineering route, long yet very scenic approach hike**
**SKILL LEVEL: Advanced +**
**TIME: Full day**
**DISTANCE: 7.5 miles round trip**
**ELEVATION CHANGE: 2,860 feet total gain**
**STARTING ELEVATION: 9,460 feet**
**AVALANCHE TERRAIN: Mostly avalanche terrain; wait for spring consolidation**
**USGS 7.5 MINUTE MAP: McHenrys Peak, 1957**
**MAP: page 24**

Tyndall Glacier is a steep and seriously challenging descent that lies in an unusual location. The glacier sits at the head of the valley that separates precipitous Hallett Peak from jagged Flattop Mountain. During the spring this valley is filled with snow, which reaches from the top of the glacier virtually to Emerald Lake. While the upper section of this tour is continuously steep for about 400 feet, the majority of the route lies on the more moderate valley bottom, making for enjoyable skiing in an extremely steep-walled canyon. It is truly a unique experience to be carving turns on perfect springtime snow with Hallett Peak's soaring rock walls so close that you can almost reach out and touch them.

The route to Tyndall Glacier begins at Bear Lake parking lot. As with all tours originating from here you must leave Estes Park and drive to the Beaver Meadows entrance. Once past the entrance make the first lefthand turn, which will put you on the road to Bear Lake. Follow the road to its terminus at the Bear Lake parking area.

The fastest route to the top of the glacier is to follow the Flattop Mountain Trail, which begins on the eastern side of Bear Lake. This trail is wide, heavily traveled and well marked, so route finding should not be a problem. In the spring some sections of the trail may be choked with large drifts of soft snow, hence you may be forced off course. Do not worry about these deviations; the trail makes many enormous switchbacks throughout the climb of Flattop Mountain and is easy to relocate. After you break out to treeline, you will be hiking along the north side of Flattop Mountain then along the gently graded summit ridge. The inconspicuous summit lies at the 4-mile mark. Stop and peer off the southern escarpment of Flattop, and you will see the sheer north face of Hallett Peak and Tyndall Glacier to the south and west.

The descent of the glacier itself is quite steep, so you should traverse along the top to get a feel for where the best route is. Many times there is a faint depression toward the southern half which gives a more reasonable line. (Do not traverse too far to the south, as you will encounter very steep slopes as you begin to reach Hallett Peak.) If it's any consolation the runout at the bottom of this section is fairly flat.

Once you reach the valley bottom, ski through a series of more moderate snowfields interspersed with rock outcrops. This portion of the trip is enjoyable and in no time you will reach the limits of the snow. Normally this leaves you several hundred yards above and west of Emerald Lake. A short hike down a talus slope will gain the lake and the wide trail back to Bear Lake (roughly 0.5 miles from the snow to Emerald Lake).

# 7 EMERALD LAKE

**DESCRIPTION: Winter ski tour, narrow trail**
**SKILL LEVEL: Novice to intermediate**
**TIME: Half day**
**DISTANCE: 3.5 miles round trip**
**ELEVATION CHANGE: 660 feet total gain**
**STARTING ELEVATION: 9,460 feet**
**AVALANCHE TERRAIN: Some avalanche terrain encountered; easily avoided**
**USGS 7.5 MINUTE MAP: McHenrys Peak, 1957**
**MAP: page 24**

Emerald Lake lies in the heart of Rocky Mountain National Park's rugged landscape. During summer the trail leading from Bear Lake west is inundated with hikers; however, when snow blankets the terrain, the number of travelers drops significantly and it is possible to enjoy a ski outing accompanied by only the wind and snow. The Emerald Lake Trail climbs from the south side of Bear Lake and ascends over a series of three steps, each of which contains a small alpine lake. On clear days Hallett Peak's monolithic north face towers to the west, while the Longs Peak massif dominates the southern skyline. The mileage is short and the climbing moderate, making for a fantastic novice to intermediate trip. The return trip will test your snowplow technique as you cruise back down to the parking lot.

To reach Bear Lake parking area and the Emerald Lake Trailhead, leave Estes Park and drive west to the Beaver Meadows entrance to Rocky Mountain National Park. Once past the entrance booths take the first left. This will place you on the road to Bear Lake which lies 9 miles away.

The tour begins with a short section of trail from the parking lot up to the edge of Bear Lake. As you approach the lake the main trail is to your left. Large and well marked, it is bordered by a split-rail fence on the left and a ranger's cabin on the right. Very quickly you will reach a fork in the trail. Take the right fork, which climbs moderately up the south slope of a large forested knob. After about one-third of a mile the angle of the trail lessens as it contours around to the west side of the knob. Directly to the west of this feature is diminutive Nymph Lake, which is 0.5 miles from the parking lot.

From Nymph Lake the route leaves the north edge and climbs to the northwest on the south side of a tiny rocky ridge/outcrop, which eventually deposits you below and to the right of an exposed treeless slope. This barren spot is small but can slide, so take care when crossing it. If you do not feel comfortable with its condition, you may circle around to the north, arriving on top of this rocky buttress. Normally this spot is safe, but care should always be exercised when conditions are questionable. If conditions allow, traverse this section and follow the trail as it skirts the south flank of this step.

The next objective, Dream Lake, is roughly 0.2 miles west of the second step. Approaching the lake the trail re-enters the woods and climbs up past the turnoff to Lake Haiyaha (to the left or south), eventually reaching the eastern shore of Dream Lake. Ski across the lake and climb out of its small basin to the northwest.

It is virtually impossible to follow the exact summer route on the final leg from Dream Lake to Emerald Lake, so be creative in your route selection. The shortest route leaves the lake on the northwest and follows the path of least resistance along the north side of the creek as you climb over, around and through many trees, rocky outcrops and small knolls. The last few yards to Emerald Lake actually descend to the shore of the lake just north of the creek. Feel free to ski out onto the lake and circumnavigate its boundaries (if the ice is thick enough).

# 8    LOCH VALE

**DESCRIPTION: Winter ski tour, moderate length, very scenic trail skiing**
**SKILL LEVEL: Advanced**
**TIME: Full day**
**DISTANCE: 5.4 miles round trip**
**ELEVATION CHANGE: 940 feet total gain**
**STARTING ELEVATION: 9,240 feet**
**AVALANCHE TERRAIN: Some avalanche terrain encountered; easily avoided**

**USGS 7.5 MINUTE MAP: McHenrys Peak, 1957**
**MAP: page 24**

Loch Vale provides skiers with an adventure into the rugged backcountry of Rocky Mountain National Park. Although shorter than its sister tour through Glacier Gorge (tour 10), it provides equally impressive alpine vistas and downhill fun with slightly more technical skiing. This is an excellent spring tour.

The trail to the loch begins at the same point as the trail to Glacier Gorge to Black Lake, but at that trail junction this tour strikes off to the west and climbs into a beautiful valley of frozen lakes and glacial tarns. On windy winter days this is a valley to avoid; however, on a fair day you'll be treated to the finest scenery that the park has to offer.

This tour begins at the Glacier Gorge parking lot on the road to Bear Lake. Leave Estes Park and drive west to the Beaver Meadows entrance. Once past the entrance booths, take the first left to Bear Lake and Glacier Gorge. After 8.3 miles, park in the small plowed parking area enclosed in the sharp hairpin curve. The tour begins directly across the hairpin. Start skiing on the usually well-traveled path and pass a park service information display containing maps and other data concerning backcountry travel and safety. Cross over Chaos Creek on a small wooden bridge and ski along the large summer trail.

The route between its starting point and the Glacier Gorge–Loch Vale trail junction can be done in either of two ways. The first option is to simply follow the large well-traveled summer trail. The second is to turn up the first major drainage to your right after crossing Chaos Creek (near a second bridge). The turn is approximately one-eighth of a mile from the start of the trip. There is a nonmaintained summer trail through this tiny valley, but the trail and its turnoff can be hard to locate during winter unless someone has skied it recently. Just remember to turn upstream (west at the second small bridge). Once in the drainage, follow it as it contours around the northwest side of the first Glacier Knob. Stay low in the valley and ski on the northwest side of the creek until you contour south and climb toward the main summer trail.

The two trails merge in a flat forested spot several hundred feet to the east of the Glacier Gorge–Loch Vale trail junction. Glide west through the trees and take the right fork, which begins to climb up the righthand side of Icy Brook. This section rises through a small yet rugged ravine which deposits you on the eastern lip of the loch after several steep switchbacks (or climb straight up the creekbed if sufficient snow exists). If the weather is clear, this scenic spot affords fine views of the high glacial cirques to the west. Loch Vale can be quite windy when cold winter winds descend off Andrews Glacier and Taylor Peak and funnel through this narrow spot. Cross the lake either by skiing around the north side through the trees or claw your way directly across the frozen ice. Sheltered by the forest on the west bank, follow the valley bottom and turn up the lefthand alpine valley. Timberline Falls, a nice destination, lies about 0.2 miles past the junction of Andrews Creek and Icy Brook.

Those with enough time and energy can push the tour into the upper valley. This frozen environment lies well above treeline; expect extremes in weather and terrain. After your short steep climb past the rock benches near Timberline Falls, the topography will flatten out as you ski to Glass Lake and Sky Pond. Sky Pond sits alone with commanding views of Taylor Peak's east face, the Cathedral Spires, Shark's Tooth and the slender Petit Grepon.

No matter how far you ski up into this valley, you will be rewarded with a thrilling return trip to the car (especially when tail winds rocket you back across the loch).

# 9    ANDREWS GLACIER

**DESCRIPTION: Spring ski descent, long approach hike**
**SKILL LEVEL: Intermediate to advanced**
**TIME: Full day**
**DISTANCE: 7.2 miles round trip**
**ELEVATION CHANGE: 2,800 feet total gain**
**STARTING ELEVATION: 9,240 feet**
**AVALANCHE TERRAIN: Mostly avalanche terrain; wait for spring consolidation**
**USGS 7.5 MINUTE MAP: McHenrys Peak, 1957**
**MAP: page 24**

The upper section of Andrews Glacier makes a good introduction to spring ski descents. It starts out gently, so you can build confidence and get into the flow of cranking turns before tackling the steep section below Andrews Tarn. The only drawback is that it is a long walk in for a relatively short descent. If you plan on taking several runs on the upper section and then enjoying a leisurely lunch beside the tarn, the excursion will be well worth the effort.

The approach starts from the Glacier Gorge turnoff on the road to Bear Lake. Leave Estes Park and drive west to the Beaver Meadows entrance to Rocky Mountain National Park. Once past the entrance booths, take the first left to Glacier Gorge and Bear Lake. Proceed 8.3 miles to a small parking area hemmed in by a sharp hairpin curve. From the parking lot, begin the tour by following the main Glacier Gorge Trail (or the more direct, unmarked, old trail if you can find it) for 2 miles, passing the turnoff for Lake Haiyaha and the turnoff for Mills Lake and continuing up some steep switchbacks to the loch. Go around the loch and proceed up the valley 0.5 miles to the turnoff for Andrews Glacier. This trail climbs steeply into the Andrews Creek drainage. Soon you'll break out of the trees and be rewarded with some striking views of Shark's Tooth on the left and the narrow rock pinnacles known as Wham and Zowie on the right. Continue west up a steep step to Andrews Tarn. Above the tarn is the main upper section of Andrews Glacier.

Depending on the conditions and the amount of snow remaining, you may be able to ski all the way back down to the Glacier Gorge Trail before being forced to remove your skis.

# 10 GLACIER GORGE TO BLACK LAKE

**DESCRIPTION: Winter ski tour, spectacular, moderate trail**
**SKILL LEVEL: Intermediate to advanced**
**TIME: Full day**
**DISTANCE: 7 miles round trip**
**ELEVATION CHANGE: 1,380 feet total gain**
**STARTING ELEVATION: 9,240 feet**
**AVALANCHE TERRAIN: None**
**USGS 7.5 MINUTE MAP: McHenrys Peak, 1957**
**MAP: page 24**

A trip through Glacier Gorge will provide the backcountry skier with a chance to experience some of the most spectacular terrain anywhere in the Front Range of Colorado. Glacially scoured granite walls and soaring spires encircle a beautiful valley of evergreen forests, deep alpine lakes and solitude. Combine this environment with great touring and exciting downhill skiing on the return trip, and you have the ingredients for a superb outing.

As with most tours in Rocky Mountain National Park, access is from Estes Park via the Beaver Meadows entrance. From this entrance proceed west until you reach the turnoff to Bear Lake and Glacier Gorge. After 8.3 miles you will come upon a small parking area hemmed in by a sharp hairpin curve. This is the Glacier Gorge parking area and the jumping-off point for the tour.

The trail begins due south of the parking area and is well marked by a park service information board containing a map of the area and written information concerning backcountry travel and safety. Pass the display and follow the trail as it crosses Chaos Creek via a small wooden bridge. The trail here is quite wide and well traveled so it is easy to find and follow; just be sure to avoid the smaller trail, which heads east and downstream along Glacier Creek.

Once on the main trail, you have two ways of reaching the fork that separates the trails to Loch Vale and Glacier Gorge (Mills Lake–Black Lake). The first option is to simply follow the primary summer trail, which passes Alberta Falls on the left and traverses the first Glacier Knob on its southeast side. The second option follows a nonmaintained trail passing northwest of Glacier Knob and rejoins the main trail several hundred feet east of the turnoff to Glacier Gorge. This route is preferable because it is shorter, less windy and has better snow. The point at which this nonmaintained trail deviates from the main trail is hard to locate, but just remember that it follows the first major drainage to the right once you have passed Chaos Creek. When you reach the second bridge on the main trail, turn right and follow the small drainage along its north side. Contour along the creek as it heads south and ascend toward the main summer trail.

The two trails merge in a flat forested area just east of the turnoff to Glacier Gorge. Follow the left fork as it drops to Icy Brook. After this small tributary the route begins to climb up into Glacier Gorge and Mills Lake. This climb, steep but short, lies west of Glacier Creek. Pass Mills Lake and Jewel Lake on their north and east sides. The panorama here is incredible, dominated by Longs Peak, Pagoda Mountain and Chiefshead at the head of the valley to the south. Once past these lakes, glide south through the woods until you begin a noticeable climb which, after several steps, eventually brings you to Black Lake, a beautiful lunch spot surrounded by jagged alpine topography. The return trip is simply a reversal—but far more action-packed!

# 11  GLACIER CREEK

DESCRIPTION: Winter ski tour, backcountry trails, mostly downhill, car shuttle required
SKILL LEVEL: Novice
TIME: Half day
DISTANCE: 4 miles or more one way
ELEVATION CHANGE: 800 feet loss
STARTING ELEVATION: 9,460 feet
AVALANCHE TERRAIN: Some avalanche terrain encountered; easily avoided
USGS 7.5 MINUTE MAP: McHenrys Peak, 1957
MAP: page 24

This tour makes an excellent introduction to the joys of cross-country skiing. Organized with a car shuttle from Sprague Lake, the tour is virtually all downhill. The trail is, for the most part, well marked and easy to follow. Although narrow and fast in spots, the descent into the Glacier Creek valley is generally easy to control with snowplow turns, pole drags and an occasional sit-down before the sharp turn stop.

The tour begins from the Bear Lake parking lot and ends at Sprague Lake, where a car shuttle is required to return to the starting point. From Estes Park, drive west to the Beaver Meadows entrance to Rocky Mountain National Park. After passing the entrance booths, take the first left turn to Bear Lake and Glacier Gorge. Follow this road 5.5 miles to the Sprague Lake Trailhead on the south side of the road. Leave one car here and proceed 3.5 miles to the Bear Lake parking lot. There is an information station at the upper end of the lot which has a map of the area. Ski up toward the lake for a few hundred feet and make a sharp left. After skiing a short distance down this trail, take another left on the Glacier Creek Trail and begin a steady descent into the valley. This first section is the steepest part. After about 0.5 miles, you will emerge at the Glacier Gorge parking area. Ski south a short distance along the Loch Vale–Mills Lake Trail to find the continuation of the Glacier Creek Trail, and proceed the rest of the way down into the valley. After 2.3 miles from the start of the route, you'll encounter another fork with several possibilities. The quickest way out is to bear left, taking you directly to the access road for Sprague Lake. Follow this road 0.3 miles, first east, then north, to the Bear Lake road where your car shuttle is waiting.

# 12   SPRAGUE LAKE

**DESCRIPTION: Winter ski tour, backcountry trails, loop trip, mostly level terrain**
**SKILL LEVEL: Novice**
**TIME: Quarter day**
**DISTANCE: 3.7 miles round trip**
**ELEVATION CHANGE: 220 feet total gain**
**STARTING ELEVATION: 8,680 feet**
**AVALANCHE TERRAIN: None**
**USGS 7.5 MINUTE MAP: Longs Peak, 1978-PR**
**MAP: page 24**

A tour around Sprague Lake will take you out and about and into the backcountry without encountering any difficult ski terrain. There is a good chance you'll catch a glimpse of wildlife, especially waterfowl, along the way. The route follows backcountry trails over level terrain on a wide loop that circles Sprague Lake. The lake is located in the Glacier Gorge valley below Bear Lake in Rocky Mountain National Park.

The elevation of this tour is lower than most other tours described in this book. Consequently, the snowcover is often disappointing. Call or check in at park headquarters for information on trail and snow conditions prior to making the drive.

From park headquarters, west of Estes Park, proceed west to the Bear Lake–Moraine Park turnoff. Head south on this road past Moraine Park, and Hallowell Park, then bend around west into Glacier Gorge, where the marked Sprague Lake Trailhead is located on the south side of the road.

The following description is for a counterclockwise loop around the lake, but the opposite loop is no more difficult and no less enjoyable—either way works well.

From the parking area ski south on the unplowed Sprague Lake road. After a short distance the road bends north and continues to a loop turnaround. A trail takes off from here heading north. Follow it, taking left turns wherever you encounter a trail junction. This will guarantee a counterclockwise loop around the lake. After circling clear around to the south side of the valley and proceeding east downstream, you'll encounter another road. The same rule applies here—just make a left at every junction and eventually you'll complete the circuit. It is helpful, of course, to keep the map handy and chart your progress as you circumnavigate the lake.

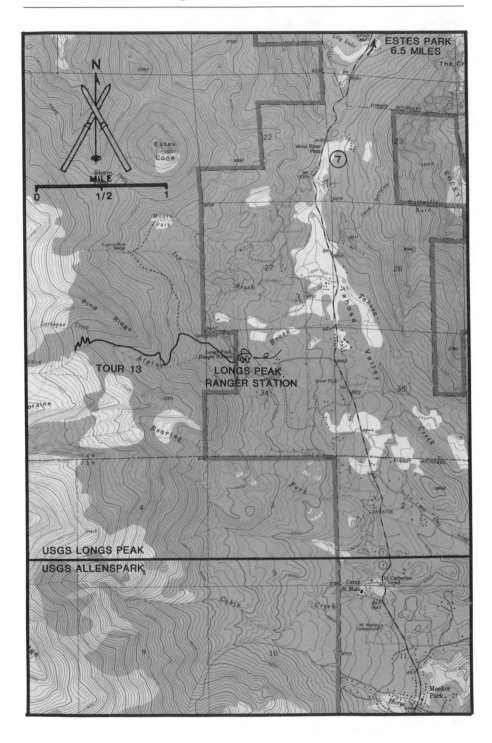

# 13 LONGS PEAK TRAIL

**DESCRIPTION: Winter ski tour, steep narrow trail, several switch-backs**
**SKILL LEVEL: Advanced***
**TIME: Half day**
**DISTANCE: 4 miles round trip**
**ELEVATION CHANGE: 1,200 feet total gain**
**STARTING ELEVATION: 9,400 feet**
**AVALANCHE TERRAIN: None**
**USGS 7.5 MINUTE MAP: Longs Peak, 1978-PR**
**MAP: page 36**

**\*INTERMEDIATE HIGHLIGHT: The alternate route to Eugenia Mine is shorter and less difficult.**

The Longs Peak Trail consistently has the best snow of any tour in Rocky Mountain National Park. The trail is steep and quite narrow, requiring a controlled, conservative descent. Unfortunately, there are also a number of sharp hairpin turns to contend with. Still, it is a worthwhile tour, especially when conditions elsewhere in the park have deteriorated into crusty windblown hardpack. Start from the Longs Peak Ranger Station, which is located at the end of a dirt access road off Colo. 7, south of Estes Park 9 miles.

The trail is both easy to find and easy to follow. Just before the second switchback (about 0.5 miles up the trail), there is a marked turnoff that leads to the old Eugenia Mine site. This makes a fine alternative tour for those who don't want to contend with the switchbacks of the Longs Peak Trail. It is not as steep and is also quite a bit shorter. From the Eugenia Mine cutoff, the Longs Peak Trail continues up a succession of

*Skiing below Notchtop Mountain to Lake Helene (tour 2), Brian Litz photo.*

switchbacks to treeline, where most parties stop. Above this point the snow is usually too windpacked and conditions too harsh to make skiing worthwhile.

The descent is via the same route.

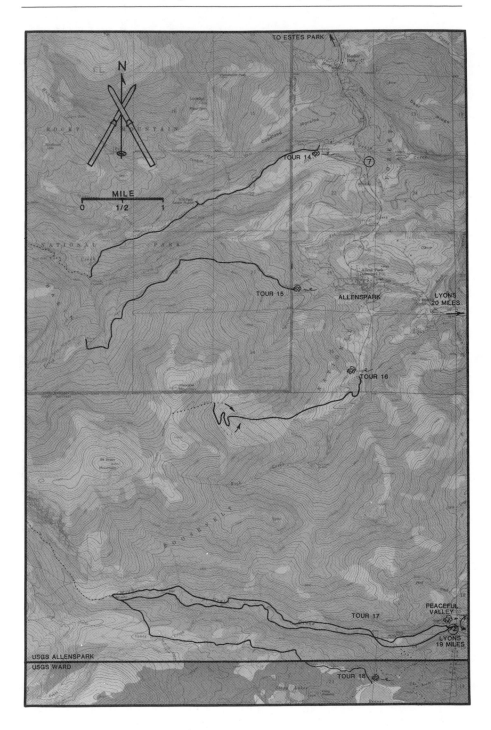

# 14 WILD BASIN (COLORADO MOUNTAIN CLUB CABIN AND CALYPSO FALLS)

**DESCRIPTION: Winter ski tour, steep and twisting trail tour, Colorado Mountain Club warming cabin
SKILL LEVEL: Advanced
TIME: Full day
DISTANCE: 9 miles round trip
ELEVATION CHANGE: 1,080 feet total gain
STARTING ELEVATION: 8,320 feet
USGS 7.5 MINUTE MAPS: Allenspark, 1978-PR, Isolation Peak, 1975-PI
AVALANCHE TERRAIN: None
MAP: page 38**

**\*NOVICE/INTERMEDIATE HIGHLIGHT: The initial few miles of this tour are only slightly inclined and make for an enjoyable and moderate trip to the Colorado Mountain Club cabin.**

The southern extension of Rocky Mountain National Park is often overlooked because of so much activity found around Bear Lake and Glacier Gorge. The most dominant topographical feature in the southern part of the park is a massive drainage known as Wild Basin. Adventuresome backcountry skiers can spend many days exploring this high-country environ, filled with a multitude of lakes, thick woods and fine ski-touring trails. The trail to Calypso Falls and Thunder Lake, which lie in the heart of Wild Basin, threads a sinuous line through dense groves of pine trees as it climbs away from the flat valley floor between Copeland Lake and the ranger station. This tour maintains a steady rate of ascent, providing a good workout and ensuring an expeditious return to civilization. Calypso and Ouzel falls make a fine destination for a day trip, while Thunder Lake awaits the advanced skier. Thunder Lake is a great spot for hearty souls to camp and enjoy the nighttime winter experience. Try this tour and discover a great winter wilderness close to home.

Of importance to all skiers is Wild Basin Cabin, which is operated by the Enos Mills Group of the Colorado Mountain Club (Estes Park). It lies roughly 2 miles from the trailhead near the ranger station. The cabin is designed primarily for day use, with overnight accommodations provided for club-member hut hosts. The cabin boasts bunks with foam pads, wood stove (etc.) and utensils for the use of the hosts, who can number up to four. Day use for all skiers is strongly encouraged by the club and hot drinks are available. For more information contact the Enos Mills Group of the Colorado Mountain Club (see Appendix 4).

Access to Wild Basin is just north of Allenspark on the Peak-to-Peak Highway (Colo. 7). The turnoff to Wild Basin Ranger Station may be approached from Estes Park from the north or Allenspark from the south. Turn west and drive until the road is no longer plowed, normally right near Copeland Lake. Don your ski gear and glide along the valley bottom. The tour begins on land outside of the park, but you will shortly pass the national park boundary. Continue skiing on the main road, passing several forks to the right that lead to private cabins. This portion is quite flat and a great spot for the novice to try out a new sport. Beyond the road's end and the ranger station, you will pass a park service information sign at Hunter Creek. From here, the Thunder Lake Trail climbs steadily and can be icy, so study trail conditions and be ready for a potentially harrowing return trip.

After a climb of roughly 200 feet, during which you cross a wooden bridge at Sandbeach Creek, the angle of the trail decreases. The trail bends south and you cross North St. Vrain Creek before a climb brings you to Calypso Falls, a cold and forbidding spot during the deep of winter. Ouzel Falls lies about 0.25 miles farther up the tightly twisting trail. Just beyond Ouzel Falls the trail makes a sharp lefthand turn on a small rock outcrop, providing a striking view back down into the valley. This is the usual turnaround point for this tour.

*Overlooking Odessa Lake (tour 2), Brian Litz photo.*

For a much more demanding outing, go to Thunder Lake, a little over 3 miles farther at the head of the valley. To reach the lake, ski beyond the scenic point near Ouzel Falls and descend down a tree-covered, north-facing slope, maneuvering past a few large rock outcrops and boulders. The descent continues until you reach North St. Vrain Creek. The trail now follows a moderate path as it crosses the valley bottom and turns off to Bluebird Lake. After crossing North St. Vrain Creek, the trail climbs up the south flank of Mount Orton. After several hundred feet the trail begins a gentler traverse of this south slope through more broken forests, with a view to the south of bulbous Mount Copeland. After traversing around to the western side of Mount Orton, the final stretch to Thunder Lake begins with a climb through the trees, crossing two small drainages higher above the lake. The two streams lie 0.25 miles east of the lake and signal the time to head directly west to the lake. When the time to depart arrives, follow the creekbed as it leaves the lake. Great powder runs may be had through this section until you meet the Thunder Lake Trail. It is important to stress that this variation is much more demanding than simply skiing into Ouzel Falls. Plan for a long day and prepare properly, or plan for a night out in a fantastic mountain setting.

# 15 FINCH LAKE AND PEAR RESERVOIR

**DESCRIPTION: Winter ski tour, remote and demanding trail**
**SKILL LEVEL: Advanced**
**TIME: Full day**
**DISTANCE: Finch Lake 7.6 miles round trip**
             **Pear Lake 11.8 miles round trip**
**ELEVATION CHANGE: Finch Lake 1,230 feet total gain/258 feet loss**
                    **to lake**
                    **Pear Reservoir additional 670 feet gain**
**STARTING ELEVATION: 8,940 feet**
**AVALANCHE TERRAIN: None**
**USGS 7.5 MINUTE MAP: Allenspark, 1978-PR**
**MAP: page 38**

The Finch Lake Trail is a scenic, isolated and demanding tour traversing the north slopes of Meadow Mountain, which lies on the edge of the southern boundary of Wild Basin and Rocky Mountain National Park. Heading west from the town of Allenspark, the route provides a mix of strenuous climbs, long stretches of kick and glide and several spots of twisting downhill adventure. On clear days the views to the north and west of the Longs Peak–Mount Meeker group and upper ramparts of Wild Basin will help you forget about your exertion.

Perhaps the most challenging part of this tour is finding the new and slightly elusive park service trailhead. To reach this spot drive on Colo. 7 and take the turnoff to Allenspark. Drive into the center of town and turn west (right). The center of town is marked by the wooden community church and the Allenspark post office. Once you have turned right follow the road through a mountain housing area on a slight uphill climb. Crest over a hill and follow the main road on its curving path to the north and west. Drop to the bottom of a hill, bypassing a turnoff to the right. Climb sharply around a switchback toward the southeast. Continue through a second switchback which leads to a steeper hill oriented toward the southwest (this switchback is very close to the 8,800-foot mark and contour line on the USGS topographic map). Finally the road bends to the south and the trailhead will be found on your right. Total driving distance is roughly 1.8 miles.

Leave the road and ski past the wooden sign and through the split-rail fence. Enter the woods and begin a gentle climb along the wide trail. Moderate climbing characterizes this initial section of trail, 0.5 miles to the first turnoff to the Wild Basin Trail, ascending steadily to the northwest through mixed stands of pine and aspen. Once past the trail junction the route heads more to the west on an increasingly steep climb. The forest becomes more dense (fewer aspen, too) as you gain altitude, though you will be able to peer through the trees and into Wild Basin below. As you approach the 1.5-mile mark, the trail veers right, climbing steeply through a labyrinth of fallen and standing timber. The normally distinct trail and ski tracks can become a confusion of tight switchbacks, snowplow zones and sitzmarks left by previous skiers who tried to negotiate this treacherous spot.

Once past this tricky ascent the trail climbs and traverses gently westward, high on the north side of Meadow Mountain. Kick and glide through this stretch, marked by silvery skeletons of dead pine trees. The 2-mile mark brings you to a hub of trails leading to Finch Lake, Calypso Cascades and Wild Basin to the east. Ski through this intersection, taking the leftmost alternative.

After passing this trail junction the tour heads toward the southwest where Finch Lake sits roughly 2 miles away. The rolling nature of the last mile gives way to steeper terrain as the trail climbs into a thicker cover of forest. The climbing becomes harder as this ascending traverse of Meadow Mountain brings you to a large, burned area. The trail continues its diagonal route, following a distinct swath cut through the dead timber. As with the rest of the tour the route here is marked by blue trail markers. Nearing the end of the burn, the tour makes a short but sharp drop to the west-northwest just before re-entering the woods.

Once again the tour begins another stretch of classic kick and glide on a moderate trail winding through large pine trees decorated with "Old Man's Beard" moss. Crossing small wooden bridges over a branch of the North St. Vrain and a branch of Coney Creek, you reach the 3.8-mile point and the final leg of the trip, which also is one of the most challenging. The last 0.25 miles, a descent to the lake's edge, may be managed in one of two ways. The first choice is to follow the marked summer trail which twists down a series of tight switchbacks. The second is to ski through the trees on a path of your choosing, eventually skiing out onto the shores of this serene lake hemmed in by rolling forested mountains. Either route is thrilling and both have seen at least one set of broken ski poles.

If you wish to push on up to Pear Reservoir, cross Finch Lake and ski to the end of the meadow on the west side. Where the clearing ends, follow Coney Creek until you reach a willow-filled clearing. From here leave the creekbed and begin climbing due west. When you reach the Coney Creek tributary which flows down from Pear Reservoir, turn upstream, switchbacking on the right side, then contour along its course to the small windblown lake.

# 16   MEADOW MOUNTAIN BOWL

**DESCRIPTION: Winter ski tour, mostly forest trail, good telemark bowl**
**SKILL LEVEL: Intermediate***
**TIME: Full day**
**DISTANCE: 6 miles round trip**
**ELEVATION CHANGE: 2,500 feet total gain**
**STARTING ELEVATION: 8,580 feet**

**AVALANCHE TERRAIN: Route crosses avalanche slopes; prone to skier-triggered avalanches during high-hazard periods**
**USGS 7.5 MINUTE MAP: Allenspark, 1978-PR**
**MAP: page 38**

**\*ADVANCED HIGHLIGHT: The upper bowl has excellent telemark glades.**

This is a little-known tour just south of Rocky Mountain National Park. It follows the unplowed continuation of an access road west out of Allenspark and then splits off northwest, following a trail for several miles to a large sparsely timbered bowl on the south flank of Meadow Mountain. The trail is narrow and fairly steep along its entire length but has no switchbacks or surprises. It may be difficult to negotiate in icy spring conditions, but because of its sheltered location, it generally has more consistent snow than most of the trails in the park. The sparsely timbered bowl is potentially one of the best powder telemark runs in the area, although avalanche danger can be high during winter.

To reach Allenspark take Colo. 7 south out of Lyons and continue west up the Middle Fork of the St. Vrain, then north toward Rocky Mountain National Park. You can also reach Allenspark by heading south from Estes Park on Colo. 7, which actually bypasses Allenspark just to the east but provides access at both the north and south ends of town. From the south access, go through Ferncliffe and take the first left turn before entering the main section of Allenspark. This road cuts back across the hill heading south, then curls west before coming to a junction. Go left at the junction and continue to the end of the plowed road. This access road can also be found from the north entrance to Allenspark by taking Ski Road (Colo. 107) and winding west and south through cabins above the main part of town.

Ski up the continuation of the access road and take the first right fork. The left fork goes up Rock Creek and can also be skied. In fact, an ambitious loop trip could be put together by following the right fork (this tour) up to the saddle west of Meadow Mountain, then rounding the next hump west, all above treeline, and finally going down Rock Creek.

From the fork continue up through a succession of switchbacks to a sign marking the start of the St. Vrain Mountain Trail. Follow this trail on a diagonal course of about 2.5 miles up into the bowl below Meadow Mountain. There, with stable conditions, you can take numerous powder telemark runs down the sparsely timbered slopes of the bowl. Be wary of avalanche danger; sparsely timbered slopes can avalanche almost as easily as wide-open ones.

Return via the same route.

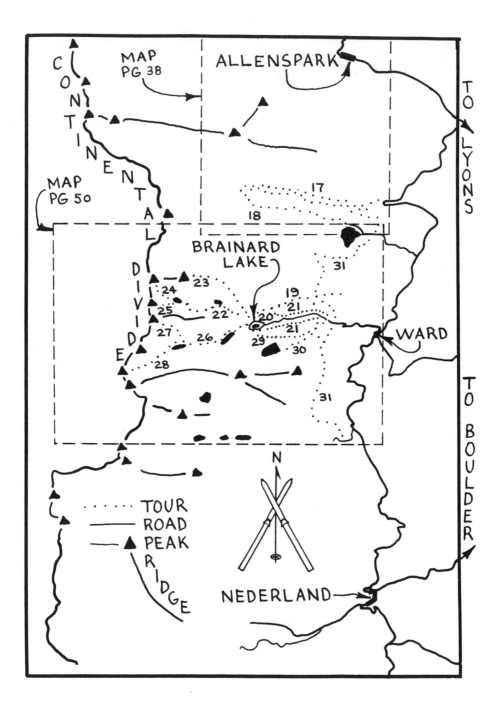

# CHAPTER TWO

# BRAINARD LAKE

## INTRODUCTION

The Brainard Lake area has been a favorite haunt of backcountry enthusiasts, both summer and winter, for many years. Virtually in the backyard of Front Range communities, the trails and peaks of the Indian Peaks have felt the passage of many Colorado skiers and hikers—of all abilities. Wintertime at Brainard Lake finds a mosaic of Nordic challenges—rolling forest tours climb up and over small hills and drainages, as skiers are treated to gentle twisting roller-coaster rides through dense trees often covered with Old Man's Beard moss. The Brainard Lake area offers trails near and around the lake that are relatively moderate, gain little elevation and consequently encounter few sustained climbs—in contrast to many Front Range trails that ascend narrow drainages and can make for difficult skiing (especially when the snowpack is shallow). Brainard Lake is a perfect destination for novice/intermediate-level skiers, families and experts desiring a nice half day of exercise. Additionally, the alpine panorama is one of the finest encountered along the Front Range.

Beyond the lake, the topography rises dramatically as you move closer to the frozen peaks. Here many beautiful mountain lakes and forgotten glacial tarns sit. Advanced skiers and the more intrepid intermediate tourer will find deep snow and exciting downhill runs en route to these frozen lakes. Combining one of the more advanced tours with any basic Brainard Lake tour will add up to a memorable trip for seasoned skiers. Also, don't forget to stop in for lunch and a rest at Brainard Lake Cabin. Owned and operated by the Colorado Mountain Club, this grand old cabin has provided a safe winter haven for generations of skiers.

Keep in mind that the weather and snow conditions at Brainard Lake are classic Front Range: either crisp clear weather and fine snow or bitter gale-force winds that drive the windchill factor well below zero and transport and compact snow into heavy drifts. If you suspect the presence of arctic conditions, plan and be prepared for a hearty adventure.

As spring brings longer days and warmer temperatures, the Front Range snowpack transforms radically. While the lower trails remain skiable for a surprisingly long time (easily into early April), the high peaks become perfect for spring ski mountaineering. Each year more and more alpine/Nordic skiers ascend these airy points in search of "spring velvet." Favorite descents include Mount Toll, Apache

Peak and Mount Audubon. Many of these alpine descents are quite spectacular while being surprisingly moderate.

## HISTORY

When one thinks of Nebraska, one hardly conjures up images of craggy mountain wilderness, gold fields and skiing. However, when the first settlers reached the area around and to the west of present-day Boulder, they were actually in the territory of Nebraska. The 40th parallel, which runs along present-day Baseline Road in Boulder, was the dividing line between the Nebraska and Kansas territories. The flood of white people into the area began when rumors of the Pikes Peak gold trickled back toward the east. Chief Niwot, famed Arapaho chief, in 1858 foretold the impending crush of people when he proclaimed to Captain Thomas Aikens, "Does the white man remember, many, many moons ago, the great light in the west, when the stars fell? The Great Spirit told us then that the white man would soon be as numerous as the falling stars." Aikens had led a prospecting party west and followed the South Fork of the St. Vrain River to the mouth of Boulder Canyon, erecting a small camp on October 17, 1858.

The first flecks of gold had been discovered near Boulder Creek during that autumn. Colorado mountain weather soon became the miners' greatest adversary as the approaching winter's frigid storms froze the ground and water solid. With the coming of spring in the year 1859, both temperatures and enthusiasm climbed. The drainages flowing down off the high Indian Peaks to the Great Plains were crawling with an ever-increasing number of meticulous prospectors who panned every creek and creeklet. These tough characters knew also that the gold lying in the streams was only a tiny hint of the vast lodes or veins that represented the source of the rare metal. The largest placer deposit was found near present-day Gold Hill; they named the area Gold Run, for obvious reasons. By employing great sluice boxes the miners exhausted the placer or free gold in roughly one year. Interest then shifted to subsurface hardrock quartz vein mining.

With the advent of hardrock mining, the entire atmosphere changed. This form of mining required much more equipment, including massive stamps to crush the ore. Large lodes of high-grade ore were discovered near Gold Hill (including the Horsfal Lode which was found on June 16, 1859, by J. D. Scott). Other lodes were exposed in the mountains west of Boulder. Ward, Colorado, named after Calvin Ward, saw several large veins exposed in the early 1860s. Mr. Ward found the Miser's Dream while C. H. Merrill found the vastly superior Columbia vein which had produced a staggering $5 million worth of gold by 1949. Today most of the old mining camps are mere shadows of their past brilliance, but their names—Jamestown, Wall Street, Crisman and Magnolia—shine on.

# 17 MIDDLE ST. VRAIN

**DESCRIPTION: Winter ski tour, flat road and rolling trail loop trip, good for skating**
**SKILL LEVEL: Novice***
**TIME: Optional, up to full day**
**DISTANCE: Optional, normal loop 9.2 miles round trip**
**ELEVATION CHANGE: 1,060 feet total gain, for first 4.6 miles**
**STARTING ELEVATION: 8,520 feet**
**AVALANCHE TERRAIN: Some avalanche terrain encountered; easily avoided**
**USGS 7.5 MINUTE MAP: Allenspark, 1978-PR**
**MAP: page 38**

**\*INTERMEDIATE HIGHLIGHT: The alternate return loop via the Coney Flats Trail, then a cutoff to the Sourdough Trail, makes a very adventurous intermediate loop.**

The Middle Fork of the St. Vrain drains an extensive section of the Indian Peaks north of Mount Audubon. It is a wide flat valley that can be skied for many miles without encountering any steep terrain. You have the choice of either following the road (great for skating) or following a trail through timber on first the south then the north side of the valley. The road and the trail merge 4.6 miles from the trailhead, so you can make a loop trip if desired. The north end of the Sourdough Trail (tour 31) can also be skied from this same access. It intersects with the valley trail 0.6 miles from the parking lot. The road is frequented by snowmobiles, leaving it nicely groomed for skating.

The trailhead is located 5.8 miles north of Ward on the Peak-to-Peak Highway (Colo. 72) at a wide, sweeping hairpin turn. The turnoff is on the west side of the highway, marked by signs indicating "Forest Access" and "Middle St. Vrain Campground." Peaceful Valley Lodge sits in the valley below the hairpin turn. Limited parking is available just off the highway on the west side.

Start by skiing west on the road, which has only a very slight uphill grade along its entire length. After 0.1 miles, the trail leaves the road, cutting left into dense timber on the south side of the valley. The trail is well marked and easy to follow. Ski past the junction for the Sourdough Trail which comes down off the hillside to your left after 0.5 miles. The next 0.5-mile section is the most difficult with short drops that could be troublesome in fast springlike conditions. At the 1-mile point the trail crosses the road, then crosses the creek to the north side of the valley. From here, proceed through intermittent meadows and trees another 3.5 miles west, up valley, staying very close to the creek. The trail ends when it again intersects the road just above the bridge 4.6 miles in. The road continues from here, west, then northwest, for another 2.5 miles. Most parties prefer to return from the 4.6-mile point using either the trail or looping back on the road.

ALTERNATE ROUTE: The Coney Flats Trail (tour 18) intersects the road 0.1 miles below the 4.6-mile point. A considerably more adventurous loop takes this trail back to a point just north of Beaver Reservoir, then cuts northeast on an unmarked trail to the Sourdough Trail. The Sourdough Trail is then descended north, back to the Middle St. Vrain Trail, completing the loop.

# 18 CONEY FLATS TRAIL

**DESCRIPTION: Winter ski tour, summer jeep road, secluded backcountry terrain, trailhead located north of Ward**
**SKILL LEVEL: Novice**
**TIME: Full day**
**DISTANCE: 7.6 miles round trip**
**ELEVATION CHANGE: 600 feet total gain**
**STARTING ELEVATION: 9,200 feet**
**AVALANCHE TERRAIN: None**
**USGS 7.5 MINUTE MAPS: Ward, 1978-PR, Allenspark, 1978-PR**
**MAP: page 38**

This tour is similar to the trails around Brainard Lake but sees far less traffic. It starts from the northwest side of Beaver Reservoir (located at the end of the next main access road north of Brainard Lake) and follows a jeep road up through heavily wooded terrain. Eventually it drops down and intersects with the Middle Fork of the St. Vrain (see tour 17) near the start of Buchanan Pass.

To find Beaver Reservoir take the Peak-to-Peak Highway (Colo. 72) to a turnoff 2.5 miles north of Ward and 3.4 miles south of the Middle Fork of the St. Vrain. The turnoff is marked by signs indicating "Camp Tonahutu." Follow the dirt road west 2.2 miles to Beaver Reservoir. The Sourdough Trail (tour 31) intersects this road just before the reservoir. The trailhead for the Coney Flats Trail is on the northwest side of the reservoir, where a limited amount of parking is available. The trail is wide and easy to follow. It gradually gains altitude for the first 3 miles before dropping down into the Middle Fork of the St. Vrain. There is one left fork that leads straight west up a different jeep road. It can also be skied for a short distance.

A patchwork loop trip can be put together by heading north on the Sourdough Trail (tour 31) from the Beaver Reservoir access road to the Middle Fork of the St. Vrain, then up the Middle Fork of the St. Vrain (see tour 17) to the Coney Flats Trail, which would then take you back to Beaver Reservoir. Either this loop or the reverse makes a pleasant backcountry tour that comparatively few people travel.

# 19 SOUTH ST. VRAIN TRAIL

**DESCRIPTION: Winter ski tour, combines well with other Brainard Lake tours, fast paced and moderately steep**
**SKILL LEVEL: Intermediate**
**TIME: Full day**
**DISTANCE: 4.3 miles one way (parking area to Mitchell Lake road where it may be combined with other Brainard Lake tours)**
**ELEVATION CHANGE: 770 feet total gain/400 feet total loss**
**STARTING ELEVATION: 10,080 feet**
**AVALANCHE TERRAIN: None**
**USGS 7.5 MINUTE MAP: Ward, 1978-PR**
**MAP: page 50**

The South St. Vrain Trail is less well known than other Brainard tours but it is highly recommended. It travels east to west staying north of the Brainard Lake road (tour 20) and the North Colorado Mountain Club Trail (tour 21). The most popular section of the trail links the north half of the Sourdough Trail (tour 31) to the Mitchell Lake road (tour 22). This section is described in detail below, along with the recommended access from Red Rock Lake parking area via the north Sourdough Trail. There is also a lower section that continues below the Sourdough Trail to an alternate trailhead at Camp Tahosa.

From the town of Ward drive north on Colo. 72 and take the first left immediately past town. This is the Brainard Lake road, marked by a large sign. Drive 2.6 miles and park at the large plowed parking area. To reach the trailhead, walk back to the east and find the brown wooden sign marking the Sourdough Trailhead. Ski into the sparse trees on the north side of the road. Continue past an old wooden sign and enter the thick tree cover on a good trail. From here the trail drops over 400 feet to the South St. Vrain Creek. Fast skiing, tight switchbacks and slightly sinuous straightaway enliven this descent.

Cross the creek via a wooden footbridge and continue along the trail until you rendezvous with the South St. Vrain Trail 50 yards away. Turn upstream (left) and begin easy climbing on the north side of the drainage. Near the 2-mile mark the tour climbs steeply away from the creek as the drainage swings more to the southwest. After several hundred yards, the angle eases off as you reach a second trail junction. To the right the Sourdough Trail heads north on its way to Beaver Reservoir. Turn left again and continue along the South St. Vrain route. Cross a small tributary creek and skirt the southern edge of a small meadow. This stretch maintains a moderately easy rate of ascent through the forest. Every so often Mount Audubon shows itself through the woods to the west.

After twisting through the woods, you will meet the Colorado Mountain Club North Trail (Harold Waldrop Trail) merging from the left (just beyond the 3.5-mile mark). Ski west and make a quick drop into a sharp creekbed containing a

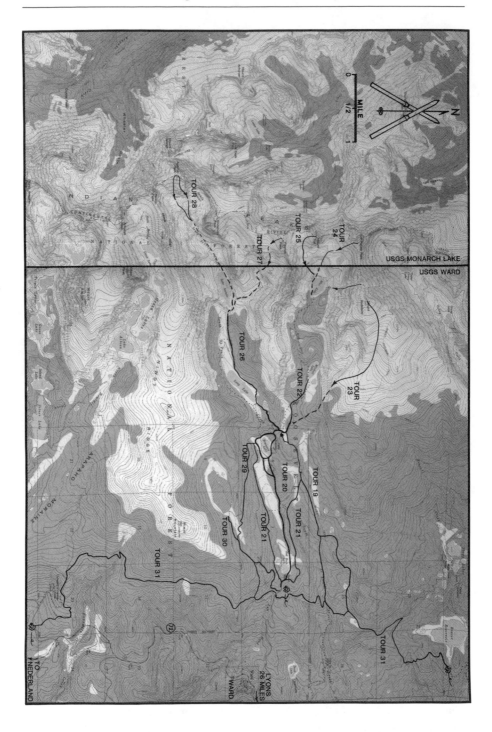

tributary of the South St. Vrain. Climb out its opposite bank (watching out for skiers dropping in from the west), contour west and ski past a marked cutoff to the Brainard Lake road. Moderate terrain carries you upward for a little over a mile until you break out of the dense forest. This area on blustery days is a natural wind tunnel, as winds shriek off Mount Toll and Paiute Peak high above Mitchell Lake to the west. When your party reaches this open spot, you can either cross the wind-tortured clearing to reach Brainard Lake Cabin or ski west along the edge of the trees reaching the Mitchell Lake road.

Reversing this tour is equally enjoyable, with many stretches of downhill skiing before crossing the bridge over the South St. Vrain. From there it's all uphill back to the parking area, but it goes quickly.

# 20 BRAINARD LAKE ROAD

**DESCRIPTION: Winter ski tour, popular family tour**
**SKILL LEVEL: Novice**
**TIME: Half day**
**DISTANCE: 2.1 miles one way to Brainard Cabin**
**ELEVATION CHANGE: 260 feet total gain**
**STARTING ELEVATION: 10,080 feet**
**AVALANCHE TERRAIN: None**
**USGS 7.5 MINUTE MAP: Ward, 1978-PR**
**MAP: page 50**

The Brainard Lake road is one of Colorado's best novice ski tours. The trip's highlights include minimal elevation gain, a superb panorama of the Indian Peaks and the warm shelter of Brainard Lake Cabin as a lunch spot. Route finding is also very straightforward, as the entire trip lies on a wide summer roadbed. This tour certainly must rank as one of the most popular tours in northeastern Colorado and is an excellent choice for a family outing. To the northwest of Brainard Lake lies Brainard Lake Cabin, owned and operated by the Boulder Group of the Colorado Mountain Club. This structure is one of the finest backcountry cabins in Colorado, featuring overnight accommodations, weekend hut hosts and a rich history. For a small fee (about $1.00) your party may stop in and eat lunch by a toasty fire while sipping hot drinks heated on the large wood-burning stoves. For more information on the cabin and the Colorado Mountain Club see Appendix 4.

Brainard Lake lies west of the Peak-to-Peak Highway (Colo. 72) immediately north of the town of Ward. The turn is well marked and the road is plowed to the parking area, 2.6 miles away. On a typical weekend this parking spot will overflow with vehicles so try to arrive early. The ski tour simply continues on the road west past the tubular-metal gate blocking winter traffic.

After you begin skiing, the road will make a very slight climb as it leaves the parking area, contouring north and west over a rise as it starts its gently undulating path to the lake. Red Rock Lake, just over the rise on the left, is a nice spot to gain an unobstructed view of the high peaks. On clear days the entire Indian Peaks wilderness breaks up the western skyline, dominated by the massive Mount Audubon (13,223 feet) to the northwest.

Brainard Lake is roughly 1.8 miles from the starting point. When you reach its shores, you may loop around it in either direction. To reach Brainard Lake Cabin ski to the west side of the lake and follow the turnoff to Blue and Mitchell lakes. This spur road heads first west, then quickly veers north. On this road you will first pass a turnoff on your left leading to the parking area for the trail to Long Lake and Isabelle Lake; continue along the road to Mitchell and Blue lakes and you will break out into the east edge of a large clearing. The cabin lies directly to your right in the woods. On most weekends an obvious packed trail will guide you to the cabin's front door.

The quickest and easiest return route is on the road; however, Brainard Lake Cabin lies at the hub of a vast network of superb ski tours. Alternate return routes are the North Trail and the South Trail (tour 21). Tours of a more advanced nature push higher west into the valleys containing Blue Lake (tour 22) and Isabelle Lake (tour 26). No matter what combination you choose, a great day is ensured for all.

# 21 COLORADO MOUNTAIN CLUB TRAILS— SOUTH AND NORTH

**DESCRIPTION: Winter ski tour, beautiful rolling trails**
**SKILL LEVEL: Novice to intermediate**
**TIME: Full day**
**DISTANCE: South Trail 2.6 miles one way**
          **North Trail 2.7 miles one way**
**ELEVATION CHANGE: South Trail 360 feet total gain**
                 **North Trail 420 feet total gain**
**STARTING ELEVATION: 10,080 feet**
**AVALANCHE TERRAIN: None**
**USGS 7.5 MINUTE MAP: Ward, 1978-PR**
**MAP: page 50**

The Brainard Lake area is one of the most popular and diverse ski-touring destinations along the Front Range. This huge basin features a classic mountain setting, good skiing conditions and a short drive from Denver and Boulder. The Colorado Mountain Club established several trails which form a large loop encircling Brainard Lake. Known descriptively as the South and North trails (the latter is also known as the Harold Waldrop Trail), these tours offer some of the best ski touring east of the Continental Divide.

These two trails are quite different in nature; the South Trail follows a more gentle path, skirting the area south of Brainard Lake, leisurely ascending and dropping off many small knolls. The North Trail places greater demands on your snow-plow skills and aerobic capacity, as it drops sharply into several drainages and then climbs back out. The North Trail is more of an intermediate ski tour, while the South Trail is well within the novice category—but both are highly recommended to skiers of all abilities. These trails may be skied in any direction, but the most popular method is to ski them in one continuous loop beginning on the South Trail, stopping for lunch at Brainard Lake Cabin, then finishing the day with an exciting return trip to the car on the North Trail.

Reach Brainard Lake from the Peak-to-Peak Highway (Colo. 72) immediately north of the small mountain community of Ward. The turnoff is well marked and the plowed road will lead you 2.6 miles to the winter parking area. On weekends this large parking area will fill, so the earlier your party arrives the better.

To begin the South Trail, pass the metal gate that blocks the road and ski west a few hundred feet. The trail starts on the left where the road begins to veer to the northwest; the trailhead is well marked. It climbs steeply where it enters the woods but with 5 to 10 minutes work, you will pass this steep section and begin gliding over rolling terrain. The majority of the route is near the forest's edge, with occasional openings to give you views of the alpine summits to the west and north. After about a mile you will look down onto the large meadow lying east of Brainard Lake. Re-enter thicker stands of timber and glide past several old fireplaces from long-abandoned structures that sit near the 1.8-mile point. At this point you will be nearing the west edge of the lake. The trail breaks out of the woods, heading to the northwest as it crosses the southwest extensions of the clearings that surround the lake. Aim for the summer roadbed, which will lead you to the turnoff to the upper parking areas (summer parking for trails to Blue Lake, Mount Audubon, Lake Isabelle, etc.). Follow the road that leads to the Blue Lake parking area. When you reach the southeast corner of a large clearing, Brainard Lake Cabin will sit to your right, hidden in the trees on a hill.

For the return trip on the North Trail return to the road and continue north toward the Blue Lake parking area. After a few hundred feet the road turns sharply west and the North Trail begins immediately to your right. It climbs slightly east onto a small rise on the north side of the windy clearing lying on the east side of the Mitchell Lake road. This area is covered by small wind-tortured trees. From that point turn into the thicker trees to the north, pick up the well-marked trail and glide effortlessly through heavier stands of trees on a long moderate decline. Near the end of this downhill section, the trail veers to the north and drops sharply into South St. Vrain Creek. Climb out of the creek to the east and begin another fast and twisting descent before crossing South St. Vrain Creek for a second time.

From here the trail snakes through the woods, crossing a small meadow before it enters thick woods festooned with ornamental clumps of Old Man's Beard moss. The route through here climbs up and over several hills; some are steep but short. The trail then leaves the narrow corridors of the trees as it drops and bends southward. Several hundred yards more of touring in a southerly direction will return you to the Brainard Lake road, a short glide away from the car. Both trails are easy to follow and well marked. Be sure to allow plenty of time to fully enjoy these fine trails.

# 22    MITCHELL LAKE AND BLUE LAKE

**DESCRIPTION: Winter ski tour, backcountry trails**
**SKILL LEVEL: Intermediate**
**TIME: Full day**
**DISTANCE: 7 miles round trip to Mitchell Lake via Brainard Lake road**
**ELEVATION CHANGE: 700 feet total gain to Mitchell Lake**
**STARTING ELEVATION: 10,080 feet**
**AVALANCHE TERRAIN: Some avalanche terrain encountered; easily avoided**
**USGS 7.5 MINUTE MAP: Ward, 1978-PR**
**MAP: page 50**

Mitchell Lake is a popular destination for those seeking a moderate but satisfying day in the backcountry. The tour is especially good during or just after a storm because there is little or no avalanche danger. Actually, the same is true of most of the other winter tours around Brainard Lake but the Mitchell Lake and Blue Lake tour takes you a little higher and a little deeper into the backcountry. The immediate area around Brainard Lake is often exposed to high wind, but the rest of the tour is well protected. For a longer tour it is possible to continue up the valley to Blue Lake. The trip can also be combined with one of the two Colorado Mountain Club trails (tour 21) or the Little Raven Trail (tour 29). All these tours funnel into Brainard Lake, which is where the Mitchell Lake Trail starts.

To get there take the Peak-to-Peak Highway (Colo. 72) to the Brainard Lake turnoff just north of Ward. Follow this west for 2.6 miles to the winter parking area at the end of the plowed road. Ski up the road for 2.5 miles or, as mentioned above, take either of the two Colorado Mountain Club trails or the Little Raven Trail to Brainard Lake. The North Colorado Mountain Club Trail is a good choice because it intersects the Mitchell Lake Tour just north of Brainard Lake.

The Mitchell Lake and Blue Lake Trail starts at the northwest side of Brainard Lake. It begins as a road that cuts back north, crosses the creek and then continues northwest up the valley. The North Colorado Mountain Club Trail intersects this road at the far end of the first large open meadow. A little farther on, the road ends at the summer parking lot for Mitchell and Blue lakes. A marked trail continues straight west from the parking lot 0.2 miles to a narrow footbridge. Beyond the bridge, the trail turns northwest, running parallel to the creek (it's easy to miss this turn). If snowcover is plentiful, the creekbed makes a fine alternate route. Either way, proceed 0.5 miles northwest to Mitchell Lake. To extend the tour to Blue Lake gain the first bench on the southwest side of Mitchell Lake by ascending a short draw; then proceed west along the general line of the creekbed for another mile. There is no marked trail above Mitchell Lake but the forest opens considerably, allowing you to navigate by using the high peaks as landmarks.

Return to Brainard Lake via the same route; then you can select one of the various alternatives for an exit.

# 23   MOUNT AUDUBON (13,223 FEET)

**DESCRIPTION: Spring ski descent, long, moderate approach hike**
**SKILL LEVEL: Intermediate***
**TIME: Full day**
**DISTANCE: 13 miles round trip from winter parking area**
**ELEVATION CHANGE: 2,140 feet from Red Rock Lake parking area**
**STARTING ELEVATION: 10,080 feet**
**AVALANCHE TERRAIN: Some avalanche terrain encountered; easily avoided**
**USGS 7.5 MINUTE MAP: Ward, 1978-PR**
**MAP: page 50**

***ADVANCED HIGHLIGHT: The south slopes of Mount Audubon hold several intriguing couloirs which offer a variety of difficult descents. Just west of the summit is a fine gully which drops straight down to the valley. These descents are narrow and steep, approaching 35 degrees. They should only be attempted under stable conditions.**

Mount Audubon is a good, moderately difficult ski-mountaineering route. In summer the route is a heavily traveled hiking trail; in spring it is a vast snowfield beckoning the adventurous ski mountaineer. From the plains, this mountain is one of the largest peaks on the western skyline and consequently, from the summit you have a spectacular panorama of Colorado's eastern rampart.

Mount Audubon is a better tour early in spring; the snow melts quickly as summer arrives. Plan to hike (or ski) the Brainard Lake road, which is normally closed until early summer. From the winter parking area, the road goes directly west to the lake. Loop around to the west side of the lake and take the turnoff to the Blue Lake–Mount Audubon parking area, which lies northwest about 0.3 miles. The trailhead is at the northwest corner of the parking area.

The well-marked trail leads north into the forest and climbs steadily for 0.5 miles to a series of switchbacks which guide you up a steep slope to treeline and the eastern expanse of the Mount Audubon massif. From here the trail leads up moderate slopes toward the saddle lying north of the summit. As you approach this saddle follow the path of least resistance to the 13,223-foot summit. The approach hike is not complicated and many variations exist. Much of the ground may still be covered with snow, so a party on skis will be free to improvise on route selection.

When it's time to leave the summit, you will have to again improvise, choosing a descent route that best suits the needs of your group. Because this peak is so gentle and broad, even novice ski mountaineers can find a pleasing "line." On one particular spring trip down Mount Audubon, it was possible to leave the summit on skis, carve turns down to treeline, continue through the woods and finally ski out on the road to the parking area east of Red Rock Lake.

# 24　PAIUTE PEAK (13,088 FEET)

**DESCRIPTION: Spring ski-mountaineering route, long approach hike**
**SKILL LEVEL: Advanced***
**TIME: Full day**
**DISTANCE: 12 miles round trip**
**ELEVATION CHANGE: 3,000 feet total gain**
**STARTING ELEVATION: 10,080 feet**
**AVALANCHE TERRAIN: Mostly avalanche terrain; wait for spring consolidation**
**USGS 7.5 MINUTE MAPS: Ward, 1978-PR, Monarch Lake, 1978-PR**
**MAP: page 50**

***INTERMEDIATE HIGHLIGHT: The huge snow-filled bowl at the end of the valley below Paiute Peak provides a vast playground of intermediate angle slopes, perfect for practicing telemark and parallel turns.**

Paiute Peak is one of the more interesting mountains in the Indian Peaks wilderness. It is linked to Mount Toll to the south and Mount Audubon to the east by ridges. Below these three mountains lies Blue Lake and farther to the east, Mitchell Lake. When spring comes this entire valley is choked with voluminous amounts of skiable snow. Paiute Peak's southeast face can be skied for several weeks before the summer sun has melted it out. The routes are steep but shorter than they look. The amphitheater between Toll and Paiute provides a fine diversion for those skiers not ready to tackle the higher peaks.

The approach is from Brainard Lake. To get there take the Peak-to-Peak Highway (Colo. 72) to the Brainard Lake turnoff just north of Ward. Proceed west 2.5 miles to the winter parking area. The remaining 2.5 miles of road to the lake is not opened to cars until very late spring, so you may have to park at the winter parking area and walk or ski up the road to Brainard Lake. From Brainard Lake take the Mitchell Lake–Blue Lake access (see tour 22) from the northwest end of Brainard Lake and continue up the marked trail to Mitchell Lake. From the south side of Mitchell Lake ascend a short draw to the south, which soon breaks out into more open country. Continue west to the head of the valley, heading directly for Paiute Peak, which lies at the northwest corner.

There are two distinct routes of descent. The first and most obvious route drops straight down to the southeast face below the summit and is the more challenging and dangerous route. The second possibility drops directly south and slightly left of the broad southeast face. A subtle, low-angled gully drops off a small shoulder of the mountain on its south side, a few hundred feet below the summit. Ski parties may hike down from the summit to this shoulder before putting on skis. While the top of this feature is steep, perhaps 40 degrees, the grade quickly becomes reasonable.

# 25 MOUNT TOLL (12,979 FEET)

DESCRIPTION: Spring ski-mountaineering descent, approach hike, beautiful route
SKILL LEVEL: Advanced*
TIME: Full day
DISTANCE: 12 miles round trip
ELEVATION CHANGE: 2,900 feet total gain
STARTING ELEVATION: 10,080 feet
AVALANCHE TERRAIN: Mostly avalanche terrain; wait for spring consolidation
USGS 7.5 MINUTE MAPS: Ward, 1978-PR, Monarch Lake, 1978-PR
MAP: page 50

*INTERMEDIATE HIGHLIGHT: The huge snow-filled bowl at the end of the valley, between Mount Toll and Paiute Peak, is a destination very worthwhile but less demanding, a perfect place to practice telemark turns in the warm spring sun.

Mount Toll ranks as one of the best ski descents in Colorado. The route follows a clean line down the triangular southeast face, clinging close to the sharp ridge of the western skyline. The face runs out into a large hanging bowl between Pawnee and Toll, which then spills down another steep runout into the main valley, a spectacular, rewarding run of over 1,600 vertical feet. The route is not for novice or intermediate skiers; slope angle approaches 35 degrees in spots.

The approach is from Brainard Lake. To get there take the Peak-to-Peak Highway (Colo. 72) to the Brainard Lake turnoff just north of Ward. Proceed west 2.5 miles to the winter parking area. The remaining 2.5 miles of road to the lake is not opened to cars until very late spring, so you may have to park at the winter parking area and walk or ski up the road to Brainard Lake. From Brainard Lake take the Mitchell Lake–Blue Lake access (see tour 22) from the northwest end of Brainard Lake and continue up the marked trail to Mitchell Lake. From the south side of Mitchell Lake ascend a short draw to the south, which soon breaks out into more open country. Continue up the valley heading directly for Mount Toll, the striking peak on your left at the end of the valley. Take the straightforward direct ascent route up into the hanging bowl just east of the peak and then climb directly to the summit; or ascend from the hanging bowl to the south ridge and then to the top. The descent plunges down the south face into the hanging bowl, then down the steep section below the hanging bowl to Blue Lake. From Blue Lake retrace the access route back to Brainard Lake and out to the parking lot.

# 26    LONG LAKE AND ISABELLE LAKE

**DESCRIPTION: Winter ski tour, trail and road**
**SKILL LEVEL: Intermediate ***
**TIME: Full day**
**DISTANCE: 9.2 miles round trip**
**ELEVATION CHANGE: 788 feet total gain**
**STARTING ELEVATION: 10,080 feet**
**AVALANCHE TERRAIN: Some avalanche terrain; easily avoided**
**USGS 7.5 MINUTE MAP: Ward, 1978-PR**
**MAP: page 50**

***NOVICE HIGHLIGHT: Less zealous skiers can terminate this tour at Long Lake, which when combined with the Brainard Lake road or the South Trail makes a nice long day of easy to moderate skiing.**

The trail to Isabelle Lake is a scenic yet moderate trip following South St. Vrain Creek as it tumbles from its glacial birthplace. Above Isabelle Lake the forested subalpine environment surrenders to a jagged and inhospitable topography of talus, ice and wind. Towering to the west over Isabelle Glacier, the stately summits of Navajo Peak and Apache Peak inspire awe of the incredible geologic forces that created the Indian Peaks wilderness. For the majority of the trip, the trail is not difficult and is sheltered by forest. You will encounter one steep section as you bypass a rocky step just before Isabelle Lake. This step is short and should not interfere with an enjoyable day of touring.

The Isabelle Lake Trail begins west of Brainard Lake. Therefore, choose a route to the trailhead: either the Brainard Lake road (tour 20) or the Colorado Mountain Club South Trail (tour 21). From the west side of the lake follow the road which leads from Brainard Lake to the summer parking area for the Isabelle Lake–Pawnee

Pass Trailhead. The trail begins at the southwest corner of the parking area and is well marked. Double-pole through the virtually flat forest for about 0.2 miles and ski out onto the northeast edge of Long Lake. Another short route to link the Brainard Lake road to Long Lake is the Niwot cutoff. This short trail, marked by a small wooden sign, leaves the Brainard Lake road immediately west of Brainard Lake.

From Long Lake the southern skyline is comprised of massive Niwot Ridge, heavily forested above Long Lake. Traverse the lake's northern shore and re-enter the cover of the woods on the west edge. The trail skirts the edge of the forest and the small meadow that traces the creekbed. Treeblazes abound to guide you along the summer route, but if you stray don't worry; the terrain will steer you west up the valley bottom to a large step 0.8 miles from Long Lake.

The step forces you to climb into the woods on the north side of the valley. Gain 160 feet of elevation through this spot, then you've reached treeline. From here a short traverse across wind-encrusted snow will bring you to the massive shelf containing frozen Isabelle Lake. Because Isabelle Lake tends to be windy, the snowpack near the lake is thin. Be careful not to destroy your ski bottoms as you push along the final few yards. Avoid climbing too high as you approach the lake, as this will carry you far above treeline and on toward Pawnee Pass to the northwest.

This tour is quite safe and the trip back to Brainard Lake goes quickly; just keep in mind that the car lies several miles east of where you regain the main road. Plan accordingly and enjoy a fine day of skiing.

# 27 PAWNEE PEAK (12,860 FEET)

**DESCRIPTION: Spring ski-mountaineering descent, approach hike, mostly moderate slopes (less than 25 degrees)**
**SKILL LEVEL: Advanced***
**TIME: Full day**
**DISTANCE: 13 miles round trip**
**ELEVATION CHANGE: 2,780 feet total gain**
**STARTING ELEVATION: 10,080 feet**
**AVALANCHE TERRAIN: Mostly avalanche terrain; wait for spring consolidation**
**USGS 7.5 MINUTE MAPS: Ward, 1978-PR, Monarch Lake, 1978-PR**
**MAP: page 50**

**\*INTERMEDIATE HIGHLIGHT: The only steep section is easily avoided by hiking the short slope that drops east off the south shoulder of Pawnee.**

Pawnee makes a good introduction to spring ski descents. It is just as far and just as long as most of the other spring ski descents but is not as steep or intimidating.

The summit snowfield makes a short picturesque sweep onto the shoulder below Pawnee Pass, providing a perfect place to practice telemark turns on spring corn in a high alpine setting. The descent generally faces south or southeast. The snow remains fairly continuous until about mid-June in most years.

To get to Pawnee turn off the Peak-to-Peak Highway (Colo. 72) just north of Ward and follow the paved road west toward Brainard Lake. Normally it is necessary to hike in the last 2.5 miles because that last section of paved road is closed until late spring (a mountain bike would save time here). Follow the road all the way around the north side of Brainard Lake, turn right (west) at the Mitchell Lake–Long Lake turnoff and then left to the Long Lake parking lot. From there follow the summer hiking trail around the north side of Long Lake. Continue up valley, following the Pawnee Pass Trail. Just below Lake Isabelle, 0.8 miles above the west edge of Long Lake, cut north and head up into a side valley below the east ridge of Pawnee. The Pawnee Pass Trail switchbacks up the shoulder east of Pawnee Pass and south of Pawnee Peak, but the easiest and most direct route to the top continues up this side valley to a point just below the peak. It then proceeds directly west up steep slopes to the shoulder and finally north up the summit snowfields to the top.

The descent starts with a short run down the summit snowfield. It then drops steeply (up to 35 degrees), heading east off the shoulder into the previously mentioned side valley southeast of the summit and continues out on lower, angled slopes to the main valley and Long Lake. If you're there early in the spring ski descent season, you may get a continuous run from the top all the way to Long Lake.

# 28   APACHE PEAK (13,441 FEET)

**DESCRIPTION: Spring ski-mountaineering descent, approach hike, steep, challenging route**
**SKILL LEVEL: Advanced +***
**TIME: Full day**
**DISTANCE: 14 miles round trip**
**ELEVATION CHANGE: 3,320 feet total gain**
**STARTING ELEVATION: 10,080 feet**
**AVALANCHE TERRAIN: Mostly avalanche terrain; wait for spring consolidation**
**USGS 7.5 MINUTE MAPS: Ward, 1978-PR, Monarch Lake, 1978-PR**
**MAP: page 50**

**\*INTERMEDIATE HIGHLIGHT: The huge snowfield bowls at the end of the valley below Navajo, Apache and Shoshoni peaks are very worthwhile but less demanding destinations, perfect places to practice telemark turns on spring corn snow.**

Apache is one of the most formidable peaks in the Front Range. Viewing its jagged isolated summit from the valley, one might wonder why any persons in their right mind would attempt to ski it. But for those with the ability, the energy and the taste for adventure, Apache is one of the truly great ski descents.

The approach is from Brainard Lake. To get there take the Peak-to-Peak Highway (Colo. 72) to the Brainard Lake turnoff just north of Ward. Proceed 2.6 miles to the winter parking area for Brainard Lake. The remaining 2.5 miles to the lake is not plowed until very late spring, so you may have to walk or ski in to the end of the road. Once there take the Long Lake–Pawnee Pass Trail from the west end of Brainard Lake. This trail passes Long Lake to the north and continues up the valley for another mile to Lake Isabelle. Navajo and Apache soon come into view, the two highest peaks at the end of the valley: Navajo is the pointed peak on the left and Apache is the next peak to the right. Navajo Glacier sits at the base between the two summits.

Apache is most easily ascended via either of two obvious snowfields (or couloirs) on its east flank. These snowfields also serve as the descent routes. The first plunges east from the very top, hugging the north edge of the main southeast snowfield. About halfway down it cuts northeast into a steep (40 to 45 degrees), narrow couloir that eventually comes out below Isabelle Glacier. The other, more direct route skis the southeast snowfield to the base of Navajo Glacier. This route also approaches 40 to 45 degrees at its steepest point.

Once down in the valley you'll have a delightful rolling descent the rest of the way to Isabelle Lake. Then retrace the access route back out to the parking lot.

# 29   LITTLE RAVEN TRAIL

**DESCRIPTION: Winter ski tour, marked backcountry trails**
**SKILL LEVEL: Intermediate**
**TIME: Half day to full day**
**DISTANCE: 2.7 miles one way (where it may be combined with other Brainard Lake tours)**
**ELEVATION CHANGE: 520 feet total gain**
**STARTING ELEVATION: 10,080 feet**
**AVALANCHE TERRAIN: None**
**USGS 7.5 MINUTE MAP: Ward, 1978-PR**
**MAP: page 50**

This trail was blazed by the Colorado Mountain Club in 1981. It is named in honor of Chief Little Raven, leader of the Arapaho during their final days in Colorado before a treaty restricted them to a reservation in Kansas. Take the Peak-to-Peak Highway (Colo. 72) to the Brainard Lake turnoff just north of Ward. Proceed 2.5 miles west to the winter parking area. The trail starts at the east end of the parking area for Brainard Lake, just a few hundred feet before the road to Left Hand Reservoir. The start is the same as for the South Sourdough Trail (tour 31) and is marked as such. It makes its way through the forest south of the main road, paralleling it just as the South Colorado Mountain Club Trail does but staying even farther south.

The trail can be broken into four sections. The first section is actually the first half mile of the South Sourdough Trail. Little Raven then splits off, climbing steeply west and gaining 380 feet in the second half-mile section before intersecting with the road to Left Hand Reservoir. This section can be treacherous in the reverse (downhill) direction. The Left Hand Reservoir road (tour 30) can also be used as a shortcut to the middle of the Little Raven Trail. The third section follows this road for 0.75 miles as it climbs gradually toward the reservoir. The fourth section breaks off from the road 0.25 miles below the reservoir and traverses west through trees to a meadow at Left Hand Creek. The trail then heads upstream a short distance before diving back into the trees. Watch for blue diamond trail markers—it's easy to miss this turn and end up skiing all the way up Left Hand Creek to the reservoir. After returning to the trees the trail continues traversing west, then gradually drops toward Brainard Lake. A marker honoring Chief Little Raven is near the junction with the South Colorado Mountain Club Trail. The Brainard Lake road is a short distance northwest across a brushy meadow.

From Brainard Lake take any one of the various alternative trails back out to the winter parking area (see tours 19, 20 and 21).

# 30   LEFT HAND RESERVOIR

**DESCRIPTION: Winter ski tour, short scenic road**
**SKILL LEVEL: Novice**
**TIME: Half day**
**DISTANCE: 3.5 miles round trip**
**ELEVATION CHANGE: 550 feet total gain**
**STARTING ELEVATION: 10,080 feet**
**AVALANCHE TERRAIN: None**
**USGS 7.5 MINUTE MAP: Ward, 1978-PR**
**MAP: page 50**

The road to Left Hand Reservoir is recommended for novice skiers and those with limited time who wish to experience the magnificent scenery of this fine touring area. The tour, following a wide road, climbs steadily through forests of spruce trees before breaking out to the east edge of Left Hand Reservoir. This spot presents one of the most unobstructed views of the high Indian Peaks. A truly grand sight.

From the town of Ward head north on Colo. 72 and make an immediate left turn, which places you on the road to Brainard Lake. This turnoff is well marked.

Drive 2.6 miles until you reach the plowed parking area. This seemingly large area will fill up very quickly on weekends, so try to arrive early.

The tour begins on the south side of the parking area. It is an obvious road and is marked by a large wooden sign. Heading into the woods, the trail is quite flat; however, after several hundred yards the skiing becomes more demanding as you begin a 0.5-mile climb, which is sustained but moderate. Once the climb is finished the grade moderates and "herringbone" climbing gives way to gentler kick and gliding. To the southwest you can see pyramidal Kiowa Peak (13,276 feet) framed by the trees lining the roadbed. Soon you will arrive at a spot where the forest begins to open up. This signals the approach of Left Hand Reservoir's earthen dam. As you approach the dam, turn south and make a very short climb up onto the east edge of the reservoir. On clear days the seemingly endless peaks of 12,000 and 13,000 feet will provide a perfect backdrop for lunch.

The return trip is a reversal of the trip into Left Hand Reservoir. However, the more adventurous might try skiing the Little Raven Trail (tour 29) which turns left roughly 0.3 miles back to the east (from the dam). This will take you to the west side of Brainard Lake, where you have a choice of several routes back to the parking area.

# 31 SOURDOUGH TRAIL

**DESCRIPTION: Winter ski tour, marked backcountry trails, rolling forested terrain, car shuttle recommended**
**SKILL LEVEL: Intermediate***
**TIME: Half to full day (one way) for either of the two halves**
**LENGTH: North half 8 miles one way, south half 5.5 miles one way**
**ELEVATION CHANGE: North half 630 feet total gain/1,530 feet total loss, south half 480 feet total gain/1,220 feet total loss**
**STARTING ELEVATION: 10,080 feet**
**AVALANCHE TERRAIN: None**
**USGS 7.5 MINUTE MAPS: Ward, 1978-PR, Allenspark, 1978-PR**
**MAP: page 50**

***NOVICE HIGHLIGHT: The first 6 miles of the north half, to the Beaver Reservoir access road, and the first 4 miles of the south half, are primarily novice terrain.**

This trail parallels the Peak-to-Peak Highway (Colo. 72) from the access road to the University of Colorado Alpine Research Station at Niwot Ridge all the way to the Middle St. Vrain. It is split into two halves, one north of Brainard Lake and one south of Brainard Lake. The tour is characterized by rolling forested terrain that is perfectly suited to backcountry ski touring. The trail is well marked with blue diamond trail markers along its entire length. The recommended way to do the tour is to pick either one of the two halves and start from Brainard Lake. With a car shuttle at either of the two ends, this makes the majority of your tour downhill.

There are four access points to the Sourdough Trail.

1. Rainbow Lakes road: approximately 7 miles north of Nederland on the Peak-to-Peak Highway (Colo. 72), turn southwest at a sign indicating "University of Colorado Research Station," proceed south, then west 0.4 miles to a trailhead marker on the right.
2. Brainard Lake: turn west off the Peak-to-Peak Highway (Colo. 72) just north of Ward, proceed 2.6 miles to the winter parking area.
3. Beaver Reservoir: 2.5 miles north of the Brainard Lake access (just north of Ward) on the Peak-to-Peak Highway, turn west at signs for Camp Tahosa and proceed 2 miles to the trailhead marker.
4. Peaceful Valley: 5.8 miles north of the Brainard Lake access (just north of Ward), park at a wide sweeping hairpin turn, ski west 0.6 miles on the Middle St. Vrain Trail to a marked trail junction for the Sourdough Trail.

*Telemark skiing below Pawnee Pass (tour 27), Brian Litz photo.*

To ski the north half, leave one car at either the Beaver Reservoir access or the Peaceful Valley access, and return to the Brainard Lake winter parking area. The trailhead is at the east end of the parking area. Ski north through sparse timber on a gradual descent into South St. Vrain Creek. At 0.8 miles the trail switchbacks before crossing the creek. Immediately on the other (north) side of the creek is a trail junction for the South St. Vrain Trail. Although other possibilities exist (see map), the quickest way to continue is to first turn right (east) on the South St. Vrain Trail and proceed 0.2 miles to another trail junction, then turn left (north) and proceed 0.3 miles to a third trail junction, which puts you back on the Sourdough Trail. From here the trail continues north on relatively level terrain. Skirt a meadow on its left side at the 1.6-mile mark. The trail then begins to drop more noticeably as it continues north.

At the 2.5-mile mark there is a trail junction for the Stapp Lakes Trail. Cut sharply back right here and proceed east on a level traverse. At the 3.5-mile mark there is an alternative cutoff (right) on a jeep road that goes directly northeast to the Beaver Reservoir access road. Most parties prefer to proceed north on the marked Sourdough Trail. At the 3.9-mile mark, just before reaching a small knob heading northwest, there is a tricky right turn, northeast, away from Beaver Reservoir, avoiding a more obvious jeep trail. Keep a close watch on the blue diamond trail markers in this section. At the 4.4-mile mark the trail crosses the Beaver Reservoir access road. If you want to continue, cross the road and ski east parallel to it for 0.2 miles before bending north. Proceed northwest, then northeast through a short switchback. Cut back west 0.2 miles, then begin a steep descent with switchbacks into the Middle St. Vrain Valley. When you reach the bottom of this hair-raising descent, turn right and ski 0.6 miles east on the Middle St. Vrain Trail to the Peaceful Valley access.

To ski the south half, leave one car at the Rainbow Lakes road access and proceed with the other car to the Brainard Lake winter parking area. The trailhead is located approximately 50 yards east of the Left Hand Reservoir road. Ski southeast through thick forest 0.3 miles to the trail junction for the Little Raven Trail. Continue southeast, then south on a high traverse at approximately the 10,200-foot level. At the 4-mile mark the trail switchbacks sharply on the north side of Fourmile Creek. Cross the creek on a narrow bridge and continue traversing south. At the 5-mile mark the trail begins a rapid descent east through sparse trees, following the general line of a ridge. Once off this section turn south and proceed another 0.5 miles to the Rainbow Lakes road.

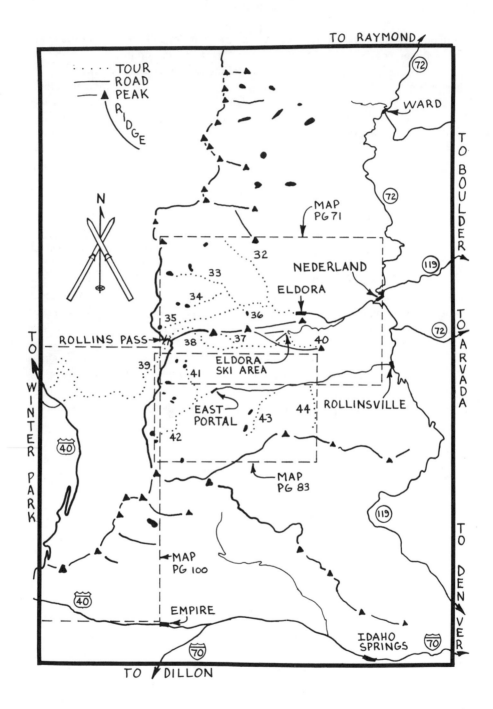

# CHAPTER THREE
# ROLLINS PASS AND ELDORA

## INTRODUCTION

The Rollins Pass–East Portal area encompasses two main drainages located on the east side of the Continental Divide, approximately 15 miles west of Boulder. Middle Boulder Creek drains an area bounded by South Arapaho Peak on the north and the Eldora ski area on the south. It is a large drainage with three main tributaries and a few side valleys, all of which offer tremendous potential for backcountry skiing.

South Boulder Creek, the other drainage, extends from the Eldora ski area on the north to James Peak on the south. One of the primary east/west railroad lines for the entire Rocky Mountain region travels up this drainage to the Moffat Tunnel, where it cuts under the Continental Divide. Rollins Pass was the original route taken over the Continental Divide before the Moffat Tunnel was built. It is now a dirt road that is only passable in summer and fall.

The combination of a wide selection of backcountry tours and quick easy access from Boulder has made this area very popular. It's only a half-hour drive from Boulder to any one of the trailheads in the area. Novice, intermediate and advanced tours are all equally represented. The Eldora Nordic Center offers an excellent system of groomed tracks and trails as well as Tennessee Mountain Cabin, a rustic backcountry hut that can be reserved for overnight use.

Backcountry enthusiasts have a choice of several trails and side valleys that emanate from three easy-to-reach access points: the Eldora Town Trailhead, the Eldora Ski Area Trailhead and the Rollinsville–East Portal access. The Eldora Town Trailhead is located at the far west end of the town of Eldora. Both it and the Eldora Ski Area Trailhead are reached by first driving up Boulder Canyon on Colo. 119 to Nederland. Then veer left as the highway proceeds through Nederland to the southwest side of town where a righthand turn, with signs indicating the way to the Eldora ski area, heads west. After 2 miles, the road forks. The left fork, which climbs steeply out of the valley, leads to the Eldora ski area. The right fork continues up valley another 2 miles through the town of Eldora to a trailhead at the end of the plowed road.

The Rollinsville–East Portal access is reached by first driving up Boulder Canyon on Colo. 119 to Nederland, veering left as the highway proceeds through Nederland and continues south on Colo. 119 to Rollinsville. From the center of Rollinsville a dirt road heads straight west, paralleling the railroad tracks. Jenny Lind Gulch, Mammoth Gulch and the tours emanating from East Portal are all accessed from this road, with the East Portal Trailhead located 10 miles from Rollinsville at the far west end of the road.

Snow conditions in this area vary considerably from one day to the next, even in midwinter, because of the frequently ferocious Front Range winds. All of the trails start high enough to receive ample snowfall— it's just a question of whether the wind has left the snow intact on the more exposed, open stretches. Conditions are always best in the densely forested back bowls, as opposed to the lower, open valleys or the exposed tundra above treeline, neither of which offer adequate protection.

## HISTORY

Rollins Pass was frequently traversed by Native Americans long before white men entered the area. The Utes, who lived on the Western Slope in what is now Grand County, crossed over the Continental Divide to hunt buffalo on the eastern plains. Arapaho and Cheyenne, whose home was already on the eastern plains, also crossed the pass in the opposite direction, in search of game and lodgepole pines for teepees. These tribes were somewhat territorial, which resulted in a number of battles and skirmishes in the vicinity of Rollins Pass. There is evidence of several rock fortifications near the top of the pass, structures uncommon in the western United States.

Pioneers and trappers visited the area sporadically during the early 1800s. John Quincy Adams Rollins, son of a New England minister, took a party of Mormons over the divide as early as 1865. With wagon loads of provisions, it was a treacherous and difficult journey with only a faint Indian path to follow. They tenaciously pushed, pulled, grunted and willed their wagons over fallen logs and large boulders as the lead men cut a wider swath through the heavy timber. Rollins later founded the town of Rollinsville, where he promoted mining ventures.

In 1866, Rollins was granted a 10-year franchise for the Middle Park and South Boulder wagon road, which later became known as the Rollins Pass road. It was a toll road, with charges of $2.50 for a single team—not a very quick way to riches even in those days. H. L. Baldwin commented on an early crossing of the pass: "My impression is that before our wagon trip across Rollins Pass, which was about July 1, 1874, none but prospectors and trappers even entered Middle Park, and I do not know why Rollins spent what must have been a considerable sum to build this toll road."

More financially unsound decisions were to follow. The construction of the Moffat Railroad began in July 1902. It was the dream of David H. Moffat, who sunk his personal fortune into the project, to connect a line from Denver to Salt Lake City crossing the Continental Divide at Rollins Pass. He eventually did it, but the cost was so great and he was so continuously fought by other railroad interests that his resources were exhausted when the tracks reached Craig. For many years it was a just a dead-end line leading to the western frontier. The railroad was eventually absorbed by the Denver and Rio Grande Western Railroad, which completed the route down the Colorado River to Utah and across the desert to California. Today it is one of the primary east-west rail lines, transporting everything from coal to automobiles to Amtrak passengers.

The section of track leading over the pass was a monumental achievement. Miles and miles of rails rounded treacherous curves through tunnels and across numerous trestles, culminating at Corona, the top of the pass and the highest point in the world to be served by a standard-gauge railroad. In winter the pass was beset by heavy snows and buffeted by ferocious gales. Trains were sometimes stranded for days at Corona while snowplows stuck on both sides of the pass struggled to clear the tracks. It was a continuously frustrating battle, for as soon as the tracks were cleared, it was often only a matter of days or even hours before winds would fill the newly ex-cavated troughs with 10 feet or more of new snow. Giant rotary plows were extremely effective for loose powder snow but occasional warm sunny days created an even more difficult problem—ice. Ice caused more lengthy delays because the giant rotaries were of little use and the only effective alternative was good old picks and shovels. Gangs of men were recruited from Larimer Street in Denver and from Middle Park on the west side of the divide to manually remove the ice and clear the tracks.

The worst blockade lasted 43 days in April and May of 1920. Ranchers in Middle Park ran out of hay and their cattle began to starve. Coal mines in Routt County closed down. In subsequent years, master mechanic Charlie Peterson came to the rescue with "the world's largest ice picks." These huge hydraulic lances, 30 inches long and 6 inches wide, were mounted on powerful engines called mallets. The mallets blasted their way through the snow and ice, snorting and spinning their wheels until they finally got bogged down in the rubble. Then the mallet would back out and let the rotary have a go at picking the ice up and hurling it out of the cuts.

Unfortunately, even with "the world's largest ice picks," snow removal was extremely expensive, so it was only a matter of time before the railroad went broke in 1921. About this time several very powerful and influential politicians began to realize that there was more at stake here than just another railroad. The future of Denver as a hub for the entire Rocky Mountain region lay in the balance. Years earlier, in 1912, a proposal to construct the Moffat Tunnel using state funding was defeated. Now, it was time to try again. The Tri-Tunnel Plan was introduced, proposing not only a Moffat Tunnel but a Cumbres Hill Tunnel and a Monarch Hill Tunnel. Politicians from the town of Pueblo, in the southern part of the state, opposed the bill, recognizing that they would probably lose much of their interstate railroad traffic. They managed to defeat the bill by a narrow margin. However, there is more than one way for savvy politicos to get their pet projects through. When the Arkansas River flooded, wiping out a large section of Pueblo, disaster relief and construction to prevent future damage were passed only in exchange for support of the Moffat Tunnel project. Pueblo's hands were tied. They couldn't possibly turn down disaster relief.

The Moffat Tunnel was completed in 1928 at a cost of over $15 million, three times the original estimate. Problems with rotten rock and water seepage were the primary reasons for cost overruns. Unbeknown to many at the time, Denver also got a water diversion tunnel (a pioneer bore running parallel to the railroad tunnel) out of the deal, securing the potential for future growth with water from the Western Slope.

# 32    FOURTH OF JULY ROAD

DESCRIPTION: Winter ski tour, long road up valley, exposed to wind
SKILL LEVEL: Novice
TIME: Half to full day
DISTANCE: Optional, up to 10 miles round trip
ELEVATION CHANGE: Optional, up to 1,300 feet total gain
STARTING ELEVATION: 8,820 feet
AVALANCHE TERRAIN: None
USGS 7.5 MINUTE MAPS: Nederland, 1972, East Portal, 1958
MAP: page 71

The Fourth of July Campground is a popular summer recreation area for picnicking and hiking. In winter the road is closed just west of Eldora and only ski tourers and snowmobilers make the 5-mile journey in. The road gradually gains elevation along its entire length and is never very steep. There may be several short stretches where the road has been blown clear of snow, but these can easily be skirted.

To reach Eldora go southwest out of Nederland and turn right just outside town, following signs to the Eldora ski area. After 1.5 miles, instead of going up the hill to the ski area, fork right and continue up the valley floor for another 1.5 miles to Eldora. The trailhead is located at the far west end of town. Park off to the side of the road where you do not block anyone's driveway.

Ski up the road 0.7 miles and take the first major right fork. The tour stays on this road for the next 5 miles, gradually gaining elevation through wooded terrain that is interspersed with open meadows. Along the way you'll pass several private cabins. Please stay on the road and respect their private property. The Fourth of July Campground is located in the woods at the end of the last major open meadow. The return trip should only take about half as much time as the trip in.

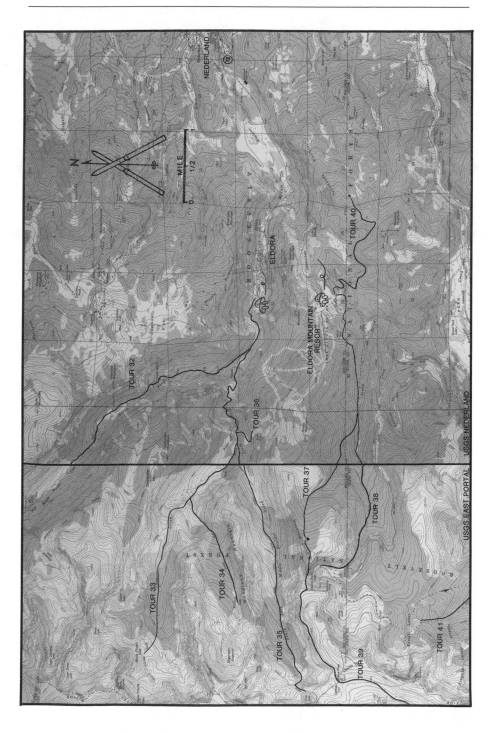

# 33  DEVIL'S THUMB LAKE

DESCRIPTION: Winter ski tour, road, remote backcountry trail and
off trail, long, strenuous
SKILL LEVEL: Intermediate*
TIME: Full day
DISTANCE: 13 miles round trip
ELEVATION CHANGE: 2,300 feet total gain
STARTING ELEVATION: 8,820 feet
AVALANCHE TERRAIN: Some avalanche terrain encountered; easily
avoided
USGS 7.5 MINUTE MAPS: Nederland, 1972, East Portal, 1958
MAP: page 71

*NOVICE HIGHLIGHT: The first section up through Hessie is nearly
level. Beyond Hessie the road gets somewhat steeper but may still be
enjoyable for novice skiers.

This lengthy, demanding tour takes you far beyond roads and packed trails,
up into some of the most isolated backcountry in the Front Range. It requires a full
day, so start early if you plan to go the distance. Few parties actually make it all the
way to the lake, so expect to break trail much of the way.

The tour starts from the far west end of the town of Eldora. To reach Eldora
go southwest out of Nederland on Colo. 119 and take the first right turn, following
signs to the Eldora ski area. At the first fork, instead of going left up the hill to the ski
area, continue straight up the valley. Eldora is reached after another 2 miles. Proceed
through town to the end of the plowed road. There is limited parking available at the
trailhead. Try not to block anyone's driveway.

Start skiing up the road and after 0.7 miles take the first left fork toward the
old townsite of Hessie. The road switchbacks just beyond Hessie, climbing up into
the South Fork of Middle Boulder Creek. When the road flattens out, you'll come to
a sign marking the start of Devil's Thumb Trail. Do not take this trail. It is much easier
to continue up the road, taking right forks past the trails to Lost Lake and King Lake
(see tours 36 and 35). Beyond these well-marked forks, the road veers north and
slowly narrows to a trail. The trail then becomes difficult to find, forcing the leader
to take the path of least resistance. Gain a steep bench and curve west up the left side
of the valley. Continue 2 more miles, breaking trail through hilly terrain. When you
finally reach what seems like the end, you must still climb one last steep section up
and right to reach the lake.

Return via the same route.

# 34 WOODLAND LAKE

DESCRIPTION: Winter ski tour, road, remote backcountry trail and off trail, long, strenuous
SKILL LEVEL: Advanced*
TIME: Full day
DISTANCE: 10.4 miles round trip
ELEVATION CHANGE: 2,170 feet total gain
STARTING ELEVATION: 8,820 feet
AVALANCHE TERRAIN: Some avalanche terrain encountered; easily avoided
USGS 7.5 MINUTE MAPS: Nederland, 1972, East Portal, 1958
MAP: page 71

*NOVICE HIGHLIGHT: The first section up through Hessie is nearly level. Beyond Hessie the road gets somewhat steeper but may still be enjoyable for novice skiers.

The first half of this tour is the same as the Devil's Thumb Lake Tour (tour 33). It follows a relatively easy road, then trail, up the South Fork of Middle Boulder Creek. The character of the tour then changes, climbing steeply into the backcountry. The tour ends at Woodland Lake in a picturesque, alpine bowl. The second half of the tour is usually untracked and may require more time and effort than planned, so get an early start.

The tour begins from the far west end of the town of Eldora. To get there, take Colo. 119 southwest out of Nederland and turn right just outside town, following signs to the Eldora ski area. Instead of going left up the hill to the ski area, fork right and continue up the valley for another 2 miles to Eldora. Proceed through town to the end of the plowed road and find a place to park where you're not blocking anyone's driveway.

Ski up the road 0.7 miles and take the first left fork toward the old townsite of Hessie. The road switchbacks just beyond Hessie, climbing up into the South Fork of Middle Boulder Creek. Just before crossing the creek, you will come to a sign marking the start of the Devil's Thumb Lake Trail. Do not take this trail. Instead, continue up the road, passing another turnoff for Lost Lake (tour 36). Soon after this turnoff you'll come into an open field where the road forks again. Take the right fork here. The left fork goes up to King Lake (tour 35). The right fork heads north into Jasper Creek and soon narrows to a trail. After about a mile, the trail crosses a small tributary that comes down through a steep gulch on the left. This is the route. Climb the steep bench to the right of the creek and continue climbing through comparatively level terrain for 2 more miles to Woodland Lake.

Return via the same route.

# 35  KING LAKE

DESCRIPTION: Winter ski tour, long and strenuous backcountry trail
SKILL LEVEL: Advanced
TIME: Full day
DISTANCE: 12 miles round trip
ELEVATION CHANGE: 2,060 feet total gain
STARTING ELEVATION: 8,820 feet
AVALANCHE TERRAIN: Some avalanche terrain encountered; easily avoided on primary tour
USGS 7.5 MINUTE MAPS: East Portal, 1958, Nederland, 1972
MAP: page 71

Fifteen million years ago the eastern escarpment of the Front Range was buried under several thousand feet of glacial ice. The incredible weight and power of these tongues of ice carved deep and dramatic valleys into the landscape. King Lake, sitting at the base of the Continental Divide high to the west of the town of Eldora, lies at the head of a textbook example of a glacially carved U-shaped valley. The trail to King Lake climbs steadily westward through elegant stands of spruce and gains over 2,000 feet in elevation in a moderate yet consistent fashion. While never very steep and rarely flat, this is one of the finest tours west of Boulder and is quite a workout!

The trailhead to King Lake is shared with the tours to Lost Lake (tour 36), Woodland Lake (tour 34) and Devil's Thumb Lake (tour 33) and is immediately west of the town of Eldora. From Nederland drive on Colo. 119 to the southwest end of town and turn right (north) onto the Eldora ski area road. Proceed past the lefthand turn to the ski area and continue west through the cabin-filled town of Eldora. Park at the plowed turnaround.

Begin skiing west along the snow-covered road. Gently climbing, you will contour west and south before heading due west, passing the righthand turnoff to the Fourth of July Campground road at 0.8 miles. The road makes a very small descent into a small meadow just beyond this intersection. Cross the meadow and ski past a group of cabins to the right. This marks the old mining town of Hessie. Ski into the woods and cross a wooden bridge over the North Fork of Middle Boulder Creek, then pass a metal gate blocking vehicular traffic.

The most difficult section of the tour now presents itself as you ascend two large switchbacks that travel through a large clearing to the northwest. This spot is fairly short and soon you will contour back to the west and re-enter the cover of trees. Kick and glide through the trees, following the trail as it curls south to a bridge over the South Fork of Middle Boulder Creek. Cross the bridge and turn right, as the trail follows the creek flowing through the small rocky gully. Gain the top of a tiny rocky point and ski past the left-forking road to Lost Lake. Ski 0.2 miles into the southeast corner of a large meadow and reach the turnoff to King Lake, marked by a large sign with trail information and a small map of the area.

Re-enter the woods and begin a moderate climb to the north of the creek on a nearly indiscernible ridge. In the upper valley the terrain is dominated by a continual series of hummocks and small slopes covered by stands of spruce intermixed with a few aspen trees. As you ski through here try to maintain as level a course as possible. The summer trail is nearly impossible to follow but the rolling U-shaped nature of this drainage allows for many possible routes. Someone may have preceded you in selecting and breaking trail; but in general, anywhere within several hundred yards north of South Fork Creek will do nicely.

King Lake sits several hundred feet above treeline on top of a large step. The skiing to the actual lake becomes more difficult and most skiers end the tour at the small willow-filled meadow (marsh) that sits at the spot where the creek turns sharply north. As you approach this small clearing you will swear that the terrain steepens. While you ski under the precipitous north face of Point 11,829, notice the wooden trestles clinging to the mountainside far above you. This is the old Rollins Pass rail line, its sinuous route carved over Corona Pass and into the Grand Valley.

Those with a taste for adventure may spend the night near the trail's end, allowing for a more leisurely trip and a chance to ski some of the steep glades near treeline. This tour also makes a nice first leg on a ski trek over Corona Pass into Winter Park. The pass is 800 feet above the marsh directly to the south. If the sparsely timbered gullies leading up to the old rail grade are passable, the remainder of the journey is all downhill into Winter Park.

# 36 Lost Lake

**DESCRIPTION: Winter ski tour, moderately long, some steep climbing**
**SKILL LEVEL: Novice to intermediate**
**TIME: Half day**
**DISTANCE: 6 miles round trip**
**ELEVATION CHANGE: 966 feet total gain**
**STARTING ELEVATION: 8,820 feet**
**AVALANCHE TERRAIN: None**
**USGS 7.5 MINUTE MAP: Nederland, 1972**
**MAP: page 71**

To the west of the mountain town of Eldora lie several classic ski tours of varying difficulty. Diminutive Lost Lake, high on the south slopes of the Middle Boulder Creek drainage, is the shortest of these tours and maintains a lively temperament. The route to Lost Lake follows an old mining road that leads through the once-bustling community of Hessie. Gaining relatively little elevation during the first half of the trip, this tour packs in nearly 800 feet of gain in the last 1.5 miles. Needless to say the descent can be fast and furious. Since the trip traces the old roadbed, however, there is plenty of room to check your speed.

To reach the trailhead drive on Colo. 119 southwest from the center of Nederland to the turnoff for the Eldora ski area. Follow the Eldora road past the turnoff to the ski area, which is on your left. Continue west up the Middle Boulder Creek road and park at the end of the plowed parking area immediately west of the town of Eldora.

Begin skiing along the snow-covered roadbed as it gently climbs away from the parking area on the north side of the valley. Follow the road as it gradually contours to the southwest then west again. This section continues its slight elevation gain before it meets the intersection with the road to Fourth of July Campground (tour 32). At this intersection, well marked by a wooden sign listing possible trip destinations, follow the road to the left, dropping a few feet before reaching the flat valley bottom. Kick and glide through the cluster of cabins that mark the old mining town of Hessie and then begin another gradual contour to the west and southwest. This section of the road will take you across a small wooden bridge over North Fork Creek, past another mileage sign and around a metal gate (this marks the end of the easy portion of the tour).

The final half of the tour begins with the ascent of two large switchbacks that climb north and west through a grove of aspen trees intermixed with clearings. At the end of these two switchbacks, the road traverses around a small promontory providing a dramatic panorama back down the valley and to the south where Bryan Mountain and the slopes of the Eldora ski area are high above you. Once past the step, which is ascended via the switchbacks, the trail re-enters mixed stands of aspen and spruce trees covering more gentle terrain. Soon the trail curls southward for several hundred yards following the natural contours in the terrain and eventually brings you to a wooden bridge crossing Middle Boulder Creek. Just before the bridge and to the right are a trail and a sign giving information on several other trails in the area. Disregard this turnoff; it is an optional summer trail that is very hard to follow in winter.

Proceed across the bridge, turn right and climb up along the lefthand side of a small rocky gully, eventually traversing west onto a small knob. On top of this knob is a major intersection marked once again by a series of signs with summer/winter mileage information. Follow the left fork, which leads you first toward the southwest then back east for several hundred yards to the lake. The last leg of the journey gains roughly 200 feet in 0.5 miles from the turnoff to the lake's shore.

# 37  GUINN MOUNTAIN (ARESTUA HUT)

**DESCRIPTION: Winter ski tour, strenuous, exciting trail to backcountry hut**
**SKILL LEVEL: Advanced**
**TIME: Full day**

**DISTANCE: 10 miles round trip**
**ELEVATION CHANGE: 1,800 feet total gain**
**STARTING ELEVATION: 9,360 feet**
**AVALANCHE TERRAIN: None**
**USGS 7.5 MINUTE MAPS: Nederland, 1972, East Portal, 1958**
**MAP: page 71**

The trail up Guinn Mountain is a variation of the Jenny Creek Tour. It is, however, much more difficult and ends high above the surrounding landscape near the windy summit of Guinn Mountain, which sits between the Jenny Creek drainage on the south and the King Lake valley on the north. Several hundred feet below this summit to the east and tucked into a stand of evergreen trees is the sturdy Arestua Hut. Operated by the Colorado Mountain Club, this intimate cabin is a great spot to eat before the return trip. The cabin's amenities include sleeping benches for seven adults, a small wood-burning stove, wood supply, an axe, pots, pans, plates, utensils and a few mice. At night the cabin's inhabitants are treated to an unobstructed view of the Great Plains. This tour is very popular, even though it is very strenuous climbing to the hut and exciting on the descent.

The trail to Guinn Mountain begins at the Eldora Nordic Center. Drive southwest on Colo. 119 from Nederland and turn right onto the well-marked Eldora ski area road. Continue 1.5 miles, then turn left onto the ski area road, which climbs steeply southwest out of the valley. Follow this until you reach the ski area; turn left again into the first parking area, which services the touring area and the eastern (beginner) part of the downhill area. The tour starts near the small trailer used as an office for the Nordic Center.

The beginning of the tour crosses the private land of the ski area via a public right-of-way. Although it is marked its beginning can be hard to locate, especially if the area is buzzing with downhill skiers. Begin skiing up the farthest east downhill run (just above the small Nordic Center trailer) and keep ascending along the left edge of this run. The chairlift will be on your right to the west. Follow signs marking the public right-of-way and enter the trees at a point just above the top of the lift. Once in the trees you will ski an undulating course into Jenny Creek. Climb over two hills and begin a steeper descent to the south, well away from the ski area. A short descent brings you to an intersection marked by several hand-painted private property signs. The public trail veers to the southwest and makes a long and fast descent into the creek bottom. It is about 1 mile from the top of the last hill to Jenny Creek, and various skiers are often climbing up and snowplowing down the trail at the same time—so be careful! This section sounds confusing but actually it is well marked and obvious.

Once everyone has made it safely to the bottom of the hill, begin skiing west up the large trail/road (Jenny Creek, tour 38). After 0.25 miles an intersection is reached where a jeep trail climbs into the trees to the right (northwest) near a white wooden post. Turn right and begin the first section of strenuous climbing on the Guinn Mountain Trail. This part is wide and easy to follow and reaches a small level spot near a white-painted trail mileage sign after roughly 0.5 miles. Turn left to the west and kick and glide over more moderate terrain and enter into thicker woods. Start climbing again up a narrower trail for another 0.75 miles until you ski onto a steep treeless slope where ruins of a large cabin sit. The cabin is halfway through the clearing and is on the right side of the trail.

Pass the cabin and ski toward the west end of the clearing into a cul-de-sac formed by the trees and a small gully. Switchback up the right side of this gully and turn back west into the trees near its top. Soon the trail crests onto flatter terrain and begins the last leg of the journey through dense forests broken occasionally by small clearings. This is one of those spots where it pays to watch carefully for the elusive trail markers. Ski west and slightly north and break into a clearing. Enter this area and begin searching to the left (south). The Arestua Hut sits to the left on a small hill, facing east. It is brown and backed by a thick stand of evergreen trees.

To visit the summit of Guinn Mountain, leave the hut, re-enter the clearing and head west to the top. James Peak is to the south, Rollins Pass west and the impressive Arapaho Peaks north. Now head back to the hut and rest up for the excursion back down the mountain.

# 38   JENNY CREEK

> **DESCRIPTION: Winter ski tour, moderate, well-marked trail**
> **SKILL LEVEL: Intermediate to advanced**
> **TIME: Full day**
> **DISTANCE: 11 miles round trip**
> **ELEVATION CHANGE: 1,451 feet total gain**
> **STARTING ELEVATION: 9,360 feet**
> **AVALANCHE TERRAIN: None**
> **USGS 7.5 MINUTE MAPS: Nederland, 1972, East Portal, 1958**
> **MAP: page 71**

Jenny Creek has been a favorite ski tour in the Front Range for many years. In the past this drainage has been reached by skiing up from Tolland and from near Petersen Lake. This tour now begins at the Eldora Nordic Center, climbing up and over a ridge before a thrilling descent drops skiers down into Jenny Creek with its large, well-marked trail. The terrain is characterized by moderate climbing through sheltering trees. Eventually your party will reach Yankee Doodle Lake, a small alpine lake sitting at the base of the Rollins Pass road. Jenny Creek makes a fine spring tour; it may be a tour to avoid on cold winter days when the Front Range winds howl.

Drive southwest on Colo. 119 from Nederland and turn right, following signs to the Eldora ski area. Follow this road for 1.5 miles, then turn left (south) onto the ski area road, which heads up a steep hill to the southwest. Turn left into the first parking lot of the ski area, which services the Nordic Center and the eastern (beginner) part of the ski area. The tour starts near the small trailer used as an office for the Nordic Center.

Start the tour from the Nordic Center and cross a public right-of-way through the downhill area. This route is marked but can be difficult to locate. Ski up the first downhill run directly to the southwest, staying on the left edge of the ski run. The chair lift will be on your right (to the west). Follow signs marking the public right-of-way, eventually skiing into the forest. After reaching the trees the tour crosses over a series of small hills, weaving through the forest. Once on the highest knoll the trail widens and begins the descent into Jenny Creek to the south. Descend until you reach an intersection marked by private property signs. The roads to the east and south are on private property and should be avoided. Follow the trail as it heads southwest down a steep narrow path. This section of trail is almost 1 mile long and is lined with sturdy trees, so be careful. Jenny Creek lies at the bottom of this trail and is roughly 2 miles from the parking area.

Turn right (upstream) and start skiing to the west on the wide Jenny Creek Trail. Gentle touring along the valley bottom takes you past the turnoff to Guinn Mountain to the right (north), through thick trees and finally to a spot where the trail begins to steepen, requiring more strenuous exertion. High to the south you will see the old Rollins Pass railroad bed, which may be accessed from higher in the valley for a fun variation to this tour. Climb up and around the southwest slopes of Guinn Mountain, touring along the north side of Jenny Creek. The easy skiing up this valley covers about 1 mile. The more strenuous climbing begins after this at the 3-mile mark. From that point to Yankee Doodle Lake is slightly over 2 more miles and nearly 700 feet of elevation gain. Tougher skiing through this section may discourage less experienced skiers from continuing to the lake. For those who reach the lake the tour can be extended to the south along the railroad grade traversing back east over Jenny Creek. It is also possible to ski to the southwest and descend to Forest Lakes and then out to East Portal. The return trip down Jenny Creek goes quickly, but keep in mind that it is a steady 1-mile climb back up to the ski area.

# 39  ROLLINS PASS

**DESCRIPTION: Winter/spring ski tour, traditional Front Range crossing to Winter Park, car shuttle required. The tour is exposed to the elements for extended periods of time.**
**SKILL LEVEL: Intermediate**
**TIME: Long day/overnight**
**DISTANCE: 15 miles one way**
**ELEVATION CHANGE: 2,450 feet total gain/2,900 feet total loss**
**STARTING ELEVATION: 9,360 feet**
**AVALANCHE TERRAIN: Route crosses avalanche slopes; prone to skier-triggered avalanches during periods of avalanche hazard**
**USGS 7.5 MINUTE MAPS: Nederland, 1972, East Portal, 1958, Fraser, 1957**
**MAPS: pages 71, 100, 110**

West of the Eldora ski area lies the Rollins Pass road, a study in the evolution of both Colorado and technology. Originally built as a wagon road to link the Front Range to Grand County, in later years the roadbed was used for David Moffat's Denver, Northwestern & Pacific Railroad—a hair-raising, high-altitude rail line. Today the train makes its way under the pass through the Moffat Tunnel; all that remains is the old roadbed. Modern travelers use cars, mountain bikes and skis. This popular winter ski tour offers a long, often unprotected crossing of the Continental Divide to Winter Park. There are several ways to begin this tour, including Jenny Creek (tour 38), Forest Lakes (tour 41) and by far the most popular method, Guinn Mountain (tour 37), where skiers can spend the night in the warmth of the Arestua Hut before committing themselves to this alpine crossing. If the weather is at all threatening, go elsewhere and leave this tour to the pleasant days of spring.

Winter Park (the final destination) is a long way from the Eldora ski area; hence return transportation must be arranged. Some ideas include arranging for someone to pick up your group at a prearranged spot in Winter Park, riding the bus back to Denver or traveling by train. Each choice has advantages and shortcomings, and you will need to research the bus and train schedules and ticket prices.

Follow tour 37 to Guinn Mountain and the Arestua Hut. Leave the hut and ski west over the summit of Guinn Mountain, then descend to the western saddle that separates Guinn from the Continental Divide. From the saddle ascend directly west over easy to moderate terrain, aiming for the obvious railroad grade which cuts from south to north (this portion of the tour crosses snow-covered tundra and follows no trail). Down to the south is Yankee Doodle Lake, while to the north tower the Arapaho Peaks. Once on the road, ski north and round the corner to the west, skiing along the edge of the steep north slopes which tumble down into King Lake valley. Continue west then contour slightly southwest, crossing several of the old trestles which supported the tracks high above the valley. Then ski (or walk) up to the top of the pass. One section of this traverse can drift in with snow, forcing skiers to cross over a steep and treacherous couloir. This spot may be easily avoided by climbing over the flat, rocky tundra of Point 11,829. To follow this easy variation, leave the roadbed near the spot where you originally reached it, after crossing the saddle west of Guinn Mountain. Ski for approximately 1 mile before returning to the road east of the pass. This area is quite exposed to winds coming from the west and often lacks adequate snow, so you may be forced to walk a bit.

Cross the pass and descend a gentle grade which crosses the frozen alpine tundra. Pass a fork that climbs left (toward the southeast) to the radio tower that sits above Forest Lakes, ski past the Corona Range Study Plot and after 2.5 miles (from the top of the pass) approach treeline and better snow. Near the 11-mile mark ski over the old trestle, then turn south and leave the road. Ski through the trees of the South Fork of Ranch Creek. Veer west where this drainage reaches the meadow on the USGS maps, crossing flat terrain before regaining the roadbed.

Follow the road west for a little over 0.5 miles on easy terrain until you reach a small forested knoll on the right (north) and the slopes to the left drop more steeply into the head of Buck Creek. Turn down this drainage and ski through thick glades

of trees before reaching a small meadow. Cross and continue down the creek a short way. Then climb the east side of the drainage to reach an old roadbed. Ski down the road until you reach an aqueduct, then turn left. Double-pole along the aqueduct for several hundred feet until you see a large cut in the trees that drops down to the right (southwest) to the base of the Winter Park ski area. Follow this cut to the highway and cross to reach the ski area.

It is also possible to continue down the rail grade to the original outlet of the road, which lies west of the above-described route. Following this path eliminates the descent down Buck Creek and maintains a more moderate level of skiing difficulty. It also adds several miles to overall skiing distance.

# 40   TENNESSEE MOUNTAIN CABIN

**DESCRIPTION: Winter ski tour, overnight cabin, access via groomed Eldora Nordic Center trails**
**SKILL LEVEL: Intermediate**
**TIME: Quarter day to cabin**
**DISTANCE: 4 miles round trip**
**ELEVATION CHANGE: 500 feet total gain**
**STARTING ELEVATION: 9,360 feet**
**AVALANCHE TERRAIN: None**
**USGS 7.5 MINUTE MAP: Nederland, 1972**
**MAP: page 71**

As the story goes, the troll of Tennessee Mountain toiled for more than a year to make this tiny ski cabin a reality. Laying the foundation, cutting and peeling logs and finally putting it all together, he finished the cabin in 1980. The troll wanted to share the cabin and the responsibility for maintaining it with visitors so they could "relax, reflect and observe nature." He writes in the cabin's log book "The cabin is not nature, but a halfway house or window where nature can breathe some life into people's smothered instincts without frightening or harming them."

The Tennessee Mountain Cabin (or Troll Cabin) is located high up on a ridge southeast of the Eldora ski area. It is a cozy cabin with a wood stove and enough bunk space for six. Essential items like pots and pans, a lantern, split, stacked wood and sleeping pads are also furnished. You need only bring a sleeping bag, some warm clothes and provisions. A small camping stove is also recommended. The cabin must be reserved for a fee (which also includes the trail fee) from the Nordic Center at the Eldora ski area. It is especially popular during weekends and holidays. Advance reservations are recommended.

From the Nordic Center at the southeast end of the Eldora ski area, it is a moderate 2-mile ski to the cabin, most of it uphill. There are several ways to get there, all of them on groomed Nordic Center trails. A Nordic Center map is essential and

makes the route self-explanatory. Rather than go into a lengthy and probably confusing description of the route and its many variations, we'll just defer to the Nordic Center map.

# 41 FOREST LAKES

> **DESCRIPTION: Winter ski tour, backcountry trail and off trail, southern exposure often gets crusty**
> **SKILL LEVEL: Intermediate\***
> **TIME: Two-thirds day**
> **DISTANCE: 6 miles round trip**
> **ELEVATION CHANGE: 1,500 feet total gain**
> **STARTING ELEVATION: 9,200 feet**
> **AVALANCHE TERRAIN: Some avalanche terrain encountered; easily avoided**
> **USGS 7.5 MINUTE MAPS: East Portal, 1958**
> **MAPS: pages 71, 83**
>
> **\*NOVICE HIGHLIGHT: The first section to the turnoff for Forest Lakes is nearly level. Beyond the turnoff the trail gets steeper but may still be enjoyable for novice skiers.**

Snow conditions on this tour vary considerably throughout the winter. Because of its southern exposure, it is often crusty or icy in spots where the sun has peeked through the trees for a few days. Generally, there is very little avalanche danger, making it a good choice during or just after a storm. Intermediate skiers may find the final steep section to the first lake a bit more than they bargained for, but the rest of the tour is straightforward intermediate skiing.

Drive to Rollinsville, located on the Peak-to-Peak Highway (Colo. 119) 4.3 miles south of Nederland and 14.2 miles north of Black Hawk in the foothills southwest of Boulder. From Rollinsville, follow a dirt road straight west for approximately 10 miles until it ends at East Portal. Park at a convenient spot along the side of the road where you do not block anyone. Carry your skis across a bridge that is just in front of the huge entrance doorway to the Moffat Tunnel and hop the fence. About the first 0.5 miles of this tour is on private land. Although the owners generally allow access, this has not always been the case. Please be courteous and respectful or you may jeopardize future access to this and other tours in the area.

Follow a road up the valley for 1.1 miles until you come to an open field. Look for a trail that cuts back east, up the slope on the north side of the valley. This narrow trail steadily climbs east out of the main valley through thick forest for about 0.75 miles before turning up into a shallow side valley. Continue up this side valley as the trail becomes less and less distinct. If no trail has been broken, just keep going

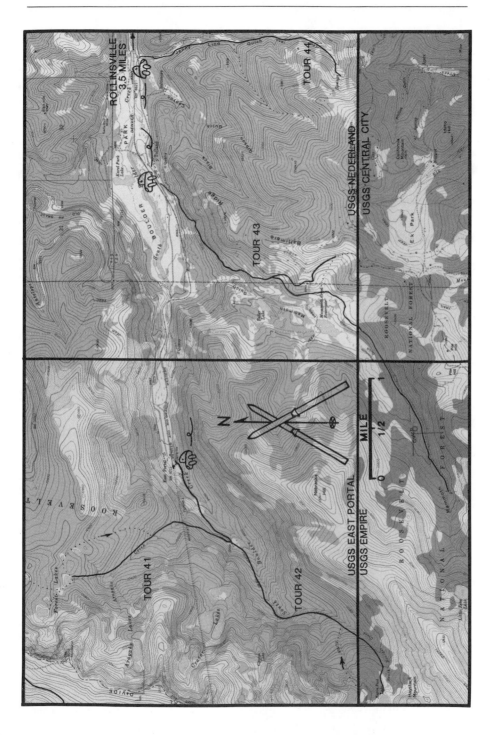

up the right side of the valley until you've gained the large bench that holds the lakes. This last stretch is steep.

Once you reach the first lake there are several good alternatives for an extended trip. You can continue west another 0.5 miles, gaining 200 feet in the process, to the largest of the Forest Lakes at treeline. Or, there are numerous glades, gullies and drop-offs that are perfect for short telemark runs. If you keep going north and west from the first lake, you'll intersect the Rollins Pass road, which can be skied for several more miles to the top of the pass, although the section above treeline rarely has adequate snow for skiing.

Most parties return by the same route. A difficult but fun alternative traverses straight east from the first lake 0.25 miles to another smaller lake at about the same elevation. Continue east past this lake until you funnel down into a draw that drops southeast through the trees. This draw eventually intersects with the trail just above the traverse. Follow it back down to the main valley and out to the car.

# 42　HEART LAKE AND ROGERS PASS LAKE

**DESCRIPTION: Winter ski tour, steep narrow trail, generally better snow than most Front Range tours**
**SKILL LEVEL: Advanced***
**TIME: Full day**
**DISTANCE: 7 miles round trip**
**ELEVATION CHANGE: 2,100 feet total gain**
**STARTING ELEVATION: 9,200 feet**
**AVALANCHE TERRAIN: Some avalanche terrain encountered; easily avoided**
**USGS 7.5 MINUTE MAPS: Nederland, 1972, East Portal, 1958**
**MAP: page 83**

**\*NOVICE HIGHLIGHT: The first mile is mostly level terrain, suitable for novice skiers.**

This is a fun trail ski with a fast and furious descent. The snow is almost always good because the route is protected from both wind and sun. Drive to Rollinsville, located on the Peak-to-Peak Highway (Colo. 119) 4.3 miles south of Nederland and 14.2 miles north of Black Hawk in the foothills southwest of Boulder. From Rollinsville, take a dirt road approximately 10 miles straight west until it ends at East Portal. Park at a convenient spot along the side of the road where you aren't blocking any driveways. Carry your skis across a bridge that is just in front of the huge Moffat Tunnel entrance and hop the fence. About the first 0.5-mile part is on private land. Although the owners generally allow access, this has not always been the case. Please be courteous and respectful or you may jeopardize future access to this and other tours in the area.

The tour follows a narrow road up the right side of the valley for approximately 3 miles. Gentle at first, the road gets steeper as you go. Toward the end it peters out, forcing you to make a few steep switchbacks to gain the last bench. Rogers Pass Lake is another 0.5 miles up near the top edge of treeline. Heart Lake can be found by contouring north from Rogers Pass Lake for another 0.5 miles.

It is possible to continue over Rogers Pass (the shortest route to Winter Park), then traverse north and west along the back side of the divide until you can drop down into Jim Creek. From Jim Creek it is only a few miles to the base of the Winter Park ski area. This is a difficult, exposed route that is sometimes done as an overnight. Snow conditions above treeline are rarely good until spring.

The return trip from Rogers Pass Lake to East Portal is usually done by simply reversing the ascent route. Watch out on your way down; it's easy to lose control and knock over some unwary skier on his or her way up.

It is also possible to cut straight down through the trees from Heart Lake. This involves a bit of timber-bashing but is well worth it for adventurous, advanced skiers.

# 43 MAMMOTH GULCH

**DESCRIPTION: Winter ski tour, huge, rarely visited valley, much skiable terrain, first mile on wind-scoured road**
**SKILL LEVEL: Novice to intermediate**
**TIME: Half day or longer**
**DISTANCE: 4 miles or more round trip**
**ELEVATION CHANGE: 900 feet or more total gain**
**STARTING ELEVATION: 8,900 feet**
**AVALANCHE TERRAIN: Route crosses avalanche runout zones; can be dangerous during high-hazard periods**
**USGS 7.5 MINUTE MAP: Nederland, 1972**
**MAPS: pages 83, 92**

The Mammoth Lakes basin is a huge area with miles of good skiable terrain. Few people visit the area, perhaps because the first mile up into the basin is on a hillside which is often windblown and unappealing. If you go when the wind is low and there is plenty of good snow, you won't be disappointed.

Drive to Rollinsville, located on the Peak-to-Peak Highway (Colo. 119) 4.3 miles south of Nederland and 14.2 miles north of Black Hawk in the foothills southwest of Boulder. From Rollinsville, follow a dirt road straight west for 5 miles to Tolland. Just past Tolland find the start of an unplowed dirt road that climbs out of the valley on the hillside to the south. There should be enough plowed parking space for several cars. Ski up the road as it climbs steadily for about a mile before turning up into Mammoth Lakes basin. After another mile, the road forks. The main road (left fork) climbs the left side of the valley 2.7 miles to a saddle at treeline. The right fork splits into two jeep trails, both of which drop down toward Mammoth Lakes. The right option goes straight to the outlet of Mammoth Creek Reservoir, where it ends. The left option contours along the east side of the valley. It continues for 3 miles up into the basin. All of these choices offer good skiing. A good option is to follow the main road (left fork) until you find a large low-angle glade that drops back down into the valley. Ski the glade (a good one for learning the telemark turn) and hook up with the left-option jeep trail. From there you can either continue up valley or contour back along the jeep trail to the fork. If you continue up valley, you'll find it goes for 3 miles before ending at some small lakes below the spectacular east face of James Peak.

# 44   JENNY LIND GULCH

**DESCRIPTION: Winter ski tour, gentle road that leads to open bowl**
**SKILL LEVEL: Novice to intermediate***
**TIME: Half to full day**
**DISTANCE: 4.2 miles round trip to bowl/5.2 miles for variation**
**ELEVATION CHANGE: Up to 1,400 feet total gain**
**STARTING ELEVATION: 8,800 feet**
**AVALANCHE TERRAIN: Some avalanche terrain encountered; easily avoided**
**USGS 7.5 MINUTE MAP: Nederland, 1972**
**MAP: page 83**

***ADVANCED HIGHLIGHT: The bowl above the upper end of the road is a fine spot for telemark skiing when the snow is fresh. Most of the bowl is safe from avalanches, but always exercise caution. Skiers can cross into the drainage to the west and return to the cars via an exciting loop.**

Jenny Lind Gulch has something to offer skiers of all abilities. The tour begins with a gentle climb up an old mining road and eventually opens into a large, sparsely wooded bowl. Novices can ski as far as they like, while those with greater endurance and downhill proficiency can spend hours skiing fresh powder in the upper reaches of the drainage. It is also possible to climb the western ridge and drop off into the head of a small tributary of the main valley, returning to the main road via an exciting schuss through scattered trees. This is one of the best short tours close to Boulder.

Drive to Rollinsville, located on the Peak-to-Peak Highway (Colo. 119) 4.3 miles south of Nederland and 14.2 miles north of Black Hawk in the foothills southwest of Boulder. From Rollinsville drive west for roughly 4 miles toward Tolland. Find a turnoff to the Melrose Mine which is blocked by a large silver metal gate. Park here as the tour follows the road behind the fence. Be sure to park in such a manner

*Arestua Hut (tour 37), Brian Litz photo.*

as not to block the gate and leave room for other cars in this slightly cramped spot.

Ski along the Melrose Mine road (approximately 0.2 miles) until a jeep trail branches off to the right crossing Jenny Lind Creek. Pass the jeep road and continue the gradual ascent through the dense spruce forest on the west side of the valley. After you pass the obvious mouth of a western tributary, the grade becomes a little steeper but is still quite moderate. The tributary can be used as an alternate ski trip; it is, however, a little steeper and the trail twists more tightly.

Dense stands of timber begin breaking up after about a mile of skiing as you enter the upper basin. At 1.5 miles is a nice lunch spot and good turnaround point. To the south the sparsely vegetated eastern extension of Colorado Mountain gives you a feeling that you have gained more elevation than you really have. Northward across the main valley, the Eldora ski area clings to the east side of Bryan Mountain.

From here, the climb becomes more demanding, as you explore the east-facing upper bowl. When the snow is fresh the skiing in this bowl is superb. Most parties return from here via the same route. Those with an insatiable appetite for tree skiing may return to the cars by skiing into the head of the small western tributary that was passed on the tour in. To reach the head of this small valley, ascend to the top of the bowl on the west side. You will now be on the north ridge of Colorado Mountain. This area is exposed to the wind and is not heavily timbered, allowing for a good look into the top of the tributary. Head off through the trees to the northwest, descending onto a roller coaster of steep slopes and little humps decorated with evergreen trees.

Keep your eyes open, as a small abandoned mining cabin may be found hiding on a tiny "shelf" or bench on the west edge of the streambed; it makes a nice spot for lunch. Continuing the descent, you are eventually funneled into the lower stream drainage, where a trail curls you back to the east, and meet the Jenny Lind Gulch Trail just south of the intersection with the Melrose Mine road.

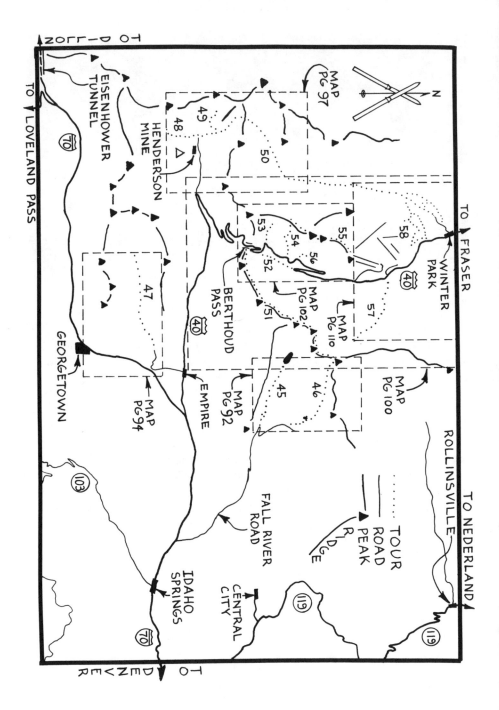

# CHAPTER FOUR

# BERTHOUD PASS AND TOURS NORTH OF I-70

## INTRODUCTION

Sinuous Berthoud Pass cuts across the Continental Divide, connecting the mountain communities of Empire and Winter Park. The terrain on this high-country passage offers some of the finest and most diverse backcountry skiing close to Denver. Novice as well as advanced skiers will find a wealth of relatively short tours that feature rolling downhill terrain and open slopes for telemark skiing. The typical Berthoud Pass tour leaves the trailhead and climbs upward over small benches. Following well-marked trails or roads, skiers can easily travel into the many small basins and find fine lunch spots. From these high points, skiers can explore the glades that carpet the landscape. Descents to the parking area are often exciting schusses and sudden sitzmarks. Ski groups of mixed abilities will find something for everyone, as novice skiers trace the primary trails and more advanced skiers tackle the steeper gradients. Of special note to the more proficient skiers are the tours that leave the top of the pass and drop down the main drainages before returning to the highway several hundred feet lower—Seven Mile Run, for example.

Remember, when planning your tour in this area: On weekends most of the well-known trails will be inundated with skiers. Also, the pass is the primary route for downhill skiers driving to and from the Winter Park–Mary Jane ski areas, so traffic increases noticeably about 8:00 a.m. and 4:00 p.m. The pass itself is narrow and twisty, so when a severe winter storm strikes, driving times can increase drastically; expect a 45-minute drive from west Denver under normal driving conditions.

## HISTORY

In 1859, Clear Creek Canyon was transformed from a quiet and pristine canyon to a hub of activity. Significant quantities of precious metals were discovered there that year. Colorado's first gold find was in the Platte River near Denver. Prospectors moved west into the mountains to follow the natural trail of these small placer (gravel/stream) deposits toward their hardrock sources (and, they hoped, more gold). An experienced mining man, George A. Jackson, collected the first traces of the malleable substance near the confluence of Chicago Creek and Clear Creek. Jackson worked under bitter winter conditions, excavating small portions of frozen fluvial debris, thawing them over fires and finally panning them with frigid water in a tin cup.

Nearly simultaneous gold discoveries to the north in Gilpin and Boulder counties, along with the Clear Creek finds, marked the beginning of Colorado's role as supplier of rare metals, healthy bank accounts and broken dreams. News of the discoveries spread quickly. A city soon sprouted near Jackson's find as the valley was inundated with miners and businessmen. The town was named Idaho Springs, in recognition of the nearby hot springs. Houses, stores, hotels and mills dotted the valley floor as "urban" life came to the mountains. Narrow-gauge rail service came during the 1870s as an ambitious service/transportation tunnel was constructed which linked Idaho Springs to Central City to the north. The Argo Tunnel, still visible across the river, ran nearly five miles and cost a whopping $10 million to build.

The valley from "Jackson's Bar" to Georgetown saw every inch of ground and stream picked at and panned. So thorough were the miners in their activities that the Georgetown–Idaho Springs district became Colorado's richest mining area during the 1860s and 1870s, producing more than $400 million worth of gold, silver, lead, zinc and copper. West and north of Idaho Springs, near Fall River Reservoir and St. Mary's Glacier, was the small community named Alice, as well as a milling site known as Fall River.

Empire sits near the confluence of the west fork of Clear Creek and Clear Creek where the Berthoud Pass road begins its ascent over the Continental Divide into Grand County. In 1860 two prospectors working their way north over Union Pass (between Georgetown and Empire) found traces of gold near Empire. Empire was populated by men staunchly in favor of the United States remaining a union, but in honor of their respective pre–Civil War politics, many names that reflected individual beliefs were bestowed upon mines and mountains. The Union District Valley City Company, Lincoln Mountain, Democrat Mountain and Douglas Mountain are names that were born during Colorado's colorful past.

Berthoud Pass, once a narrow Indian trail, was completed as a wagon road October 1, 1875, and is now a busy mountain thoroughfare. Thousands of downhill and backcountry skiers travel this pass in search of winter recreation. Berthoud Pass was also the site of some of Colorado's earliest organized ski outings. Aside from the miners and mailmen who used French–Canadian snowshoes and Norwegian "snow-shoes" (skis), many Denverites skied regularly near the summit of Berthoud and other areas around Clear Creek. St. Mary's Glacier, Chicago Lakes and Squaw Pass were popular destinations. The Colorado Mountain Club even built a ski jump on Genesee Mountain. Colorado's first rope tow was erected at Berthoud Pass; it began hoisting skiers up the mountain on February 7, 1937. During the 1938–39 season the Berthoud Pass ski area saw an estimated 50,000 skier days—a truly incredible number and indicative of Colorado's economic future.

# 45  FALL RIVER RESERVOIR

**DESCRIPTION: Winter ski tour, road up gentle valley, first section
frequently in poor condition**
**SKILL LEVEL: Novice**
**TIME: Three-quarters day**
**DISTANCE: 6.4 miles round trip**
**ELEVATION CHANGE: 1,130 feet total gain**
**STARTING ELEVATION: 9,580 feet**
**AVALANCHE TERRAIN: None**
**USGS 7.5 MINUTE MAP: Empire, 1974-PR**
**MAP: page 92**

Only a half hour from Denver, this surprisingly secluded tour makes a good morning (or afternoon) excursion when you have something else planned for the rest of the day. It follows a jeep road that parallels Fall River, a tributary of Clear Creek that joins it just west of Idaho Springs. The road continues up the Fall River valley above the point where Fall River Road, the access road, switchbacks and climbs out of the valley at a point 6.8 miles northwest of I-70. The road is gradual for the most part with a few steep sections near the end.

To get there, take I-70 to the Fall River Road exit, 2 miles west of Idaho Springs. Turn right and follow Fall River Road 6.8 miles to the beginning of a second set of hairpin turns. Park here and start skiing. The jeep road, which crosses the river almost immediately and then continues up the valley, is easy to follow and has no surprises. Expect a couple of forks and alternate roads along the

*At the trailhead, Brian Litz photo.*

way, none of which will cause any route-finding problems, as long as you take the main road at each junction and stay reasonably close to the creek. The road ends in a clearing just below Fall River Reservoir. The reservoir itself is not all that exciting but makes a good final destination.

The return trip has several nice glades and only takes about half as long as the trip in.

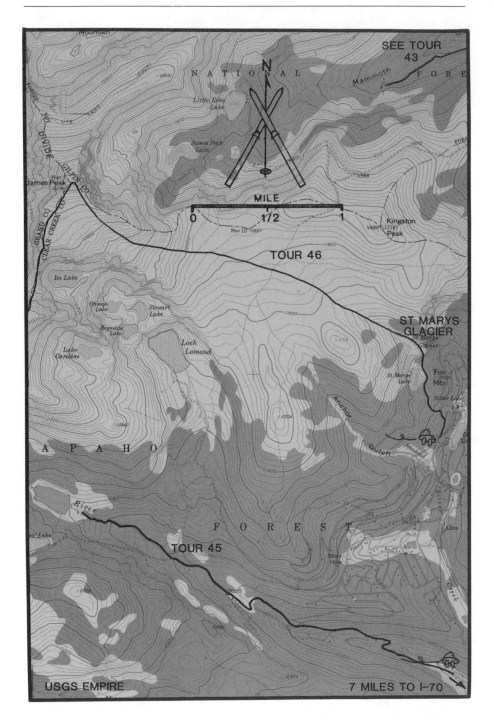

# 46 JAMES PEAK (13,294 FEET)

**DESCRIPTION: Spring (or winter) ski-mountaineering route**
**SKILL LEVEL: Advanced***
**TIME: Three-quarters day**
**DISTANCE: 6.4 miles round trip**
**ELEVATION CHANGE: 2,900 feet total gain**
**STARTING ELEVATION: 10,400 feet**
**AVALANCHE TERRAIN: Route crosses avalanche slopes; prone to skier-triggered avalanches during high-hazard periods**
**USGS 7.5 MINUTE MAP: Empire, 1974-PR**
**MAP: page 92**

**\*INTERMEDIATE HIGHLIGHT: The first two-thirds of the route is suitable for intermediate skiers. Above the bench the route gets considerably steeper.**

Quick easy access from Denver, a challenging ski descent, spectacular views and a lofty summit make this a Front Range classic. It is best done as a spring tour after the snow above treeline has changed to spring corn but can also be enjoyable in winter if snow conditions are good and avalanche hazard is low.

Take I-70 west from Denver to the Fall River Road turnoff 2 miles west of Idaho Springs. Follow this road for 9 miles up the valley, past some switchbacks, past the old St. Mary's ski area, to a small parking area opposite a four-wheel-drive access road. The parking area is 0.2 miles beyond the old St. Mary's ski area and 0.3 miles before Silver Lake Condominiums.

Ski up the four-wheel-drive road for 0.5 miles to St. Mary's Lake at the base of St. Mary's Glacier. Go around the right side of the lake and ascend the glacier near its right margin. Steepness gradually decreases as elevation increases, until the glacier opens out onto a huge flat bench at 11,600 feet. Cross the bench heading straight west and ascend the ridge or the left front side of James Peak, continuing to its summit.

The descent is quite steep at first but becomes more moderate lower down. Depending on snow conditions, you'll probably have to stay off to the south side of the ridge to get the best run. It is extremely easy to get disoriented while crossing the flat bench when visibility is low. More than one party has ended up going down the wrong valley. Always take a map and a compass.

St. Mary's Glacier has been the site of numerous accidents. It is a popular summer spot for hiking and glissading, but people occasionally misjudge their own ability to stay under control and end up crashing into the rocks below. In winter, the glacier occasionally avalanches. To be safe, ascend on the far right side, next to the rock outcrops. Don't go at all if avalanche conditions are high.

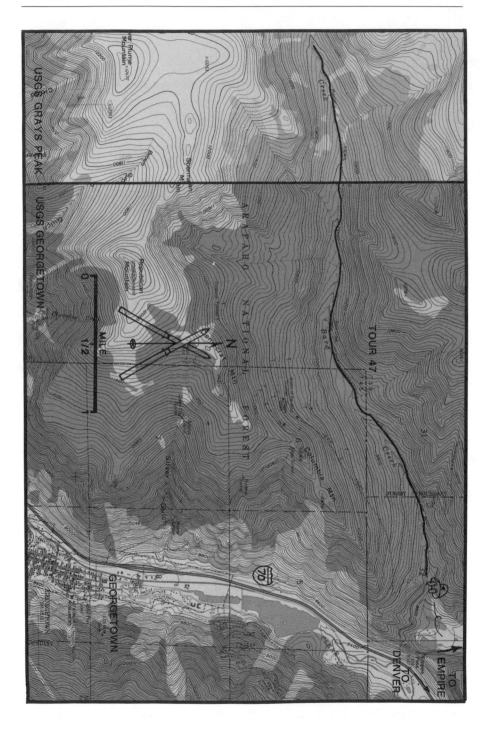

# 47  BARD CREEK

**DESCRIPTION: Winter ski tour on secluded and sheltered road**
**SKILL LEVEL: Intermediate**
**TIME: Full day**
**DISTANCE: 9 miles round trip**
**ELEVATION CHANGE: 1,750 feet total gain**
**STARTING ELEVATION: 8,940 feet**
**AVALANCHE TERRAIN: None**
**USGS 7.5 MINUTE MAPS: Georgetown, 1974-PR, Grays Peak, 1987-PR**
**MAP: page 94**

Bard Creek is a long isolated valley sitting directly southwest of the town of Empire. It is lodged between US 40 and I-70 and is often overlooked by skiers. On busy ski weekends when Berthoud Pass and Guanella Pass tours are bustling with legions of cross-country skiers, it is possible to enjoy this pleasant valley without seeing another party. The route follows an old mining roadbed, maintaining a steady yet moderate rate of ascent. Additionally, this tour boasts one of the shortest approach drives from Denver of any tour in this book.

Bard Creek is immediately to the southwest from the town of Empire, which is on US 40 a few miles west of I-70. In the middle of town turn south on Bard Creek Drive (at Jenny's Restaurant). Follow the plowed road past a narrow passage overlooking I-70 and Georgetown to the south. Just past this overlook the road turns to the west and twists along on the cold, shady south side of the valley to the small plowed parking area at the mouth of Bard Creek (a little over 2 miles from the town of Empire).

The tour usually begins near a small group of private cabins and continues along the summer roadbed on the south side of the creek. After 0.2 miles the road bears toward the northwest and crosses Bard Creek. Once past the creek the tour begins a pronounced climb through sparse timber up and past another group of cabins which are right of the road. After this climb the terrain relaxes and moderate kick and glide technique propels you through intermittent stands of spruce and aspen trees.

Bard Creek Mine appears at just under 2 miles. Named after 18th-century miner Dr. Richard Bard, this well-preserved structure is a great lunch spot. If you turn around at this point, you will have an enjoyable short intermediate ski tour. Pushing on farther up the valley to the west requires more energy, as the terrain remains moderate except for a steeper climb near the 3-mile mark. When you reach a point where the road becomes harder to follow, it is easiest to strike out on your own, staying on the north side of the creek until you reach treeline near 11,000 feet. The bowls above and west of treeline near the head of the valley should be skied only by competent backcountry skiers with thorough experience in avalanche assessment.

# 48    BUTLER GULCH

**DESCRIPTION: Winter ski tour up small side valley, good telemark glades**
**SKILL LEVEL: Intermediate***
**TIME: Half day**
**DISTANCE: 4 miles round trip**
**ELEVATION CHANGE: 1,000 feet total gain**
**STARTING ELEVATION: 10,350 feet**
**AVALANCHE TERRAIN: Some avalanche terrain encountered; easily avoided**
**USGS 7.5 MINUTE MAP: Berthoud Pass, 1957**
**MAP: page 97**

***ADVANCED HIGHLIGHT: The glades and bowls near treeline offer excellent telemark skiing.**

The bowls and glades at the head of Butler Gulch are a popular destination for telemark enthusiasts intent on sharpening their skills and having some fun. The area always seems to have great powder, on the first day of the season or the last. The short drive and moderate approach make for a delightful half day of skiing with minimal effort. If you start early, there still will be plenty of time to catch the last half of the Sunday afternoon football game.

Take US 40 west to the Henderson Mine turnoff at the first hairpin turn past Empire. Follow this to a designated parking area just past Henderson Mine. Ski up the road 0.25 miles and take the left fork, which cuts back across the creek and diagonals up the opposite hillside. The right fork leads to Jones Pass (see tours 49 and 50). After 0.5 miles of moderate climbing up a narrow road, you'll reach a small meadow in the middle of Butler Gulch. Cross the creek and continue up the left side of the valley. The trail steepens dramatically and finally switchbacks a few times before gaining the treeline glades. Most parties ski a few runs here and return but you can easily continue up into the bowl above treeline or do some runs on the right side of the valley. The return trip via the same route starts out fast and furious. Watch out for other skiers who are still on their way up. Once down to the small meadow, you will have an easy glide back to the parking lot.

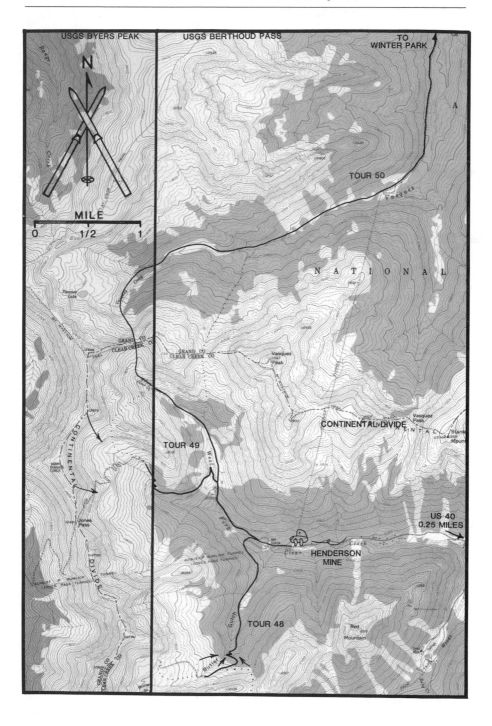

# 49   JONES PASS

**DESCRIPTION: Winter ski tour, road to high alpine bowls, excellent for spring skiing**
**SKILL LEVEL: Novice to intermediate\***
**TIME: Half to full day**
**DISTANCE: Up to 7 miles round trip**
**ELEVATION CHANGE: Up to 2,300 feet total gain**
**STARTING ELEVATION: 10,350 feet**
**AVALANCHE TERRAIN: Some avalanche terrain encountered; easily avoided**
**USGS 7.5 MINUTE MAPS: Berthoud Pass, 1957, Byers Peak, 1957**
**MAP: page 97**

**\*INTERMEDIATE/ADVANCED HIGHLIGHT: The two high bowls offer superb possibilities for above-treeline spring skiing. This is mostly avalanche terrain; wait for spring consolidation.**

This is a popular winter tour with quick, easy access from Denver. Snow conditions are usually quite good, at least until you reach treeline, where it is often blowing and windpacked in winter. The skiing is gentle and follows snow-covered roads most of the way, making it a good choice for novices. The area encompasses two short side valleys, both of which can be skied in a half day. The Butler Gulch Tour (tour 48) shares the same start and can easily be combined with these side valleys to make a longer tour.

From I-70, take US 40 west to the Henderson Mine turnoff at the first hairpin turn past Empire. Follow this to a designated parking area just past the Henderson Mine. Ski up the road 0.25 miles and take the right fork toward Jones Pass (the other fork cuts back left to Butler Gulch). After about a mile you'll break out of the trees into an open area. There are two possibilities. You may continue up valley or follow the Jones Pass road as it cuts back left across the creek, makes a switchback on the hillside to the south and traverses through trees up and into the Jones Pass bowl. This road eventually breaks out of the trees after another 0.5 miles. The skiing gets a little steeper here as the road switchbacks a couple of times to gain elevation. Once above treeline, advanced skiers may continue all the way up and over Jones Pass.

The other option, the right side valley, continues up through intermittent meadows and forest. It can be followed above treeline to another high bowl. Be cautious of the large avalanche paths on the right side of the valley.

If snow conditions above treeline are good, it is possible to connect the two valleys via a high saddle, thus making a loop trip. The slopes off either side of the saddle are gentle enough to be negotiated by intermediate skiers, if the snow isn't too windpacked.

# 50   JONES PASS TO WINTER PARK

**DESCRIPTION: Winter ski tour, very long route, crosses over high pass, car shuttle required**
**SKILL LEVEL: Intermediate**
**TIME: Full day or longer**
**DISTANCE: 13 miles**
**ELEVATION CHANGE: 1,700 feet total gain**
**STARTING ELEVATION: 10,350 feet**
**AVALANCHE TERRAIN: Route crosses avalanche slopes; prone to skier-triggered avalanches during high-hazard periods**
**USGS 7.5 MINUTE MAPS: Berthoud Pass, 1957, Byers Peak, 1957, Fraser, 1957**
**MAPS: pages 97, 100, 110**

This tour starts from the Henderson Mine access to Jones Pass, makes its way over the ridge into Vasquez Creek and then continues down Vasquez Creek to Winter Park. The pass is well above treeline but the terrain is generally moderate. The descent into Vasquez Creek is excellent with long stretches of open glade skiing. Lower Vasquez Valley is much like the popular Shrine Pass Tour—a long, arduous glide on a road that gradually loses elevation.

Take US 40 west to the Henderson Mine turnoff at the first hairpin turn past Empire. Follow this to a designated parking area just past Henderson Mine. Ski up the road 0.25 miles and take the right fork toward Jones Pass (the other fork cuts back left to Butler Creek). After about 1 mile you'll break out of the trees into an open area. Here, the Jones Pass road cuts across the creek, makes a switchback on the hillside to the south and traverses back around toward the upper Jones Pass bowl. Instead of following the Jones Pass road, keep going up the main valley staying right of the creek. The normal route continues up about 2 miles and eventually curves right toward a pass at 11,950 feet. Once over the pass ski the glade of choice down toward Vasquez Creek. Stay on the left side of the creek as you continue down valley.

An alternate route, which goes over a different pass to reach Vasquez Creek, takes the first low point on the right ridge. This route encounters a little more advanced terrain. It starts with a steep climb to the pass and continues on the other side with a good open run and then some fast tight alleys through the trees as you drop into Vasquez Valley.

The routes converge a short distance down Vasquez Creek. Snowmobiles are not uncommon along the entire route. The nasty beasts are noisy and annoying but following their tracks can eliminate a lot of hard trail breaking. This tour could easily turn into a grueling marathon if you have to break trail all the way down the Vasquez drainage. Fortunately, this is rarely the case, unless you go during or just after a big storm.

Continue down the left side of the valley until you find the road. Follow this

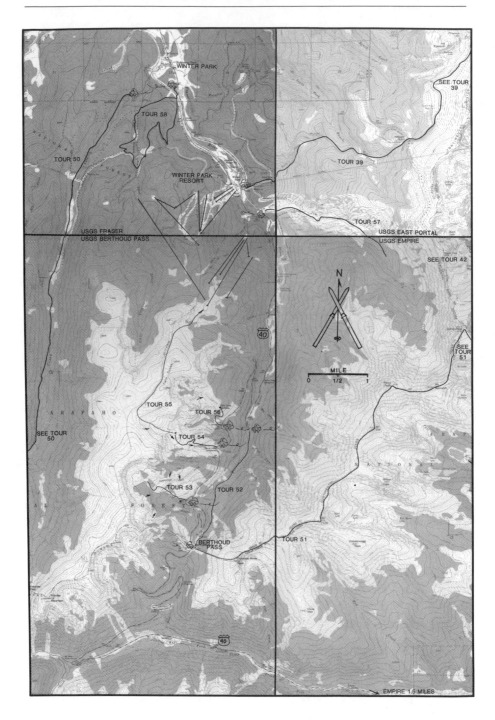

for several miles, passing forks that take off both to the left and to the right. Eventually you'll run into a housing development at the low end of the valley. From here it's a short distance to the town of Winter Park. A shuttle bus makes a loop through the high end of the housing development, picking skiers up and dropping them off at the Winter Park ski area. So, you can ride up from Denver with friends who plan to ski Winter Park, have them drop you off at the Jones Pass parking area and then meet them later at the bottom of the slopes for après ski.

# 51   SKYLINE TRAVERSE

DESCRIPTION: Spring ski-mountaineering route, long and strenuous, car shuttle required
SKILL LEVEL: Advanced
TIME: Full day or longer
DISTANCE: 17.6 miles one way
ELEVATION CHANGE: 4,182 feet total gain/5,647 feet total loss
STARTING ELEVATION: 11,315 feet
AVALANCHE TERRAIN: Mostly avalanche terrain; wait for spring consolidation
USGS 7.5 MINUTE MAPS: Berthoud Pass, 1957, Empire, 1974-PR
MAPS: pages 100, 102

This 17-mile endurance test leaves the summit of Berthoud Pass and makes its way to the northeast, terminating at the base of St. Mary's Glacier. The day's agenda includes some hiking, spectacular springtime skiing and even a shot of scrambling as you traverse a medley of 13,000-foot peaks. The tour gets its name from the view you see heading west on I-70 under the overpass at the Genesee Park–Lookout Mountain exit, for the entire route is visible on the western skyline from here. These peaks also compose the horizon east of the Winter Park ski area. A long and demanding trip, it requires a very early (or "alpine") start. At the end of the day as you leave the summit of James Peak on the final 2,500-foot descent, you will agree that this special trip is one to remember.

A car shuttle is necessary since the tour ends a long way from its start. The best place to leave a car is just below St. Mary's Lake, where an old jeep trail leaves the paved road and climbs to the base of the glacier. To reach this spot, drive on I-70 and take the Fall River exit, which is immediately west of Idaho Springs. Follow this road for 19 miles and park on either side of the road where a small jeep road descends from the left (northwest). The jeep road is 0.2 miles beyond the old St. Mary's ski area and 0.3 miles before Silver Lake Condominiums. Go back to I-70, head west to the turnoff to Berthoud Pass (US 40) and drive to the summit of the pass.

From the moment you leave the car you will be climbing. Head east and climb the ski area run. Once past the ski area head several hundred yards up toward

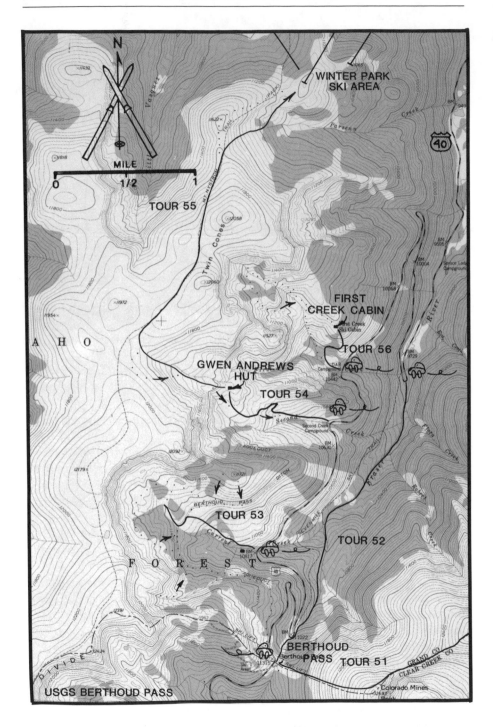

the summit of Colorado Mines Peak, then begin an ascending traverse across its north slopes toward the saddle on its northeast side. After gaining the saddle follow the ridge as it gently rolls up to the summit of Mount Flora (13,132 feet). Drop off this peak and head in a more northerly direction as the route now heads toward Mount Eva (13,130 feet), 2 miles away. Moderate hiking up the wind-scoured southeastern summit cones and easy skiing down cornices on the leeward ridges characterize this portion of the tour.

Mount Eva stands near the halfway mark on the traverse of the peaks. Additionally it divides the relatively easier first half of the tour with the more difficult second half. Leaving the summit of Mount Eva, ski the cornice snowfield which drops to the saddle at the base of Parry Peak (13,391 feet). The ascent of Parry is nothing more than a stiff hike as you climb the 700 feet to its summit, which is also the high point of the trip. The alpine panorama from the top takes in Winter Park and the Grand Valley to the west, Longs Peak and the Indian Peaks to the north and the Mount Evans–Grays Peak group to the south.

Ascending Mount Bancroft (13,250 feet) to the east does not require an extreme drop in elevation for its ascent but is simply a traverse along a breathtaking ridge before a short slope brings you to its peak. Cross over the summit and link turns down the northeast spur. This short slope ends quickly on the edge of rocky cliffs which fall down to Ice Lake and Loch Lomond. From this perch head west-northwest and follow the path of least resistance down the steep snowfields. These are probably the most difficult downhill sections of the tour as they are steep, somewhat discontinuous and bordered by talus islands.

The final unclimbed summit, James Peak (13,294 feet), lies roughly 0.75 miles north of you at this point. Rough is a good adjective for the ascent of the peak, which requires some scrambling to reach the large snowfield occupying its southeast face. From the low point on the saddle drop off the ridge to the west (this is the head of Jim Creek) and go directly north, bypassing a series of rocky outcrops and towers. After several hundred feet search for one of several moderate passages through the outcrops to the right which allow you to regain the crest of the ridge. Then climb a short but steep snow step before reaching the large snowfield. This section is not very difficult but it crosses steep talus slopes. Good route finding ensures a safe passage through this spot. James Peak's summit is a straightforward hike from the edge of the plateaulike snowfield.

The final descent off James Peak begins with an immediate drop onto the superb southeast face. After descending several hundred feet, contour naturally along the eastern ridge. When the slope angle eases off and you merge with the vast plateau head straight east toward the large ravine holding St. Mary's Glacier. Easy gliding across this huge alpine meadow quickly deposits you on top of the glacier and the final chance for telemark turns. At the bottom, head south and pick up the jeep road which begins on the east edge of St. Mary's Lake. Hike or ski the remaining 0.3 miles to the waiting autos and the cooler of beer.

# 52  SEVEN MILE RUN

DESCRIPTION: Winter ski tour, fun and relatively short downhill run, car shuttle required, very popular
SKILL LEVEL: Advanced
TIME: Quarter day or less (roughly one hour for descent to highway)
DISTANCE: 3.2 miles one way
ELEVATION CHANGE: 1,500 feet total loss
STARTING ELEVATION: 11,315 feet
AVALANCHE TERRAIN: Some avalanche terrain encountered; easily avoided
USGS 7.5 MINUTE MAP: Berthoud Pass, 1957
MAPS: pages 100, 102

Seven Mile Ski Run stands as a tribute to the timelessness of the sport of skiing. In the 1940s this route was state-of-the-art in this winter sport. From the summit of Berthoud Pass the route drops over 1,500 feet along Seven Mile Creek, meeting the highway at the last hairpin curve. It is a fast and challenging descent that will force you to draw upon all of your cross-country downhill techniques. Whether you are on wooden skis or modern single-camber wonders with cable bindings and telemark boots, this tour is fun and will bring out the kid in everyone. The entire run should take about 45 minutes to complete, so you can ski Second Creek in the morning and have plenty of time to enjoy this historic tour in the afternoon.

Begin on the summit of Berthoud Pass. From the north edge of the parking area a small snowfield fans out to the north, reaching an obvious hairpin curve. Known as Hell's Half Acre, this is the beginning of the tour. This open slope can vary from superb powder to days-old crud; however, beyond this point the tour lies in the cover of the trees so more consistent snow conditions prevail. As you drop north off the pass and approach the first major switchback, veer toward the east (right) and skirt the edge of the road's snowbanks before dropping into the steep head of the drainage. From here on out the tour lies below the level of the highway. Historically the tour followed a trail maintained by the U.S. Forest Service that ran west of the creek at the base of the steeper slopes. Most skiers today, however, use a route that follows the creekbed very closely, where the terrain is faster and more challenging. Below the chute ski along the creek, following a rough trail that is usually well traveled. The next section that can be difficult is another drop through a bottleneck along the creek. It is noticeable in that it bends west and has a steep and more open left face that skiers use to make a traversing descent to the bottom. This chute spits you out at high speed onto a fast, narrow section of trail characterized by a long series of washboardlike bumps. From here on out you will maintain a steady descent through the woods along a gentle trail. The topography on the lower stretches, although more moderate than the initial one-third of the tour, is still very pleasing.

The tour ends at the final switchback on US 40. If you haven't left a shuttle car here it is normally quite easy to flag a ride back to the top of the pass (and another trip down Seven Mile Creek). For your information this tour is not 7 miles long but actually only 3.2 miles. The misleading name is derived from the fact that it was 7 miles from the top of the pass to the first stage station on the old Berthoud Pass wagon road. If you feel deprived, feel free to ski it twice!

# 53  Current Creek

**DESCRIPTION: Winter ski tour, open terrain and bowl for telemarking**
**SKILL LEVEL: Intermediate***
**TIME: Half day**
**DISTANCE: 1.8 miles round trip**
**ELEVATION CHANGE: 800 feet total gain**
**STARTING ELEVATION: 10,800 feet**
**AVALANCHE TERRAIN: Some avalanche terrain encountered; easily avoided**
**USGS 7.5 MINUTE MAP: Berthoud Pass, 1957**
**MAPS: pages 100, 102**

**\*ADVANCED HIGHLIGHT: This area has good telemark glades and bowls.**

Current Creek is the first major drainage to the west once you have crossed over Berthoud Pass while traveling north into the Fraser Valley. Shaped like an enormous bowl, the actual skiable distances in Current Creek are fairly short; however, its circular geometry provides many acres of enjoyable backcountry skiing. It is possible to spend an entire day exploring the glades and rolling hills that abound in this small valley. If you are lucky enough to encounter powder snow conditions, you will be in for an exceptional outing. A well-hidden cabin on forest service land lies at the base of the densely wooded south slopes. It is a perfect spot to spend the night, allowing for an early start on your morning figure eights.

Reach Current Creek by driving on US 40 west and north from Empire or south from Winter Park and Fraser. Roughly 1 mile north of the summit of Berthoud Pass, Current Creek flows from its cirque and crosses the highway near a plowed parking area large enough for about 10 cars. This parking area lies west of US 40 and on the outside radius of a sharp turn.

The tour begins by skiing southwest on a small road. Just before you reach the creek, turn west and climb toward the trees. Continue west climbing along the north side of the creekbed skiing in and out of stands of timber. If you stay high on the slope from the creek, you will ski into larger clearings until you reach the Berthoud Pass Ditch Aqueduct at about 10,300 feet. Follow the aqueduct south until you return to Current Creek. Turn upstream following the creek as it continues to pass in and out of the trees. Eventually you will approach treeline. At this spot the steep and ominous west wall of the basin towers above and to the west, just beyond the edge of treeline. With massive overhanging cornices, the base of this escarpment is not a spot to while away idle moments.

Remain in the trees and you can loop more to the south, climbing through the small clearing that follows the creek. Current Creek's source is a small tarn lying in the southwest corner of the main basin above treeline. It is a safe spot to break out of the trees for an unobstructed view down valley and across Fraser Creek to Parry Peak. For the return trip you can follow your tracks or search for uncut powder which always seems to be hiding among the trees in this valley.

This trip is a good path to follow if you have never skied Current Creek; it follows the primary drainage and climbs the full length of the valley. However, feel free to explore. The north side of the valley features sparse glades, which when covered with new snow, provide fine slopes to link telemark turns. The cabin sits on the south side of the valley; the trees are much thicker here and the skiing is more challenging.

The quaint Current Creek Cabin is hard to locate, but it lies south of the creek on a small flat spot within a small clearing. This little wooden cube holds three to four adults comfortably. Inside is a small stove and the basic amenities necessary for a warm night out. To reach the cabin follow the creekbed on the south side and after about 20 minutes of climbing, search to the south at the base of the steeper southern valley wall. More information on the cabin may be obtained from the forest service or the ski area at Berthoud Pass.

# 54   SECOND CREEK (GWEN ANDREWS HUT)

**DESCRIPTION: Winter ski tour, small valley, overnight shelter/cabin, good telemark skiing**
**SKILL LEVEL: Intermediate***
**TIME: Half day**
**DISTANCE: 1 mile to cabin, another 0.75 miles to end of valley**
**ELEVATION CHANGE: 750 feet total gain to cabin**
**STARTING ELEVATION: 10,580 feet**
**AVALANCHE TERRAIN: Some avalanche terrain encountered; easily avoided**
**USGS 7.5 MINUTE MAP: Berthoud Pass, 1957**
**MAPS: pages 100, 102**

**\*ADVANCED HIGHLIGHT: This area has excellent telemark glades and bowls.**

Second Creek is a favorite place for a short day tour or an overnight cabin trip. The cabin is maintained by the Colorado Mountain Club and is open to the public for both day and overnight use on a first come/first served basis. Although it has very few amenities and can be rather drafty, it is still much better than camping in a snowdrift. The cabin is a small A-frame with a wood stove and enough bunk space for four. There are a few pots and pans but it's recommended that you bring your own stove and cook set. Also, there may be some dry wood early in the season but don't count on having a cozy wood fire unless you haul up some wood yourself.

Second Creek is the second drainage from the top of Berthoud Pass as you head north toward Winter Park. Plowed areas for parking are on both sides of the highway. To get to the cabin most people head up the right side of the creek. After 0.5 miles you must switchback up a steep section and then round a bald knob to the left. This puts you in a bowl below a steep face that drops off from the high corniced ridge to the west. From here, the cabin is in the trees up on the knoll to the right between the First and Second Creek drainages.

Great skiing surrounds the cabin. The run back down valley over the steep section is challenging enough for even the hottest skier but manageable enough for intermediate skiers. Above the cabin you can ski to the end of the valley and then up onto the main ridge. This area is often windblown, but if you're there when snow conditions are good, the skiing can be outstanding.

# 55  SECOND CREEK TO WINTER PARK

**DESCRIPTION: Winter ski tour, mostly above treeline, finishes by skiing to Winter Park or Mary Jane ski areas, car shuttle required**
**SKILL LEVEL: Intermediate to advanced**
**TIME: Three-quarters day**
**DISTANCE: 8 miles**
**ELEVATION CHANGE: 1,500 feet total gain/2,780 feet total loss**
**STARTING ELEVATION: 10,580 feet**
**AVALANCHE TERRAIN: Route crosses avalanche slopes; prone to skier-triggered avalanches during high-hazard periods**
**USGS 7.5 MINUTE MAP: Berthoud Pass, 1957**
**MAPS: pages 100, 102**

This adventurous tour starts with a climb through the sparsely timbered glades of Second Creek, then makes a high traverse north along a ridge well above treeline and finishes with a run down the slopes at the Winter Park ski area. Views from the ridge are spectacular, with the Williams Fork Mountains to the west, the Fraser Valley to the north and the entire string of Indian Peaks to the northeast. The ridge is also wide and flat and extremely exposed to high winds. It would be very easy to get lost in a whiteout, so it's best to pick a calm day with good visibility.

Second Creek is the second drainage down from the top of Berthoud Pass as you head north toward Winter Park. There should be a plowed area for parking on either side of the road. Follow the Second Creek valley for 2 miles up to the main ridge (see tour 54 for a more detailed description). Head north along the ridge for 2 miles, staying just left of two high knobs. If you get too far to the left, you'll end up on a spur ridge that eventually drops down into the Vasquez Expansion of the Winter Park ski area. This route works but there is a steep, rocky section through thick trees that must be negotiated before reaching the ski runs. If you stay on the right ridge, you'll be able to see the top of Mary Jane after rounding the second knob. Once around this knob you can either drop into Parsenne Bowl or continue along the ridge to the top of the lifts. The ski area has been very agreeable about allowing people to descend without a lift ticket, but to avoid any liability problems, you should talk to the ski patrol before descending and, if necessary, sign some sort of waiver.

# 56  FIRST CREEK (COLORADO MOUNTAIN CLUB CABIN)

DESCRIPTION: Winter ski tour, cozy cabin, short, steep approach
SKILL LEVEL: Intermediate
TIME: Quarter day
DISTANCE: 1 mile round trip
ELEVATION CHANGE: 500 feet total gain
STARTING ELEVATION: 10,400 feet
AVALANCHE TERRAIN: Route crosses avalanche slopes; prone to skier-triggered avalanches during high-hazard periods
USGS 7.5 MINUTE MAP: Berthoud Pass, 1957
MAPS: pages 100, 102

The Colorado Mountain Club maintains several rustic cabins on forest service land for both summer and winter use. The First Creek Cabin is one of the nicest. It has six roomy bunks, a good wood stove, an outhouse and plenty of pots, pans and cooking utensils. First Creek is the third drainage down from the top of Berthoud Pass as you head toward Winter Park. The cabin is located on a spur ridge just north of First Creek, overlooking the highway. During the summer there is a trail that angles up the valley a few hundred yards and then heads almost straight up the hillside to the cabin. Most parties use this direct approach in winter as well as summer, but it is very steep. Skins or snowshoes are recommended unless the trail has been packed down enough to walk on. You can also reach the cabin by heading up the right fork of the creek for 0.5 miles and then cutting back along a bench at the level of the cabin. It is located in fairly dense trees and may be difficult to find. Pay close attention to the map.

Skiing from the cabin is somewhat limited. There are several avalanche slopes that come into the valley from the ridge above. Best bets are to take a short tour to the end of the valley where there are some good glades for telemarking or just play around on the slopes near the cabin. Although the trip is steep and avalanche-prone, you may also climb onto the main ridge and follow it to Winter Park (see tour 55).

The cabin can be reserved from the Colorado Mountain Club for a small fee (see Appendix 4). They ask that at least one person from each party be a member. Volunteers maintain the cabin and stock it with wood for the winter. A lot of work goes into keeping the cabin in good shape; please keep it that way. When you leave, clear the cabin, remove all trash and make sure the windows are shuttered and the door is securely closed.

# 57  JIM CREEK

**DESCRIPTION: Winter ski tour, narrow road up scenic side valley**
**SKILL LEVEL: Intermediate***
**TIME: Three-quarters day**
**DISTANCE: 5 miles round trip**
**ELEVATION CHANGE: 840 feet**
**STARTING ELEVATION: 9,220 feet**
**AVALANCHE TERRAIN: Some avalanche terrain encountered, easily avoided**
**USGS 7.5 MINUTE MAPS: Fraser, 1957, East Portal, 1958, Empire, 1974-PR**
**MAPS: pages 102, 110**

**\*NOVICE HIGHLIGHT: The first 0.5 miles up to the aqueduct road and the alternate routes on the aqueduct road itself are suitable for novice skiers.**

This is a very enjoyable tour up a scenic side valley located on the east side of US 40 directly across from the Winter Park ski area. The route follows a narrow jeep road that climbs steadily south (right) of the Jim Creek valley. The road peeks in and out of the trees at several points along the way, revealing ever more impressive views of the huge west flanks of James Peak. The road itself consistently challenges the intrepid skier, presenting numerous opportunities for head-deep plunges into deep powder on the return trip. The only minor drawback is the rather unimpressive final destination. The road merely ends in the middle of the forest, halfway up the valley at a point that has no landmarks or distinguishing characteristics whatsoever. It just ends.

To reach the trailhead, take US 40 over Berthoud Pass to the southernmost entrance to the Winter Park ski area (not the Mary Jane entrance but the main entrance

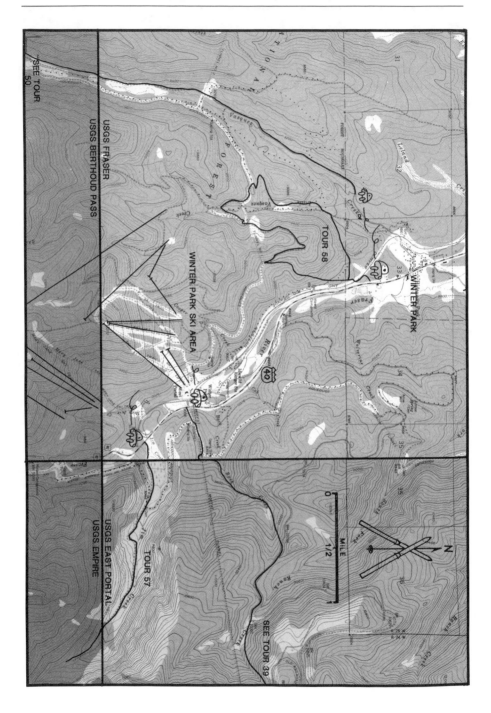

to the Winter Park ski area proper). A trail begins directly across the highway from the ski area turnoff (parking is available at the turnoff). This, however, is not the recommended trail—it dead ends after only 0.2 miles. Instead, hike about 100 yards south (toward Berthoud Pass) along the highway to an inconspicuous narrow road that burrows east through dense trees. After skiing 0.2 miles on this road, you will encounter a huge, somewhat offensive-looking water pipe. This pipe is part of a large system that collects and diverts water through the Moffat Tunnel to the Eastern Slope. Ski under the pipe, continuing a gradual ascent east another 0.5 miles to an intersection with a nearly level aqueduct road. There is a small water diversion gate located where Jim Creek intersects the aqueduct. Alternate routes, explained at the end of this tour description, follow the aqueduct road north or south from this point.

To proceed up Jim Creek, find the continuation of the narrow access road as it forges ahead through the brush a short distance to the right of the water diversion installation. At times the road becomes difficult to find as it steadily climbs through intermittent meadows and trees. After another 1.6 miles the last of the open meadows is encountered directly across Jim Creek from an obvious avalanche trough (the trough poses little or no danger as long as you stay on the south side of Jim Creek). The road continues above this meadow for another 0.25 miles before coming to a dead end in the middle of the forest.

The return trip via the same route may require some quick reflex reactions from your weary legs as you navigate through tight corridors at high speed, hopefully demonstrating at least a hint of grace, form and control. If not, so what? At least you got down in one piece.

ALTERNATE ROUTES: Novice skiers will find the snow-covered aqueduct road makes a very pleasant alternate tour. The aqueduct road traverses into Jim Creek from the south, then continues north toward the Moffat Tunnel. Turning southwest (right) from the intersection of the aqueduct road with the Jim Creek road, novice skiers can diagonal stride southwest (back toward the water pipe), then south for up to 1.5 miles before dropping back to US 40 about a mile above the ski area turnoff. It is also possible to turn left on the aqueduct road, thus traversing north out of Jim Creek. Eventually this will lead to the Rollins Pass road some 3.5 miles to the north, but most skiers prefer to return before reaching that point. Either of these alternate routes provides scenic views of the Fraser Valley without encountering any steep or difficult terrain.

# 58   WINTER PARK TRAIL SYSTEM

**DESCRIPTION: Winter ski tour, system of quiet and secluded backcountry trails**
**SKILL LEVEL: Novice to intermediate**
**TIME: Half to full day**
**DISTANCE: Optional, 6.5 miles round trip for route described**
**ELEVATION CHANGE: Optional, 800 feet total gain for route described**
**STARTING ELEVATION: 8,860 feet**
**AVALANCHE TERRAIN: None**
**USGS 7.5 MINUTE MAP: Fraser, 1957**
**MAPS: pages 102, 110**

This trail system takes advantage of a complex array of Denver Water Board roads, U.S. Forest Service roads and old ski-touring trails located between the town of Winter Park and the ski area. These trails can be connected in a number of different ways, making short, moderate or long tours possible with a variety of loop trips and side excursions. The system of ski-touring trails was set up several years ago by a local ski-touring shop. The touring shop no longer exists but the trails are still in good shape and accessible to the general public. They have names like Cherokee, Ice Hill, Blue Sky, Sunset Pink, Chickadee, Gold Dust and Serenity. The loop described here is a recommended route known as the Great Viewpoint Loop. Interested skiers are encouraged to try some of the other possibilities.

The trailhead for this tour (there are several others) is located 50 yards south of and across the highway from Beaver Lodge, which is at the south end of the town of Winter Park. After obtaining permission from Beaver Lodge to park at either the lodge or one of the other lots nearby, cross the highway and walk south

*Front Range trail skiing, Brian Litz photo.*

to the old trailhead sign. The trail starts by climbing west 100 yards to the railroad tracks. It then parallels the tracks, heading south for 100 yards before crossing to the other side, where the trail splits. The right fork is the Ice Hill Trail, used for the return trip. The left fork is the Cherokee Trail, which leads up a diagonally ascending course to a water board road. Along the way pass a junction for the Serenity Trail. The Serenity Trail continues south toward the ski area. At the water board road turn right and ski north to the Great Viewpoint. Here a wide panorama of peaks surrounding the Fraser Valley comes into view. The road continues winding around and eventually traverses into Little Vasquez Creek. There is an obvious water diversion pipe that dips down into Little Vasquez Creek from the opposite side of the valley. It serves as an easily recognizable landmark. Several forks are encountered near Little Vasquez Creek. The route described here continues a level traverse past the water diversion pipe and around the next corner. Immediately after rounding the corner turn right on the Chickadee Trail, which takes off down through the trees. The Chickadee Trail eventually intersects with and then parallels Little Vasquez Road. The Ice Hill Trail intersects Little Vasquez Road a little farther down. Take the Ice Hill Trail back to the railroad tracks for the last leg of the loop.

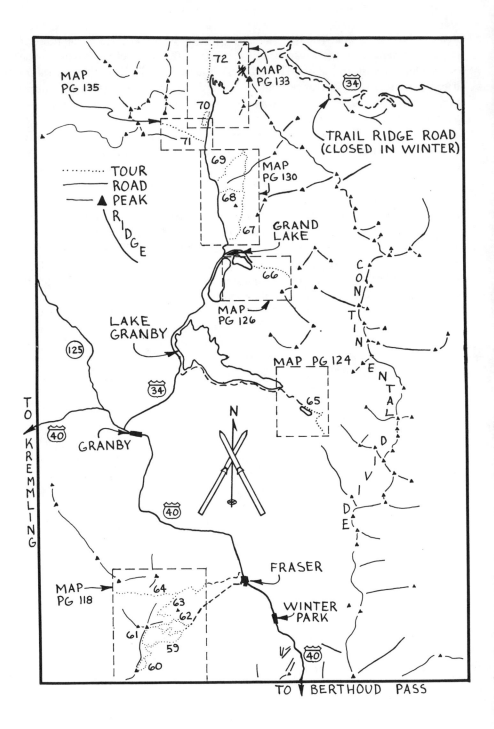

MAP
PG 135

72

MAP
PG 133

US 34

TRAIL RIDGE ROAD
(CLOSED IN WINTER)

70

71

······· TOUR
——— ROAD
——▲ PEAK

R
I
D
G
E

69

MAP
PG 130

68

67

GRAND
LAKE

C
O
N
T
I
N
E
N
T
A
L

66

MAP
PG 126

LAKE
GRANBY

125

MAP PG 124

D
I
V
I
D
E

65

US 34

TO
KREMMLING

US 40

GRANBY

N

US 40

FRASER

MAP
PG 118

64

63

62

61

59

WINTER
PARK

US 40

60

TO ▼ BERTHOUD PASS

between the Utes and raiding Arapaho braves who came over the Continental Divide from the plains. In the mid-1800s the Utes were forced onto the Ute Indian Reservation in the northwestern corner of the state. The Utes, accustomed to roaming and hunting wherever they pleased, were, to say the least, disturbed at being restricted to a reservation. The loss of their hunting and fishing grounds and the curtailment of their freedom provoked many acts of violence.

During these unstable times the settlers knew that killing an Indian would prompt swift retaliation. One evening in the late summer of 1879, just west of the present townsite of Tabernash, a stagehand was threatened and badly frightened by a band of Utes who had strayed from the reservation. The stagehand managed to slip away and inform the authorities. A posse of 18 or 20 men was organized to drive the Utes back to their reservation. One member of the posse recognized one of the braves as the killer of his father and brother several years before. He fired at the brave, killing him instantly. The murdered brave's name was Chief Tabernash. For a while there was tense anger and excitement but eventually the Utes headed back to the reservation. A few days later a settler near the Blue River was ambushed and killed. A life for a life.

Grand Lake's first permanent white settler, Joseph L. Wescott, arrived in 1867 and built a homestead on the west shore of Grand Lake. For years he led a solitary life, hunting, fishing and trapping until the mining boom brought gold seekers. Grand Lake became the outfitting point for prospectors heading up to the boom towns of Lulu City, Gaskill, Pearl and Teller. Lulu City typifies the boom-bust scenario of a town built on dreams of gold, silver and riches. The boom only lasted four years, from 1879 to 1883, and the bust was swift and complete. What remains of the town lies about 3 miles north of the Phantom Valley Ranch below the west side of Trail Ridge Road.

One notable story from this era tells of a lost gold cache dating back to the late 1850s. Where it lies nobody knows. It is buried in a large Dutch oven, so the story goes, and marked by a hunter's knife stuck deep into the trunk of a jack pine. The miners who left it there were attacked by Indians; the lone survivor managed to tell his story but did not live much longer. Many have searched, but to this day, the hunting knife and the Dutch oven with its treasure of gold dust never have been found.

When the gold-mining boom collapsed, Grand Lake became almost a ghost town until the railroad and improved highways came. Word spread of the outstanding hunting, fishing and recreation in the area, and the town was soon transformed into a tourist resort. Other towns sprang up along the railroad line, including Granby, Tabernash and Fraser. Winter Park developed from what was once the Idlewild Stagecoach Station on the old Berthoud Pass wagon road.

# CHAPTER FIVE
# FRASER VALLEY AND GRAND LAKE

## INTRODUCTION

While you're driving up I-70 during the typical weekend rush of ski traffic, wired from too much coffee, with bleary eyes glued to the bumper in front of you, wondering whether the guy behind you has had his share of coffee, so when everybody slams on the brakes at once he doesn't T-bone your back end, bound for a day spent standing in the lift line, the cafeteria line and then the lift line again, it's no wonder you get the feeling that you never left the city. There is no sense of isolation, no buffer from the intense hustle-bustle of city life. It's as if Denver stretched a long bloodthirsty tentacle up into the heart of the mountains.

Once you get over Berthoud Pass and past Winter Park, that feeling changes. You can once again gaze at the horizon without having to worry about the traffic. The few small towns that do exist are separated by large distances with just a scattering of ranches and cabins in between. The snowy peaks of the Continental Divide stretch north endlessly. The ski tours of western Rocky Mountain National Park and the Fraser Valley offer a sense of isolation and solitude that is rare on the eastern side of the divide.

## HISTORY

The first visitors probably came to Grand County between A.D. 900 and 1300. Excavations conducted by the Smithsonian Institution in 1948 just prior to building the dam at Lake Granby uncovered many artifacts from prehistoric times. The finds were by no means extensive—a few fragments of cord-marked pottery, fireplaces, flaked stone projectile points and fragments of milling stones. The bulk of the material suggested an affiliation with prehistoric Plains cultures. It appears there was only casual intermittent occupation of the sites, probably during the warm summer months.

In more recent times (still well before the turn of the century) the Ute Indians occupied the area. Many fearsome battles were fought in the Middle Park valley

# 59  WEST ST. LOUIS CREEK

**DESCRIPTION: Winter ski tour, isolated logging road, moderate grade**
**SKILL LEVEL: Novice**
**TIME: Full day**
**DISTANCE: 10 miles round trip**
**ELEVATION CHANGE: 1,700 feet total gain**
**STARTING ELEVATION: 9,032 feet**
**AVALANCHE TERRAIN: None**
**USGS 7.5 MINUTE MAP: Bottle Pass, 1957**
**MAP: page 118**

This tour is recommended for those seeking a novice tour in a relatively isolated setting. The tour gradually but steadily gains elevation on a road that makes its way up toward treeline along St. Louis Creek west of Fraser. From Winter Park drive 1 mile north on US 40 to Fraser. Take the first left turn after curving right as you enter town (Eisenhower Drive). This turn is marked by a convenience store on the left and a sign pointing to the library located half a block west. Cross the railroad tracks, then jog left two blocks on any of three side streets that divide up the small housing development on the west side of Fraser. Continue west on County Road 107 to a designated cross-country skiers' parking area 4.8 miles from the railroad tracks.

From the far end of the parking area, ski past an old building on a wide track which soon merges with the West St. Louis Creek road. Follow this road another few hundred yards, taking the main left fork (the right fork goes up Deadman Creek and Morse Mountain, see tour 62). Continue up the road, steadily gaining elevation, first on the left side of the creek and then on the right. Soon you'll come to another fork, where you should veer right. The left fork loops back around the hillside into the main fork of St. Louis Creek. Another fork is encountered a little higher up: Turn right again here. The left fork is just a subsidiary loop that crosses to the left side of the creek and rejoins the main road higher up. The road now switchbacks a couple of times as it climbs into the upper reaches of West St. Louis Creek. At the head of the valley the road crosses the creek for the last time and traverses out along the hillside to the left. After another 0.25 miles the road comes to a dead end several hundred yards below the east ridge of Byers Peak. This is about as far as anybody ever travels in winter, although Byers Peak does see a handful of winter ascents each year.

To return, follow your tracks on a gently descending glide back down the valley to the parking area.

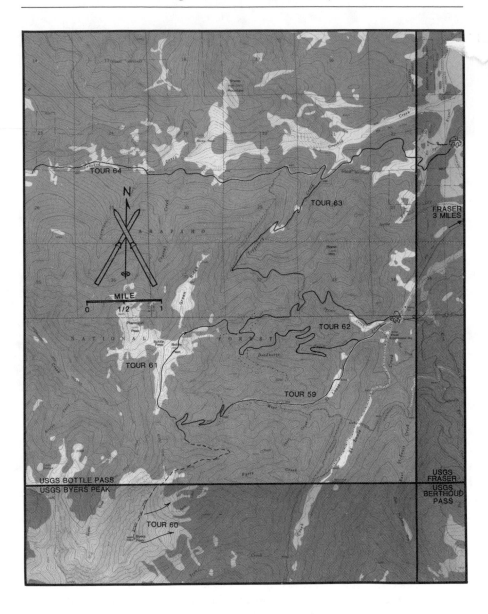

# 60  BYERS PEAK (12,804 FEET)

**DESCRIPTION: Spring ski-mountaineering descent, approach hike, access road not clear of snow until early summer**
**SKILL LEVEL: Advanced**
**TIME: Full day**
**DISTANCE: 6 miles round trip**
**ELEVATION CHANGE: 2,300 feet total gain**
**STARTING ELEVATION: 10,580 feet**
**AVALANCHE TERRAIN: Mostly avalanche terrain; wait for spring consolidation**
**USGS 7.5 MINUTE MAPS: Byers Peak, 1957, Bottle Pass, 1957**
**MAP: page 118**

Byers is the majestic peak overlooking Fraser from the southwest. Its giant east-facing double bowl holds snow until late June. Unfortunately, the access road usually isn't clear until early June, which leaves a window of only a few weeks for finding both good skiing and easy access. The trip can be made before the road opens, but the approach is longer.

The access road follows West St. Louis Creek and is actually a good novice ski tour in winter (see tour 59). Drive north on US 40 from Winter Park to Fraser. Take the first left turn after curving right as you enter town. Cross the railroad tracks then jog left two blocks on any one of three side streets that divide up the small housing development on the west side of Fraser. Continue west on County Road 107 past the experimental forest station and the winter ski-touring parking area (4.8 miles past the railroad tracks). The West St. Louis Creek road comes in just beyond the experimental forest station. The lower part of the West St. Louis Creek road is usually blocked off, making it necessary to take the water board access road from the main fork of St. Louis Creek. This access road intersects the main road a few miles past the winter ski-touring parking area. It traverses around a ridge that separates the main and west forks. Once on the West St. Louis Creek road follow it for 4 miles to its end. The road is rocky but passable for most passenger cars.

From the end of the road begin the tour by following the Byers Peak Trail as it traverses up onto the east ridge. Continue up the ridge past treeline to the summit, a stiff but straightforward hike. It's also possible, and perhaps preferable when the snow below treeline is still deep, to leave the road where it crosses the creek, well before the parking area, then proceed up to the north ridge and on to the summit. This approach is a little shorter but does not have a trail.

Once on top pick any one of several inviting descent lines. The longest comes right off the top. Late in the season it may be necessary to hike down a bit before putting on your skis. After making the descent it is necessary to climb out of the bowl. By hitting the spur ridge between the two bowls and ascending it, you can get another good run down the second more northerly bowl. From there traverse up and out to the east ridge and follow the trail back out.

# 61 BOTTLE PEAK LOOP

**DESCRIPTION: Winter ski tour, strenuous backcountry/trail route**
**SKILL LEVEL: Advanced**
**TIME: Full day**
**DISTANCE: 10 miles round trip**
**ELEVATION CHANGE: 2,552 feet total gain**
**STARTING ELEVATION: 9,032 feet**
**AVALANCHE TERRAIN: Some avalanche terrain; easily avoided**
**USGS 7.5 MINUTE MAP: Bottle Pass, 1957**
**MAP: page 118**

A winter ascent of this small peak begins with a tour up the road through West St. Louis Creek then strikes out on its own, ascending the south ridge of Bottle Peak. This windswept summit looms above the Fraser Valley and is an excellent vantage point for viewing the backside of the Front Range to the east, Byers Peak to the south and the Williams Fork Mountains and the Gore Range to the west. The descent off the summit is fantastic, featuring powder skiing through perfectly spaced evergreen trees. Amazingly, a strong party can complete this tour in a day, even with a start from Denver. This tour is a must for advanced backcountry skiers.

The tour begins in the Fraser Experimental Forest 4.8 miles west of the town of Fraser. To reach this point drive on US 40 to the middle of town. Turn west at the wooden "Town of Fraser" sign, which is on Eisenhower Drive. Proceed west over the railroad tracks and turn left (south) on the Fraser Experimental Forest Road. This road heads south for two blocks then curves to the right (west) where a huge meadow stretches out to the south. From this point it is a straight shot to the end of the plowed road in the experimental forest. At the end of the road, it forks near some cabins. Take the right fork (which ends immediately) and park in the plowed parking area.

The skiing begins by following the snow-covered road to the southwest past a small log cabin. Once past this cabin remain on the main road up West St. Louis Creek (tour 59), avoiding the right fork into Dead Horse Creek. It is important to note that the 1957 USGS map "Bottle Pass" is seriously out-of-date. While it is reliable for the trip up the West St. Louis Creek road, the descent is a confusing maze of logging roads and clear cuts. These logged areas do not even appear on the 1957 quadrangle.

Follow the West St. Louis Creek road to the head of the valley, a distance of 5 miles. Near its end where it crosses West St. Louis Creek, leave the road and begin a steep climb into the woods to the northwest. This first section is steep and follows no trail but the grade begins to taper off quickly. A faint but definite trail can be found hiding in the trees here but don't worry if you don't find it. After roughly 0.3 miles the trees begin to break up as you reach the ridge. Directly south is the impressive Byers Peak, with Mount Nystrom standing behind. From this point to the summit of Bottle Peak the wind tends to scour snow from the ridge, so when you reach treeline you may want to carry your skis. This slope is gentle and the summit is reached quite rapidly. Once on the summit be sure not to stray too close to the cornices that overhang the east face or you might be in for an unexpected trip into Dead Horse Creek!

While lunching on top of Bottle Peak, study the drainage to the east, taking note of the road and clear-cut system. Of special interest is the highest clear-cut area on the left (north) side of the creek. It lies just below the saddle west of the 10,750-foot forested knob on the east ridge and contains a logging road which can be followed easily to a rendezvous with the West St. Louis Creek road.

The actual descent begins with a short walk north along the summit ridge. A very small bowl lies on the east side of the ridge about 40 yards below the summit. It points north and begins at treeline. Drop into this bowl and ski north. Where the bowl ends, a steep gully-type feature drops to the east. Traverse carefully across the top of this feature and reach the ridge which drops to the east-northeast. It is also possible to just follow the ridge proper until you reach the east ridge.

Once on the ridge you can ski excellent evergreen glades until you reach the aforementioned saddle. Keep a sharp eye peeled to your right as the cleared area is somewhat hard to spot. When you reach the clearing, ski along the road which switchbacks down through the clearing then heads directly to the east for about 150 yards until you reach the main logging road. There are usually ski tracks down this road and it is steep enough to allow for a quick return trip to the car.

# 62  MORSE MOUNTAIN LOOP

**DESCRIPTION: Winter ski tour, secluded backcountry logging roads and trails, loop trip**
**SKILL LEVEL: Intermediate***
**TIME: Full day**
**DISTANCE: 8.5 miles**
**ELEVATION CHANGE: 1,600 feet total gain**
**STARTING ELEVATION: 9,032 feet**
**AVALANCHE TERRAIN: Some avalanche terrain encountered; easily avoided**
**USGS 7.5 MINUTE MAP: Bottle Pass, 1957**
**MAP: page 118**

***NOVICE HIGHLIGHT: The first half of the route follows a gentle, graded logging road. Ski it as far as desired and then reverse the route to make an enjoyable novice tour.**

This is a good tour that makes its way through a confusing array of logging roads to eventually form a loop. It slowly gains elevation on a winding gentle road that wanders up Dead Horse Creek and then returns via an old partially overgrown road that follows Spruce Creek.

From Winter Park drive north on US 40 to Fraser. After curving right as you enter town take the first left turn on Eisenhower Drive. This turn is marked by a convenience store on the left and a sign pointing to the library half a block west. Cross the railroad tracks, then jog left two blocks on any of three streets that divide the small housing development on the west side of Fraser. Continue west on County Road 107 to a designated cross-country skiers' parking area approximately 4.8 miles from the railroad tracks.

From the far end of the parking area ski past an old building and up a trail which intersects with the West St. Louis Creek road. Follow this road a few hundred yards to a fork. Veer right (the left fork leads up West St. Louis Creek (see tour 59), cross the creek and gradually gain elevation on a winding course leading up Dead Horse Creek. After 2.5 miles you'll come to the first of many forks. All of them dead-end eventually—some after only a few hundred yards, others after up to 2 miles. The best way to find your way through the maze is to look for the black-and-orange arrow markers indicating the main road. Eventually, after four successive forks, even the main road dead-ends. Just 50 yards or so before its end, look for a black diamond ski trail marker on the right side of the road. An inconspicuous, overgrown jeep road descends from this marker, traversing a spur ridge into the upper end of Spruce Creek. Continue down the road until it intersects with the access road just below the parking area. There is one fork on the Spruce Creek road but it's obvious that the right fork leads downhill into the main valley. The uphill fork continues over the ridge into Tipperary Creek (see tour 63). It makes an excellent longer tour but requires a car shuttle to return from the Tipperary Creek access.

# 63  TIPPERARY CREEK

**DESCRIPTION: Winter ski tour, secluded logging road, snowmobiles common on first 2.5 miles**
**SKILL LEVEL: Intermediate***
**TIME: Full day**
**DISTANCE: 12 miles round trip**
**ELEVATION CHANGE: 1,200 feet total gain**
**STARTING ELEVATION: 8,780 feet**
**AVALANCHE TERRAIN: None**
**USGS 7.5 MINUTE MAP: Bottle Pass, 1957**
**MAP: page 118**

***NOVICE HIGHLIGHT: The first 2.5 miles are nearly level, up to the turnoff for Tipperary Creek. Beyond that, the road gets steeper but may still be enjoyable for novices.**

This little-known tour starts on the Crooked Creek road west of Fraser (see tour 64) and follows a side road up Tipperary Creek to about 10,000 feet. The road gains elevation quickly and provides an exciting run back to the flats. Intermediate skiers looking for new alternatives won't be disappointed by this tour.

From Winter Park drive north on US 40 to a point 0.3 miles past the north edge of Fraser. Turn left (west) on County Road 50, cross the railroad tracks, proceed 100 yards and turn left again. Continue 3.4 miles to a cattle guard that marks the end of the plowed road 0.4 miles past the entrance to Tally Ho Lodge.

Ski west along the flat Crooked Creek road past the entrance to Arapaho National Forest. The side road up Tipperary Creek is reached after a quick 2.4-mile ski. Turn left up Tipperary Creek and begin a steady climb. The road stays left of the creek for a few hundred yards, then crosses to the right. Two successive series of switchbacks will soon be encountered. Each has beautiful open glades between the switches—perfect for short telemark runs on the return trip. Near the head of the valley the road crosses the creek and traverses left onto a saddle just southwest of Morse Mountain. The road continues down into West St. Louis Creek (see tour 59) but most parties prefer to stop at the saddle. With a car shuttle it is possible to connect this tour with Morse Mountain Loop (tour 62).

# 64   CROOKED CREEK

> **DESCRIPTION: Winter ski tour, gentle road**
> **SKILL LEVEL: Novice**
> **TIME: Half to full day**
> **DISTANCE: Up to 15 miles round trip**
> **ELEVATION CHANGE: 1,120 feet total gain**
> **STARTING ELEVATION: 8,780 feet**
> **AVALANCHE TERRAIN: None**
> **USGS 7.5 MINUTE MAP: Fraser, 1957, Bottle Pass, 1957**
> **MAP: page 118**

Crooked Creek climbs westward from the Fraser Valley into the northern reaches of the Vasquez Mountains. Along the north side of the valley a road parallels the drainage, following a twisted path. The road climbs moderately for most of its length, which is roughly 7.5 miles from the plowed parking area near the Tally Ho Ranch to the tour's termination in Church Park. In the last few years Crooked Creek has become a favorite haunt for lightly clad skaters (racers) who use the normally packed road for a training run. One thing to keep in mind is that this road is packed because it is a popular snowmobile tour; if you ski here, you will have to be patient with these cacophonous contraptions. However, you will rarely have to break a trail!

The turnoff to Crooked Creek is immediately north of Fraser. Drive on US 40 across the West St. Louis Creek bridge, continue 0.3 miles, then turn west. Cross the railroad tracks, then take the next possible left. After a few hundred yards the road

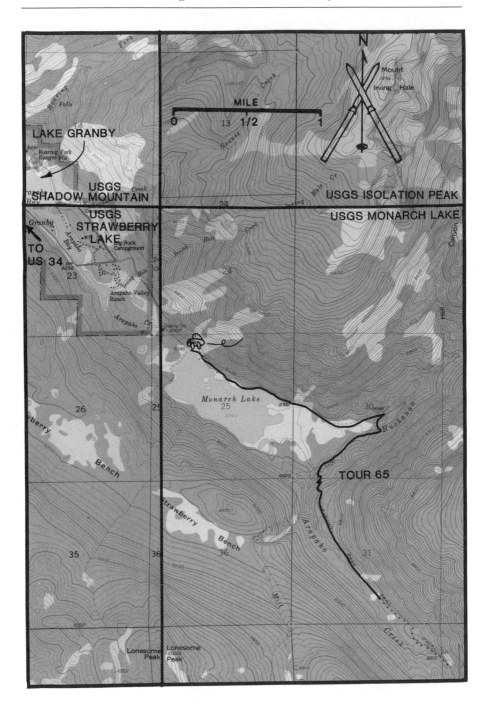

bends to the west. From here follow the main road as it leads you through a sparse housing development mixed into the trees until you reach the plowed turnaround just past the Tally Ho Ranch and near a cattle guard.

The actual directions for the tour are simple: Point your skis west and go. Except for a sustained incline just past the turnoff to Tipperary Creek, the road gains elevation in a relaxed manner. At the 5-mile mark the road crosses Crooked Creek and reaches Church Park on the north side of the valley. When you reach this spot be sure to look back east to where Rollins Pass crosses the divide and south to the treeless summit of Ptarmigan Peak at 11,773 feet.

# 65 ARAPAHO CREEK

**DESCRIPTION: Winter ski tour, moderate backcountry trail**
**SKILL LEVEL: Novice to advanced**
**TIME: Half to full day**
**DISTANCE: 7 miles round trip**
**ELEVATION CHANGE: 375 feet total gain**
**STARTING ELEVATION: 8,346 feet**
**AVALANCHE TERRAIN: None**
**USGS 7.5 MINUTE MAP: Monarch Lake, 1978-PR**
**MAP: page 124**

Arapaho Creek flows off the west side of the 13,000-foot Arapaho Peaks in the Indian Peaks wilderness area and eventually drains into Monarch Lake. This long linear valley is isolated and is the perfect environment for those desiring a peaceful escape. Seldom will skiers encounter other backcountry visitors except on the most crowded of weekends. The terrain is moderate so skiers of all abilities can explore this drainage, pushing as deep into the backcountry as they wish.

The tour's trailhead is on the northwest corner of Monarch Lake, which is approached from US 34 between Granby and Grand Lake. Turn east onto the Lake Granby road, 5.5 miles north of US 34's intersection with US 40. Once on the Lake Granby road, drive 10 miles (crossing the dam, etc.) and park at the end of the plowed road near Monarch Lake.

The skiing follows the Arapaho Pass Trail, which begins at Monarch Lake near the ranger's cabin. It may be necessary to ski a short distance on the road to reach the cabin if the snowplows haven't cleared the road completely to the lake. At Monarch Lake the trailhead is well marked with forest service information signs.

The trail begins as an old roadbed and follows this feature for roughly 0.75 miles before becoming a trail. Remain on the north side of the lake as the trail gently undulates through thin pine forests until you reach a large willow-choked meadow on the east side of the lake. Continue along the north edge of the meadow to a point where Buchanan Creek flows from the high peaks to the northeast.

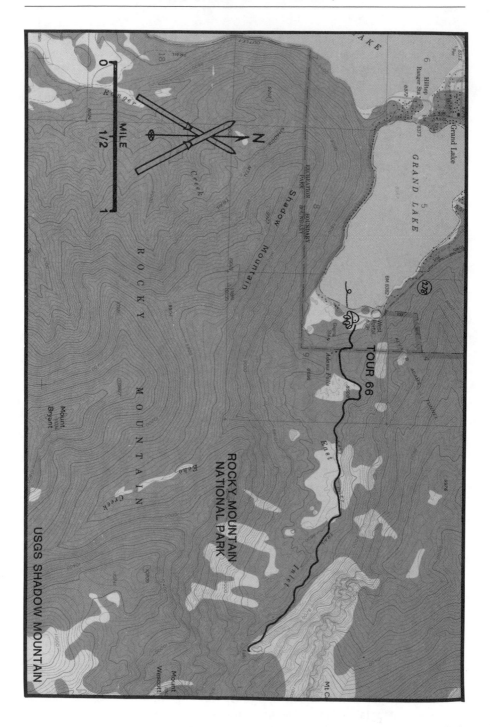

The meeting with Buchanan Creek marks a change in the general direction of the route; it now heads more to the south to reach the mouth of Arapaho Creek. Follow the trail past the forest service trail mileage signs marking the point where the trails to Buchanan Pass and Arapaho Pass diverge. Take the right fork and follow it until you have crossed Buchanan Creek. Contouring to the southwest, traverse the east edge of the meadow, staying within the woods that climb the mountainside.

At the 2.5-mile mark you will once again reach a trail junction. The terrain begins to change at this spot so if you are not ready to challenge intermediate skiing, this is a good turnaround spot. If you do push on, you will ascend a series of switchbacks and enter the long valley containing Arapaho Creek. Near the 3-mile mark make a short descent onto the floor of the valley. The floor is generally flat, so experienced skiers will have no trouble making fast progress toward the head of the valley. This upper valley is several miles in length; hence this can be a long day of touring. It is also a remote spot to spend the night.

# 66 EAST INLET

**DESCRIPTION: Winter ski tour, moderate, well-marked trail**
**SKILL LEVEL: Intermediate**
**TIME: Full day**
**DISTANCE: 6.4 miles round trip**
**ELEVATION CHANGE: 780 feet total gain**
**STARTING ELEVATION: 8,391 feet**
**AVALANCHE TERRAIN: None**
**USGS 7.5 MINUTE MAP: Shadow Mountain, 1978-PR**
**MAP: page 126**

Skiers venturing onto the East Inlet Trail will be treated to a fine short tour on the less-visited side of Rocky Mountain National Park. From the trailhead the tour climbs quickly on a sinuous path through trees and rocky outcrops. After this harrowing 0.5 miles the trail breaks into a serene alpine meadow hemmed in by steep canyon walls. Through this meadow meanders East Inlet Creek, which provides an alternate ski route if the trail is lacking in adequate snowcover. Glide effortlessly along the creek with Mount Craig soaring at the head of the valley. For those skiers with enough time and endurance the tour can be extended beyond the falls at the end of the meadow and into the upper valley containing Lake Verna. This valley is a nice choice for an afternoon tour when the winter alpenglow illuminates the high peaks to the east.

The tour begins east of Grand Lake. To reach this, drive on US 40 to its intersection with US 34, just west of Granby. Turn north and drive to the town of Grand Lake, a distance of roughly 14.5 miles. When you reach the town turn right (east) on Colo. 278 and proceed toward the center of town. When you reach an intersection follow the road to the left, which will put you on the "tunnel" road while the right fork would take you into the center of Grand Lake. Continue on the tunnel road until you drive past the west portal of the Adams Tunnel. Drive down toward the flat parking area east of the lake. To the east you will see the large park service information board. The trail climbs into the trees directly behind the sign.

The initial section is the hardest for both ascending and descending, so remember its nuances for the return trip. At 0.3 miles a wooden marker announces the turnoff to Adams Falls. This is a pleasant side trip for those who have had enough climbing already. When the climbing eases off at 0.3 miles, you will approach the first meadow. Often the snow is much better on the valley floor than on the south-facing trail so don't be shy about following the river's course. Either way you will re-enter the woods before reaching the second and larger meadow. Again it is possible to ski the trail or continue along East Inlet Creek.

Before the end of the second meadow it is best to resume skiing on the trail because the creek becomes steeper and congested with boulders and small falls. At the 2-mile mark the trail ascends along the north side of the creek and becomes much more strenuous. The higher in elevation you climb, the better are the views of Mount Craig and the four-pronged shape of Mount Cairns to the northeast.


# 67  TONAHUTU CREEK

**DESCRIPTION: Winter ski tour, gentle, secluded backwoods trail**
**SKILL LEVEL: Novice**
**TIME: Full day**
**DISTANCE: 6 miles round trip**
**ELEVATION CHANGE: 680 feet total gain**
**STARTING ELEVATION: 8,720 feet**
**AVALANCHE TERRAIN: None**
**USGS 7.5 MINUTE MAP: Grand Lake, 1978-PR**
**MAP: page 130**

This tour is typical of the backcountry trail skiing found in the western part of Rocky Mountain National Park. It follows a gentle valley with very little vertical relief. Its beauty lies not in the fast downhill runs or spectacular scenery that other tours offer but in the serenity found only deep in the backwoods in midwinter.

The trail begins from the south end of the parking lot at the West Unit Office of Rocky Mountain National Park. To get there go north from Granby on US 34 past Lake Granby and Shadow Mountain Reservoir. Turn left just before reaching the town of Grand Lake and proceed to the turnoff for the West Unit Office. The trail heads east from the parking lot to a junction with the main Tonahutu Creek Trail (this junction can also be reached from the Grand Lake entrance to the park). Turn left at the junction and follow orange trail markers on a gentle climb into the Tonahutu

Creek Valley. After 3 miles of touring through dense forest the trail suddenly opens up at the south end of Big Meadows. It is possible to continue north along the west edge of Big Meadows and hook up with the Green Mountain Trail (tour 68) to a car shuttle loop tour but most parties prefer to return the same way they came in.

# 68   GREEN MOUNTAIN TRAIL

**DESCRIPTION: Winter ski tour, short but steeply twisting trail**
**SKILL LEVEL: Intermediate**
**TIME: Half day**
**DISTANCE: 3.6 miles round trip**
**ELEVATION CHANGE: 680 feet total gain**
**STARTING ELEVATION: 8,780 feet**
**AVALANCHE TERRAIN: None**
**USGS 7.5 MINUTE MAP: Grand Lake, 1978-PR**
**MAP: page 130**

Green Mountain Trail is the shortest route into the large flat nonforested feature known as Big Meadows. From the trailhead on Trail Ridge Road skiers climb through heavy woods for 1.8 miles onto the west edge of the meadow. It can be a stiff climb early in the morning with a commensurately quick return trip. The tour takes roughly half a day to complete (depending on how much time you spend exploring Big Meadows) and combines nicely with the Tonahutu Trail or the Onahu Creek Trail for a long day of skiing.

To reach the Green Mountain Trailhead drive on US 40 to the west end of Granby, turn north onto US 34 and drive 14 miles until you reach the turnoff into the town of Grand Lake. Stay on US 34 and follow this road (Trail Ridge Road) to Rocky Mountain National Park. Stop in at park headquarters to find out about daily skiing conditions, then proceed through the entrance gate and drive 2.5 miles north to the small plowed parking area on the right side of the road.

The trail begins directly behind the large informative park service sign. It starts to ascend immediately but moderately as it runs along the north side of the creek. Climb east and slightly north along the twisting trail. The second half of the trail, although the steepest portion of the tour, is very easy to follow.

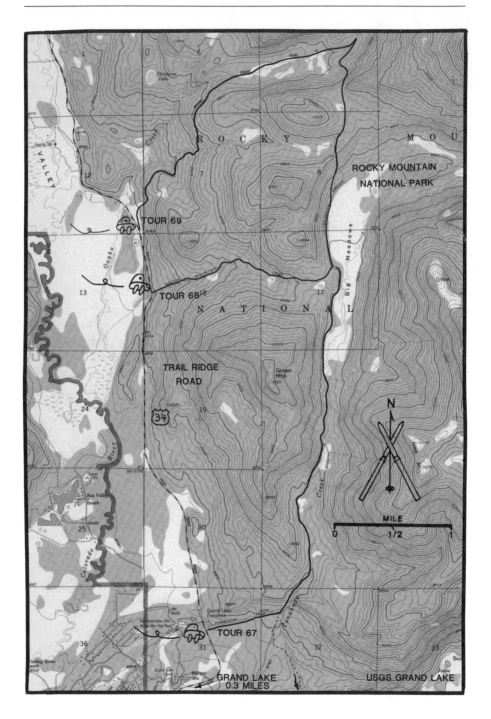

# 69   ONAHU CREEK

**DESCRIPTION: Winter ski tour, remote and strenuous trail, can be difficult to follow**
**SKILL LEVEL: Advanced**
**TIME: Full day**
**DISTANCE: 10.6 miles round trip**
**ELEVATION CHANGE: 880 feet total gain**
**STARTING ELEVATION: 8,780 feet**
**AVALANCHE TERRAIN: None**
**USGS 7.5 MINUTE MAP: Grand Lake, 1978-PR**
**MAP: page 130**

Onahu Creek is the most challenging winter ski tour on the west side of Rocky Mountain National Park. While it only gains 880 feet the trail is tricky to follow, rarely has a trail already broken and climbs steadily throughout the first half of the trip. From the trailhead to the point where Onahu Creek is reached (near a small bridge), the trail is not obvious and locating it will keep your attention. The forest that covers this part of Rocky Mountain National Park is dominated by evenly spaced lodgepole pines and trails seem to branch off everywhere. Excellent route-finding skills are a must. The trip up this drainage may be easily extended into a classic loop by climbing over into Big Meadows and then back to the parking area via a final descent down the Green Mountain Trail (tour 68).

Drive on US 40 west of Granby and turn north onto US 34. Proceed 14 miles until you reach the turnoff to Grand Lake. Keep to the left and drive into the west entrance of Rocky Mountain National Park. Stop in at the visitors center, then continue past the guard station and drive roughly 3 miles to the trailhead for Onahu Creek. The park service does not plow out a parking area so skiers must parallel park against the snowbank near the trailhead.

Ski over to the wooden trail-information sign and gain the trail as it climbs into the trees to the east. Onahu Creek actually is several hundred feet to the north, so for the first half of the tour, the trail traverses northeast in an effort to reach the main creek. Study the map to gain a feel for how far it is until you reach Onahu Creek. For 2 miles the trail climbs, traverses and descends continuously. There are trail markers here but still it is not easy to follow the route. You will know when you have reached Onahu Creek when you cross it on a small bridge.

After you reach Onahu Creek the trail heads more to the east and the terrain becomes much more moderate. Double-pole through thick stands of lodgepole pines, once again following the trail markers on their elusive route. Near 5.3 miles the trail forks. To the left is Upper Onahu Creek while to the right is the trail that connects Lower Onahu Creek with Big Meadows to the south (Tonahutu and Green Mountain trails). If you decide to ski into Big Meadows, a 250-foot climb takes you onto the ridge above the meadows. Drop down into the flat basin and either ski straight across until you reach the corner of the forest that pokes out into the meadow or follow just along the edge of the trees until you reach a small corral hidden in the woods near the turnoff to the Green Mountain Trail. Descending the Green Mountain Trail will return you quickly to the Onahu parking area, several hundred feet north on Trail Ridge Road, and rarely takes longer than 30 to 40 minutes.

# 70  KAWUNEECHE VALLEY LOOP

DESCRIPTION: Winter ski tour, gentle and easy-to-follow trail
SKILL LEVEL: Novice
TIME: Quarter to half day
DISTANCE: 2.6 miles round trip
ELEVATION CHANGE: 75 feet total gain
STARTING ELEVATION: 8,940 feet
AVALANCHE TERRAIN: None
USGS 7.5 MINUTE MAPS: Grand Lake, 1978-PR, Fall River Pass, 1977-PR
MAPS: pages 133, 135

Kawuneeche Valley Loop is the easiest trail in the northwestern section of Rocky Mountain National Park. The elevation hardly changes and the open-meadow skiing will delight neophyte skiers. Carving a small circle on the floor of the Colorado River valley, this wonderful jaunt is a perfect tour to take your friends and family on who are just learning the art of ski touring. Kawuneeche is Ute for "the valley of the wolves." It'll make you howl!

To reach the trailhead, drive on US 40 to the west edge of Granby, then turn north onto US 34. Drive 16 miles, passing the turnoff into Grand Lake and proceed into Rocky Mountain National Park. Stop in at the visitors center to obtain current weather and snow conditions and to check to see if a permit is necessary for that particular time of year. Continue north for 8 miles until you reach the Timber Creek Campground and park near the amphitheater.

Begin skiing north and west, following trail markers. Easy kick and glide will carry you through a few scattered trees and across frozen beaver ponds and elk meadows. Approaching the west edge of the valley the trail re-enters thicker stands of trees before reaching a small, hidden meadow where you contour south. This tiny meadow melts into the main valley as you continue south, tracing the edge of the thick woods.

The Never Summer Ranch (Holzworth Homestead) lies near the 1.4-mile point of the tour and marks the spot where the trail begins its swing back to the parking area. Near the ranch follow the markers as they carry you onto a road that squiggles back to the east and into the heart of Kawuneeche Valley. The final leg begins when you reach the far east edge of the meadow. From here it is slightly over 0.5 miles back north to the cars.

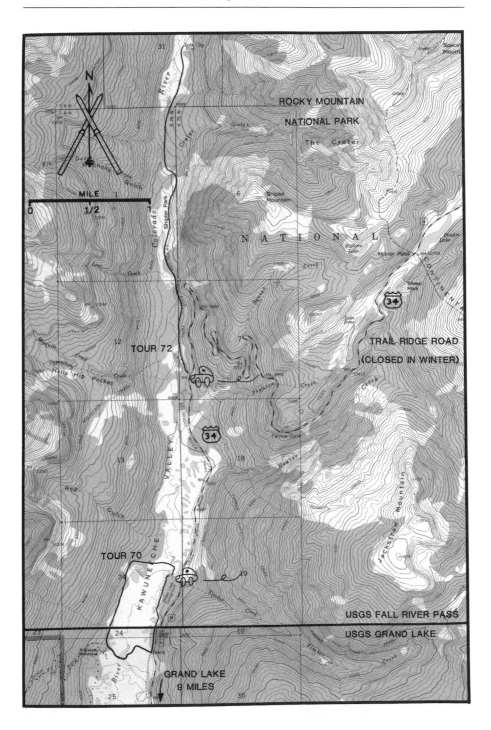

# 71   BAKER GULCH

DESCRIPTION: Winter ski tour, isolated backcountry trail
SKILL LEVEL: Intermediate to advanced*
TIME: Two-thirds day
DISTANCE: 7 miles round trip
ELEVATION CHANGE: 1,500 feet total gain
STARTING ELEVATION: 8,840 feet
AVALANCHE TERRAIN: Route crosses avalanche runout zones; can
be dangerous during high-hazard periods
USGS 7.5 MINUTE MAPS: Grand Lake, 1978-PR, Bowen Mountain,
1977-PR
MAP: page 135

*NOVICE HIGHLIGHT: The first mile is not steep; suitable for novice
skiers.

This tour begins from the west edge of Rocky Mountain National Park and
heads up Baker Gulch into the Never Summer Range. The trail is flat and easy at first
but gradually becomes steeper as you get farther up into the gulch. The Great Ditch
(a water diversion project) traverses from the upper end of the gulch around the
mountainside to the north. It is possible to make a long loop trip by skiing out along
the Great Ditch and then descending a water road back into the valley, but the
avalanche danger on the traverse is often high until very late in the season.

From Granby go north on US 34 past Lake Granby and Shadow Mountain
Reservoir to the fork just before the town of Grand Lake. Go left here and continue
into Rocky Mountain National Park. Register at the West Unit Ranger Station and
drive several more miles to the Bowen Gulch–Baker Gulch Trailhead where a plowed
parking area is available.

The tour starts by crossing the wide Kawuneeche meadow. Jog right on the
opposite side of the meadow and follow signs through the trees to the park boundary
and the Baker Gulch Trail. The trail stays on the right side of the gulch the entire way.
It begins in a moderate and easy fashion but soon becomes steeper and more difficult
to find. Stay on the same general course, making occasional switchbacks and crossing
two small tributaries along the way. The trail eventually breaks out into some open
meadows in the upper end of the gulch just below the Great Ditch. These meadows
sit at the base of some huge avalanche paths and should not be crossed in unstable
conditions. The return trip back down the same route is fast and enjoyable.

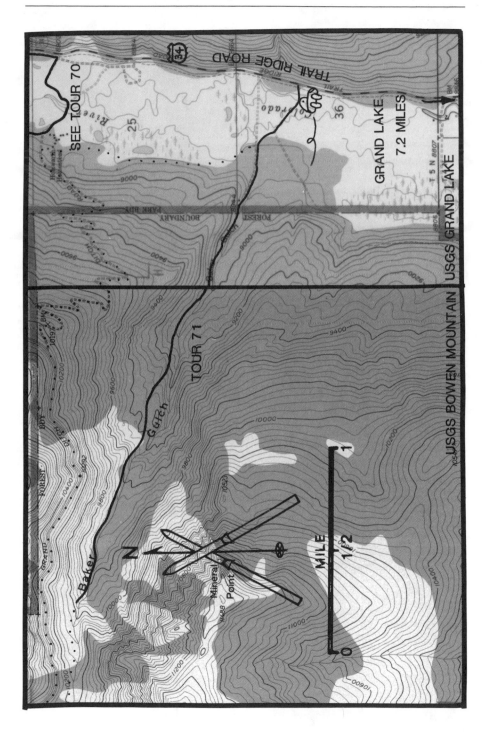

*Solitary skier crossing Big Meadows above Tonahutu Creek (tour 67), Brian Litz photo.*

# 72 SHIPLER PARK AND LULU CITY

**DESCRIPTION: Winter ski tour, gentle valley tour, well marked**
**SKILL LEVEL: Novice**
**TIME: Full day**
**DISTANCE: 8.5 miles round trip**
**ELEVATION CHANGE: 320 feet total gain**
**STARTING ELEVATION: 9,080 feet**
**AVALANCHE TERRAIN: None**
**USGS 7.5 MINUTE MAP: Fall River Pass, 1977-PR**
**MAP: page 133**

In the quiet northwestern corner of Rocky Mountain National Park, there are several fine ski tours at the novice to intermediate level. The trail to Shipler Park and the abandoned mining townsite of Lulu City leaves the plowed end of Trail Ridge Road and explores the upper reaches of the Colorado River and the Never Summer Range. Along with minimal elevation gain, this valley features gentle snow-covered meadows, a meandering stream and no crowds. About the only drawback is the distance from Denver. If you are not staying in the Fraser River valley or the Grand Lake area, plan on an early start.

The tour is approached from the west entrance to Rocky Mountain National Park, which lies north of the town of Grand Lake. It takes about 45 minutes to reach the parking area from Winter Park on US 34. Since this tour is in the park, you need to stop and purchase an entrance permit (if necessary, depending on the time of the year) plus you can inquire about the daily skiing conditions. Drive on to the end of the plowed road and park.

The trailhead is to the west, near the plowed parking area. Begin by crossing open terrain from the parking area over to the west, reaching the Colorado River and the Colorado River Trail. The tour follows this summer route for the entire trip. It is a large well-marked trail in typical park service fashion. After 2.8 miles you will reach Shipler Park with its abandoned cabins. If you continue along the gentle valley floor, you will reach the townsite of Lulu City, named after a girl who lived in this now-abandoned mining community. Lulu City lies 4.3 miles north of the trailhead but the moderate terrain allows for a quick round trip.

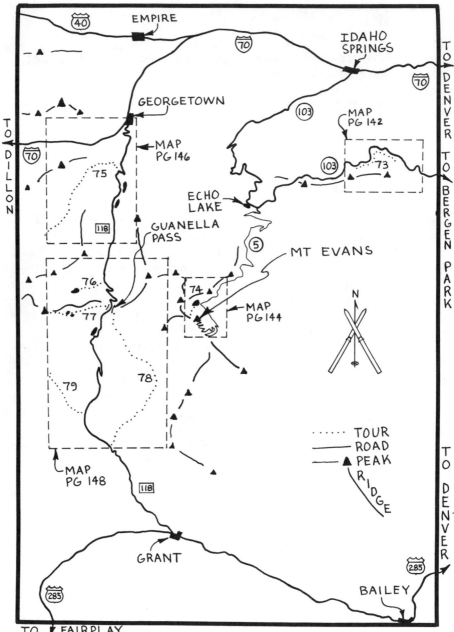

# CHAPTER SIX

# MOUNT EVANS TO GUANELLA PASS

## INTRODUCTION

The closest ski touring to the Denver metropolitan area is found in the region lying between Idaho Springs, Mount Evans, Georgetown and Guanella Pass. Mount Evans, easily seen on the western skyline from Denver, is the hub of this touring area. On its north flanks lie the Squaw Pass Trail and a difficult spring descent off its summit. West of the mountain, Guanella Pass climbs south from Georgetown into the alpine world before descending to the South Platte drainage to the south. Along the Guanella Pass road novice skiers will find several tours with moderate skiing conditions and short approach drives. Just the drive to the top of Guanella Pass is worth the effort, for the dramatic views of Mount Evans and Mount Bierstadt and the approach into the forbidding world of frozen tundra and shattered talus.

Skiers can strike it rich exploring the roads leading to the numerous abandoned mining communities that bravely cling to the high slopes above Clear Creek. This historic area provides the opportunity to explore some of the Front Range's hardrock mining history while enjoying Colorado's mountains in winter. Trails such as the Waldorf road follow old roadbeds to reach the high mines and passes that originally linked the Front Range to Summit County. Today they make excellent ski tours wide enough to allow ample room for snowplowing!

These tours provide good early- and late-season skiing because they begin at a higher elevation than most novice and intermediate routes. This often means a relatively deep snowpack from November to April. Be prepared, however, for extreme and rapidly changing weather conditions during storms. Additionally, skiers accustomed to lower elevations should proceed at a more relaxed pace to allow themselves to acclimatize. On clear days and especially during spring be sure to carry sunscreen; these routes are not well protected by forest cover.

## HISTORY

The land that stretches from Mount Evans to Guanella Pass is part of the

Clear Creek drainage both physically and historically (readers are encouraged to see Chapter 4 for more information). Forming the southern watershed of Clear Creek, this high mountain area underwent the same human and industrial development as the area near Idaho Springs and Empire. The massif of Mount Evans and Mount Bierstadt delineates the course of the creek and dominates the landscape covered by this chapter. Mount Evans (14,264 feet) was named in honor of Colorado's second territorial governor, while Mount Bierstadt's (14,060 feet) namesake was Alfred Bierstadt, the famous landscape painter of the mid-1800s. Mount Evans features a paved road to the summit, making it one of the highest paved roads in the world. The summit has hosted scientists from all over the world who have studied everything from high-elevation human and animal physiology, astrophysics and meteorology to aviation. Mount Evans was first climbed by Alfred Bierstadt and Fitz-hugh Ludlow in 1863. Mount Bierstadt was climbed initially by miners searching for gold (maybe a little recreation, too) and perhaps even Native Americans.

West of these two peaks are two more of Colorado's famous mountains— Grays and Torreys peaks (14,270 feet and 14,267 feet, respectively). Grays and Torreys were named after Asa Gray and John Torrey, who were noted botanists of the 19th century. They led many field expeditions to these peaks and coauthored publications on botany. Their most famous work is *Flora of North America*, published in 1841.

Dividing these alpine couples is Guanella Pass, which climbs from the south end of Georgetown up a spectacular series of switchbacks. Georgetown, sitting in a flat basin surrounded by steep mountain walls, lies several miles south and west of Empire. In June 1859, a party of prospectors arrived in this valley. Two brothers from Kentucky, George and David Griffith, were among this group and within two days had uncovered a gold-bearing vein which they named the Griffith Lode. The boys set up camp on a spot where 17th and Main streets would eventually intersect. Georgetown took its name from George Griffith—the brothers' tent site was commonly referred to as "George's Town." Unlike many mountain mining communities, which were ramshackle assortments of dull brown cabins and false-fronted stores, Georgetown was planned to be special from its inception. Early homesteaders and miners took great pains to create a beautiful village with exquisite Victorian homes, two operas, wrought-iron fences and streets lined with sturdy shade trees.

Georgetown grew as more people came to prospect and mine. Although the Griffith claim continued to pay well, the entire area never quite produced the gold that the early miners had sought. The gold-bearing ore found in the area required more extensive mechanical and chemical processing than was available at the time. The town's fortunes were erratic until September 1864 when silver was discovered. Georgetown's mining community originally had failed to realize that this area was a predominantly silver-bearing geologic formation. When gold's cousin had been located in paying quantities, the area prospered. Georgetown's silver boom lasted until 1893 when the Sherman Act was repealed, returning the United States to a strict gold standard. Today Georgetown remains a frequented tourist spot because of its charm and authentic character.

Southwest of Georgetown, off Guanella Pass near the head of Leavenworth Creek, is Waldorf, a treeline camp servicing a very productive but inhospitable mining area. Like Georgetown and Silver Plume, the town lying immediately west of Georgetown, Waldorf was primarily a silver-producing district. At 11,666 feet the Waldorf Mining and Milling Company held claim to over 80 veins. To access many of the lodes deep under McClellan Mountain to the west, a tunnel was driven straight through the massive pile of stone to reach the famed Stevens Mine in the drainage below Grays and Torreys peaks! Stevens Mine's ore was actually removed through the bore and then shipped out via the Argentine Central Railroad. This narrow-gauge line crept up from Georgetown, passed Waldorf and ended on the summit of McClellan Mountain. Needless to say, riding the Argentine Rail was also a smash with the tourists of the era as well as with the hard-working miners.

The Leavenworth Creek drainage and Waldorf also served as the most direct line of travel (via Argentine Pass) into the Snake River valley and Summit County before Loveland Pass was opened. Argentine Pass left the head of the Leavenworth Creek valley and snaked treacherously over the alpine barricade where it dropped into the head of Peru Creek and the Argentine Mining District near Montezuma. Many Coloradans braved lightning, hail, snow, thin air and buffeting winds crossing this pass dividing the Eastern and the Western slopes.

# 73   SQUAW PASS TRAIL

**DESCRIPTION: Winter ski tour, enjoyable roads, half hour from Denver**
**SKILL LEVEL: Novice**
**TIME: Half day**
**DISTANCE: Optional, up to 4 miles**
**ELEVATION CHANGE: Up to 1,000 feet total gain**
**STARTING ELEVATION: 10,620 feet**
**AVALANCHE TERRAIN: None**
**USGS 7.5 MINUTE MAPS: Squaw Pass, 1974-PR, Idaho Springs, 1974-PR**
**MAP: page 142**

This is a good choice if you're tired of dealing with the ski traffic or you just don't want to drive very far. It takes about 30 minutes to get from the El Rancho exit on I-70 to the trailhead. The tour follows an old road that parallels the Squaw Pass road for several miles as it climbs toward Echo Lake. The road has a gentle uphill grade with no sharp turns or surprises. The summit of Squaw Pass is an inconspicuous low point on the ridge separating Clear Creek from Bear Creek. The Squaw Pass road traverses high along the shaded north side of this ridge. The road comes to within 0.2 miles of the summit of the pass but does not go through it. Instead, it continues travers-

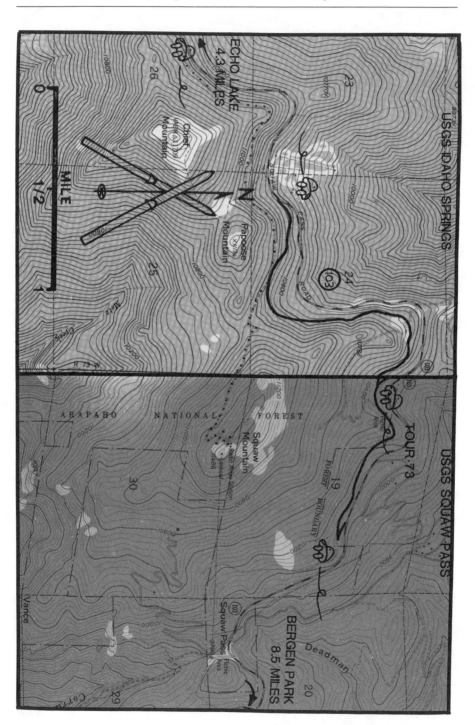

ing west on the north side of the ridge, eventually dropping southwest to Echo Lake.

To get to the Squaw Pass road take the El Rancho exit off I-70 and head south toward Evergreen. At Bergen Park bear right onto Colo. 103 (the Squaw Pass road) and drive approximately 10 miles. Because the tour parallels the Squaw Pass road, there are several convenient places to start. With a car shuttle you can start at the top end and cruise downhill most of the way to the lowest access point. All of the access points are fairly inconspicuous. You just have to look for small turnouts with a road cutting uphill toward the ridge. The first one is approximately 10 miles from the turnoff at Bergen Park. The last one is another 3.8 miles farther up the road. In between these are three other access points. The middle one is also the access road for the Squaw Mountain Fire Lookout, which makes a good short ski in itself.

# 74  MOUNT EVANS (14,264 FEET)

**DESCRIPTION: Spring ski descent, no approach hike, car shuttle required**
**SKILL LEVEL: Advanced +**
**TIME: Quarter day**
**DISTANCE: 1.4 miles**
**ELEVATION CHANGE: 1,300 feet total loss**
**STARTING ELEVATION: 14,120 feet**
**AVALANCHE TERRAIN: Mostly avalanche terrain; wait for spring consolidation**
**USGS 7.5 MINUTE MAP: Mount Evans, 1974-PR**
**MAP: page 144**

For those who like to expend a minimum amount of energy, Mount Evans comes close to being the ultimate ski descent. Drive to the top, walk five minutes, don skis, plunge 1,300 feet to Summit Lake and car shuttle or hitchhike back to the top. Downhill skis are no more hassle than telemark or mountaineering skis because the approach and finish are so short. It's possible to do several action-packed runs on a good day. Also, the descent itself is one of the best in the area. It is steeper (approaching 45 degrees) and a bit more advanced than most of the other ski descents in this book, so it is not recommended for ski-mountaineering novices. Still, any expert downhill skier with a sense of adventure should have little trouble, although it may require some nerve to commit to those first few turns.

Reach Mount Evans from either Idaho Springs or from the El Rancho exit off I-70 by taking the Squaw Pass–Mount Evans fork at Bergen Park. The road above Echo Lake is usually not plowed until early June. There is a sign at Bergen Park indicating whether the road is open. If you're coming from Idaho Springs check at forest service headquarters at the second (west) exit just off I-70. Drive to Echo Lake, then turn south and proceed 9.3 miles to the Summit Lake parking lot where you can

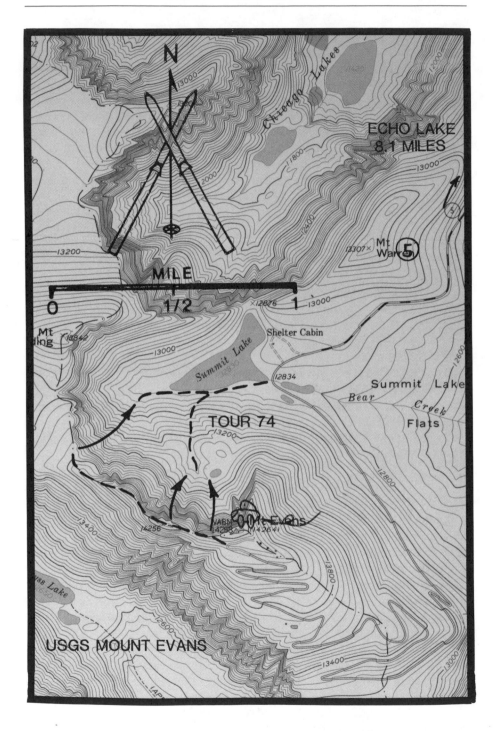

survey the route. There are really three good descent possibilities. The best is a finger of snow that diagonals up left from the right center portion of the main snowfield. The top part of this finger is not visible from the lake. It is a narrow couloir with steep rock walls on either side and is filled with snow to within 100 feet of the top. A short scramble is required to get into the gully. The large main snowfield on the left is another possibility. It is a bit steeper but more wide open. The snowfield at the saddle between Evans and Spalding, the mountain just north of Mount Evans, has also been skied. The longer approach and huge nasty-looking cornice at the top make it a much less appealing route.

The approach for all options starts from the parking lot at the top of Mount Evans or from the last hairpin turn (a slightly shorter walk). Contour west around the top. The finger descent starts from the second highest point just west of the main summit. The wide open snowfield route can be reached by scrambling down between the two summits. Early on, just after the road opens, you may be able to ski all the way to Summit Lake. After reaching the lake make a quick shuttle back to the top for another run.

# 75  WALDORF ROAD

**DESCRIPTION: Winter ski tour, wide, gentle road in historic mining area, close to Denver**
**SKILL LEVEL: Novice**
**TIME: Half to full day**
**DISTANCE: 7 miles round trip**
**ELEVATION CHANGE: 1,170 feet total gain**
**STARTING ELEVATION: 9,800 feet**
**AVALANCHE TERRAIN: None**
**USGS 7.5 MINUTE MAPS: Georgetown, 1974-PR, Grays Peak, 1987-PR**
**MAP: page 146**

The road to the Waldorf Mine, which sits high on the north slopes of Argentine Peak, meanders through delightful stands of spruce trees as well as through some of Colorado's richest mining history. Dotted with old structures, mine shafts and tailings piles, the Leavenworth Creek drainage was the sight of near-frenzied silver-ore exploration and extraction. As you ski up this large valley, look high on McClelland Mountain's east slopes and you will see the old railroad grade that carried a small cog rail line (the Argentine Central Railroad) into the alpine zone in the early 1900s. This journey was very popular with miners and city folks alike. That frantic period in Colorado's history lives on in books, photos and the ghosts that inhabit places such as the Waldorf road.

To get to the Waldorf road drive to Georgetown and proceed to the south

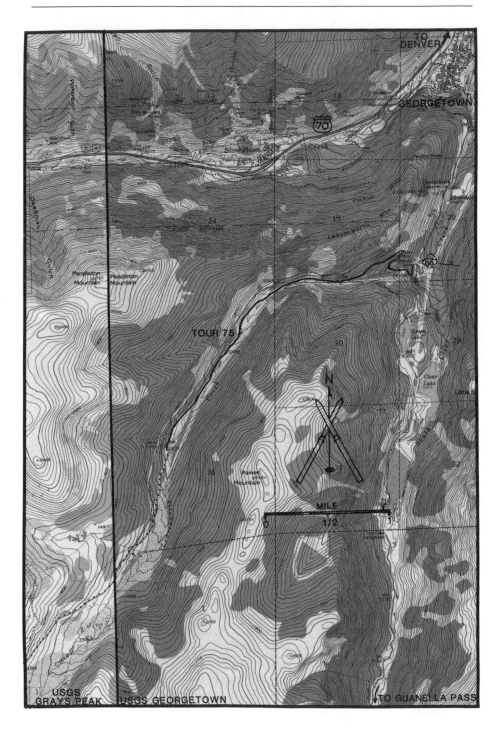

edge of town. From here gain the narrow Guanella Pass road which climbs precipitously up the steep mountainside. Now, pay close attention to the next section as there are some major discrepancies between the 1974 photo-revised topographic map and what exists today. After 2.5 miles, the road switchbacks from south to north and back to south as it continues to the pass. As you head into the second switchback a small plowed parking area lies on the outer edge of the turn. This is the parking area that you want. The topo map shows the turnoff lying well below this series of switchbacks and not within them.

Begin the tour by following the wide snow-covered roadbed as it leaves the parking area and climbs gently, initially paralleling the Guanella Pass road. Pass under the huge high-tension power lines and ski around a switchback which takes you north. Contour west into the creekbed, then climb out toward the north-northeast, gaining the south-facing side of the Leavenworth Creek valley. Ski out around a second treeless switchback which swings you to the west-southwest and back into the main valley. This all takes place within the first 0.5 miles of the tour.

Continue along the main road as it dives deeper into this narrower section of the valley. Pass a smaller road that merges in from the left and begin a steeper climb. After several hundred yards the grade relaxes and maintains a moderate rate of climb for the remainder of the tour. Ski through a series of clearings and stands of pine trees. Several hundred feet up the slope to your right, hidden in the trees, is the old railroad grade that climbed from the town of Silver Plume and traversed around Leavenworth Mountain before meeting the Waldorf road farther up valley.

Ski along the road as it heads south and west, providing a superb view of 13,000-foot Argentine Peak at the head of the drainage. On the far side of Argentine Peak is Peru Creek (tour 91), which is near Montezuma. Shortly after the 2-mile mark the road abruptly crosses over to the left (southeast) side of the creek and remains there for several hundred yards. After you cross back to the right side of the valley, easy skiing brings you to the collapsed shaft of the Sidney Mine. A tailings pile protrudes from the road opposite the shaft, making a nice spot for lunch on clear days.

The Sidney Mine, 3.5 miles from the trailhead, is a common resting point before returning home. However, if you decide to continue to the Waldorf Mine, stay on the gentle roadbed. You'll notice as you approach the mine that large willow-filled clearings begin to appear more frequently near the creek as the forests finally disappear near the 4-mile mark. Pass under the high-tension power lines again and ascend to the group of buildings near the mine (11,594 feet). You are now 6 long miles from the car. For the majority of the return trip, the moderate grade of the road requires only pole-powered glides and goes quickly.

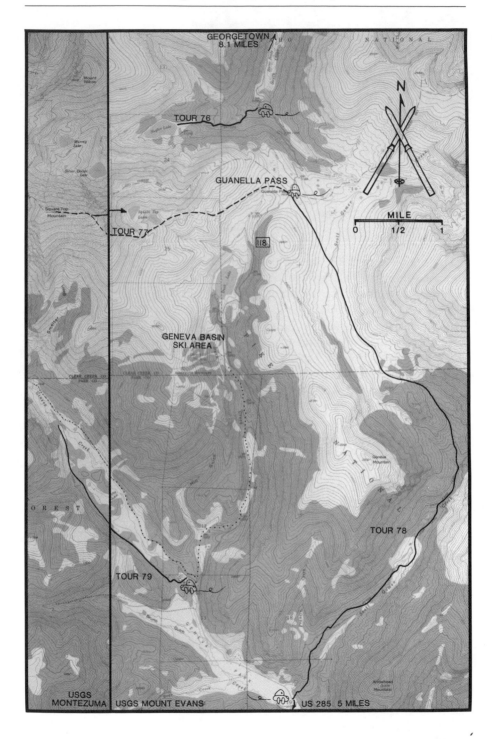

GEORGETOWN
8.1 MILES

TOUR 76

GUANELLA PASS

N

MILE

0          1/2          1

TOUR 77

118

GENEVA BASIN
SKI AREA

TOUR 78

TOUR 79

USGS
MONTEZUMA | USGS MOUNT EVANS          US 285  5 MILES

# 76   NAYLOR LAKE

> **DESCRIPTION: Winter ski tour, enjoyable and close to Denver**
> **SKILL LEVEL: Novice**
> **TIME: Half day**
> **DISTANCE: 2.6 miles round trip**
> **ELEVATION CHANGE: 512 feet total gain**
> **STARTING ELEVATION: 10,860 feet**
> **AVALANCHE TERRAIN: None**
> **USGS 7.5 MINUTE MAPS: Mount Evans, 1974-PR, Montezuma, 1974-PI**
> **MAP: page 148**

The Naylor Lake Tour is an excellent novice ski that combines minimal mileage, a short approach drive and an exciting return trip to the parking area. Climbing to 11,372 feet, this tour is one of the highest "introductory" tours in this guide, giving novices a taste of the Colorado alpine world. Because of its high elevation, this tour maintains good skiing conditions for much of the winter, with fine early- and late-season days. Remember, however, that winter ski tours that climb to treeline can present a myriad of weather conditions, ranging from subzero wind-driven blizzards to skin-scorching, high-elevation sun. Be prepared.

Reach the Naylor Lake Tour from I-70 at the Georgetown exit. Drive through Georgetown to its south end and find the well-marked Guanella Pass road. As you leave town the narrow road immediately begins climbing a series of switchbacks. After the switchbacks, the road courses along the valley bottom, passing the Cabin Creek Power Station and a series of small reservoirs before reaching the plowed parking area just short of 9 miles from Georgetown. The parking area is on the right at the outer edge of a small switchback and is marked by a brown metal sign listing "Silver Dollar Trail—1 mile."

The tour leaves the parking area with a short but steep climb before relaxing into its consistent and more moderate climb to the west-southwest along the summer roadbed. Walled in by thick stands of pine, the route is obvious and easy to follow, even during inclement weather. For the first 0.5 miles the tour remains on the south side of Naylor Creek; then it crosses to the opposite side, striking off directly west. When you reach the 0.75-mile mark you face two alternatives for the final leg to the lake, roughly 0.3 miles away. The simplest and safest route continues along the roadbed, breaking out of the trees several hundred yards east of the lake's east edge. The second option is to follow the Silver Dollar Lake Trail, which skirts south of the lake through more challenging and dangerous terrain. The turnoff is approximately 0.8 miles from the parking area and branches off to the left. This trail climbs up a gentle subsidiary drainage and over a small knoll on the southwest corner of Naylor Lake before it is possible to drop down to the lake through stunted alpine trees.

West of Naylor Lake lies Silver Dollar Lake, which sits above treeline just over 1 mile farther. It is a beautiful alpine lake at the foot of Squaretop Mountain (see tour 77) to the southwest. The route to Silver Dollar Lake follows the creek drainage for approximately 0.75 miles, then climbs south-southwest to the lake's edge. This popular intermediate extension will nearly double both the distance and the elevation gain of the base tour and should be attempted by competent parties with plenty of time and backcountry experience. Whichever destination you choose, the return trip is a simple reversal of the trip in but is much faster and more fun!

# 77   SQUARETOP MOUNTAIN (13,794 FEET)

**DESCRIPTION: Spring ski-mountaineering descent, approach hike, high, seldom-visited summit**
**SKILL LEVEL: Advanced**
**TIME: Full day**
**DISTANCE: 7 miles round trip**
**ELEVATION CHANGE: 2,200 feet total gain**
**STARTING ELEVATION: 11,670 feet**
**AVALANCHE TERRAIN: Mostly avalanche terrain; wait for spring consolidation**
**USGS 7.5 MINUTE MAPS: Mount Evans, 1974-PR, Montezuma, 1974-PI**
**MAP: page 148**

Squaretop is located a few miles west of the summit of Guanella Pass. It is not quite a "fourteener," so compared to Evans and Bierstadt, which are on the opposite side of Guanella Pass, it sees very few visitors. But Squaretop is a wonderful mountain, every bit as beautiful and imposing as its more popular neighbors to the east and west. The ski descent route is picturesque and challenging. It comes straight down a narrow ridge from the top and then drops toward two beautiful alpine lakes at the base of the peak. If you don't get bogged down in the willows, the approach is relatively moderate.

Guanella Pass can be reached from either I-70 or US 285. It is plowed all winter long and there is ample parking at the highest point, which is where the route starts. The summit of Squaretop is visible from the pass: When you look west, it is situated left of and slightly behind a false summit. From the parking lot, ski southwest across the flats, heading for an east-facing bowl below the summit. The willows in this section can be troublesome and it may be better to bypass them, as much as possible, by heading straight west up the ridge. This means having to regain a little elevation after reaching the false summit east of Squaretop. If you take the direct route into the bowl, you'll find the two picturesque Squaretop lakes nestled at the base of the peak. The descent route comes down a narrow snowfield directly west of and above the highest lake. To reach the summit from the lakes, take either the left or right skyline ridge.

From the top you can see a wide array of peaks. There is an unobstructed view south to Pikes Peak. Grays and Torreys are not far to the west and Evans and Bierstadt are just across the valley to the east. After the descent, which plunges east down the ridge and then drops into the bowl, it's an easy but tedious slog across the flats to the top of the pass.

# 78  SCOTT GOMER CREEK

**DESCRIPTION: Winter ski tour, long descent from Guanella Pass, requires car shuttle**
**SKILL LEVEL: Intermediate to advanced\***
**TIME: Half day**
**DISTANCE: 8.2 miles one way**
**ELEVATION CHANGE: 2,050 feet total loss**
**STARTING ELEVATION: 11,669 feet**
**AVALANCHE TERRAIN: Some avalanche terrain encountered; easily avoided**
**USGS 7.5 MINUTE MAP: Mount Evans, 1974-PR**
**MAP: page 148**

**\*NOVICE HIGHLIGHT: If skiers begin at the finish of this tour and ski upstream, they can enjoy gentle to moderate terrain with the added benefit of forest protection.**

Scott Gomer Creek is the southernmost ski tour in the Front Range covered in this guidebook. This tour is unusual in that it leaves the summit of Guanella Pass and drops continuously for over 8 miles through a stunning Front Range valley before reuniting with the Guanella Pass road in Geneva Park. Additionally, this trail maintains a constant southern exposure throughout its fast and twisting course. Crossing exposed alpine tundra for several miles, skiers will reach the protection of the forest below the south slopes of Mount Bierstadt. On days when the wind drives normal humans below treeline, skiers can easily reverse the trip's direction and ski up out of Geneva Park protected from the elements by the deep valley walls and the thick forest.

To reach Guanella Pass leave I-70 and drive south through Georgetown and continue up the Guanella Pass road for 10.7 miles to the top of the pass. If you are approaching from the south (US 285), turn north at Grant and drive past the tour's endpoint at 5.3 miles and continue a total of 8.3 miles to the summit of the pass. The top of the pass is marked by a wooden sign. Directly east across the tundra and the upper headwaters of Scott Gomer Creek is the jagged Sawtooth, connected by a long ridge to Mount Bierstadt on the right. A shuttle car may be left downstream at a large and well-marked parking area 18.7 miles from Georgetown and 5.3 miles from Grant on US 285.

The tour begins directly east of the small summit parking area. The idea is to reach the deepening drainage which drops from the huge bowl sitting at the base of Mount Bierstadt down to the south. The first few miles of this tour cross the tundra and are quite exposed to the elements, so attempt this route only when conditions allow. Leave the cars and ski to the east-southeast, descending slightly over the wind-blown willow-covered landscape and heading for the Scott Gomer Creek drainage located below and southwest of Mount Bierstadt. Contour south on a gradually descending course, staying left of the creek and head for a shallow saddle between Mount Bierstadt and a small tree-covered knoll (2.4 miles from Guanella Pass).

From this saddle, descend first to the east, then to the south where the trail heads into the forest. Roughly 1 mile below the saddle, the trail rejoins the creek near a spot where several trails lead to the east toward Abyss Lake. In the next section the grade steepens and the skiing takes you through stands of aspen trees and around the side of a small knob covered with boulders and aspen. This section ends with a quick bend to the southeast and a tiny bridge which crosses the creek. Continue south on the east side of the creek and enjoy great views of the entire valley, including Mount Evans and Mount Bierstadt. Recross the creek in a small clearing near mile 6. Back on the west side of Scott Gomer Creek, re-enter the trees and cruise the enjoyable 2-mile drop to the parking area in Geneva Park.

# 79   GENEVA CREEK

**DESCRIPTION: Winter ski tour, marked backcountry trail valley tour**
**SKILL LEVEL: Novice**
**TIME: Half to full day**
**DISTANCE: 6 miles round trip**
**ELEVATION CHANGE: 270 feet total gain**
**STARTING ELEVATION: 9,730 feet**
**AVALANCHE TERRAIN: None**
**USGS 7.5 MINUTE MAPS: Mount Evans, 1974-PR, Montezuma, 1974-PI**
**MAP: page 148**

Novices will find this tour highly enjoyable. It retains the quiet, secluded feel of a good backwoods tour despite the windy conditions often encountered in this area. The tour is mostly flat trail skiing with very little elevation gain overall but a few short downhill sections to make things interesting.

The access road and trailhead are located on the south side of Guanella Pass approximately 7 miles from US 285 and 6 miles from the top of the pass. The turnoff (west) is at the north end of a huge, flat, open meadow (Geneva Park). It is usually plowed for a short distance up to the entrance for Duck Creek Campground. This road continues up Geneva Creek for several miles and is an alternate route.

Ski the road into and through Duck Creek Campground to a trailhead at the west end. From here, the tour is marked throughout by blue diamond trail markers and remains on the south side of the valley in the trees. There is one fork that climbs steeply up the hillside to the left which eventually leads to Bruno Gulch. After approximately 3 miles the trail crosses a footbridge to the north side of the creek, where it intersects with the continuation of the access road. It is possible to ski back on this road but most parties prefer to return via the trail.

*Scott Gomer Creek (tour 78), view toward Mount Evans and Mount Bierstadt, Brian Litz photo.*

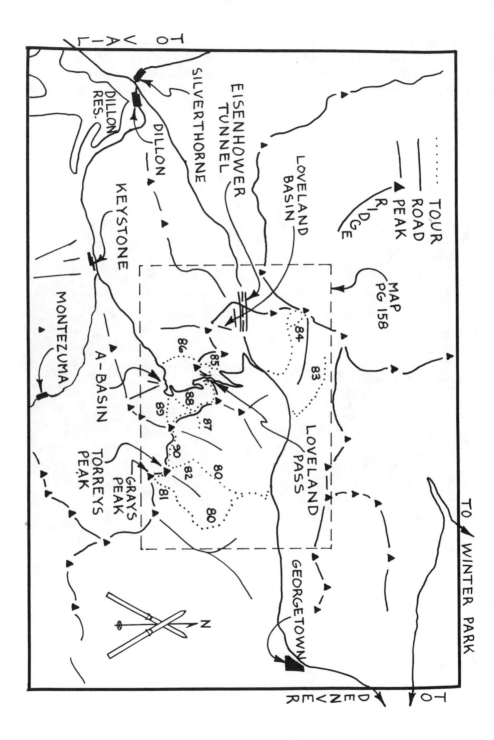

# CHAPTER SEVEN

# LOVELAND PASS AND
# UPPER CLEAR CREEK

## INTRODUCTION

At an elevation of 11,992 feet, Loveland Pass is the loftiest, wintertime maintained highway in the United States. It provides the ski mountaineer easy access to a vast amount of high alpine terrain as well as short approaches to several high peaks. A wide selection of outstanding ski descents is available. Many start a short distance from the top of the pass. With a car shuttle pickup, a minimum amount of time and effort is expended, leaving more time for additional runs later on. Because of intermittent high avalanche hazard throughout the winter, many of these descents are only possible in spring, after the snow above treeline has consolidated and strengthened. Others, such as the popular run from the top of the pass down the east side, can be skied in winter as well as spring.

Also included in this section are the more traditional winter ski tours found in the upper Clear Creek valley with access from I-70. These generally start in the trees and make their way up side valleys, staying below treeline most of the way to their destination.

## HISTORY

In 1879 the "High Line" wagon road was constructed over Loveland Pass. It connected Georgetown with the valleys of the Western Slope and provided a much-needed alternative route to Leadville, then in its second year of what became one of the biggest mining booms in Colorado history. Previously the only viable route to Leadville was through South Park and over Mosquito Pass. The "High Line" road provided a shorter alternative route from Denver. It was used to transport everything from heavy mining equipment to soap and candles until the railroads reached Leadville in 1880. A highway was eventually constructed over the pass and was named after William A. H. Loveland, a key figure in the development of Colorado's railroad system.

Loveland Pass was a favorite hangout for Colorado's earliest ski enthusiasts. The Zipfelberger Club, an early ski-racing club founded by Thor Groswold and Dick Thompkins, often used the east side of Loveland Pass for a race course. In 1938, Groswold and J. C. Bickensderfer set up a portable ski tow in Porcupine Gulch on the west side of Loveland Pass, across the valley from what is now Arapahoe Basin. It used a 4.5-horsepower engine mounted on a toboggan, with 1,000 feet of rope strung down the slope through pulleys anchored to trees and poles. The whole contraption fit in the back of a station wagon. They called it the "Little Sweden Freezer Company."

In 1946, Arapahoe Basin Inc. was formed by Larry Jump, a Tenth Mountain Division veteran of World War II, Sandy Schauffler, who skied for Amherst College before the war, Max Dercum, an ex–Pennsylvania State ski coach and proprietor of the Ski Tip Ranch near what is now Keystone, Thor Groswold, a Denver ski manufacturer, and Dick Durrance, a national ski champion. Their original setup hauled skiers from the base lodge to a rope tow midway up the slope in an old war surplus truck. By the 1948–49 season Arapahoe Basin had two chairlifts. An inexpensive Poma lift, invented and marketed by Larry Jump, was added in 1954.

Meanwhile, Loveland Basin in 1947 erected one of the first double chairlifts in the nation; Berthoud Pass also installed one during that same year. Relatively easy access from Denver and excellent snow conditions throughout the winter made Loveland Pass an ideal location for development of these early ski areas. It was not, however, an ideal location for a major interstate thoroughfare. Avalanches closed the pass on a regular basis and the narrow circuitous route had only one lane in each direction. As a result, traffic was often either stopped or backed up by slow-moving vehicles. With increasing amounts of traffic, a major interstate highway was a logical, if not essential, step in Colorado's future development. Several options were considered, including expanding one of the existing highways, US 6 over Loveland Pass or US 40 over Berthoud Pass, or bypassing these routes via long tunnels under the Continental Divide. The Eisenhower Tunnel, which bypasses the highest portion of Loveland Pass, received the go-ahead and the first bore was completed in 1973 at a cost of more than $1,000 per inch.

The new interstate highway was a boon to Summit County ski resorts and destinations farther west such as Vail and Beaver Creek. These resort areas expanded during the mid-1970s and early 1980s at a rate reminiscent of the days of early gold mining. In contrast, Grand County and Estes Park, which previously had been the premier resort destinations in Colorado, saw very little expansion during this same period. This is attributable in large part, if not exclusively, to the construction of I-70 and the Eisenhower Tunnel.

# 80   Stevens Gulch and Grizzly Gulch

**DESCRIPTION: Winter ski tour, old mine roads up large side valleys, quick access from I-70**
**SKILL LEVEL: Intermediate***
**TIME: Half or full day**
**DISTANCE: Optional, up to 6 miles round trip**
**ELEVATION CHANGE: Optional, up to 1,400 feet total gain**
**STARTING ELEVATION: 9,800 feet**
**AVALANCHE TERRAIN: Route crosses avalanche runout zones; can be dangerous during high-hazard periods**
**USGS 7.5 MINUTE MAP: Grays Peak, 1987-PR**
**MAP: page 158**

**\*NOVICE HIGHLIGHT: Novice skiers eager for a bit more challenge will find these routes enjoyable, even though they require intermediate skills on a few short stretches.**

Driving up I-70, about halfway between Georgetown and the Eisenhower Tunnel, you get a quick glimpse of the north flanks of two massive mountains on the left side of the highway. They are Kelso Mountain and Torreys Peak. The deep side valleys on either side of these peaks are Stevens Gulch and Grizzly Gulch. Both gulches offer enjoyably moderate tours with spectacular scenery. Both routes follow a roadcut for most of their length. They can be combined for a full-day tour or taken by themselves for a half-day tour.

Take I-70 to the Bakerville exit between Georgetown and the Eisenhower Tunnel. Park in an open area just south of the highway at the bottom of an unplowed road that cuts diagonally southeast up through the trees. Follow this road as it switchbacks up the south side of Clear Creek valley and then heads south toward the base of Kelso Mountain. At the base of the mountain you'll come to a fork. The right fork leads to Grizzly Gulch. The left fork leads to Stevens Gulch.

The road to Grizzly Gulch drops toward the creek for a few hundred feet to some old houses and mine ruins. It then crosses the creek and continues up the west side of Grizzly Gulch for another 2 miles. Grizzly Peak is at the end of the valley along with Torreys, whose massive north flank rises over 3,000 feet from the valley floor.

The road to Stevens Gulch continues from the previously mentioned fork up the valley on the left side of Kelso Mountain. Treeline is reached after 1.5 miles. Most parties turn back here, preferring to stay out of the wind and exposed conditions that usually dominate above treeline. The road continues above this point by first crossing the creek and then heading another 1.5 miles up the right side of the valley into a bowl below Grays Peak.

The glide back down either of these two gulches requires some control but is never too steep to negotiate with moderate snowplow turns and occasional bailouts into the powder.

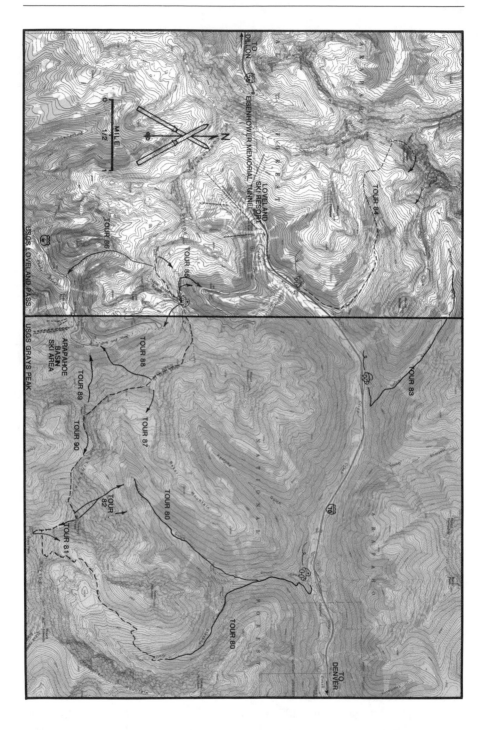

# 81 GRAYS AND TORREYS PEAKS
## (14,270 FEET AND 14,267 FEET)

**DESCRIPTION: Spring ski-mountaineering descent, approach hike, two Front Range "fourteeners"**
**SKILL LEVEL: Advanced**
**TIME: Full day**
**DISTANCE: 7 miles round trip**
**ELEVATION CHANGE: 3,070 feet total gain**
**STARTING ELEVATION: 11,200 feet**
**AVALANCHE TERRAIN: Mostly avalanche terrain; wait for spring consolidation**
**USGS 7.5 MINUTE MAP: Grays Peak, 1987-PR**
**MAP: page 158**

Grays and Torreys are two of the most frequently climbed "fourteeners" in the state. Easy access from Denver and a relatively straightforward approach make them very attractive targets for summer hikers and climbers. Most people wait until the snow is essentially gone, then trudge up and back over endless fields of talus. Many would never consider climbing these peaks in the spring with the subsequent descent on skis. But late spring/early summer may be the best time to climb these peaks. The landscape is more spectacular in spring; the peaks seem to come alive with brilliant white snowfields that contrast strikingly against a deep blue sky. Best of all, on skis, the descent only takes a matter of minutes—and it's fun! One note of caution—parts of the descent off Grays are quite steep, approaching 35 degrees in spots. Therefore, it is only recommended for advanced skiers with previous experience on steep terrain.

Approach by driving up I-70 to the Bakerville exit, located between Georgetown and the Eisenhower Tunnel. Turn south and follow a dirt road that climbs out of the valley up several switchbacks into Stevens Gulch. Soon after entering Stevens Gulch, avoid a right fork which leads across the creek into Grizzly Gulch. Continue up the main road past several small cabins until further progress is blocked by snow. The road goes all the way into the bowl below Grays Peak but it is usually impassable until much later in the summer. Park in a convenient spot off to the side of the road.

Ski or hike up the road, aiming for a small spur ridge that comes down off the summit of Grays into the main valley. Grays is the more rounded left summit of the two high peaks at the end of the valley. Ascend the spur ridge and traverse the top of the bowl to the saddle between Grays and Torreys. If you plan to do both peaks, it's better to do Torreys first, so that you can get a long continuous run down from the top of Grays. The ridge from the saddle to the summit of Torreys takes surprisingly little time to climb. The ski descent back down to the saddle may not be continuous but is worth the effort. Grays is the real plumb. After plodding up the ridge to the summit pick a direct line straight down into the bowl. Wet-snow avalanches are common in this bowl so be extremely cautious. If you wait until late spring there should be no problem. After reaching the bowl it is an enjoyable cruise back out to the car.

# 82  TORREYS PEAK—NORTH COULOIRS
## (14,267 FEET)

**DESCRIPTION: Spring ski-mountaineering descent, approach hike, steep, challenging route, big vertical drop**
**SKILL LEVEL: Advanced +**
**TIME: Full day**
**DISTANCE: 7 miles round trip**
**ELEVATION CHANGE: 3,940 feet total gain**
**STARTING ELEVATION: 10,335 feet**
**AVALANCHE TERRAIN: Mostly avalanche terrain; wait for spring consolidation**
**USGS 7.5 MINUTE MAP: Grays Peak, 1987-PR**
**MAP: page 158**

The north couloir on Torreys is a first-rate ski descent. It is one of the more serious routes covered in this book—some might classify it as borderline extreme. Continuously steep for almost 3,000 vertical feet, it is certainly not one for the faint of heart. The period of time when snow conditions are good is rather short—three to four weeks in June at the most. Attempt the route only after the snow has completely consolidated, so there is little or no chance of avalanches. Even a small sluff could be very dangerous.

The approach is from either Grizzly or Stevens Gulch, both accessed from the Bakerville exit off I-70 (tour 80). Although more difficult and time-consuming, the Grizzly Gulch approach is recommended because it allows you to scout the descent. There are actually two or three couloirs that can be skied. The one that starts from the very top is the most esthetic but it has a narrow section located about halfway down that may melt out in late June. The couloir farthest east is more moderate lower down but is difficult to get into and has a rocky section that may require removing your skis. For this reason it is not recommended. The couloir just down the ridge west of the summit is a clear, straight shot from top to bottom. Looking down any one of these alternatives and committing to that first turn will undoubtedly get the adrenaline flowing. Once the bottom is reached there is a jeep road a few hundred feet up on the opposite side of the creek that goes back to the junction between Grizzly Gulch and Stevens Gulch.

# 83   HERMAN GULCH

> **DESCRIPTION: Winter ski tour, road and off-trail backcountry, quick access from I-70, vulnerable to large avalanches**
> **SKILL LEVEL: Intermediate**
> **TIME: Quarter day**
> **DISTANCE: Optional, up to 5 miles round trip to treeline**
> **ELEVATION CHANGE: Optional, up to 1,300 feet total gain**
> **STARTING ELEVATION: 10,300 feet**
> **AVALANCHE TERRAIN: Route crosses avalanche runout zones; can be dangerous during high-hazard periods**
> **USGS 7.5 MINUTE MAPS: Loveland Pass, 1987-PR, Grays Peak, 1987-PR**
> **MAP: page 158**

Access to this tour is so easy that most people pass it up without even knowing it exists. The tour starts not more than 50 yards from I-70, but once you get up into the gulch, you feel as if you're totally isolated. Situated in a hanging valley, rung with high peaks, it is no less spectacular than any of the other tours in the Front Range. The only drawback is that you must cross some large avalanche runout areas in order to go more than 0.5 miles up into the valley. Do not attempt this tour if avalanche hazard is high and/or if visibility is poor. Call the avalanche recording for current conditions before you begin your tour.

*Spring skiing on Loveland Pass, Brian Litz photo.*

Traveling west on I-70, between Georgetown and the Eisenhower Tunnel, take the first available exit after the exit for Bakerville, 1.9 miles before the Loveland Pass–Loveland Ski Area exit. Turn right and cut back around on a short access road to the parking area. The tour starts as a trail that diagonals up and east for a few hundred yards past some cabins to a jeep trail. The jeep trail is steep for the first 0.25 miles until you get up into the hanging valley, where it opens up and flattens out. Here you must cross the first of several large avalanche runout areas. Evaluate the conditions before crossing and turn back if the snow is at all unstable. Continue up the valley 2 miles to treeline or as far as desired. Return via the same route.

# 84   HAGAR MOUNTAIN (13,195 FEET)

**DESCRIPTION: Spring ski-mountaineering route, beautiful setting**
**SKILL LEVEL: Advanced***
**TIME: Full day**
**DISTANCE: 7 miles round trip**
**ELEVATION CHANGE: 2,595 feet total gain**
**STARTING ELEVATION: 10,600 feet**
**AVALANCHE TERRAIN: Mostly avalanche terrain; wait for spring consolidation**
**USGS 7.5 MINUTE MAP: Loveland Pass, 1987-PR**
**MAP: page 158**

***INTERMEDIATE HIGHLIGHT: Those skiers not ready to climb directly to the summit of this peak can find a wealth of intermediate terrain to ski throughout this valley.**

This exploration into the land of alpine tundra is a fine outing for spring ski mountaineers of all abilities. While more intrepid skiers will want to challenge themselves by attacking the eastern rampart of Hagar Mountain, those with more limited skill, endurance and zeal can satisfy themselves telemarking in the almost limitless bowls that lie at the head of Dry Gulch at the base of the higher surrounding peaks. Interestingly, this drainage sees few skiers, even though the approach is relatively short and the opportunities for skiing vast. Visiting the narrow summit peak is alone worth the trip up this valley.

Take I-70 to the Loveland Pass exit. Immediately after exiting the highway turn right on a gravel frontage road that cuts back along the north side of I-70. Drive 100 yards to a locked gate and park off to the side of the road. Hike up this road into Dry Creek. The road ends after 0.2 miles at a hillside scarred by heavy equipment during the construction of I-70 and the Eisenhower Tunnel. Proceed from here up first the right side of the creek, then the left, 2 miles to treeline. From treeline continue west up the lowest part of the creek and begin contouring northwest at about 12,000 feet. Cross the moderate tundra slopes, aiming for the obvious saddle found at the base of Hagar's southern summit ridge. Once at the saddle turn north and scale the aforementioned ridge.

For the descent it is best to scramble from the summit north along the often tantalizingly narrow ridge. To the right or east lies the broad east slope. There are many points of entry onto the snow; some are very steep. The most moderate skiing begins several hundred feet beyond the highest point of the peak near a faint buttress, which is discernible on the topographic maps. Once on the snow the skiing is consistently steep, about 35 to 40 degrees, but the runout at the bottom is good. From the base of the mountain, traverse south over rolling and descending terrain until you drop back down into Dry Creek.

# 85   LOVELAND PASS RUNS

**DESCRIPTION: Winter/spring descents, no approach hike, car shuttle required**
**SKILL LEVEL: Intermediate to advanced**
**TIME: One hour to full day**
**DISTANCE: Optional, 0.5 to 1 miles**
**ELEVATION CHANGE: North Run 730 feet total loss**
                              **South Run 990 feet total loss**
**STARTING ELEVATION: 11,990 feet**
**AVALANCHE TERRAIN: Routes cross avalanche slopes; prone to skier-triggered avalanches during high-hazard periods**
**USGS 7.5 MINUTE MAPS: Loveland Pass, 1987-PR, Grays Peak, 1987-PR**
**MAP: page 158**

Skiing off the summit of Loveland Pass has been a popular winter pastime for decades. Many skiers have cut their "off-piste" teeth on these high-elevation runs. Ease of access and short car shuttles (or hitches) back to the top allow for numerous repetitions in only a few hours. The terrain is never extremely steep, so skiers of all abilities can enjoy these runs. With highly variable snow conditions ranging from hardpack and windblown crust to deep powder, this is a perfect area to introduce oneself to the vagaries of backcountry telemark skiing. Care should always be exercised, as these slopes can hide dangerous pockets of wind-deposited snow vulnerable to skier-triggered avalanches—don't let the large numbers of skiers lull you into imprudence.

The north face of the pass is the most heavily traveled and normally possesses better snow conditions. This huge bowl has moderate slopes (15 to 30 degrees) which eventually funnel into a creek drainage ending at the second large switchback north from the top of the pass. A complex assortment of small glades and little chutes hide nice powder skiing; no definite route exists. Cross the highway from the parking area and walk down to the west. Mount up and begin traversing west away from this wind-scoured spot. After traversing several hundred yards the terrain opens and you can ski wherever your ability will take you. It is possible to trace the contours far out to the west and descend from there. The standard run will take about 15 to 20 minutes.

The south side of the pass is less complicated but sometimes more dangerous because of the leeward aspect of the slopes, increasing the potential for avalanches. You can hike east from the parking area along the crest of the ridge and choose many lines to ski. The steep nature of the initial drop is slightly more challenging and can hold dangerous slabs of snow if the wind has been blowing. At the foot of these slopes the angle reclines and you can ski to many rendezvous points. Following the creekbed, it is possible to ski down to the Arapahoe Basin ski area.

# 86   TUNDRA RUN

**DESCRIPTION: Winter/spring ski descent, moderate approach hike, car shuttle required**
**SKILL LEVEL: Intermediate to advanced**
**TIME: Half day**
**DISTANCE: 2.3 miles one way**
**ELEVATION CHANGE: 424 feet total gain/2,014 feet total loss**
**STARTING ELEVATION: 11,990 feet**
**AVALANCHE TERRAIN: Route crosses avalanche slopes; prone to skier-triggered avalanches during high-hazard periods**
**USGS 7.5 MINUTE MAP: Loveland Pass, 1987-PR**
**MAP: page 158**

The Tundra Run is another enjoyable "off-piste" ski descent off the summit of Loveland Pass. From the parking area on the summit of the pass, this tour heads west-southwest, gaining slightly in elevation before dropping off into the large bowl draining into the North Fork of the Snake River, exiting just west of Arapahoe Basin ski area. When compared with the North Face and South Face routes on Loveland Pass, this tour is longer and more complicated, requiring greater skiing proficiency and skills in backcountry route finding and avalanche hazard evaluation. This is a fine short tour that combines nicely with other routes in the area to provide a day of diverse ski adventure.

Place a shuttle car at the Arapahoe Basin ski area on the west side of US 6. Then drive on US 6 to the summit of Loveland Pass and park on the east side of the road in the small parking area. Cross the road and begin hiking southwest, traversing along the moderate north slopes of Point 12,585. After roughly 0.5 miles, intersect the ridge that runs to the northwest of Point 12,585. Below lies a vast bowl of rolling terrain for telemark skiing with many possible routes. The main considerations in determining your descent are the ability of the skiers in your party and the stability of the snowpack. A good choice for those who have not skied here before is to drop off Point 12,414 and ski its convex southwest side. This route is technically moderate and is relatively safe from slides. This slope blends into lower-angled alpine tundra that separates the two creeks draining this basin. From here ski down to the east, reaching the trees in the eastern of the two creeks. Follow the creekbed to the highway.

# 87   GRIZZLY BOWL

**DESCRIPTION: Spring ski descent, moderate approach hike**
**SKILL LEVEL: Intermediate to advanced**
**TIME: Optional, half day or longer**
**DISTANCE: Optional, 1.5 miles to the skiing, up to 3 miles round trip**
**ELEVATION CHANGE: Optional, 1,200 feet to the skiing, up to 2,700 feet total round trip gain**
**STARTING ELEVATION: 11,990 feet**
**AVALANCHE TERRAIN: Mostly avalanche terrain; wait for spring consolidation**
**USGS 7.5 MINUTE MAP: Grays Peak, 1987-PR**
**MAP: page 158**

Hidden to the east of the summit of Loveland Pass is a large cirque that forms the headwaters of Grizzly Gulch. Grizzly Bowl, as it is known, affords excellent springtime skiing for intermediate to advanced skiers. It lies at nearly 12,000 feet and remains skiable even into late June and early July. Although it may be reached by a long hike up Grizzly Gulch from the Stevens Mine road (see Stevens and Grizzly gulches, tour 80), the shortest approach is to park on the summit of Loveland Pass and hike along the crest of the ridge to the south and east. The routes in the bowl are short; however, this will allow you to ski them more than once in a day. Other possibilities include skiing out Grizzly Gulch or hiking back to the ridge and skiing Dave's Wave (tour 88) or the west face of Grizzly Peak (tour 89).

Drive on US 6 to the summit of Loveland Pass and park on the east side. The routes drop off at various spots along the east face of Point 13,117, which may be reached two ways. The first is to simply leave the cars and hike east along the crest of the ridge, crossing Point 12,915, then turn southeast and follow the ridge until you ascend Point 13,117. The second route is more direct, contouring across the southwest side of Point 12,915 before reaching Point 13,117. This eliminates an unnecessary gain and loss of elevation. The entire hike is a little over 1.5 miles and easily managed.

When you stand on the summit of Point 13,117 facing east, the entire bowl curls out and around to your right and left with the impressive north side of Torreys Peak towering across Grizzly Gulch to the east. There are many descents possible from this point. In general though, to the far left and slightly to the right, easier lines exist, with steeper slopes dropping directly to the east off the top of Point 13,117. Normally, dangerous cornices overhang the bowl far off to the right as you approach Grizzly Peak. Aside from these hazards, this area is safe for skiing after spring snowpack consolidation. Enjoy!

# 88 DAVE'S WAVE

DESCRIPTION: Spring ski descent, short approach hike, also popular
with downhill gear, car shuttle required
SKILL LEVEL: Advanced
TIME: Quarter day
DISTANCE: 2.5 miles one way
ELEVATION CHANGE: 1,000 feet total gain/2,000 feet total loss
STARTING ELEVATION: 11,990 feet
AVALANCHE TERRAIN: Mostly avalanche terrain; wait for spring
consolidation
USGS 7.5 MINUTE MAP: Grays Peak, 1987-PR
MAP: page 158

This is one of the best spring ski descents in the state, fun and quite popular.
The approach, from Loveland Pass east, then south along the crest of the ridge, is
relatively short and straightforward. The ski descent itself is a wild, challenging
plunge down the edge of a shallow trough with what is best described as a wave
running down the length of its windward edge. The route finishes at the first hairpin
turn above the Arapahoe Basin ski area. A car shuttle is required to return to the
starting point at the top of Loveland Pass. Because of its relatively short approach,
many choose to ski it using downhill gear rather than telemark or ski-mountaineering
equipment.

Leave one car at the first hairpin turn above the Arapahoe Basin ski area and
return to the summit of Loveland Pass. There is parking available here for approximately a dozen cars. From the parking lot hike east up the ridge 0.5 miles, heading
for the summit of an unnamed 12,915-foot mountain. Before reaching the summit,
traverse right to a saddle on the main north-south ridge (cutting off the last 200 feet
of the 12,915-foot mountain). Proceed south along the ridge to the summit of a second
mountain at 13,117 feet. The descent begins here on a gradual slope that quickly
steepens to 35 degrees. Hidden from view at first, the route unfolds as a shallow
trough that drops 2,000 feet to the hairpin turn above the ski area. The route's
characteristic "wave" of snow runs parallel to the trough along the entire upper
portion of the route. Ski the wave on its right edge. The lower portion of the trough
as it enters the trees is somewhat ragged and less well defined. It is better to jog left
to the next trough south for a more continuous run. At the bottom of the trough a short
slog across buried willows takes you to the road. Car shuttle or hitch back to the top
of the pass.

# 89  GRIZZLY PEAK (13,427 FEET)

**DESCRIPTION: Spring ski descent, approach hike, car shuttle required**
**SKILL LEVEL: Advanced**
**TIME: Half day**
**DISTANCE: 3 miles one way**
**ELEVATION CHANGE: 1,587 feet total gain**
**STARTING ELEVATION: 11,990 feet**
**AVALANCHE TERRAIN: Mostly avalanche terrain; wait for spring consolidation**
**USGS 7.5 MINUTE MAPS: Loveland Pass, 1987-PR, Grays Peak, 1987-PR**
**MAP: page 158**

Majestically standing guard over the upper reaches of the North Fork of the Snake River, the smooth and conical Grizzly Peak (13,427 feet) is an often-overlooked telemark challenge. Carved into its west flank is a long and continuously steep couloir hiding a beautiful ski descent that remains skiable well into July. Late-spring conditions find nearly 2,000 feet of intermediate to advanced telemark paradise awaiting those with the gumption to travel the 2.5 miles from the pass to the route's start.

Place a shuttle car at the Arapahoe Basin ski area on the west side of US 6. Then drive on US 6 to the summit of Loveland Pass and park on the east side in the small parking area. Leave the cars and hike east, either following the crest of the ridge or traversing along the southwest slopes of Point 12,915. After attaining this gentle ridge which runs from Mount Sniktau on the north to Grizzly Peak on the south, traverse it south, crossing Point 13,117 as well as several other minor bumps. Because this ridge presents no more of a challenge than a stiff alpine walk, you will soon be at the base of Grizzly Peak's northwest ridge.

To the right of the final summit ridge is the west face and the snow-filled couloir. The top of the snowfield reaches only to within several hundred feet of the summit and varies in height throughout the season. Hence it is generally not necessary to ascend directly to the summit. Instead, hike up the ridge and then traverse onto the west face at a level closest to where the good skiing begins.

Once you hit the snow the descent is straightforward and exciting. When you have dropped to below 12,200 feet, the best route traverses onto the rounded ridge forming the south side of the couloir. Traverse out to the west and then drop back into the couloir on a descending traverse to the north and west. When you reach treeline the skiing becomes more confined and tricky but soon you will reach US 6 directly across the road from the Arapahoe Basin parking lots.

*Massive spring avalanche on Hagar Mountain (tour 84), Brian Litz photo.*

# 90   LOVELAND PASS TO GRAYS PEAK TRAVERSE

**DESCRIPTION: Spring ski-mountaineering route, high ridge traverse with much elevation gain but even more elevation loss, car shuttle required**
**SKILL LEVEL: Advanced**
**TIME: Full day**
**DISTANCE: 8 miles**
**ELEVATION CHANGE: 4,400 feet total gain/5,200 feet total loss**
**STARTING ELEVATION: 11,990 feet**
**AVALANCHE TERRAIN: Mostly avalanche terrain; wait for spring consolidation**
**USGS 7.5 MINUTE MAP: Grays Peak, 1987-PR**
**MAP: page 158**

This is an exceptional ski-mountaineering adventure. Altogether the route traverses three major peaks, covers 8 miles and gains 4,400 feet of elevation. For all that work there is ample reward—as much as 5,000 feet of outstanding ski-descent terrain. A car shuttle is required for the return trip.

Start from the top of Loveland Pass. Hike east up the ridge to the first major high point and turn south, heading toward Grizzly Peak. You can avoid gaining the last 300 feet of this first high point by traversing right at the level of the next saddle. Continue down the ridge over two more high points and then up the last steep grade to the summit of Grizzly Peak. The descent to the saddle between Grizzly and Torreys peaks is fast and fun. Once at the saddle you must contemplate the long, arduous trudge to the top of Torreys. If your enthusiasm is waning, you may descend from this saddle down Grizzly Gulch instead of continuing to Torreys. You'll come out at the junction of Grizzly Gulch and Stevens Gulch 1.5 miles above Bakerville. The traverse from Torreys to Grays is comparatively easy and well worth the extra effort. From the summit of Grays step into your skis and prepare for the big plunge north into the cirque below Grays and Torreys. The angle gets steep and fairly serious toward the bottom of this run. Once you are safely in the bowl ski down the left side of the valley until you hook up with the Stevens Gulch jeep road. Depending on how late in the season you do this route, it may be possible to drive your shuttle car all the way up Stevens Gulch to treeline.

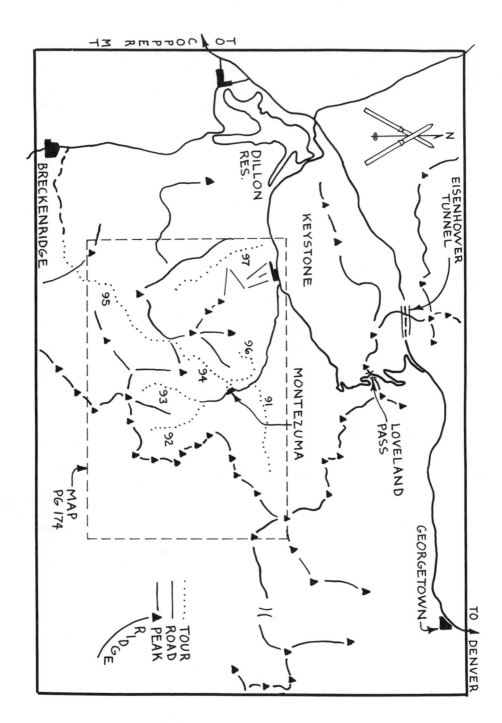

TO COPPER MTN.

DILLON RES.

BRECKENRIDGE

EISENHOWER TUNNEL

N

KEYSTONE

97

95

96

94

93

92

91

MONTEZUMA

LOVELAND PASS

MAP PG 174

GEORGETOWN

TO DENVER

RIDGE

······· TOUR
——— ROAD
▶ PEAK

# CHAPTER EIGHT

# Montezuma and Keystone

## Introduction

The east edge of Summit County, near the headwaters of the Snake River, is characterized by deep gentle valleys and massive rolling alpine peaks. Pleistocene glaciers (less than 3 million years old) at one point covered this entire area, leaving behind long U-shaped valleys and smoothly contoured uplands. Nordic skiers will find this terrain to be just right for novice and intermediate trail skiing. The typical tour in the Keystone–Montezuma area ascends gradually along the bottoms of the drainages which feed into the Snake River and eventually, Lake Dillon. Scenic, consistently moderate and possessing many fine trails easily reached from several relatively central locations, this is a good place to bring new skiers. Montezuma's only drawback is its popularity—it is often crowded on weekends. Also, if Loveland Pass is closed, Denver skiers must drive through Dillon. This can add at least 30 to 45 minutes to the trip.

Cross-country skiing at Montezuma is enhanced by its historic past, which manifests itself in the mining shacks, tailings piles and the stoic ghost camps residing in this mountain environment. Old mining roads crisscrossing the topography create the tours here as they snake their way across the slopes to now-silent towns such as Sts. John and Decatur. Instead of tightly wooded trails, most Montezuma routes are roadbeds, easy to follow and generally wide enough for the widest of snowplow turns. The Wild Irishman Mine, above and west of Sts. John, sits near treeline in a beautiful bowl. Skiers who make this their stopping point for the day will find acres of powder skiing a short distance from the mine's cabins—a classic day trip.

Montezuma sits at roughly 10,300 feet. All trails that begin from near the town easily reach treeline. While this treeless land is stark and very different from the protected forests, it may be enjoyed by even novice skiers because of its close proximity. If you plan on skiing above treeline, be prepared for all weather conditions. Bitter storms can move in from the west quickly, and skiers may not notice the changing weather patterns. Suddenly, orientation can become very difficult and temperatures can plummet, turning a leisurely tour into an ordeal.

An unusual feature of skiing at Montezuma is the Inn Montezuma. Owned and operated by Rob Ilves, this rustic mountain bed-and-breakfast is a Nordic skier's backcountry haven. Beds and rooms may be procured, as well as food and drink. Day skiers are invited to stop in for lunch and hot drinks. Ilves intimately understands every nook and cranny of the upper Snake River basin and can provide the latest trail, snow and avalanche conditions (as well as a welcome rest). During the summer of 1988, Ilves moved his inn west into the abandoned townsite of Sts. John. Accessible now only to skiers, its charm and backcountry ambience remain intact, a stopover highly recommended. See tour 94 for more information.

## HISTORY

Breaking rock at 11,000-plus feet with a pickaxe, dodging avalanches in the heart of the winter, carrying out ore by wagon and mule—this was life in Montezuma in the late 1800s. This mining district, set almost entirely above treeline, was as remote and rugged as it was prosperous. During the height of its activity, Montezuma's rich silver veins produced high-grade ore in quantities rivaled by few other mines in the country. The district was originally named after the Aztec leader by D. C. Collier, a prospector who arrived in the upper Snake River valley in 1865.

The town of Montezuma served as a hub for the mining district. The radial alpine valleys to the east, south and west were filled with productive silver mines, mining camps and upstart towns. For a time Montezuma contained the only smelter in the district. Montezuma's prosperity, like all mining towns, fluctuated with the economy of the nation and the price of silver (as well as gold). The booms and busts continued until 1893, when the U.S. government devalued silver and returned to the gold standard. The downturn that followed this woeful news tested the little town. The area rebounded once more in 1905, when the price of silver rose again.

The first silver ore discovered in Colorado came from the Montezuma district, near the ghost town of Sts. John. The lode was named the *Comestock* by John Coley, who uncovered it in 1863. Nearby a camp was erected which quickly became a town. Originally named Coleyville, its name was changed by the Mason who helped establish the community to Sts. John (for their patron saints St. John the Baptist and St. John the Evangelist). While the lodes were numerous and of high quality, the silver was difficult to separate from the associated minerals and ores. The ores needed to be roasted at high temperatures to release the silver. Eventually, in 1872, a group of eastern investors known as the Boston Silver Mining Association built a mill and smelter capable of separating the silver in a cost-effective manner. Sts. John then was sold to the Boston Mining Company, which created both a state-of-the-art mining operation and a town of some culture in a land of brothels, bars and beer. They imported libraries of books, built beautiful homes and buildings and even collected the latest eastern newspapers.

Since the early 1900s when the Montezuma–Sts. John area experienced the last great days of silver mining, the valley has declined steadily in population. The historic railroad town of Keystone has obviously been reborn since the opening of the ski area in 1970, but the upper Snake River drainages have remained relatively undeveloped commercially. Today this beautiful area is accessible for winter and summer mountain recreation and adventure.

# 91 PERU CREEK

**DESCRIPTION: Winter ski tour, scenic and generally gentle road in historic mining area**
**SKILL LEVEL: Novice\***
**TIME: Full day**
**DISTANCE: 8 to 12 miles round trip**
**ELEVATION CHANGE: 900 feet total gain**
**STARTING ELEVATION: 10,004 feet**
**AVALANCHE TERRAIN: Route crosses avalanche runout zones; can be dangerous during high-hazard periods**
**USGS 7.5 MINUTE MAP: Montezuma, 1974-PI**
**MAP: page 174**

**\*INTERMEDIATE HIGHLIGHT: Three alternate side valleys, Chihuahua Gulch, Warden Gulch and Cinnamon Gulch, emanate from Peru Creek and offer more intermediate (and advanced) terrain.**

The Peru Creek Trail leaves the road to Montezuma and climbs east, following a gentle roadbed with plenty of room for snowplow maneuvers on the descent. The basic tour ends near the Pennsylvania Mine but can easily be extended up into Horseshoe Basin, far above treeline and surrounded by 13,000- and 14,000-foot peaks. On weekends this valley is inundated with skiers, so if you don't like crowds, try it during the week.

Drive on US 6 to the east entrance to the Keystone ski area. Turn south towards the ski area, then take the first left onto County Road 5, which is the road to the town of Montezuma. Follow this road 4.9 miles and park in a parking area on the left side of the road, immediately past the sharp switchback that crosses the Snake River. This parking area is large but will fill on busy days.

Leave the parking area and ski north to the Peru Creek road. It is very flat at the start but soon climbs gently as it contours from north to east. Just past the 1-mile mark the tour breaks from the trees as the road jogs left, crossing the creek to the north side. Continue along the north bank, passing the mouth of Chihuahua Gulch, a fine intermediate alternate route high to the left.

Re-enter the trees at the 2.5-mile mark, then contour close to the creekbed. At 3 miles the road forks. Either route may be chosen: The right variant leads to the Pennsylvania Mine, a total distance of 4 miles from the parking area; the left route bypasses the mine, remaining on the north side of the valley along the base of Cooper and Ruby mountains.

If your party wants to ski into Horseshoe Basin, continue on either road,

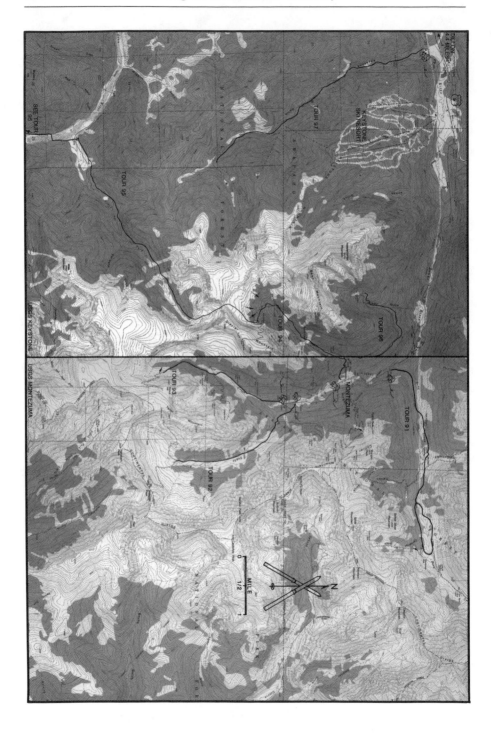

passing a point where they join. Pass the small but well-constructed stone building marked "Decatur" on the USGS map, and begin to contour north. High above to the east is Argentine Peak with Argentine Pass to its left. Argentine Pass is the old route used by miners and settlers to cross the divide into Waldorf Mine–Leavenworth Creek and Georgetown (see tour 75). Continuing on this tour, follow the road along Peru Creek. Cross the creek and climb the last easy yards to the National Treasury Mine, a good spot to turn around. Return over the same route.

This extension into Horseshoe Basin is easy but it pushes far into the alpine world and crosses several avalanche slopes on the north in the process. Attempt it only when the weather and snowpack are stable.

# 92  WEBSTER PASS

**DESCRIPTION: Winter ski tour, mine road up valley to high pass**
**SKILL LEVEL: Novice to intermediate**
**TIME: Three-quarters day**
**DISTANCE: 6 miles round trip**
**ELEVATION CHANGE: 1,000 feet total gain**
**STARTING ELEVATION: 10,530 feet**
**AVALANCHE TERRAIN: Route crosses avalanche runout zones; can be dangerous during high-hazard periods**
**USGS 7.5 MINUTE MAP: Montezuma, 1974-PI**
**MAP: page 174**

This tour starts just beyond the town of Montezuma and travels up the very last bit of the Snake River valley to Webster Pass. It follows a relatively tame jeep road but the route does gain elevation steadily and provides a quick, exhilarating return trip.

To get to Montezuma take US 6 to the easternmost turnoff for the Keystone ski area. Immediately after turning off the highway take the first left turn onto County Road 5 and follow it for approximately 6 miles to Montezuma. Continue through town and follow the road another 0.9 miles to a sign indicating "Webster Pass" on the left side of the road. There is usually plowed parking for several cars off to the right. If you come to the end of the road, you've gone too far by about 0.25 miles.

The tour starts out gaining elevation quickly as it winds up through a heavily wooded section into the upper valley. Here the tour opens up into large meadows and gentler terrain. After another mile the road crosses the creek and continues up the right side of the valley. Near treeline, at the end of the valley, the road steepens as it switchbacks up toward Webster Pass high on the ridge to the left. Most parties prefer to stop at treeline before actually reaching Webster Pass because the winds above are often harsh and unpleasant. The return trip is a peaceful glide back down the same road.

# 93   DEER CREEK

**DESCRIPTION: Winter ski tour, mine road up valley beyond Montezuma**
**SKILL LEVEL: Novice to intermediate**
**TIME: Three-quarters day**
**DISTANCE: Up to 6 miles round trip**
**ELEVATION CHANGE: Up to 1,000 feet total gain**
**STARTING ELEVATION: 10,560 feet**
**AVALANCHE TERRAIN: Some avalanche terrain encountered; easily avoided**
**USGS 7.5 MINUTE MAP: Montezuma, 1974-PI**
**MAP: page 174**

Another fine tour in the Montezuma area, this is characterized by moderately steep terrain, large open meadows and good telemark glades at the end of the valley.

To get to Montezuma take US 6 to the easternmost turnoff for the Keystone ski area. Immediately after turning off the highway take the first left turn onto County

*Lunch break at the Wild Irishman Mine (tour 94), Brian Litz photo.*

Road 5 and follow it for approximately 6 miles to Montezuma. Continue through town to the end of the plowed road. The tour starts on the unplowed continuation of this road as it crosses Deer Creek and makes its way up the right side of the valley. The tour crosses two large meadows en route to the final steep section below treeline at the end of the valley. Here, you can take some quick telemark runs before returning via the same route. There are some inviting but potentially dangerous avalanche paths at the end of the cirque—be cautious.

An alternate finish, which is also intermediate level, leaves the main road two-thirds of the way up the valley, cutting back northeast on another old mining road to the Mohawk Mine.

# 94 STS. JOHN AND WILD IRISHMAN MINE

**DESCRIPTION: Winter ski tour, good telemark skiing at end of bowl**
**SKILL LEVEL: Intermediate***
**TIME: Three-quarters day**
**DISTANCE: Up to 8 miles round trip**
**ELEVATION CHANGE: Up to 1,500 feet total gain**
**STARTING ELEVATION: 10,300 feet**
**AVALANCHE TERRAIN: Some avalanche terrain encountered; easily avoided**
**USGS 7.5 MINUTE MAPS: Montezuma, 1974-PI, Keystone, 1974-PR**
**MAP: page 174**

**\*NOVICE HIGHLIGHT: The first section to Sts. John and the Inn Montezuma is a wide road with two switchbacks. Novice skiers should find it challenging but manageable.**

**\*ADVANCED HIGHLIGHT: There are excellent telemark glades near treeline at the west end of Sts. John Creek. Also see the advanced alternatives that follow the normal description.**

This tour will become an old favorite the very first time you try it. The snow conditions in Sts. John Creek always seem to be as good as, if not better than, they are anywhere else in the Front Range. The terrain is generally moderate, with just enough variety and steepness to keep you interested. The Inn Montezuma, one of several local bed-and-breakfast establishments, recently relocated partway up valley, at the site of the old Sts. John ghost town. It offers a warm fire, food and hot drinks to passersby as well as overnight accommodations and helpful advice on backcountry conditions.

The tour begins from the center of Montezuma. To get to Montezuma take US 6 to the easternmost turnoff for the Keystone ski area. Immediately after turning off the highway take the first left turn onto County Road 5 and follow it for approximately 6 miles to Montezuma. Park in a plowed parking area near the center of Montezuma, just off the main road at its intersection with County Road 275. Ski up the continuation of County Road 275 as it crosses the creek and diagonals up the hillside just south of town. The road makes one double switchback before rounding the corner into Sts. John Creek. After another 0.25 miles of relatively easy going, you'll reach the Inn Montezuma and the ruins of the abandoned Sts. John mining operation. The road continues, winding through trees up the right side of the valley. After another mile, the road crosses the creek and curves southeast, eventually ending at the ruins of the Wild Irishman Mine. For those who wish to go farther, there are excellent powder glades from here to treeline.

The return trip goes so quickly that you may have plenty of time to ski one of the other fine tours in the area.

ALTERNATE ROUTES (ADVANCED): Weather permitting, it is possible to connect the Sts. John Creek drainage with a route that ends at Keystone. There are two good alternatives. One climbs to the saddle at the far west end of the Sts. John Creek drainage, then goes north over Keystone Mountain and two lower summits, to the summit warming house at the Keystone ski area. With ski patrol permission, you can then finish by skiing down ski-area slopes to the base lodge.

The second alternative goes over the saddle at the west end of Sts. John Creek and then drops down into Keystone Gulch. From there, ski out the Keystone Gulch Tour which comes out just south of the ski area (see tour 97).

With a car shuttle between Keystone and Montezuma, these make fine extended backcountry routes.

# 95   MONTEZUMA TO BRECKENRIDGE

**DESCRIPTION: Winter ski tour, long and strenuous, car shuttle required**
**SKILL LEVEL: Advanced**
**TIME: Long day**
**DISTANCE: 17.8 miles**
**ELEVATION CHANGE: 3,027 feet total gain/3,786 feet total loss**
**STARTING ELEVATION: 10,300 feet**
**AVALANCHE TERRAIN: Route crosses avalanche slopes; prone to skier-triggered avalanches during high-hazard periods**
**USGS 7.5 MINUTE MAPS: Montezuma, 1974, Keystone, 1974-PR, Breckenridge, 1987-PR**
**MAPS: pages 174, 288**

The Montezuma to Breckenridge Tour is a mountain marathon that covers over 17 miles and includes a whopping 3,000 feet of accumulated elevation gain. The majority of the tour traces old jeep roads in the historic mining areas that filled the mountains of eastern Summit County. While the tour follows mostly moderate terrain, crossing of the pass above and to the west of Wild Irishman Mine, sheer distance and overall commitment elevate this trip to advanced status. Check on avalanche conditions before you undertake this tour. The descent west of the Wild Irishman Mine into the North Fork of the Swan River crosses avalanche terrain. A car shuttle is essential. Start early if you are coming from the Denver area. This is a good tour for later in the season, when days are longer and the snowpack above treeline has stabilized. The route described leads into the center of Breckenridge; however, it is possible to place the shuttle cars up French Gulch, shortening the trip by several miles.

The tour begins in Montezuma, which sits near the head of the Snake River southeast of the Keystone ski area. Drive on US 6 to the easternmost entrance of the ski area and turn south. Take the first left on County Road 5 and continue approximately 6 miles to Montezuma. Park near the head of the road to Sts. John, County

Road 275, where there is ample parking.

The first leg of the journey follows the road to Wild Irishman Mine (see tour 94) which is wide and well traveled. After leaving the parking area the road climbs steeply around two switchbacks before heading southwest along the moderate valley bottom. Pass the ruins of Sts. John near the 1.5-mile mark and begin a slightly steeper climb. Continue along the road as it contours southeast in the trees that fill the beautiful upper basin. Cross Sts. John Creek and climb moderately to the cabins of the Wild Irishman Mine, which are just past the 3-mile point.

Leave the cabins and climb south before cresting onto the vast alpine plateau which encircles the upper basin. To the north stands graceful Bear Mountain (12,585 feet) and to the northeast across the Snake River are Grays (14,270 feet) and Torreys (14,267 feet). Double-pole southwest, aiming for the obvious sharp saddle that breaks the ridge at the south corner of the basin. Ski up onto the saddle (at 12,020 feet, the highest point on the tour) and enjoy the panorama of alpine peaks to the south and west. The traverse from the cabins at Wild Irishman Mine to this saddle runs in close proximity to the steep northwest face of Glacier Mountain, which holds potentially dangerous avalanche slopes: Remain well away from this feature.

From the saddle, the route drops south into the head of the North Fork of the Swan River; this is the most hazardous spot to negotiate. The initial 200 feet of the slope is steep enough to avalanche and can be unstable. Analyze for avalanche potential. If conditions are unstable, perhaps you should turn around and opt to spend the rest of the day skiing the glades in Sts. John drainage, as there is not an alternative route to bypass the descent into the North Fork. If conditions are stable, drop off the saddle and ski down into the south-facing bowl. Follow the natural contour of the valley as it hooks west-southwest. Ski into the woods on the north (right) side of the creek and search for a scant trail that quickly turns into a distinct jeep path that is also traveled by snowmobiles. A quick 4-mile descent along this road drops through thick trees to the wide Swan River valley, marked by large mine tailings from 19th-century placer mining.

Turn upstream and make your way along the flat, snowmobile-packed road on the east side of the tailings piles. Cross to the west side of the Swan River at the first possible road crossing. Once across follow the road to the left and begin the next section of climbing (up Georgia Gulch). This leg of the trip gains over 1,500 feet of elevation in a relatively short time and should not be underestimated. Climb directly up the gully on the left side of the creek and mine tailings. After 400 feet of elevation gain the strenuous climb breaks to the southeast out of Georgia Gulch and onto the ridge on its southeast side. Contour back up along the ridge and pass over Humbug Hill and a trail intersection leading off to the northeast (right). This second pass is over 11,000 feet and overlooks French Gulch and the Tenmile Range to the west. Leave the shelter of the woods and descend into French Gulch along a treeless slope.

Once on the floor of French Gulch it is a long 4-mile skate or double-pole into town. If you haven't left a car here, proceed (ski or walk) west on the wide plowed roadbed. When you reach a big intersection marked by a high-tension power line tower, follow the road to the left, which quickly reaches the city limits marked by the re-entry into thicker trees, houses and condominiums. This is Wellington Avenue, which leads directly into the center of town (hot tub time!).

# 96  HUNKIDORI MINE

**DESCRIPTION: Winter ski tour, narrow mine road that traverses north-facing hillside into small side valley**
**SKILL LEVEL: Intermediate***
**TIME: Three-quarters day**
**DISTANCE: Up to 6 miles round trip**
**ELEVATION CHANGE: 700 feet total gain**
**STARTING ELEVATION: 10,300 feet**
**AVALANCHE TERRAIN: Some avalanche terrain encountered; easily avoided**
**USGS 7.5 MINUTE MAPS: Keystone, 1974-PR, Montezuma, 1974-PI**
**MAP: page 174**

***NOVICE HIGHLIGHT: The first 2 miles, to the turnoff into Hunki-dori basin, are more gentle than the rest of the tour. Novice skiers should find this section challenging but manageable.**

This is one of the lesser-known alternatives in the Montezuma area. It begins on the Sts. John road, then traverses west above the main Montezuma valley into the Hunkidori drainage. Most of the tour is in dense trees on a north-facing slope, so snow conditions are good throughout the season. The upper section in Hunkidori Creek is somewhat steep, requiring solid intermediate skills and a controlled descent, but the rest of the tour is suitable for novices.

Take US 6 to the easternmost turnoff for the Keystone ski area. Immediately after turning off the highway, take the first left turn onto County Road 5 and follow it for approximately 6 miles to Montezuma. The tour starts from the center of Montezuma and takes the Sts. John Creek road, County Road 275 (see tour 94) past the first switchback into the Sts. John valley. As you round the corner into the Sts. John valley take a right fork down and across the creek. Shortly after crossing the creek this road descends a bit and traverses around the hillside heading west. After approximately 2 miles of traversing through dense forest, the road turns up into Hunkidori Creek. Continue up the left side of the creek for another mile past some switchbacks before crossing to the right side of the valley where the old Hunkidori Mine is located. There are some potentially dangerous avalanche paths that come right into the old mine site: Although tempting for a short telemark run, they should be approached with caution.

The return trip is via the same route.

# 97  KEYSTONE GULCH

DESCRIPTION: Winter ski tour, moderately inclined road
SKILL LEVEL: Novice to intermediate
TIME: Full day
DISTANCE: 11.4 miles round trip
ELEVATION CHANGE: 1,570 feet total gain
STARTING ELEVATION: 9,230 feet
AVALANCHE TERRAIN: None
USGS 7.5 MINUTE MAP: Keystone, 1974-PR
MAP: page 174

Keystone Gulch cleaves deeply into the landscape immediately west of the Keystone ski area. The route follows an old mining road through thick stands of timber, eventually climbing to the Erickson Mine, high on the southwest side of Keystone Mountain. Though the tour gains nearly 1,600 feet in elevation, the gentle road makes a perfect outing for novices and intermediate skiers alike. It is also a nice sheltered spot for advanced skiers and ski racers to put in a few hours of exercise.

The trailhead lies west of the ski area on Keystone Road. Drive on US 6 and take one of many exits that access the ski area road. Whether you are coming from Loveland Pass or Summit County, a simple route takes you to the stoplight on US 6 just west of the ski area administration building (near the gas station/food mart). Turn south toward the ski area and the Snake River. Drive to a fork and turn right. Proceed to the small parking area (plowed along the road) directly across from the Flying Dutchman Condominiums (0.75 miles west of the ski complex and 0.6 miles east of the old townsite of Keystone). Park alongside the road or in a small parking area on the south side of the road.

Leave the parking area and ski into the woods to the south along the obvious roadbed. Stay on the east side of the creek and double-pole up the gentle grade, eventually crossing a tiny meadow at 1.2 miles. The road makes a tiny dogleg from south to southeast at the edge of a second, larger meadow. Re-enter the thick trees and maintain the gentle climb to the southeast, crossing to the west side of the drainage for a brief spell.

Now the road climbs slightly east and runs farther away from the creek. Your solitude is interrupted near the 3.4-mile mark, as you pass the base of the North Peak extension of the Keystone ski area—peculiar to see in an area seemingly miles from civilization. High on the right are large patches of stunted timber and roads where loggers once operated. After passing the ski area begin a large circular contour around Point 11,661 ("North Peak"). As you swing around to the east the road climbs more steeply north of the creek. Continue east until you reach the first sharp switchback.

This last section is more intermediate in nature and is fast on the descent. If you have enough time, push farther up the road or leave the road and explore the creekbed as it heads toward treeline high to the east.

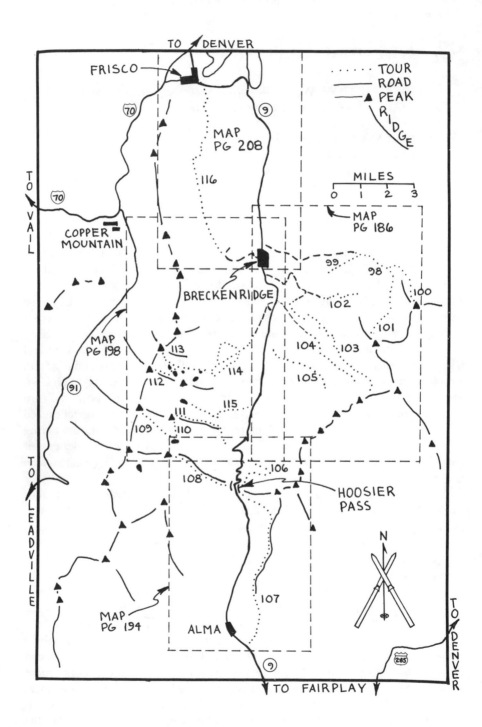

# CHAPTER NINE

# BRECKENRIDGE AND HOOSIER PASS

## INTRODUCTION

The Breckenridge–Hoosier Pass area contains a superb selection of out-standing tours: everything from track skiing to powder bowls to high peaks, all within a very compact area. Throughout the winter, Hoosier Pass holds consistently good powder. If you don't have time for a full tour, just drive to the pass and take a few powder runs on either side of the road. Those looking for track skiing will find that the trails leading north from Breckenridge to Frisco are usually in good condition and very pleasant. When spring arrives, the peaks of the Tenmile Range, along with Bald Mountain and Mount Guyot, offer some of the most classic ski descents in Colorado.

Ski conditions in the Breckenridge area are generally very good, but they can vary quite a bit from place to place, year to year, and even day to day. It is possible for marginal conditions to exist in the lower valleys while at the same time the powder is great on Hoosier Pass. Usually, the area is not as windy as the Front Range, but this too can vary. Boreas Pass and the high peaks can be exceptionally windy on any given day, and the next day be absolutely calm. The best way to gauge the conditions is to pay close attention to the ski report for the Breckenridge ski area. If there is adequate depth and powder or packed powder conditions, the skiing will probably be good. When you are considering spring ski descents, "Baldy" and Guyot tend to have softer, slushier snow than the more windpacked peaks of the Tenmile Range.

## HISTORY

Evidence of Breckenridge's colorful mining history can be seen throughout the area. Almost every valley contains the remnants of forgotten dreams. The town, now transformed into a ski resort, still retains much of the original architecture and flavor of a small mining community. Quaint Victorian boutiques and shops, adorned with carved wooden icing and gingerbread trim, line Main Street. But scars of the mining era remain too. Huge unsightly rock piles line the Blue River basin from Breckenridge to Frisco. They are the remains of Breckenridge's third mining boom—

dredging. The first prospecting began in 1859, when Ruben Spalding recovered 13 cents worth of gold from his first pan. The second pan yielded 27 cents. That was it. Spalding traded his mule for two sacks of flour and some lumber. Working in ankle-deep water, with his feet wrapped in saddle blankets, Spalding netted a chilly $10 his first day. William Iliff did much better, scratching out $7,000 in gold from a 40-square-foot section of riverbed. The next spring, Iliff spilled the beans in Denver, and several thousand men stampeded into the area.

In the 1860s early placer mining (mining of sand or gravel beds containing gold and other minerals extracted by washing) used powerful hydraulic hoses to flush the ore into sluices. One of these relics remains standing in front of the Breckenridge courthouse. The profitable beds played out quickly and most of the miners soon moved on to better prospects.

To improve its chances of getting a U.S. Post Office designation, the young town named itself after Vice President John C. Breckinridge. When the Civil War broke out, and Breckinridge sided with the South, the *i* in the town's name was changed to an *e* to avoid any association with the rebels' cause. In 1862, Breckenridge became the county seat of Summit County, after its residents sneaked in by moonlight and stole the records from nearby Parkville, the original county seat.

The discovery of gold in veins and fissures brought Breckenridge's second gold rush in the 1880s. By 1885 there were 2,000 residents. Log cabins were replaced by the more elaborate, gingerbread-trimmed Victorian houses and false-fronted stores. In 1891, Colorado enacted a saloon law that closed all saloons on Sundays and weeknights after midnight. The law was especially unpopular in Breckenridge. In fact, an editorial in the *Summit County Journal*, August 1, went so far as to say "The law was conceived in the brain of a fanatic, enacted by a body of imbeciles, signed by a dough face and in a camp like Breckenridge would be enforced only by an impracticable enthusiast." Florida Passmore, the resident Methodist minister, was ardently in favor of the law and successfully crusaded to have it enforced. But his crusade did not go without retaliation: A few weeks later an unidentified gang of vandals dynamited the church bell.

In 1898, Pug Ryan and his gang robbed the Denver Hotel. Tracked to a cabin near Kokomo, a small mining town located on Fremont Pass, the gang was appre-hended and the ensuing shootout left four dead. Ryan escaped, but was caught four years later in Seattle when the tattoo "Pug" on his left arm gave him away.

It was during the same year of 1898 that Ben Stanley Revett launched the first dredge. Huge conglomerations of buckets and machinery churned up mountains of streambed and deposited them on the banks of the Blue River. Dredging produced as much as $20,000 per week and ran for many years. The dredges finally ceased operating during World War II, and the town's population quickly diminished. Then in 1962 the ski area was opened. Breckenridge was revitalized and gradually transformed into the fashionable community we recognize today.

# 98 FRENCH GULCH AND LITTLE FRENCH GULCH

**DESCRIPTION: Winter ski tour, pleasant mining roads up side valleys**
**SKILL LEVEL: Novice***
**TIME: Half day or more**
**DISTANCE: Optional, up to 7 miles round trip**
**ELEVATION CHANGE: Up to 1,200 feet total gain**
**STARTING ELEVATION: 10,280 feet**
**AVALANCHE TERRAIN: Route crosses avalanche runout zones; can be dangerous during high-hazard periods**
**USGS 7.5 MINUTE MAP: Boreas Pass, 1957**
**MAP: page 186**

**\*INTERMEDIATE HIGHLIGHT: The alternate route up Little French Gulch is shorter but quite a bit steeper.**

This scenic winter tour will suit a wide range of abilities and tastes. It is a good choice for large groups. The tour follows a gentle road up the north side of French Gulch. Open glades at the end of the valley will please telemark enthusiasts, and some good short runs will please those just learning how to maneuver their skis in powder. A good side-trip variation up Little French Gulch offers a more challenging downhill trail run.

To find the trailhead, turn off Colo. 9 onto County Road 450 just north of Breckenridge. After a few hundred feet, take County Road 460 under an ore-cart gateway. Go through a housing subdivision and continue east up the main valley to the trailhead parking lot. Ski around the gate and follow the road as it makes its way up a densely forested valley. When you've gone 1.2 miles, you'll come to the turnoff for Little French Gulch. This variation follows a steep narrow road for another 1.5 miles, ending at treeline in the narrow bowl below Mount Guyot. It is unwise to venture any farther, as this area is vulnerable to very large avalanches.

Continuing up the main French Gulch Tour, you'll slowly gain elevation as you alternate through wide open meadows and thickly timbered forest. As you get farther up valley, it is necessary to cross under some rather large avalanche paths that come off Mount Guyot. The upper bowl and glades below Bald Mountain (the high peak to the right at the end of the valley) have potential for some good telemark skiing.

Return via the same route.

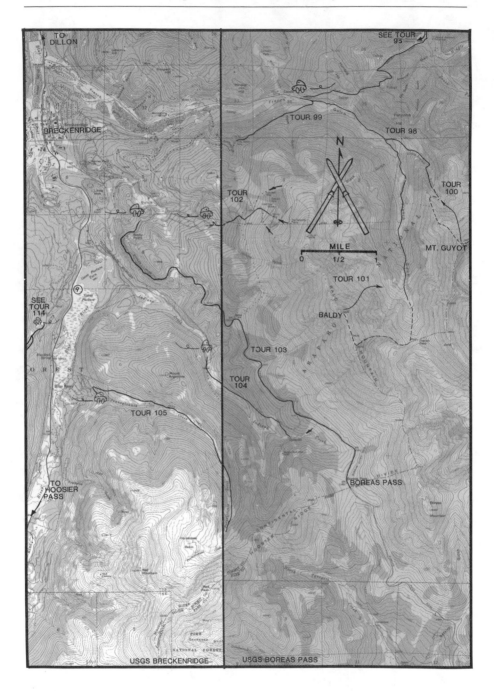

# 99 Sally Barber Mine

**DESCRIPTION: Winter ski tour, gentle, secluded mine road**
**SKILL LEVEL: Novice**
**TIME: Quarter to half day**
**DISTANCE: 2.6 miles round trip**
**ELEVATION CHANGE: 400 feet total gain**
**STARTING ELEVATION: 10,280 feet**
**AVALANCHE TERRAIN: None**
**USGS 7.5 MINUTE MAPS: Boreas Pass, 1957, Breckenridge, 1987-**
**PR**
**MAP: page 186**

The secluded old road up to the Sally Barber Mine makes a perfect setting for a short, relaxed family outing in historic Summit County. It is an excellent introduction to cross-country skiing. The tour is short and may only take a few hours to complete. It has a northern exposure, which means there is usually plenty of snow from November through May. You may extend the tour to make a loop trip.

To reach the trailhead turn off Colo. 9 onto County Road 450 just north of Breckenridge. After a few hundred feet go right, taking County Road 460 under an ore-cart gateway. Go through a housing subdivision another half mile to an intersection. Bear left and continue east up the valley 3 miles to the end of the plowed road.

From the parking area ski up the unplowed road a few hundred yards to a road that cuts down and right toward the creek. Follow this road as it crosses the creek and gradually gains elevation, cutting back west across the opposite hillside. After another mile of pleasant forested road, you'll reach the Sally Barber Mine. From here you can either return along the same route or keep going. If you keep going and take a right at either the first or second fork, you'll end up in French Gulch about 2 miles below the parking area.

*Sally Barber Mine, Kurt Lankford photo.*

# 100 MOUNT GUYOT (13,370 FEET)

**DESCRIPTION: Spring ski-mountaineering route, beautiful peak east of Breckenridge**
**SKILL LEVEL: Advanced**
**TIME: Full day**
**DISTANCE: 5.6 miles round trip**
**ELEVATION CHANGE: 2,990 feet total gain**
**STARTING ELEVATION: 10,280 feet**
**AVALANCHE TERRAIN: Mostly avalanche terrain; wait for spring consolidation**
**USGS 7.5 MINUTE MAP: Boreas Pass, 1957**
**MAP: page 186**

The southern skyline of Summit County is broken by two pronounced solitary summits. The peak on the left with the slightly tilted, truncated summit is Mount Guyot. Its broad north face holds a snowfield visible to most of Summit County for most of the year. This snowfield makes for a superb late spring/early summer ski descent while providing an equally fine panorama of the entire Blue River valley. The approach hike is somewhat long but the nearly 1,800-foot plunge into Little French Gulch makes this trip well worth the effort.

Approach Mount Guyot via French Gulch road by turning east off Colo. 9 just north of Breckenridge on County Road 450. Turn right on County Road 460, pass through the French Gulch housing subdivision and continue up valley through a plethora of tailings piles, mining scars and obsolete ore-extraction equipment. The road here is quite good, and soon you will arrive at a metal gate preventing further vehicular progress onto private property. Many local skiers advance farther up the valley on mountain bikes, carrying their skis.

Either way, once you are on foot, proceed to the junction of French Gulch and Little French Gulch roads. Little French Gulch road splits off to the left and climbs to some old mining structures that sit at the base of the north face snowfield. Mount Guyot is a relatively simple mountain with many possible ascent routes. The least complicated is to attain the northwest ridge. This presents a straightforward climb to the summit, crossing an abrupt shoulder before the final summit cone is attacked. An alternative method for climbing Mount Guyot is to walk the well-worn French Gulch dirt road past cabins and houses scattered throughout the trees. Carry on until you reach a point in the valley directly west of the shoulder on the northwest ridge. You can now attain the northwest ridge by climbing straight up the treeless, grassy and rocky avalanche slopes, staying close to the remaining trees to the left. Although arduous and steep, this approach is quick and avoids the problem of tackling Little French Gulch road, which is usually choked with late-season snowbanks.

Continuing to the summit, you will notice that the snowfield does not completely reach the top, usually ending a hundred or so feet below the unusually trapezoidal summit ridge. Leave your skis at the top of the snowfield and scamper up to the summit cairn for tremendous views of the Blue River valley to the north, South Park (to the south) and the Tenmile Range to the west. The precipitous southern cirque is worth peering into also.

On skis, you will find the massive snowfield a giant playground for carving turns. Time your descent to strike a balance between early-morning crust and late-afternoon bottomless "mashed potato" spring crud. Toward the bottom of the descent the north face funnels through a ravine before fanning out into the forest below. This entire area is still relatively wide and of a moderate grade (20 to 30 degrees), but stay alert to spring sluffs which can pass through this area. Descend as far as possible (a good rule of thumb for all skiers!). Pass the old mining structures and aim for the prominent road on the west side of Little French Gulch that leads back to French Gulch. On the road, ski as far as the snowpack allows. The parking area is usually about a half hour's walk away.

# 101 BALD MOUNTAIN—"BALDY CHUTES"

## (13,684 FEET)

**DESCRIPTION: Spring ski-mountaineering descent, approach hike, long north-facing couloir**
**SKILL LEVEL: Advanced**
**TIME: Full day**
**DISTANCE: 9.5 miles round trip**
**ELEVATION CHANGE: 3,400 feet total gain**
**STARTING ELEVATION: 10,280 feet**
**AVALANCHE TERRAIN: Mostly avalanche terrain; wait for spring consolidation**
**USGS 7.5 MINUTE MAP: Boreas Pass, 1957**
**MAP: page 186**

Bald Mountain is, as the name implies, a rather bland mountain with acres of tundra, and a long rolling summit. It does, however, have one outstanding feature—a long snow couloir leading from the summit all the way down to the trees on the north side. This makes it an excellent choice for a spring ski descent.

The normal approach is from French Gulch. Turn east off Colo. 9 just north of Breckenridge on County Road 450. After a few hundred feet, take County Road 460 under an ore-cart gateway. Go through a housing subdivision, and continue east up the main valley as far as possible to a locked gate. Leave your car and continue on foot up valley, passing several private cabins. You'll soon break out of the trees and get a glimpse of the spectacular descent couloir. The quickest way to the top is to go all the way up the valley to French Pass, then follow the east ridge up the summit.

The descent is straightforward, once you find the couloir and muster the confidence to make that first turn. It is not as steep as it looks from the valley, but be cautious and knowledgeable about avalanches—this couloir is prone to large wet slides. Plan your descent for the safest part of the day, generally in the early morning.

An alternate approach for this route starts from Boreas Pass. This is a little shorter on the way up but requires a car shuttle or lengthy traverse around the mountain to get back out.

# 102 Bald Mountain—"Baldy Bowl"

**DESCRIPTION: Winter ski tour, short and mildly strenuous trail to high-mountain telemark area**
**SKILL LEVEL: Intermediate***
**TIME: Half day**
**DISTANCE: 3 miles round trip**
**ELEVATION CHANGE: 1,440 feet total gain**
**STARTING ELEVATION: 10,680 feet**
**AVALANCHE TERRAIN: Route crosses avalanche slopes; can be dangerous during high-hazard periods**
**USGS 7.5 MINUTE MAPS: Breckenridge, 1987-PR, Boreas Pass, 1957**
**MAP: page 186**

**\*ADVANCED HIGHLIGHT: This tour features a large slope for downhill telemark action. Above the main mining structures are a large bowl and several glades to ski.**

Bald Mountain sits above the town of Breckenridge to the southeast. Along this mountain's southwest flank, the Boreas Pass Railroad grade creeps over the divide toward South Park, while to the north and east, French Gulch carves into the landscape. On the west side of its north ridge lie the remains of several mines, including the Carbonite, the Gold Eagle, the Tommy Mine and the Corporal. In addition to the weathered buildings and the ore tram which climbs the mountain to the Carbonite Mine, a beautiful bowl features a mixture of open slopes, timbered glades and a relatively short approach. Bald Mountain is not only bathed in Colorado mining history but it is often drenched with light powder snow and is a fantastic spot to immerse oneself in the joys and gymnastics of backcountry telemark skiing.

"Baldy Bowl" is reached by driving to the south edge of Breckenridge and turning left (east) onto the Boreas Pass road. Follow this road for 2 miles until the second crossing of Illinois Gulch. Once past the small bridge over Illinois Gulch take the first left onto County Road 525. Drive east up this steep road, passing many small mountain homes hidden in the trees. After several hundred yards the road switchbacks to the southwest. At the apex of the switchback is a tiny parking spot where an old mining road leads off to the east.

Park here and begin skiing east in a small meadow. Aim for two weathered mining cabins sitting right next to Illinois Gulch. Double-pole past the cabins, then quickly switchback northwest, after crossing the creek. This switchback climbs a small open hill and re-enters the trees at the top of the embankment. At this spot a little road cuts back directly to the right (east). Hop on this and ski into thicker woods. Try to follow the main road through here as you aim for the bowl, which is sitting high to the east and marked by several large mining structures standing on the ridge. A maze of small roads and trails (not marked on the map) crisscross through this area. The shortest route, aside from bushwhacking, heads east, turns left at a "T" intersection, then turns right at a second fork and climbs to the base of the bowl. The total distance is under 0.5 miles.

The base of Baldy Bowl contains the skeleton of a large and partially destroyed mine building and an old but well-maintained (private) cabin. The Carbonite Mine is the brown building near the crest of the ridge, well above treeline. Skiers can choose between many routes up and down on this slope—they are all superb when avalanche hazard is low. Just be careful of tree stumps! To the left of the line of bleached wooden towers that rise up to the Carbonite Mine is a large patch of trees. These trees hide some fine glades that always seem to contain powder snow. With an early start, you can easily wear yourself out climbing and descending.

# 103 BOREAS PASS

**DESCRIPTION: Winter ski tour, gentle railroad grade, good scenery**
**SKILL LEVEL: Novice**
**TIME: Full day**
**DISTANCE: Optional, up to 11 miles round trip**
**ELEVATION CHANGE: 840 feet total gain**
**STARTING ELEVATION: 10,360 feet**
**AVALANCHE TERRAIN: Route crosses avalanche runout zones; can be dangerous during high-hazard periods**
**USGS 7.5 MINUTE MAPS: Breckenridge, 1987-PR, Boreas Pass, 1957**
**MAP: page 186**

When the wind is calm and the snow is plentiful, there is no better novice tour in the Breckenridge area than the Boreas Pass road. The route up follows the gentle 2.8-percent grade of the old Denver, South Park and Pacific Railroad bed. Although most of the route is below treeline, it's best to pick a calm day when the road is not being raked by high winds.

Take Colo. 9 to the Boreas Pass road, the first main intersection south of

Breckenridge. Turn east and proceed 3.4 miles up the main road, a circuitous route that climbs first north then back south, to the plowed winter parking area. The tour starts by rounding Rocky Point and passing through a large roadcut, where you can get spectacular views of the Tenmile Range and Breckenridge ski area across the valley. Bakers Tank at 2.3 miles makes a good stopping point for a half-day tour. If you have time, the road continues for 3 additional miles to the top of Boreas Pass, where ruins of the old railroad station still stand. The last mile up to the pass has very sparse ground cover, so be sure to take adequate clothing to protect from the wind.

# 104 INDIANA CREEK

**DESCRIPTION: Winter ski tour, gentle mine road**
**SKILL LEVEL: Novice**
**TIME: Half day**
**DISTANCE: 3.2 miles round trip**
**ELEVATION CHANGE: 500 feet total gain**
**STARTING ELEVATION: 10,400 feet**
**AVALANCHE TERRAIN: Some avalanche terrain encountered; easily avoided**
**USGS 7.5 MINUTE MAPS: Breckenridge, 1987-PR, Boreas Pass, 1957**
**MAP: page 186**

This tour is not as well known as other novice trails in the area but the terrain and the skiing are every bit as good. The tour starts on the private land of the Spruce Valley Ranch. The owners discourage snowmobiles but have allowed access to cross-country skiers.

To reach the trailhead go south from Breckenridge toward Hoosier Pass and turn left after 1.2 miles. This is the first left turn past the turnoff for Boreas Pass. Continue up this road, bearing left at every fork, for about 3 miles to the entrance to Spruce Valley Ranch, where parking for a small number of cars is available. Begin skiing up the continuation of the road through private land. The route stays on the left side of the creek all the way up valley to the old abandoned mine site of Dyersville. There is a right fork about 0.25 miles up as you enter a large open meadow. This fork crosses the creek and heads up onto the ridge between Indiana Creek and Pennsylvania Creek. Although not the normal route (the left fork is), this makes an enjoyable tour with more intermediate skiing. There is another fork a little farther up valley that leads to some private cabins on the hillside to the left below the Boreas Pass road. Go past this fork, right, staying down in the valley on the left side of the creek.

Dyersville, at the end of the valley, has several interesting old cabins and ruins. It was the residence of Father John Lewis Dyer, the "Snowshoe Itinerant" who skied and preached to the miners of this area during the early gold rush days.

It is possible to extend the trip up to Boreas Pass (an additional 1.7 miles) by taking a short steep road north from just below Dyersville. This road climbs up the hillside to the Boreas Pass road, where you turn right and continue 1.2 miles to the top of the pass. The bowl between Dyersville and Boreas Pass has some nice open glades for an enjoyable downhill run on the return trip.

# 105 PENNSYLVANIA CREEK

DESCRIPTION: Winter ski tour, moderate mine road up side valley
SKILL LEVEL: Novice to intermediate
TIME: Two-thirds day
DISTANCE: Up to 8 miles round trip
ELEVATION CHANGE: 1,340 feet total gain
STARTING ELEVATION: 10,300 feet
AVALANCHE TERRAIN: Some avalanche terrain encountered; easily avoided
USGS 7.5 MINUTE MAPS: Breckenridge, 1987-PR, Boreas Pass, 1957
MAP: page 186

This is a good tour when the avalanche danger is running high. Once you gain the first half mile, the tour settles into an easy, gradual climb into Horseshoe Basin at the upper end of the valley. Snowmobiles occasionally tour the valley too, but their trails make the return trip faster and more enjoyable.

Finding the trailhead can be a bit confusing, so pay close attention to the map. Take Colo. 9 south out of Breckenridge to Blue River Estates. Turn left and proceed to the third (main) right turn. Continue up over a hill and around a bend. Here you take a sharp right onto a branch road. Bend left, go straight across Pennsylvania Creek and eventually switchback right to a limited parking area near the end of the plowed road 1.1 miles from Colo. 9. Take care not to block anyone's private driveway.

The first switchback of the tour is steep, but from there it is straightforward and enjoyable, following a road most of the way up valley. You can stay on the road and go only a short distance, making this a novice tour, or continue into Horseshoe Basin for a lengthier intermediate tour.

The return trip is back down the road via the same route.

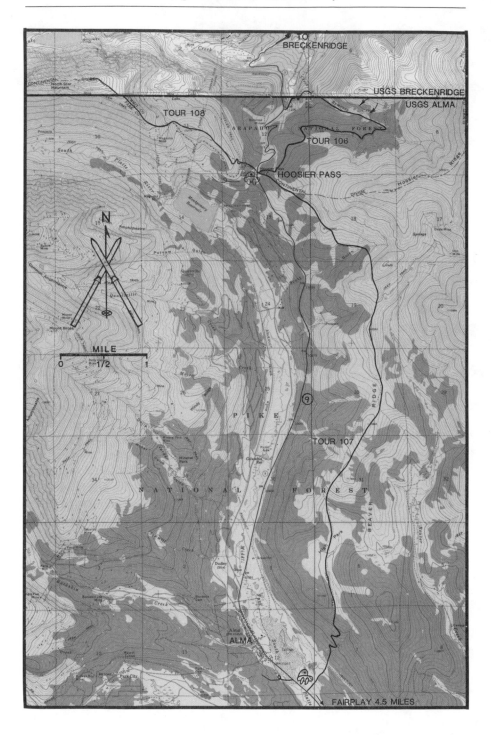

# 106 THE FLUME (BEMROSE CREEK)

·DESCRIPTION: Winter ski tour, all downhill from summit of
Hoosier Pass, car shuttle recommended
SKILL LEVEL: Novice*
TIME: Quarter day
DISTANCE: 4 miles
ELEVATION CHANGE: 450 feet loss
STARTING ELEVATION: 11,539 feet
AVALANCHE TERRAIN: Some avalanche terrain encountered;
easily avoided
USGS 7.5 MINUTE MAP: Alma, 1970, Breckenridge, 1987-PR
MAP: page 194

*INTERMEDIATE/ADVANCED HIGHLIGHT: There are some good
telemark glades midway through the tour at the high northeast end of
Bemrose Creek.

This is a great little run for those days when you crawl out of the sack at the
crack of noon. The snow is always good, and there should be plenty of time for making
turns in the glades of the spectacular alpine bowl midway through the route.

Leave a shuttle car on the north side of Hoosier Pass at a point marked "BM
11,106" on the USGS Alma topographic map (see map, page 194). There are two
abandoned mining cabins at this plowed unmarked turnout. It is located 9 miles from
Breckenridge past the first set of hairpin turns and 0.7 miles above the sharp left curve
at Monte Cristo Creek. The tour starts from the parking lot at the top of Hoosier Pass.
Cross the road to the east and find the forest service sign that points out the route to
Bemrose Creek. It follows a road that contours around the side of the mountain,
heading northeast. After traversing clear around into Bemrose Creek the route drops
down through open glades into a shallow bowl. Once in the bowl, follow the creek
out to an unplowed road that curves back left toward the summit of Hoosier Pass.
Leave this road when it drops down and right, cutting instead 100 yards across an open
meadow to the Hoosier Pass road where the tour ends and your car shuttle awaits.

# 107 BEAVER RIDGE

**DESCRIPTION:** Winter ski tour from Hoosier Pass to Alma, much unmarked backcountry terrain, mostly intermediate, car shuttle required
**SKILL LEVEL:** Advanced
**TIME:** Full day
**DISTANCE:** 8 miles
**ELEVATION CHANGE:** 900 feet total gain/2,300 feet total loss
**STARTING ELEVATION:** 11,539 feet
**AVALANCHE TERRAIN:** Route crosses avalanche slopes; prone to skier-triggered avalanches during high-hazard periods
**USGS 7.5 MINUTE MAP:** Alma, 1970
**MAP:** page 194

Imagine linked telemark turns down glade after glade along sparsely wooded treeline knolls; add a few short stretches exposed to the elements above treeline; then break trail through deep powder in the trees, all the while a little unsure whether you're on the right track. That is what this outstanding tour has to offer.

The tour ends at an unplowed access road on the east side of Colo. 9, 0.4 miles south of Alma. A car shuttle must be arranged to return from this point to the summit of Hoosier Pass where the tour begins.

From the parking lot at Hoosier Pass, cross the road and ski east through the trees, heading for treeline. Before you reach treeline, begin contouring around to the right. Follow the line of least resistance and head for a gentle point on the spur ridge to the south. This point is marked as a prospect on the map. From the prospect point, continue up and across the Scott Gulch bowl, heading for the ridgetop knoll that is the top of Beaver Ridge. A few sections along this first part of the tour traverse avalanche slopes: When conditions are unstable, avoid these by staying farther down in the trees.

Once you are on the ridge follow it south, going over and around several gently rolling knolls. From a saddle 2.5 miles down the ridge, descend through a large open glade into a small valley, heading for a line of high-tension wires. This small valley is marked "High Park" on the map. Where it begins to spill out into the large valley below Alma, pick up a road that switchbacks down the last steep section at the bottom. Cross the main valley to the highway 0.4 miles south of Alma. Car shuttle to get back to the top of the pass.

# 108 NORTHSTAR MOUNTAIN (13,350 FEET)

**DESCRIPTION: Spring (or winter) ski-mountaineering route**
**SKILL LEVEL: Mostly intermediate with a few advanced stretches**
**TIME: Two-thirds day**
**DISTANCE: 5 miles round trip**
**ELEVATION CHANGE: 1,900 feet total gain**
**STARTING ELEVATION: 11,540 feet**
**AVALANCHE TERRAIN: Route crosses avalanche slopes; prone to skier-triggered avalanches during high-hazard periods**
**USGS 7.5 MINUTE MAPS: Alma, 1970, Breckenridge, 1987-PR**
**MAP: page 194**

A good spring tour, it can also be excellent in midwinter, if conditions above treeline are not too windy and avalanche hazard is low. Northstar is located along the ridge running west from the top of Hoosier Pass. Except for three moderately steep sections—one at the beginning, one midway and one at the top—the ridge is relatively gradual along its entire length. Because the approach starts high and the ascent remains gradual, this tour requires less effort than most of the other mountaineering tours in this book. When conditions are favorable, it is highly recommended as a good introduction to ski mountaineering.

The route is straightforward. Park at the top of Hoosier Pass and head west up the ridge all the way to the top. Descend via the same route. A mining road that contours along below the first half of the ridge on the south side makes a good alternative when the ridge crest is blown clear of snow. For those who can't resist the temptation, there are beautiful open glades that drop off into the valleys on either side of the ridge. If you decide to descend these, just remember that you have to climb back up to the pass.

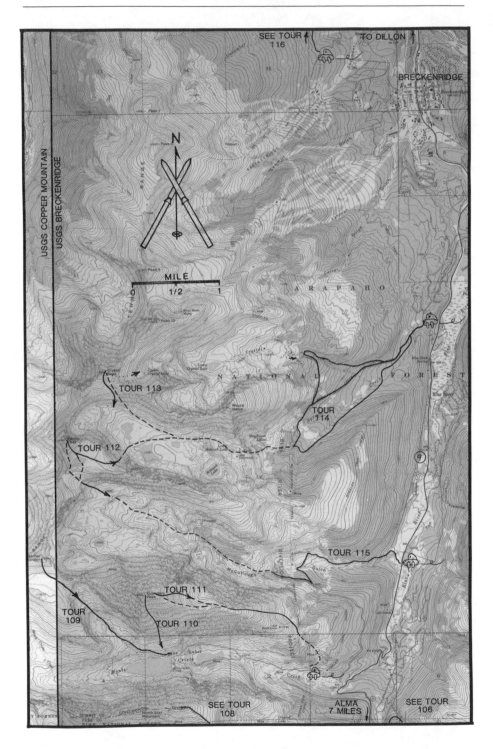

# 109 FLETCHER MOUNTAIN (13,951 FEET)

**DESCRIPTION: Spring ski-mountaineering descent, approach hike, high peak above huge snow-filled bowl**
**SKILL LEVEL: Advanced**
**TIME: Full day**
**DISTANCE: 4 miles or more round trip**
**ELEVATION CHANGE: 3,751 feet total gain**
**STARTING ELEVATION: 10,720 feet (dam spillway)**
**AVALANCHE TERRAIN: Mostly avalanche terrain; wait for spring consolidation**
**USGS 7.5 MINUTE MAPS: Breckenridge, 1987-PR, Copper Mountain, 1987-PR**
**MAP: page 198**

The summit of Fletcher Mountain is nearly 14,000 feet, but it rarely sees an ascent, because it is situated right behind (to the west of) the imposing mass of Quandary Peak. It really deserves more attention. The descent off Fletcher is a varied and enjoyable ride down a succession of spectacular hanging valleys. A southeastern exposure and plentiful winter snow ensure good ski conditions throughout the spring season.

From Breckenridge, drive south on Colo. 9 up the Blue River valley. As the road begins to climb, pass the first pair of hairpin turns and continue for another mile to Monte Cristo Creek. This is the first valley north of Hoosier Pass on the west side of the road. Turn off and follow a dirt road west through a small development of cabins as far as possible. Late in the season you should be able to drive almost all the way to the spillway at upper Blue Lake Reservoir. As you go up valley, be sure to notice the old mine ruins some 500 feet up on the sheer north side of Northstar Mountain. Remnants of a time when gold fever swept the Rockies, these old mines are excellent examples of how tenacious and determined these miners were.

The route begins from the northeast corner of the reservoir and contours up into a narrow hanging valley on the southwest side of Quandary Peak. Head straight up this valley, eventually topping out in another secondary hanging valley. Continue up the final 700 feet to the summit. The angle of the descent is steepest near the top, approaching 30 degrees. You may want to descend a bit before putting your skis back on, but once you do, it's a fairly continuous schuss all the way back to the upper end of the reservoir.

# 110 QUANDARY PEAK—SOUTH COULOIR
## (14,264 FEET)

**DESCRIPTION: Spring ski-mountaineering route, spectacular and difficult**
**SKILL LEVEL: Advanced +**
**TIME: Full day**
**DISTANCE: 1.6 miles round trip from spillway**
**ELEVATION CHANGE: 2,545 feet total gain**
**STARTING ELEVATION: 11,720 feet (dam spillway)**
**AVALANCHE TERRAIN: Mostly avalanche terrain; wait for spring consolidation**
**USGS 7.5 MINUTE MAP: Breckenridge, 1987-PR**
**MAP: page 198**

To put it simply, a ski descent of Quandary Peak's south gully is a spectacular and exciting event. Dropping over 2,000 feet directly off the 14,265-foot summit, this couloir will test your edging skills, turning ability and bravado. Fortunately, the overall angle of the descent rarely exceeds 35 to 40 degrees, with the most difficult section pushing approximately 45 degrees for roughly 200 feet. This route is not for the neophyte ski mountaineer, and it behooves prudent skiers to familiarize themselves with the route before committing to this adventure. However, for those comfortable skiing at this level, a successful descent is a rewarding achievement.

This tour begins on the summit of Quandary Peak, necessitating an ascent of the peak itself. Quandary ranks as one of the simpler 14,000-foot peaks to approach and climb, with the east ridge the most popular route. A direct ascent of the south couloir, however, can provide valuable information on the route's nature and daily condition.

Both the east ridge and south gully ascent routes begin in the Monte Cristo Creek valley, approached from Colo. 9. The turnoff lies roughly 10 miles south of Breckenridge and a little over 7 miles north of Alma on the north side of Hoosier Pass.

For the quickest access to the east ridge, drive about 0.4 miles west and park near where an old mining road climbs north into the forest above the new housing developments. On foot, follow the road as far as possible, then strike out cross-country, aiming for the gentle eastern extension of the east ridge. There is no exact route here but the forest is broken by many clearings that allow for easy visual route finding. Once you are on the treeless east ridge, gaining the summit is a matter of following the ridge to the top, passing a large flat shoulder at about 13,150 feet.

If you prefer to climb the south gully itself, drive on the same road as far west as the late spring snowpack allows. From there, continue west on foot until you reach upper Blue Lake's dam and spillway. From here the route towers above in the shape of an hourglass.

The descent begins on an easterly, angling snowfield. You can start off carving nice warm-up turns; after several hundred feet, begin to swing back toward the west as the ski route drops through a narrow traversing passage to the top of the couloir proper. The angle of the slope increases noticeably at this spot, where the most challenging and confined section begins. After this crucial section is passed, the skiing once again becomes less demanding and quite enjoyable as you descend hundreds of feet with renewed confidence. The descent ends wherever the snow meets the summer tundra—normally requiring only a short walk back to the lake.

It is important to mention that the exact conditions of this ski descent can change daily. The later in the year, the greater the probability that you will encounter a few protruding rocks and small patches of ice. With the coming of summer the snowpack tends to stabilize and the frequency of snow sluffs decreases. Inspect the conditions and proceed with caution.

# 111 QUANDARY PEAK—EAST RIDGE (14,264 FEET)

**DESCRIPTION: Spring ski-mountaineering route, very popular**
**SKILL LEVEL: Intermediate to advanced**
**TIME: Full day**
**DISTANCE: 5 miles round trip**
**ELEVATION CHANGE: 3,265 feet total gain**
**STARTING ELEVATION: 11,000 feet**
**AVALANCHE TERRAIN: Mostly avalanche terrain; wait for spring consolidation**
**USGS 7.5 MINUTE MAP: Breckenridge, 1987-PR**
**MAPS: pages 194, 198**

Quandary Peak is perhaps the most well known Colorado spring ski tour; many have experienced ski mountaineering on its graceful east flank. The route blends a relatively short hike, a 14,000-foot summit and moderate slopes into a memorable ski outing. From the moment you leave the summit, the slopes are never steeper than 35 degrees. The descent over two massive steps makes for perfect turns. For much of the year it is possible to carve a steady series of turns from the mountain's top to your car door. If you haven't skied this mountain, put it on your list.

The tour begins in the Monte Cristo Creek valley, accessed via Breckenridge from the north and Alma from the south. Follow Colo. 9 to a point approximately 2 miles north of the summit of Hoosier Pass and about 9 miles south of Breckenridge. The Monte Cristo road heads west through a small housing development and up into a large, barren valley. Park near the end of the houses where an abandoned mining road heads north into the forest. Walk or ski along the road until it ends. From this point you can easily proceed cross-country northwest through scattered trees and clearings. This area is the eastern extension of the ridge and on clear days the route ahead is quite obvious. As you break out above treeline, follow the gradual ridge upward over two massive steps divided by a flat shoulder at about 13,150 feet. From the step, the peak pierces the sky in a white conical silhouette. Climb to its top via the left edge. If this final pitch appears too challenging to ski, it is possible to leave your gear on the flat shoulder and climb to the summit, retrieving it on the return trip.

The descent to the east begins by traversing the short summit ridge. This ridge steepens and fans out into a large skiable face. Many parties ski this superb face for hours: descending, climbing and descending over and over.

The descent continues over the shoulder on an easterly path down over the next large treeless slope. Continue through treeline into the sparse forest and start to curl back south to the mining road. On an average spring day when the snowpack is good, Quandary will treat you to seemingly endless turns on a slope of firm alpine snow.

# 112 PACIFIC PEAK (13,950 FEET)

**DESCRIPTION: Spring ski-mountaineering descent, approach hike**
**SKILL LEVEL: Advanced**
**TIME: Full day**
**DISTANCE: 7 miles or more round trip**
**ELEVATION CHANGE: 3,000 feet total gain**
**STARTING ELEVATION: 11,060 feet**
**AVALANCHE TERRAIN: Mostly avalanche terrain; wait for spring consolidation**
**USGS 7.5 MINUTE MAP: Breckenridge, 1987-PR**
**MAP: page 198**

This striking peak is situated between Fletcher Mountain and Crystal Peak at the south end of the Tenmile Range. When viewed from the southeast its sharp angular ridges converge to form a classic pyramid summit. From Mohawk Lakes to the northeast, its imposing north face and notched summit ridge comprise an equally impressive alpine vista.

There are two ways to approach the peak from the east. Both make for excellent ski descents. The Mohawk Lakes approach is a bit shorter than the McCullough Gulch approach, and has a more continuous ski descent late in the spring season. To approach from Mohawk Lakes, take Colo. 9 south out of Breckenridge. After 2.4 miles, turn west at the Crown subdivision across the road from the upper end of Goose Pasture Tarn. The road first cuts back up the slope a few hundred feet, passing some private driveways. Two successive left forks put you on County Road 800. Continue up the road, passing a confusing array of subdivision turnoffs by following road signs for County Road 800 and blue diamond trail markers leading toward the national forest. You should run into the Spruce Creek Trailhead 1.3 miles from the highway. Continue past this, and past a turnoff for the Lower Crystal Lakes jeep trail at 1.5 miles. Pass one more turnoff for the Wheeler Trail at 2.5 miles before dipping down into Spruce Creek. In winter, this road is only plowed past the subdivision, so you may have to leave your car well before the end of the road, depending on the amount of snow left. When clear, the road is marginal only for Cadillac-sized cars. Other vehicles should have little trouble.

From the end of the road, the trail leads straight up valley, passing several abandoned miners' cabins, one of which has been renovated enough to provide overnight emergency shelter. Gain a steep head wall onto a bench that holds Lower Mohawk Lake. Then continue straight up the valley to the upper lakes. From here you can see the north face of Pacific Peak to the left at the end of a huge snow-filled bowl. Continue up the bowl and take the line of least resistance to the ridge that comes east off the summit pyramid. Once on the ridge, you will see a frozen lake that sits in a tiny bowl directly below the summit. Follow the east ridge to the top.

The other approach is from McCullough Gulch. Take Colo. 9 out of Breckenridge for 5.5 miles to the end of a flat, open meadow. Leave your car just across the road from the Skiers Edge lodge. Find a road that starts from the southwest corner of the meadow and heads up the north side of McCullough Gulch. Follow it for approximately 0.5 miles, then jog south 0.2 miles on the Wheeler Trail, a road at this point, and pick up another road that continues up the south side of the valley. Bear right at the end of the valley, heading for a saddle on the right ridge. Once on the saddle, go directly up the ridge north and then west to the summit, or drop down into the frozen lake bowl and then proceed directly up to the summit.

The descent for both routes starts by skiing from very near the summit down a fantastic little run (slope angle is 25 to 30 degrees) into the frozen lake bowl. Regain the ridge if you're going back to McCullough Gulch, and ski the remainder of that route back out. If you've approached from Mohawk Lakes, there is a steep borderline extreme chute (slope angle is 40 to 45 degrees) at the end of the frozen lake bowl that can be skied down into the Mohawk Lakes valley. If you do plan to ski the chute, be sure to scout it for avalanche conditions on the way up, and recheck on the way down.

# 113 CRYSTAL PEAK (13,852 FEET)

**DESCRIPTION: Spring ski-mountaineering route**
**SKILL LEVEL: Advanced**
**TIME: Full day**
**DISTANCE: 6 miles round trip**
**ELEVATION CHANGE: 2,892 feet total gain**
**STARTING ELEVATION: 11,060 feet**
**AVALANCHE TERRAIN: Mostly avalanche terrain; wait for spring consolidation**
**USGS 7.5 MINUTE MAP: Breckenridge, 1987-PR**
**MAP: page 198**

While crystals are not gems, the south face of Crystal Peak is—a gem to ski, that is! From the head of the Mohawk Lakes–Spruce Creek drainage, a large snowfield climbs nearly 1,200 feet up the southern exposure of this 13,852-foot peak, reaching nearly to the small desolate summit. In late spring this slope becomes a beautifully firm run nearly devoid of avalanche danger. Crystal Peak's slightly clandestine location belies its commanding position in the Tenmile Range. Clear Colorado skies reveal magnificent views of the Maroon Bells and the Sawatch Range to the southwest, the rugged Gore Range to the north and the Front Range to the east. As you descend from the summit, Quandary Peak (14,265 feet) and the precipitous north face of Pacific Peak (13,950 feet) will be your visual companions to the south. Skiing Crystal is a must for anyone who seeks excellent skiing in a slightly more remote situation.

Crystal Peak is easily approached from Breckenridge on Colo. 9. As you head south, turn right (west) at the Crown subdivision across the road from the upper end of Goose Pasture Tarn. Two successive left forks put you on County Road 800. Drive as far as the late spring snowdrifts allow, then continue on foot until the road ends and a trail begins. Pass a forest service registration sign and hike west up through the forest past a variety of old cabins and abandoned mining relics hidden among the trees. As you cross above treeline, switchback past a series of small waterfalls, which eventually crest onto the east lip of Lower Mohawk Lake. This spot is marked by a huge bull wheel and its wooden support structure. Hike along Lower Mohawk Lake's south shore and follow Spruce Creek as it carves its way through rocks and tundra. After ascending a small step you will enter a large, flat-bottomed cirque with two unnamed lakes. Pacific Peak's sweeping ridges dominate the western skyline.

Crystal Peak lies hidden on the right side of the upper valley. From a spot above the lakes, climb toward Crystal Peak, following the path of least resistance (normally a talus slope to the right of a small tongue of snow that connects the upper snowfield to the valley bottom). The remainder of the ascent is straightforward as you wander up the moderate slopes on a path of your choosing. For the descent, simply point your skis down and go! Under normal spring conditions you can ski to well below treeline. Note: If you are feeling energetic, this tour can easily be combined with a ski descent of Pacific Peak (tour 112).

# 114 SPRUCE CREEK LOOP

> **DESCRIPTION: Winter ski tour, primarily backcountry trails and jeep roads, loop trip**
> **SKILL LEVEL: Intermediate***
> **TIME: Two-thirds day**
> **DISTANCE: 6.5 miles round trip**
> **ELEVATION CHANGE: 1,000 feet total gain**
> **STARTING ELEVATION: 10,180 feet**
> **AVALANCHE TERRAIN: None**
> **USGS 7.5 MINUTE MAP: Breckenridge, 1987-PR**
> **MAP: page 198**

> ***NOVICE HIGHLIGHT: Only the last quarter of the loop is intermediate. This may be eliminated by returning via the Spruce Creek road, effectively cutting the normal loop in half.**

This is one of the best winter ski tours in the area. The first half gradually gains elevation on a narrow trail through thick forests of spruce and lodgepole pine. The second half, which can be avoided, traverses north on a wide aqueduct road and is followed by a thrilling descent down a steep narrow jeep trail which leads back to the Spruce Creek road. Combining the two halves into a loop makes for a delightfully satisfying outing.

Take Colo. 9 south out of Breckenridge 2.4 miles to the Crown subdivision. Turn west, cutting back up the slope a few hundred feet past some private driveways. Two successive left forks put you on County Road 800 heading southwest. Continue up this road, passing a confusing array of subdivision turnoffs by following road signs for County Road 800 and blue diamond trail markers leading toward the national forest. After 0.6 miles, you'll reach the end of the plowed road.

The tour starts on relatively flat ground, following the unplowed continuation of the road. After 0.7 miles, you'll come to a turnoff, left, for the Spruce Creek Trail. Take this and proceed on a narrow rolling course up valley parallel to the road. The trail eventually crosses to the south side of Spruce Creek and soon intersects with the Wheeler Trail. Continue straight ahead up the Spruce Creek Trail, making a wide arc through the trees above a large open meadow. The trail comes out at the end of the Spruce Creek road where the valley gets considerably steeper. Follow the Spruce Creek road back down toward the meadow and then climb up and east heading back out the valley. It's also possible and perhaps easier, to take a shortcut directly across the open meadow, following the Wheeler Trail north from where it intersects with the

Spruce Creek Trail. An aqueduct road, which comes down off the hillside to the north, intersects with the Spruce Creek road a few hundred yards after climbing out of the meadow. Follow this road for 0.75 miles to its end. Here you have to cross the creek and cut north through the trees for about 50 yards to get to the Crystal Lake jeep trail. This is the route back down. It's fast and exciting, but doesn't hold many surprises so you can disengage the brakes and really let go. The jeep trail comes out at the Spruce Creek road about a mile above the parking area.

For those with a little more energy, the jeep trail continues up into the basin. Crystal Lake is about another mile above treeline. As you begin your ascent and break out of the trees, there are some fantastic little glades that are great for telemarking. This alternative excursion, not part of the normal loop, takes you into terrain with potential for small avalanches. The return trip back to the car from Crystal Lake will probably take only about half an hour.

For a shorter loop, it's possible to ski up the Spruce Creek road and take either one of the two halves back out, cutting the time required by about a third.

# 115 McCullough Gulch

DESCRIPTION: Winter ski tour, steep road into high valley
SKILL LEVEL: Intermediate*
TIME: Half day
DISTANCE: 4 miles or more round trip
ELEVATION CHANGE: 800 feet or more total gain
STARTING ELEVATION: 10,300 feet
AVALANCHE TERRAIN: Route crosses avalanche runout zones; can be dangerous during high-hazard periods
USGS 7.5 MINUTE MAP: Breckenridge, 1987-PR
MAP: page 198

*NOVICE HIGHLIGHT: The first mile is not as difficult as the rest so is suitable for novice skiers.

This is a large side valley that very few skiers visit. It extends into the heart of the Tenmile Range just north of Quandary Peak. On a good day you can ski clear to the end of the valley well above treeline, but in general the best skiing is found in the lower half of the valley.

The trailhead is indistinct. It is located 5.5 miles south of Breckenridge on the way to Hoosier Pass, just across the highway from a large hotel/lodge, the Skiers Edge. Park in the hotel lot, then cross back over the highway and ski west and slightly north along a road that crosses the Blue River at the upper end of a large meadow. The road soon crosses to the north side of McCullough Creek and then heads west up through the trees into McCullough Gulch. After 0.5 miles the road breaks out of the trees and connects with another road that traverses in from the south. This other road is part of the Wheeler Trail, which extends from Monte Cristo Creek, one drainage to the south, over into Spruce Creek, one drainage to the north, and beyond. The Wheeler Trail might make a good ski for those with a thirst for the untracked backcountry.

To continue up McCullough Gulch it is easiest to jog south along the Wheeler Trail road for 0.5 miles until you reach a fork. Then cut back west heading up the south side of the gulch. The road ends after another 0.5 miles but you can continue cross-country above this to treeline. The return trip is back along the same route and should be fast and exciting.

# 116 BRECKENRIDGE TO FRISCO

**DESCRIPTION: Winter ski tour, rolling trail, car shuttle required**
**SKILL LEVEL: Advanced**
**TIME: Full day**
**DISTANCE: 9.2 miles one way**
**ELEVATION CHANGE: 880 feet total loss**
**STARTING ELEVATION: 10,000 feet**
**AVALANCHE TERRAIN: None**
**USGS 7.5 MINUTE MAPS: Breckenridge, 1987-PR, Frisco, 1987-PR**
**MAPS: pages 198, 208, 214**

This trail, along the eastern foot of the Tenmile Range, is a great choice for an early-season ski tour or for days when avalanches threaten the higher elevations. The Breckenridge to Frisco trail traverses moderate rolling terrain hidden in the depths of dense pine forests. Unfortunately, the forest protection also blocks most views of the surrounding mountains, including the serrated summits of the Tenmile Range only a stone's throw away. This tour is best skied from south to north, as the steady series of moderate hills and vales gives way to a fun 1,000-foot drop into Frisco via Miner's Creek at the end of the tour. While this tour has a "full day" time rating because of the total mileage covered, a fast group can complete it in several hours, making for a pleasant morning or afternoon of exercise. This route is popular and is usually tracked.

As the name implies, this route leads from the town of Breckenridge to the town of Frisco. Skiers must either arrange a car shuttle or plan the trip around the scheduling of the shuttle buses that run between these communities during most of the day. Most local businesses have bus schedules.

The most difficult part of this tour is locating the trailhead, which lies deep in the maze of small roads and developments covering the mountains west of Breckenridge. Drive south on Colo. 9 to the south end of Breckenridge. Turn right (west)

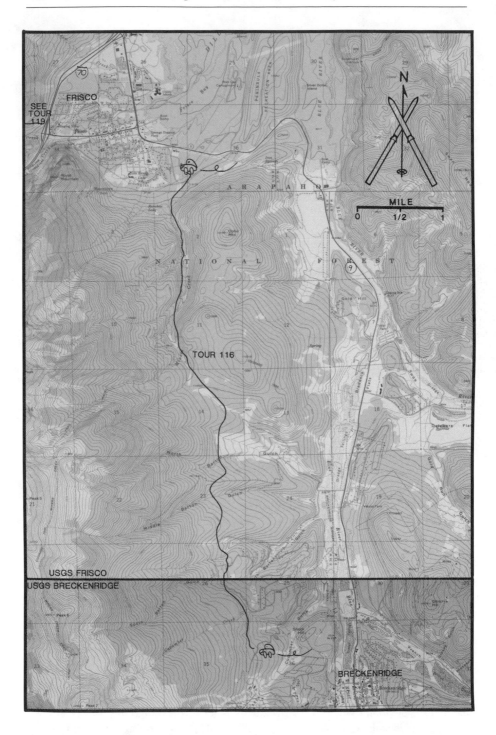

on Ski Hill Road (at a stoplight) and drive west, following the curvy road up toward the ski area. This road heads west, then swings sharply north, passes the touring center, runs past the base of Breckenridge's Peak 8 lift area and courses around a second sharp switchback. After this switchback the road leads west for a short distance, then turns northeast and begins a noticeable descent to the north and east. The trailhead will be on the left (northwest) side of the road and has a large plowed parking area.

After leaving the trailhead the tour heads north on a moderate course rising over many small hills and drainages. The trail is marked with a variety of flags, yet it possesses few distinct landmarks to use in navigating. However, the trail is easy to follow and is normally well tracked. The first half of the tour ends at an obvious (on the map) saddle where the long descent into Frisco begins. This descent begins as a fast ride down the head of Miner's Creek and a meeting with the Miner's Creek road, which is generally packed by snowmobiles. Once you are on the road it is nearly impossible to get lost, as it is quite wide. When you approach Frisco the road switchbacks east, then north. Search for one of several roads leading through the houses of Frisco and back to Colo. 9. A shuttle car may be left on any of the streets near the south end of town (off Colo. 9).

*Approaching Baldy Bowl, Breckenridge ski area in the background, Kurt Lankford photo.*

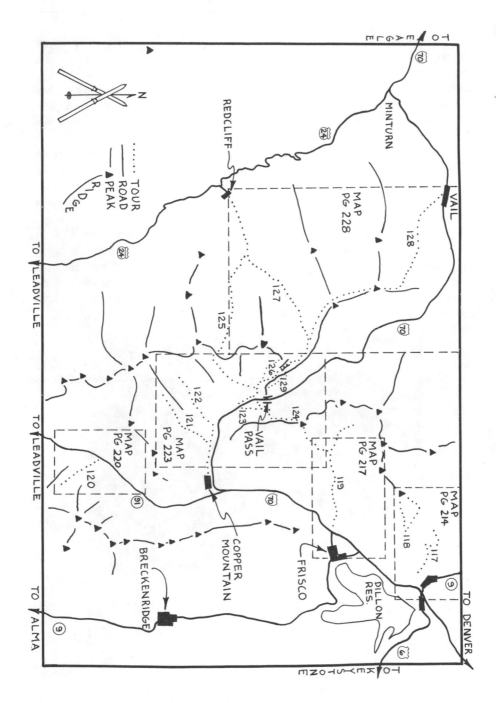

N

TOUR
ROAD
PEAK
Ridge

REDCLIFF

MINTURN

MAP
PG 228

VAIL

128

127

125

126

129

124

123
VAIL
PASS

122

121

MAP
PG 223

MAP
PG 220

120

MAP
PG 217

119

MAP
PG 214

118

117

COPPER
MOUNTAIN

FRISCO

DILLON
RES.

BRECKENRIDGE

TO EAGLE

TO 70

24

70

TO LEADVILLE

24

TO LEADVILLE

91

70

9

TO ALMA

9

TO DENVER

6

TO KEYSTONE

# CHAPTER TEN

# VAIL PASS AND THE SOUTHERN GORE RANGE

## INTRODUCTION

The Vail Pass area, in the heart of northern Colorado ski country, possesses some of the finest Nordic backcountry skiing in the state. Situated between the Gore Range to the north and east and the Tenmile Range to the south, the Vail Pass area offers incredible vistas and fantastic touring. There are many highly recommended tours in the area and several, including the classic Shrine Pass route and 18-mile Commando Run (named in honor of the Tenth Mountain Division), are some of the most popular cross-country ski outings in this guide.

Vail Pass touring is typified by trails that climb gradually through acres of fire-cleared slopes. Each tour, whether novice, intermediate or advanced, quickly gains access to unobstructed lookout points. The stepped and hummocky texture of the landscape and the area's frequent snowstorms create superb telemarking terrain. Black Lakes Ridge, Shrine Bowl, Corral Creek and Commando Run all offer limitless days of powder skiing. Shrine Pass road and Corral Creek also give novice skiers the high-country atmosphere and exciting descents.

Included too in this section are a selection of tours around Dillon and Frisco (the Southern Gore area), Copper Mountain and Fremont Pass. While the Vail Pass trails explore sparsely timbered uplands, most of these routes typically follow long open (and more protected) valleys at lower elevations. The trails up drainages such as Stafford Gulch, Guller Creek and North Tenmile Creek all ascend gentle valleys, then return to the cars on fun, long and easy drops—great novice and intermediate trips for spring and winter.

You can reach the ski tours in the Vail Pass area easily from I-70. Also, the summit parking lot features a state-of-the-art rest house with a large community room that is ideal for groups to rendezvous or wait while car shuttles are arranged (this is important for parties skiing one-way tours such as Shrine Pass and Commando Run, as they end in Redcliff and Vail, respectively, and require lengthy car shuttles). Perhaps the only drawback for individuals coming from the Denver metropolitan area is the long drive. Under good conditions it takes roughly 1 hour and 45 minutes, under poor conditons or if heavy ski traffic is encountered, it can take considerably more time. The drive is definitely worth it, as the scenery is unsurpassed and the snow always deep.

## HISTORY

Historically the area west of Dillon served as much as a transportation corridor as a major mining district. Ute Indians were the first to cross into the area now known as Summit County. Sources place the date of this migration roughly around 4800 B.C. Camping in the Blue River valley, the Utes hunted through Tenmile Gorge to Vail Pass. Bone fragments and arrow points discovered during the building of Vail Pass evidence the native American's passage today.

White people entered the picture first as explorers, then trappers who traversed the Great Plains headed for the mountains in search of beaver pelts. These brave men lived and worked throughout the Rockies under the harshest of conditions. In 1855 an unusual character came west from Ireland. Sir St. George Gore was his name and it seems that environmental carnage was his game. Gore was a wealthy baronet who enjoyed hunting for sport (and occasionally for sustenance). Across the great American desert he traveled with an entourage that included such basics as 28 wagons, 112 horses, oxen, 50 hunting dogs, about 90 guns, including both rifles and shotguns, and 40 servants. Before his three-year sojourn had ended, reputedly he killed over 6,000 buffalo, 1,600 elk and 100 bears. The rugged mountains north and west of Dillon and north and east of Vail were named to "honor" this "great" man of means.

Immediately east of the mouth of Tenmile Canyon are Frisco and Dillon. Frisco, at the mouth of the canyon, was a silver-mining town established in 1873 when H. A. Recen built the first house where present-day Frisco sits today. The Tenmile Mining District contained highly profitable silver lodes that were located throughout the valley from Frisco to its headwaters below Fremont Pass, which was constructed to connect Summit County to the fledgling mining district of Leadville.

Vail Pass is the traditional route into the headwaters of the Eagle River, Grand Junction and the western desert. Before the 1960s when travelers passed over into the Eagle Valley, they encountered a sleepy sheep pasture and tiny agricultural communities. Towering above the valley floor to the south were beautiful forest-covered mountains flanked on their south sides by massive open expanses, reputedly cleared when native Americans set large fires to strike back at white men who were steadily encroaching on their life and land. In the late 1950s, Earl Eaton, while prospecting for uranium in this area, observed that the terrain was perfect for the booming sport of downhill skiing. Eaton brought in Tenth Mountain Division veteran Pete Seibert to show him this potential ski area. Seibert concurred and the Vail ski area was born under Seibert's direction. Opened on December 15, 1962, Vail has become one of the world's great ski resorts.

# 117 SOUTH WILLOW CREEK

**DESCRIPTION: Winter ski tour, interesting and moderate trail into the southeastern Gore Range**
**SKILL LEVEL: Intermediate**
**TIME: Full day**
**DISTANCE: 8 miles round trip**
**ELEVATION CHANGE: 560 feet total gain/240 feet total loss**
**STARTING ELEVATION: 9,220 feet**
**AVALANCHE TERRAIN: None**
**USGS 7.5 MINUTE MAPS: Frisco, 1987-PR, Dillon, 1987-PR**
**MAP: page 214**

Not many tours in this book take skiers into the rugged beauty of the Gore Range proper. On the west side of Vail Pass trails are steep and menaced by avalanches, while on the east side access is difficult and trails are steep and treacherous. This is unfortunate because the Gore Range represents some of Colorado's finest alpine splendor. The South Willow Creek Trail takes skiers into the mouth of the incredible chasm that separates the domed monolith of Buffalo Mountain from the core of the Gore Range. An intermediate trail, it climbs and descends over a series of hills and drainages while only accumulating 600 feet in elevation. This deceptive trip, however, will always keep you on your toes (three-pins), wondering what's around the next bend. The terminus of the trail, a small cabin at the west edge of a small meadow, is a perfect spot for lunch.

The route begins in a housing development hidden in the woods directly west of Silverthorne. The trailhead is somewhat tricky to locate, so pay close attention to these directions. Leave I-70 at the Silverthorne exit and head north, taking the first left onto Wildernest Road, which takes you on a winding course into the Mesa Cortina development. Head west, then south before the road turns west and climbs along the creek. Follow this main road until you reach the first turn to the north. Make this turn and follow the road as it runs north. You will be able to overlook Silverthorne to the northeast. This road heads north for 0.2 miles then switchbacks south. After 0.3 miles it begins to curl west again. At this point, stop and park in the plowed parking area on the right. A wooden trail sign marks the actual trailhead.

The tour begins in the woods on a gentle traverse to the north-northwest and follows the well-marked trail (actually a jeep road for a short distance). A short, gradual descent carries you into a clearing with views of I-70 and the Blue River valley to the east and Buffalo Mountain high to the west. The traversing nature of the tour continues as you climb easily across the meadow, crossing two small drainages. Re-enter the woods and ascend due west up a moderate, rounded ridge separating two creekbeds. Pass two small switchbacks, rise over the crest of the ridge, then cruise along its north side to a meeting with the third and larger creekbed.

Once past this drainage the trail ascends on a nearly flat incline to the

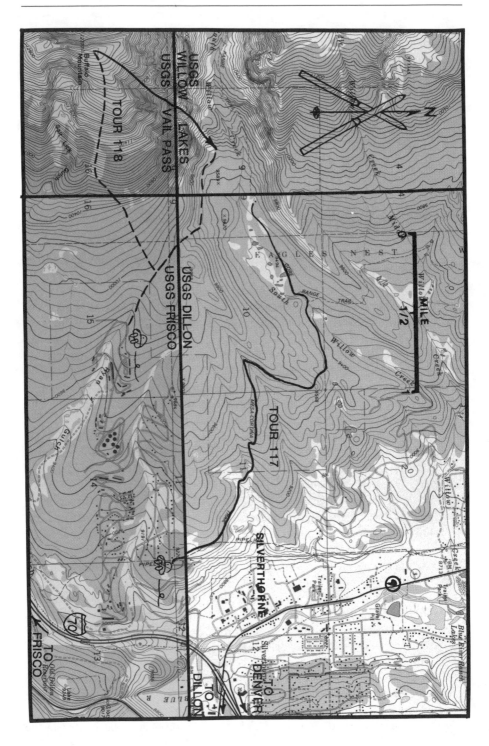

northeast. This long traverse climbs through tall lodgepole pines and ends where the trail crosses over a ridge marking the final descent into South Willow Creek. The traverse that you just completed is deceptively fast on the return; the tree trunks lining the trail serve as a powerful impetus to remain on the trail and in control.

From the top of the ridge make the steep drop into South Willow Creek. You will meet with an obvious jeep road that climbs up from the Blue River valley to the east (right). Merge with the road and descend with it west (left) for another 0.5 miles, until it blends with the flat floor of this major Gore Range drainage. Head west along the gentle rolling valley bottom, cross South Willow Creek and reach a forest service sign with Gore Range trail information. Proceed past the sign and climb around a small knob. Double-pole west through the mixed woods and traverse along the northern fringe of a large clearing. Pass this clearing, remaining in the trees, then cross a second clearing as the trail bends to the right. The trail continues up into the woods and becomes increasingly difficult. While most parties begin the trip home at this point, more experienced skiers can challenge the steep trail above.

This trip is quite popular, usually well packed and easy to follow. When you reach South Willow Creek, you can see the north side of Buffalo Mountain dropping steeply into the upper confines of the valley. Remember that several hills must be climbed on the return to the parking area so plan accordingly.

# 118 Buffalo Mountain—North Couloir
## (12,777 feet)

**DESCRIPTION: Spring ski-mountaineering descent, approach hike, steep narrow couloir, big vertical drop**
**SKILL LEVEL: Advanced +**
**TIME: Full day**
**DISTANCE: 6.4 miles round trip**
**ELEVATION CHANGE: 3,200 feet total gain**
**STARTING ELEVATION: 9,760 feet**
**AVALANCHE TERRAIN: Mostly avalanche terrain; wait for spring consolidation**
**USGS 7.5 MINUTE MAPS: Vail Pass, 1987-PR, Frisco, 1987-PR, Dillon, 1987-PR**
**MAP: page 214**

This is one of the best advanced ski descents in the state. It starts from the rounded summit of Buffalo Mountain west of Silverthorne on a wide convex snowfield that gradually gets steeper while narrowing to a 50-foot-wide chute that drops 3,200 feet into South Willow Creek. The descent is steep, technical and continuous, requiring expert skill and a lot of nerve. The severe gradient and funnel shape at the top of the couloir create a particularly hazardous configuration for wet-snow avalanches. The route should only be attempted after it has truly consolidated (early to mid-June in most years). The route gets skied more often with downhill gear than it does with telemark or ski-mountaineering gear.

Buffalo Mountain is located just west of Silverthorne. The descent couloir is visible from the north end of town. The quickest way to the summit is via the Buffalo Cabin Trail, which leads to a path that ascends a wide avalanche swath on the east side of the mountain. To reach the trailhead take I-70 to the Silverthorne exit and go north a short distance on Colo. 9 toward Silverthorne. Take a left at the first intersection and proceed southwest, then west, up Wildernest Road for several miles to a point just past the last condominium complex. The Willow Creek Trail starts here. Follow it 0.25 miles to its intersection with the Buffalo Cabin Trail. Go left (uphill) here for 0.5 miles to Buffalo Cabin (nothing more than a single old, one-room homestead). A path goes from here up to the wide avalanche swath and continues straight up the swath, wasting no time with switchbacks (the swath is clear or mostly clear of snow by the time the couloir is in good condition to ski). The summit is reached after a grueling 2,000-foot climb. Most parties start the descent just below the summit, taking a line down the main snowfield and funneling into the couloir from the west. There are two or three short sections, including the funnel section at the top of the couloir, that seem a little steeper than the rest. At the bottom the couloir fans out, cutting a wide swath through the trees. Follow the right edge of the swath to its base, where an aqueduct/trail contours in from the east. Follow the aqueduct/trail a short distance, then cut steeply uphill on the Willow Creek Trail, which takes you back out to the trailhead.

# 119 NORTH TENMILE CREEK

DESCRIPTION: Winter ski tour, moderate trail with strenuous start
SKILL LEVEL: Intermediate
TIME: Full day
DISTANCE: 8 miles round trip
ELEVATION CHANGE: 1,060 feet total gain
STARTING ELEVATION: 9,140 feet
AVALANCHE TERRAIN: Some avalanche terrain encountered; easily avoided
USGS 7.5 MINUTE MAPS: Frisco, 1987-PR, Vail Pass, 1987-PR
MAPS: pages 208, 217

North Tenmile Creek drainage is a long, lovely valley in the southern Gore Range. The mouth of this large feature lies immediately west of I-70 at the Frisco exit. The route climbs steeply for the first 0.5 miles before the gentler upper valley is entered. The return trip features a brisk descent with a large cleared slope at the 2-mile mark providing an excellent area to practice telemark turns. High to the west Uneva

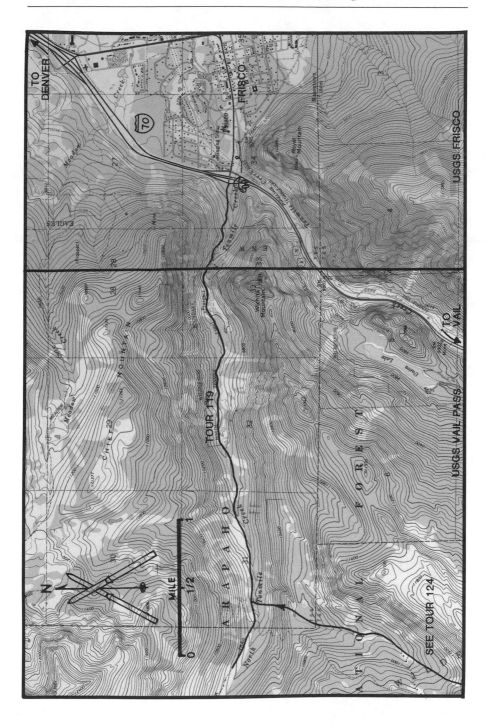

Peak rises like a lone sentinel far above the thickly forested valley. North Tenmile is a refreshing example of classic Colorado touring and a recommended intermediate trip.

Drive west on I-70 to the second Frisco exit, which lies west of the town's main street. Park on the west side of the interstate near the end of the plowed road. The tour takes off from here, following the summer roadbed.

The North Tenmile Creek Tour follows a distinct trail for its entire length, so route finding is straightforward, even for novice skiers. From the parking area ski onto the obvious roadbed heading west. The climbing is gentle for the first 0.3 miles as you ascend along the north side of the creekbed. Past this stretch the grade becomes moderately steep until you cross a small tributary flowing from the northeast (right). The trail begins to run closer to North Tenmile Creek; near the 1-mile mark it enters a clearing that contains a grouping of small ponds. When you reach this point, you have finished the most strenuous portion of the trip. Ahead lie miles of fine cross-country skiing.

Re-enter the woods after only a few hundred yards and ski on a flat trail through the woods to another clearing. Pass a small beaver pond and continue west on the trail, skiing in and out of tiny clearings. On your right near the 2-mile mark is a good spot for eating lunch and making face plants while practicing your telemark turns. Continue following the trail through a series of clearings and stands of timber, passing more small telemark practice runs on your right. Crossing the last of these meadows, the route now bends southwest and crosses the creek, remaining on the north side of the drainage for 0.3 miles. Ski into another clearing with views of the peaks surrounding the upper head of the valley. The trail then drops to the creek and then crosses back north. Skirt the very edge of a large, treeless slope that rises to the right and climbs gently through the woods following near the creek. Pass trail signs for the Wheeler Trail, skiing through one last large stand of trees before the vast nonforested upper meadow is reached. It is an interesting ecological area with dense forests south and west of the creek and sparse timber dominating the northeast slopes. Push on as far as you like through this area; the skiing remains moderate, with the only limiting factor being the daily weather conditions.

# 120 MAYFLOWER GULCH

**DESCRIPTION: Winter ski tour, short picturesque valley between Copper Mountain and Leadville, usually has excellent snow**
**SKILL LEVEL: Novice to intermediate**
**TIME: Half day**
**DISTANCE: 6 miles round trip**
**ELEVATION CHANGE: 1,000 feet total gain**
**STARTING ELEVATION: 10,980 feet**
**AVALANCHE TERRAIN: Some avalanche terrain encountered; easily avoided**
**USGS 7.5 MINUTE MAP: Copper Mountain, 1987-PR**
**MAP: page 220**

This beautiful little valley has all the right ingredients for a pleasant half-day tour. It starts with a short, relatively moderate climb and ends in a huge snow-filled bowl below two spectacular peaks. The snow conditions are always good because the route starts at almost 11,000 feet and keeps to the shaded, north-facing side of the valley most of the way.

Take I-70 to the Copper Mountain exit, then proceed south toward Leadville on Colo. 91 for approximately 6 miles to a turnoff with a small plowed parking area on the southeast side of the highway. The tour starts by following a road up the right side of the valley for about 2 miles. The road soon breaks out into the open just below the old Boston Mine site. There is a cluster of old buildings here. The Colorado Mountain Club and others restored at least two of these buildings and equipped them with wood stoves, bunk beds and other amenities. Unfortunately someone took the stoves, and the buildings quickly deteriorated so much that they are now hardly even worth entering.

Above the building site the bowl opens into a huge white expanse, a great place to take pictures or get a sunburn. The lower bowl is generally safe from avalanches because it is not steep enough to slide but if you travel up the steeper side slopes, the danger quickly increases. To return, ski back down the valley via the same route.

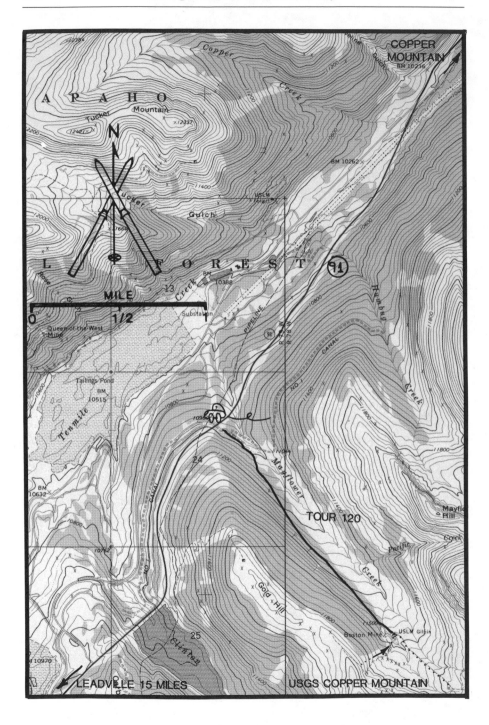

# 121 GULLER CREEK

DESCRIPTION: Winter ski tour, remote trail in large, open valley
SKILL LEVEL: Intermediate*
TIME: Full day
DISTANCE: 11.6 miles round trip
ELEVATION CHANGE: 1,520 feet total gain
STARTING ELEVATION: 9,800 feet
AVALANCHE TERRAIN: Some avalanche terrain encountered; easily avoided
USGS 7.5 MINUTE MAPS: Vail Pass, 1987-PR, Copper Mountain, 1987-PR
MAP: page 223

*NOVICE HIGHLIGHT: The initial few miles of this tour cross very moderate terrain, excellent for novice skiers.

Guller Creek is the first large valley immediately west of the Copper Mountain ski area. It is straight and long, deceptively long. Fortunately its bottom is flat and climbs toward the higher peaks in a gentle manner. The first leg of the tour is on the prepared ski tracks of the Copper Mountain Touring Center (free of charge if you intend to only use the main valley trail for access to Guller Creek). Past these tracks the tour follows the Colorado Trail toward Searl Pass and Jacque Peak. This valley is wide open with mountain meadows often drenched with warm Colorado sunshine. Guller Creek may be used as the first leg of an adventurous loop tour that crosses into and down Stafford Creek. This tour is highly recommended for the long warm days of spring.

Drive on I-70 and take the Copper Mountain exit. Drive into the Copper Mountain complex and follow the main road as far west as possible, until you reach the parking area for the touring center. The trails start a short walk west of the parking area and are well marked. On the USGS 7.5 minute map the trail leaves the end of the photo-revision's purple road and is marked as the Colorado Trail. Hop on the packed trail and follow it west, curving over a bridge and past a summer barn and corral. Continue, skiing under the overpass of I-70, and double-pole until you reach the turnoff back south into the mouth of Guller Creek. There are many touring center trails in this area but all are well marked and the wide Guller Creek Trail is hard to miss. This turnoff is roughly 1 mile from the parking area.

In Guller Creek the trail splits the narrow valley right up the middle on a marked and normally tracked path. Follow the valley toward the south, then begin to ski southwest and into the mouth of the upper valley. The upper valley contains one huge meadow, nearly level and straight, making for fast progress to the head of the drainage. The head of Guller Creek opens into a larger bowl with Jacque Ridge on the left and a thickly forested ridge to the right. On the far side of the forested ridge is

Stafford Creek. A small saddle separates these two drainages: If your party still has an appetite for climbing it is possible to cross this small pass and descend into the upper head of Stafford Creek. Otherwise the return trip is a straightforward descent back down your tracks.

# 122 STAFFORD CREEK

DESCRIPTION: Winter ski tour, moderate trail up wide drainage
SKILL LEVEL: Novice
TIME: Full day
DISTANCE: 12 miles round trip
ELEVATION CHANGE: 1,360 feet total gain
STARTING ELEVATION: 9,800 feet
AVALANCHE TERRAIN: None
USGS 7.5 MINUTE MAPS: Vail Pass, 1987-PR, Copper Mountain, 1987-PR
MAPS: pages 223, 250

Moderate and often deserted, Stafford Creek is a great tour for novice skiers. The first mile shares common ground with Copper Mountain ski area's cross-country trails (free of charge if you intend only to use the main valley trail for access to Stafford Creek) before striking off boldly to the southwest. Stafford Creek is wide open and ascends over gentle hummocky terrain—the return trip can be very fast indeed. Near the head of the valley the forests cover the upper basin, where powder-hounds can telemark in the rarely skied, powdery glades.

To reach Stafford Creek take I-70 to the Copper Mountain exit. Turn into the ski area, following the main road west as far as possible, until you reach the parking area for the touring center and the last ski lift. Grab your skis and walk the short distance to the beginning of the packed and groomed touring trails. Begin skiing west and contour around to the south (over a small bridge) past a small barn and corral. Resume skiing west, eventually passing under the I-70 overpass and over West Tenmile Creek. Double-pole on the wide south-facing trail, pass the turnoffs leading to Guller Creek and other touring center trails, and finally reach the mouth of Stafford Creek after roughly 1.5 miles. Stafford Creek, easily identified by the signs, lies immediately south of a tall I-70 overpass.

Cross under the overpass and enter the wide mouth of Stafford Creek. If no tracks exist to point the way, follow the right side of the valley over easy terrain. Approximately 1.3 miles up valley the steeper righthand slopes begin to close in on the creek, necessitating a crossing of the creek onto the southeast bank. The valley bottom becomes slightly more hummocky but easy passages circumnavigate all obstacles. The steeper righthand slopes make for superb powder skiing after a storm but should only be skied by experienced and knowledgeable backcountry skiers, as they can

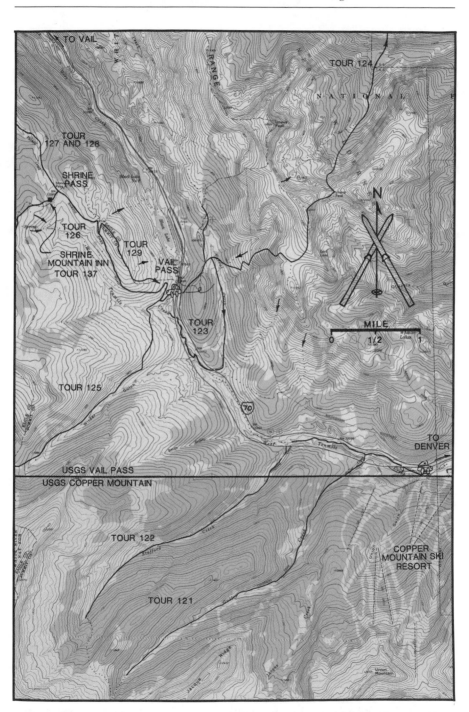

avalanche. Follow the contours of the valley to the west and back to the southwest, aiming for the trees that close off the end of the valley. When you reach these trees it is possible to climb south and ski several fine glades hidden throughout this area. The return trip simply retraces your tracks but is much faster and far more exciting.

# 123 CORRAL CREEK

**DESCRIPTION: Winter ski tour, no particular destination—just good, frolicking fun in the backcountry**
**SKILL LEVEL: Novice to advanced**
**TIME: Quarter day or more**
**DISTANCE: 2 miles or more round trip**
**ELEVATION CHANGE: 600 feet or more total gain**
**STARTING ELEVATION: 10,600 feet**
**AVALANCHE TERRAIN: Some avalanche terrain encountered; easily avoided**
**USGS 7.5 MINUTE MAP: Vail Pass, 1987-PR**
**MAPS: pages 225, 250**

This tour follows no particular route and has no particular destination; it's just a great place to tour around for a few hours. There are many glades to choose from for some fine powder runs. Or, if you just want to get off the beaten path and enjoy the backcountry, the terrain is moderate and the scenery is spectacular.

Corral Creek is located about 0.5 miles east of the summit of Vail Pass. Leave your car at the main Vail Pass rest area parking lot and cross back over the bridge to the east side of the highway. Climb diagonally left through the trees for 0.25 miles to the small ridge that separates Corral Creek from the highway. Here you can survey the whole area and decide where you want to go. Several miles of moderate rolling terrain extend north, parallel to the highway with potential for hours of fine touring. To the south the wide open meadows of lower Corral Creek gradually descend toward Copper Mountain. The creek intersects the highway about a mile below the top of the pass. You can make a small loop trip by going down the creek to the highway and then back up to the top of the pass via the summer bike path.

The wide open hillside on the opposite (east) side of Corral Creek is an excellent place to practice telemark turns. Be cautious when avalanche danger is running high—this slope is steep enough to release a slab avalanche.

For a longer more adventuresome tour, it's possible to diagonal southeast from Corral Creek all the way up onto the main ridge. From there you can head south toward Copper Mountain and pick any one of a number of sparsely timbered slopes to get back to the highway. This option is much more difficult than the others: It requires advanced route finding, downhill touring skills and experience and competency in assessing avalanche hazard.

# 124 VAIL PASS TO FRISCO (NORTH TENMILE CREEK)

**DESCRIPTION: Winter ski tour, adventurous, off-trail route over high ridge, car shuttle required**
**SKILL LEVEL: Advanced**
**TIME: Full day**
**DISTANCE: 8 miles**
**ELEVATION CHANGE: 1,800 feet total gain/2,260 feet total loss**
**STARTING ELEVATION: 10,600 feet**
**AVALANCHE TERRAIN: Route crosses avalanche slopes; prone to skier-triggered avalanches during high-hazard periods**
**USGS 7.5 MINUTE MAPS: Vail Pass, 1987-PR, Frisco, 1987-PR**
**MAPS: pages 217, 223**

This is a classic tour. The terrain is varied, the views are spectacular and the downhill runs are steep and challenging. The first half of the tour climbs 1,800 feet to a ridge crest east of Vail Pass. From there it drops down the back side into Tenmile Creek and follows this out to the second (farthest west) Frisco exit on I-70, altogether a descent of over 2,000 vertical feet. A car shuttle is then required to get back to the start of the route.

Leave one car at the second (farthest west) Frisco exit on I-70 and proceed to Vail Pass. Park the second car in the main Vail Pass rest area parking lot on the west side of the highway and cross back to the east side to begin the tour. Ski northeast from the top of the overpass, contouring up and left around a small hump that sits between Vail Pass and Corral Creek. Before dipping down into Corral Creek, look across (east) at the sparsely timbered slopes below the main skyline ridge and plan your ascent route to the high point directly above the head of Corral Creek. Perhaps the best choice is a diagonal line up and directly across an open slope, heading for the dense trees that sit below and right of the righthand summit ridge. This moderate slope (never exceeding 23 degrees) can be dangerous during periods of high-avalanche hazard but is much better than the steep ridge on the left or the slopes farther up in the bowl. After gaining the ridge, head directly to the unnamed summit at 12,363 feet.

From the top of this peak, on a clear day, you'll be treated to a spectacular panorama of peaks. The jagged Gore Range lies north, Holy Cross and the Sawatch Range are southwest, Copper Mountain and the west side of the Tenmile Range are directly across the valley to the southeast and the Front Range and Williams Fork Mountains are visible to the east.

You have two choices for the descent into the upper bowl above Tenmile Creek. When avalanche conditions are stable, usually in spring, it is possible to descend north along the ridge to the next saddle and then drop straight down into the bowl. When conditions dictate a more conservative approach, it's better to take the east ridge to Uneva Pass and then drop down into the bowl. Either way, beautiful open slopes are encountered. Exercise caution, for both alternatives cross potentially dangerous avalanche terrain.

Once in the bowl, follow a creekbed through pleasant, intermittent meadows, then descend a final steep drop-off into Tenmile Creek. The last 500 feet of drop-off requires some steep timber-bashing. The Tenmile Creek Trail is a short distance up on the opposite side of the creek. Turn right on the trail and cruise 4 miles to the second (farthest west) Frisco exit on I-70. Then car shuttle back to the top of Vail Pass.

# 125 WILDER GULCH TO WEARYMAN CREEK

**DESCRIPTION: Winter ski tour, backcountry road and off trail, Vail Pass to Redcliff, car shuttle required**
**SKILL LEVEL: Advanced\***
**TIME: Full day**
**DISTANCE: 10 miles**
**ELEVATION CHANGE: 800 feet total gain/2,240 feet total loss**
**STARTING ELEVATION: 10,600 feet**
**AVALANCHE TERRAIN: Route crosses avalanche slopes; prone to skier-triggered avalanches during high-hazard periods**
**USGS 7.5 MINUTE MAPS: Vail Pass, 1987-PR, Redcliff, 1987-PR**
**MAPS: pages 223, 228, 250**

**\*INTERMEDIATE HIGHLIGHT: The first half of the tour, from Vail Pass into Wearyman Creek, is very scenic, sparsely timbered, rolling terrain—excellent for an intermediate half-day tour.**

This tour starts from the rest area at Vail Pass and finishes at Redcliff. Although it parallels the Shrine Pass road (see tour 127) and has similar terrain, the flavor of the tour is entirely different. The first half does not follow an established road or trail; it just takes off cross-country. More often than not, you will have to break trail most of the way. In addition there may be some route finding involved in picking the right spot to cross over the ridge. These factors contribute to an air of backcountry adventure that far exceeds that of the normal Shrine Pass route. Be sure to check on avalanche conditions before you set out on this tour.

Redcliff, where the tour ends, is a unique little mining community nestled in a narrow side canyon between Vail and Leadville. A car shuttle is required to return from Redcliff to Vail Pass. The drive takes roughly 45 minutes each way, so plan an early start. To reach Redcliff drive west from the summit of Vail Pass, proceed through Vail, then exit I-70 at Minturn. Drive south from Minturn on US 24 approximately 10.3 miles. Then, just before crossing a bridge suspended over the rugged Eagle River Gorge, turn left on a narrow road. This road leads straight into

Redcliff. The tour finishes on the Shrine Pass road at the northwest corner of Redcliff. Simply drive straight through to the east side of town, then drive one block left. The Shrine Pass road is sometimes plowed a short distance up valley to a small parking area. Parking is also available on side streets in town or in the parking area at the marshall's office.

Start from the rest area parking lot near the summit of Vail Pass. Drop southeast into Tenmile Creek and contour out the opposite side. Next, round the sparsely timbered hillside again, heading southeast toward Wilder Gulch. From directly above the gulch pick a good diagonal line and drop into the upper end of the valley. Follow the gulch for another 1.5 miles until it splits. Here, take the left side of the right fork, climbing more steeply now through dense trees toward a low saddle on the ridge. This saddle is the highest point on the tour. It's all downhill from there to Redcliff via Wearyman Creek. Another way to reach Wearyman Creek is to go to the top of Shrine Pass and then follow the Tenth Mountain Association Trail past the Shrine Mountain Inn southeast over the main ridge. After crossing the ridge drop down and contour around in a sparsely timbered bowl that drains into Wearyman Creek.

Returning to the normal route, at the saddle above Wilder Gulch, drop straight south toward Wearyman Creek. Before reaching the creek you'll intersect with a road. Follow the road down Wearyman Creek for 4.2 miles to where it intersects with the Shrine Pass road. Turn left and follow the Shrine Pass road out to Redcliff.

# 126 SHRINE BOWL

**DESCRIPTION: Winter ski tour, off-trail tours through gladed bowl**
**SKILL LEVEL: Intermediate**
**TIME: Half to full day**
**DISTANCE: Optional, up to 6 miles one way**
**ELEVATION CHANGE: Up to 1,040 feet total gain**
**STARTING ELEVATION: 10,600 feet**
**AVALANCHE TERRAIN: Some avalanche terrain encountered; easily avoided**
**USGS 7.5 MINUTE MAPS: Vail Pass, 1987-PR, Redcliff, 1987-PR**
**MAPS: pages 223, 250**

Shrine Bowl is the name used to describe the vast area lying southwest of Shrine Pass road, before crossing over Shrine Pass. Bounded on the west by a large cornice-capped white ridge, this area is a veritable playground for skiers of all abilities, with special emphasis on intermediate-level skiing. You can spend many hours playing on the moderate gladed hills covering the bowl's floor. The topography is actually a little too convex to be called a true bowl but it is a nice approximation.

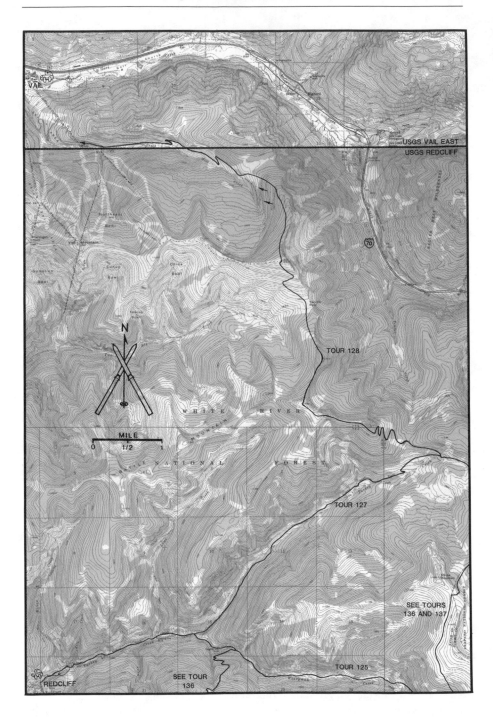

Like most Vail Pass tours the snow tends to be consistently good, making this tour worth the drive.

Drive on I-70 and take the Vail Pass–Shrine Pass exit just south of the actual summit of Vail Pass. Park on the west side of the highway in the large plowed parking area, complete with an ultramodern, solar-powered, heated restroom facility.

The many possible variations for touring in this bowl are what make this area so conducive to interesting skiing. The following route descriptions briefly cover two popular methods of exploring this area. If you are particularly adventuresome, feel free to improvise and follow your own instincts. Remember to remain well away from the corniced ridge to the west; it holds textbook examples of slopes of wind-loaded snow just waiting to be disturbed by an unwary soul.

If you want to tour around the area north of the central creekbed, follow the Shrine Pass road from the parking area toward the summit of the pass. This portion of Shrine Pass is quite obvious, climbing in a continuous yet moderate style. From the pass or a point slightly before it, leave the road and head cross-country toward the southwest. The terrain is rolling here, with clearings and forested areas. Contour around the head of the basin in the protection of the trees, remaining well away from the dangerous avalanche slopes to the west.

Traverse south, covering easy terrain, and then begin a southeasterly descent toward a branch of the West Fork of Tenmile Creek. Follow this drainage on an enjoyable rolling descent, skiing in and out of timbered glades. Reach the large clearing near the parking area and return to the cars.

Another route, which is slightly more difficult, leaves the parking area and heads straight south toward the ridge overlooking Wilder Gulch. It begins with a nearly horizontal traverse contouring around the gently bulging ridge that lies south of the branch of the West Fork of Tenmile Creek. This entire area was burned by a huge fire, so the landscape is speckled with sparse trees and aging tree snags. As you approach the escarpment that drops into Wilder Gulch, veer directly to the west and go straight up the apex of the bulging ridge. Climb west into

*Powder skiing on Black Lakes Ridge (tour 129), Brian Litz photo.*

thicker trees, skiing to a point well away from the avalanche runouts at the base of the west ridge. From here it is best to drop off to the northeast and ski the hummocky terrain lying on the south side of the creek, following this feature back to the clearing before the parking area.

# 127 SHRINE PASS ROAD

**DESCRIPTION: Winter ski tour, classic connection between Vail Pass
and Redcliff, very popular, car shuttle required
SKILL LEVEL: Intermediate\***
**TIME: Full day**
**DISTANCE: 12.2 miles one way**
**ELEVATION CHANGE: 509 feet total gain/2,429 feet total loss**
**STARTING ELEVATION: 10,600 feet**
**AVALANCHE TERRAIN: Some avalanche terrain encountered; easily
avoided**
**USGS 7.5 MINUTE MAPS: Vail Pass, 1987-PR, Redcliff, 1987-PR**
**MAPS: pages 223, 228, 250**

**\*NOVICE HIGHLIGHT: The initial climb to Shrine Pass makes an
enjoyable jaunt for those not wishing to commit to the entire route.**

Shrine Pass must certainly rank as one of the most popular ski tours in
Colorado. Cross-country skiers from all over the state converge on the summit of Vail
Pass each weekend to cross this celebrated mountain road. Shrine Pass's name
originates from its close proximity to Mount of the Holy Cross (which lies to the west)
and a shrine that was proposed for the summit of this pass. Mount of the Holy Cross
is one of the state's most beautiful and historic landmarks, visible on clear days
throughout the tour. The skiing is as exciting as the panorama and features a 2,400-
foot drop into the town of Redcliff. From the summit of the pass the road drops
continuously for nearly 10 miles, testing the leg strength and snowplow of most
skiers. This run is especially fast after the road has been packed by snowmobiles,
which unfortunately share the route. Shrine Pass is one of the finest intermediate ski
tours in this book and is a great trip for groups.

The Shrine Pass Tour involves a car shuttle with roughly a 45-minute drive
separating the trailhead from the finish. A drop-off car must be left just east of the
town of Redcliff on the Shrine Pass road. To reach Redcliff from Vail Pass drive west
on I-70 past Vail to Minturn, then south on US 24 for 10.3 miles to a bridge over the
Eagle River. Turn left onto a narrow, snowpacked road that leads from the north end
of the bridge into the center of Redcliff. Turn left again onto the marked Shrine Pass
road, driving as far as possible before parking (or park in town on a street or in the
parking lot by the marshall's office). The trailhead is on top of Vail Pass and lies on
the west side of the Vail Pass overpass north of the large parking area and modern rest
facilities.

The first leg of the tour involves climbing 2.5 miles to the summit of Shrine
Pass. This moderate and steady grade leaves the Vail Pass parking area near a large
highway department sign and proceeds around two switchbacks before contouring
around the south slopes of Black Lakes Ridge. On the west side of the ridge the road

traverses up toward the pass high above West Tenmile Creek (although the creekbed may be skied too). Rise up onto the top of Black Lakes Ridge and drop into a saddle, climbing out the other side. The view is as fine a panorama as you will encounter on any tour in this book, with the wildly serrated Gore Range filling the northern and eastern horizons and the Tenmile Range and Copper Mountain ski area to the southeast. Once you are past the saddle glide gently over the nearly flat clearing to the summit of Shrine Pass. From here on it's all downhill.

From the summit of the pass the road drops immediately to the northwest into Turkey Creek. The road follows the creekbed quite closely on its east side through a meadow. After several hundred yards veer west and ski through a narrow passage of trees before dropping steeply into a large flat meadow. The road contours along the north edge of this meadow before reaching the trees near the celebrated view of Mount of the Holy Cross. This is a pleasant rest spot for a snack or drink and to contemplate this special mountain standing majestically to the southwest.

The descent continues as you ski into the trees along the road and quickly turn the corner to the north, bypassing the turnoff to Timber Creek, which veers right at 4 miles. As you bypass this fork, the Shrine Pass road heads west and drops through stands of trees. A summer trail switchbacks through here but most folks cut telemark turns (or try to) directly down this clearing. Ski along the road close to the creekbed and curve north (right) before swinging back west and into another clearing. Pass through a small group of trees, then break out into a long section of straight road. This section is very scenic, with widely scattered trees and a panoramic view into the lower valley with its steep aspen-covered north slopes.

The road and the creek meet again at the 7.5-mile point. Follow the road across the creek, past several long-abandoned mining cabins and into the thicker stands of evergreen trees. The tour's tempo now picks up again as you descend the often heavily traveled road high on the hill above the creek. This exciting grade melds into gentler terrain, and after recrossing the creek, passes by the obvious bridge and turnoff to Wearyman Creek, where tour 125 exits onto the Shrine Pass road at 9.4 miles and finally enters onto the lower section of the tour. From here until the finish the tour follows the more heavily traveled and flatter section of the road. It is possible to ski right into the center of town (or wherever the cars are parked) under normal snow conditions.

*On Commando Run (tour 128), Gore Range in the distance, Brian Litz photo.*

# 128 COMMANDO RUN

> DESCRIPTION: Winter ski tour, classic and strenuous route, great
> telemarking, car shuttle required
> SKILL LEVEL: Advanced
> TIME: Full day or overnight
> DISTANCE: 18.7 miles one way
> ELEVATION CHANGE: 2,819 feet total gain/5,159 feet total loss
> STARTING ELEVATION: 10,600 feet
> AVALANCHE TERRAIN: Route crosses avalanche slopes; prone to
> skier-triggered avalanches during high-hazard periods
> USGS 7.5 MINUTE MAPS: Vail Pass, 1987-PR, Redcliff, 1987-PR,
> Vail East, 1987-PR
> MAPS: pages 223, 228, 250

Commando Run, named in honor of the Tenth Mountain Division troops, runs from the summit of Vail Pass to the town of Vail and represents the finest in Colorado backcountry skiing. This tour's ever-increasing reputation is well deserved as it possesses many stellar qualities, including maximum distance, voluminous gains and drops in elevation, unsurpassed alpine vistas and exceptional telemark skiing through superb wooded glades. Since this tour has become quite popular in recent years, the trail is usually packed for much of the season. While it is possible for a very strong party to complete this tour in 5 hours, you should plan on a long day, especially if it is your first attempt or if the conditions are not optimal. Although this tour has several variations, only the most frequented and scenic route is covered here. Whichever path you choose, be prepared for a memorable day of skiing.

The tour begins from the top of Vail Pass and ends on the ski runs at the base of the Vail ski area. Leave a shuttle car in Vail (at the parking facilities near the center of town; fee charged) and return to the summit of Vail Pass. Park on the west side in the large parking area near the solar-powered rest facility. The first part of this tour shares common ground with the Shrine Pass Tour (tour 127) to the 4-mile mark. Leave the parking area and begin skiing the well-marked Shrine Pass road. This obvious and well-traveled section passes quickly around two switchbacks then resumes its straightforward 500-foot climb to the top of the pass. When you arrive at the pass, note the line of timbered and nontimbered peaks lying directly west-northwest above the clearing at the summit of the pass. These are the mountains that you will be ascending today. The first peaks are the unnamed and forested summits lying between the Timber Creek turnoff and Two Elks Pass. Farthest away is the barren and windblown peak marked as "Red" on the topographic maps but more commonly referred to as "Siberia" Peak.

From the pass drop off to the northwest, staying on the Shrine Pass road into the upper reaches of Turkey Creek. Moderate gliding downhill will take you along the roadbed, contouring north and back west. As you head west the road punches through a thick stand of pine trees, then drops more steeply along the north edge of a large meadow. At the west end of this clearing double-pole past the famed Mount of the Holy Cross viewpoint, marked by a small outhouse hidden in the trees, then drop around a corner on a quick descent to the turnoff to Timber Creek. This snow-covered road forks to the right at 4 miles.

Follow this gently graded road as it traverses high above Turkey Creek, providing an even more grandiose view of Holy Cross. Ski past a turnoff to the north (right) for Timber Creek and continue on this road, which appears in purple on the new photo-revised 1987 Redcliff USGS map (the Lime Creek road). Begin curving southwest, then search for an inconspicuous point of entry into the woods to the right. As you contour along the road the trees on the right begin to thin out on the slope on the east side of Point 11,611. If no tracks are set, search for a wooden post on the right side of the road. This post marks the turnoff point where you leave the road and begin switchbacking cross-country up the east flank of Point 11,611. Near the top of this grueling climb, skirt the tiny corniced summit by making a moderate traverse a few hundred feet from the summit on its south side.

Ski into the saddle lying west of Point 11,611, then kick and glide along the flat, twisting trail that follows the crest of the ridge, aiming for the not-so-obvious Point 11,710. As you approach the end of the ridge, climb through the trees and reach the large clearings that cap Points 11,710 and 11,696. One of the most impressive points on Commando Run, this is a fine spot to drink some fluids and have a snack. An unobstructed 360-degree panorama, including the Gore Range to the north, the Tenmile Range to the southeast and the Sawatch Range high to the southwest, awaits you on this summit. Far down to the east is busy I-70.

Ski across the summit clearings, following the ridge to the northwest, cross over Point 11,696 and ski down the small powderfield dropping off its north side. Between this point and the next summit, Point 11,618, which lies between you and Two Elks Pass, is a graceful and heavily timbered ridge that contains the challenging and slightly difficult-to-follow trail. The trail lies very near the east edge of the ridge and is easily followed if someone has skied it recently (if you can't find it, timber-bashing will get you down). When you reach the saddle before Point 11,618, you have two options for passing this peak to reach Two Elks Pass. Many traverse west of the peak through dense trees. The other option continues on a trail directly over the top. Although more strenuous, this trail is more spectacular, and the descent to Two Elks Pass maximizes the superb tree skiing necessary to reach the pass. If you opt for the traverse, just remember to remain high enough to allow a descent through the nice glades to Two Elks Pass.

Above Two Elks Pass looms Siberia Peak, windblown and forbidding. Normally the snow covering its south face is hard and wind-crusted, which allows for rapid ascents. Your exact route up the peak will be influenced by whether you are using wax or climbing skins. In general, the climb up Siberia (or Red Mountain on the topographic maps) requires a slight traverse to the northwest. Often the slope just west of the south ridge is the most wind-scoured and easiest to climb. Beware of the huge cornices that often overhang the east face; they can be very dangerous!

North of Siberia Peak is a feature known as Mushroom Bowl. This vast circular bowl forms the head of Mill Creek and contains acres of exceptional terrain and consistently good powder. The farther your path of descent swings west from the north ridge, the steeper, more heavily wooded and increasingly difficult the skiing becomes. Additionally, there are intermittent rock bands that ring the upper head of the valley which must be negotiated.

For a superb, scenic and moderate descent into Mill Creek, first ski the open slope directly north of the peak. Resist the temptation to continue straight down to the west and begin a descending traverse to the right, aiming for the roadbed evident on the USGS map. Follow the road or ski right along the edge of the east face, dropping onto the road before the first small switchback. Ski around the first switchback, then around the second switchback (you are now heading north again). After rounding this second switchback, ski for 10 to 30 yards, then strike off directly west and attack the beautiful powder glades that drop nearly 700 feet to the valley floor and the roadbed leading to the ski area.

After reaching the Mill Creek roadbed, speed along the last 3 miles to the ski area. Cross the first run that you encounter, which leads from the top of Gold Peak on your right (north) down to the left to the base of upper Vail Mountain. Continue along the service road around to the north, where you will reach an entire network of trails leading to the base of the ski area. Choose a downhill run (or the service road) to finish the day, depending on your group's temperament and energy reserves. Telemark, parallel, snowplow and crash your way down the last few hundred feet into the center of Vail Village.

# 129 BLACK LAKES RIDGE

**DESCRIPTION: Winter ski tour, high ridge trail, optional telemark runs**
**SKILL LEVEL: Novice***
**TIME: Half day**
**DISTANCE: Optional, up to 5 miles round trip**
**ELEVATION CHANGE: 745 feet total gain**
**STARTING ELEVATION: 10,600 feet**
**AVALANCHE TERRAIN: Route crosses avalanche terrain; prone to skier-triggered avalanches during high-hazard periods**
**USGS 7.5 MINUTE MAP: Vail Pass, 1987-PR**
**MAPS: pages 223, 250**

**\*INTERMEDIATE/ADVANCED HIGHLIGHT: The east slopes of Black Lakes Ridge offer a bewildering array of steep and enjoyable advanced telemark runs.**

The small sparsely forested ridge that rises high above Black Lake to the west is capped by rolling terrain and can be reached easily from the Shrine Pass road. A ski loop around the top of the ridge is a fine novice ski tour that maintains the excellence of other more advanced Vail Pass ski tours. Within a mile of the parking area, you will be greeted by the wild Gore Range to the north and the Tenmile Range to the southeast. The basic tour can easily be completed in half a day, which gives you plenty of time to lunch on the summit and take in the views. Advanced skiers can be challenged by dropping off the ridge at several points to the east, skiing the steep rolling knolls that descend to the foot of Black Lake. These slopes provide perfect telemark powder skiing. Be sure to check avalanche conditions before you venture onto these slopes.

Drive on I-70 and take the Vail Pass rest area–Shrine Pass exit just south of the actual summit of Vail Pass. Proceed to the west side and park in the large plowed parking area. Walk back north and cross over the road to the summer Shrine Pass roadbed, marked by a large sign. Begin skiing on the road and pass a forest service avalanche danger zone display. Climb around two switchbacks and follow the road as it winds northwest around the southern extension of Black Lakes Ridge. The road ascends moderately until it reaches a small saddle marked by many gnarly tree snags. Drop into the saddle and either ascend directly up the other side, leaving the road on its right side, or follow the road as it begins its nearly imperceptible descent to Shrine Pass. If you leave the road simply ski up onto the ridge, a straightforward route that brings you face to face with the entire breadth of the Gore Range.

If you follow the road, after reaching the sign and small snow-covered outhouse marking the top of the pass, strike off to the east-northeast and climb the west slopes of the ridge. This 200-foot-plus ascent is easier if you leave the road several hundred yards before the pass and make a more gradual rising traverse to the top of the ridge. From the summit of the ridge ski back to the southeast along the crest. When it begins to drop off toward the parking area and the Shrine Pass road, follow a route of your choosing through the beautiful glades adorning the south face of the ridge.

For advanced or strong intermediate skiers who wish to ski the east face of the ridge, there are many possible descents. A superb line drops directly from the aforementioned saddle and follows the natural depression of the faint streambed flowing to the lakes. This is best skied under fresh powder conditions, as it is moderately steep and can be slow in older snow. Another intermediate or advanced possibility is to begin your tour by skiing directly up the south face of the ridge, which is not too strenuous. When you reach treeline contour onto the east shelf, which sits below a small but potentially dangerous wind-loaded slope that guards the crest of the ridge on its east side. Many fine lines drop off to the east; all of these variations end in a steep step that culminates the descent.

To return to the parking area cross the treeless valley bottom and intercept the old highway grade below the interstate. Follow this 0.5 miles back to the cars.

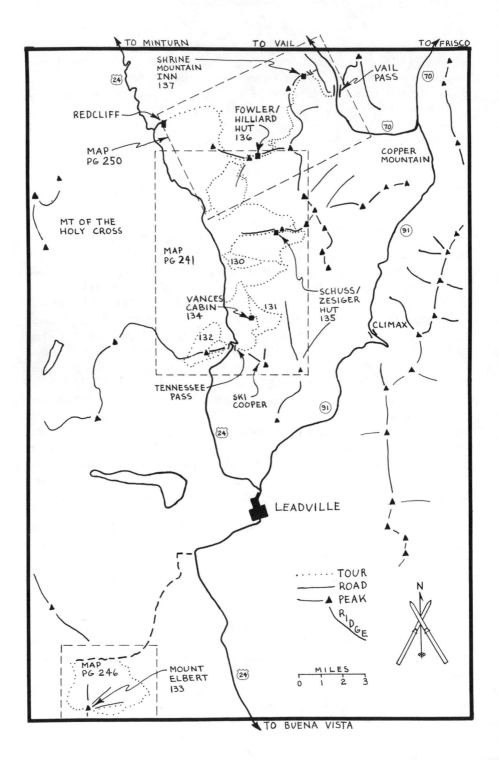

TO MINTURN    TO VAIL    TO FRISCO

24

SHRINE
MOUNTAIN
INN
137

VAIL
PASS

70

REDCLIFF

FOWLER/
HILLIARD
HUT
136

70

MAP
PG 250

COPPER
MOUNTAIN

MT OF THE
HOLY CROSS

MAP
PG 241

130

91

SCHUSS/
ZESIGER
HUT
135

VANCES
CABIN
134

131

CLIMAX

132

TENNESSEE
PASS

SKI
COOPER

91

24

LEADVILLE

TOUR
ROAD
PEAK
RIDGE

N

MILES
0  1  2  3

MAP
PG 246

MOUNT
ELBERT
133

24

TO BUENA VISTA

# CHAPTER ELEVEN

# TENNESSEE PASS AND THE TENTH MOUNTAIN TRAIL ASSOCIATION HUTS

## INTRODUCTION

### HUTS

The Tenth Mountain Trail Association (TMTA) maintains and operates what has become the finest and most extensive hut system in the United States. Fritz Benedict, a member of the elite Tenth Mountain Division during World War II, started planning and fundraising for the project in 1980. Robert S. McNamara, former Secretary of State, and Dr. Ben Eiseman actively raised funds for the first two huts, McNamara Hut and Margy's Hut, built in summer 1982. They were dedicated in memory of Robert McNamara's wife, Margaret McNamara. From these modest beginnings, the system was extended north along the west side of the Holy Cross wilderness with the addition of the Peter Estin Hut and the Harry P. Gates Hut. The Diamond J Ranch and Polar Star Inn, two private operations, were also incorporated into the system, making one long uninterrupted route with six possible stopovers between Aspen and Edwards.

Four new huts were added to the system in 1988. They make up what is for now a completely separate route. They are located between Vail and Tennessee Pass, on high ridges, just east of US 24, which runs north-south between Leadville and Minturn. These four new huts, Vance's Cabin, Schuss–Zesiger Hut, Fowler–Hilliard Hut and Shrine Mountain Inn, are within the geographic range of this book. The original six huts are not, but are covered in other publications. Contact the Tenth Mountain Trail Association for details (see Appendix 4).

The U.S. Forest Service has approved plans to build more huts north of I-70, connecting Polar Star Inn to Shrine Mountain Inn. In addition, several more huts are proposed on the south end that would connect Vance's Cabin to Diamond J Ranch, thus closing a huge loop that essentially circles the Holy Cross wilderness.

All the huts in the TMTA system are exceptionally well constructed and well maintained. Many have unexpectedly nice amenities such as saunas, solar lighting and propane stoves. Two of the huts described here, Shrine Mountain Inn and Vance's Cabin, are accessible to novice as well as intermediate and advanced skiers. The other two, Fowler–Hilliard Hut and Schuss–Zesiger Hut, are more difficult to reach. They involve serious backcountry skiing over long distances with considerable elevation gain. Skiers planning trips to any of the huts must understand that they'll be weighed down with extra food and gear, they may have to break trail through deep snow, they may encounter blizzard conditions and they may have a difficult time finding their way, even though all of the routes are marked with blue diamond trail markers. You don't have to be an expert to enjoy these huts but to be safe you should at least be in good condition, stable on your skis and properly equipped: Enthusiasm is no substitute for experience. Excellent guide services are available; inexperienced parties are encouraged to use them (see Appendix 4).

## TENNESSEE PASS

Tennessee Pass is located between Leadville and Vail on the Continental Divide. If you come from Denver there are two ways to get there. The quickest is to take I-70 to Copper Mountain, then head southwest on Colo. 91 over Fremont Pass to Leadville and finally drive north on US 24 to Tennessee Pass. The other way is to take I-70 over Vail Pass to Minturn, then drive south on US 24 to Tennessee Pass. Either way is a long drive from Denver but the tours are worth it: plenty of snow and very little wind. Novice and intermediate skiers will find that the Tennessee Pass trail system has a wonderful selection of enjoyable half-day loop trips. The Cooper Nordic Center at the Ski Cooper area has a wide selection of trails for novice through advanced skiers. One of these, the loop around the Ski Cooper ski area, is highly recommended. Backcountry enthusiasts should include the Trail of the Tenth on their list of tours that "must be skied." For advanced ski mountaineers, Mount Elbert, along with several of the other fourteeners farther south along the Sawatch Range, makes an outstanding spring ski-mountaineering descent.

## HISTORY—TENTH MOUNTAIN DIVISION

Camp Hale, located just north of Tennessee Pass, is the birthplace of modern skiing in Colorado. Selected as the best mountain infantry training site for the 87th Regiment, which later became the elite Tenth Mountain Division, the encampment held as many as 10,000 troops during World War II. The idea of training an elite unit, skilled in the rigors of winter mountain travel, was initiated by Minot Dole, founder of the National Ski Association, who recognized the value of such a unit after Finnish ski troops had effectively stopped an invasion of Russian soldiers during an early World War II conflict. He convinced Army Chief of Staff George C. Marshall of the need for such a unit and the 87th Mountain Infantry Regiment was born.

The site near the mining camp of Pando was selected because of its convenient access to rail and highway facilities as well as its isolated mountainous terrain. Camp Hale became one of the toughest training centers in the nation. Troops were often required to spend the night out in the dead of winter when temperatures dipped to minus 40 degrees F. Most troops were issued a pair of skis in addition to their uniforms and rifles. The training paid off when the men were called into the heart of the action and assigned to spearhead some of the deadliest conflicts of World War II. They took Riva Ridge, Baio, Prada, Mount Belvedere, Mount Della Vedetto and finally led the conclusive Po River valley attack. Although casualties were high (a total of 992 men were killed), the unit was extremely successful and General Mark Clark called the Tenth the finest division he'd ever seen.

After the war Camp Hale was dismantled but the veterans of the Tenth Mountain Division went on to become extremely influential in the development of Colorado's ski industry. Aspen, Vail, Arapahoe Basin, Loveland, Breckenridge, Steamboat and Winter Park were all either started or heavily promoted by Tenth Mountain Division veterans. Their combination of entrepreneurial finesse and deep love for skiing transformed Colorado into the ski mecca it is today.

## HISTORY—LEADVILLE

Leadville, situated in the upper end of the Arkansas River valley at an elevation of 10,000 feet, was the site of one of the biggest mining booms in Colorado history. The rush began in spring 1878 after word of rich silver strikes spread to Denver. The mountains surrounding Leadville were instantly invaded by thousands of hopeful prospectors with visions of untold riches. The first year saw some $2 million worth of ore extracted; the take increased to over $9 million the following year and in the decade from 1879 to 1889, more than $82 million worth of silver was mined and smelted.

Horace Austin Warner Tabor came from a modest background and launched a career in the Arkansas Valley that would make him one of the wealthiest and most legendary figures in Colorado history. For years Tabor could do no wrong in mining or investments. He speculated with abandon, purchasing the Matchless Mine for "pocket change" and turning it into a steady producer that lasted for nearly a decade. Eventually his financial recklessness led to his downfall, but not before he was elected to the U.S. Senate and married Elizabeth McCourt, better known as Baby Doe. The marriage was disapproved of by a large portion of the upper-class citizenry and created one of the era's juiciest social scandals.

For all his rash financial and social dealings, Tabor was a conscientious leader who worked hard to promote and shape the community. Leadville was growing so rapidly that to organize and structure it into a respectable town was nearly impossible. It soon surpassed all other Colorado communities except Denver in population. Profiteering, turmoil and disarray were the rule rather than the exception. A business census of 1879 listed 4 banks, 17 barber shops and 120 saloons for a population of 24,000. At night the gambling halls, variety houses and bars came alive. All types of entertainment were available, from the rankest dive to the epitome of high society at the Tabor Opera House.

With the closing of the Little Pittsburg and Chrysolite mines, Leadville's boom ended almost as abruptly as it had started. Stocks plummeted and prospectors left, seeking more profitable opportunities in Aspen, Creede and Breckenridge. Several of the largest mines continued operation but never again would the town see the frenzied profit taking and inflation of those first few boom years.

# 130 CAMP HALE TRAIL SYSTEM

**DESCRIPTION: Winter ski tours, system of interconnecting trails and roads on moderate terrain**
**SKILL LEVEL: Novice**
**TIME: Two to five hours (varies with route)**
**DISTANCE: East Fork Valley 7.1 miles round trip**
              **South Fork Road 2.6 miles one way**
              **Resolution Creek 5.3 miles round trip**
**ELEVATION CHANGE: East Fork Valley 360 feet total gain**
                     **South Fork Road 550 feet total loss**
                     **Resolution Creek 410 feet total gain**
**STARTING ELEVATION: East Fork Valley 9,280 feet**
                   **South Fork Road 9,832 feet**
                   **Resolution Creek 9,250 feet**
**AVALANCHE TERRAIN: None**
**USGS 7.5 MINUTE MAP: Pando, 1987-PR**
**MAP: page 241**

During World War II Camp Hale served as the training base for America's mountain fighting group known as the Tenth Mountain Division. Today all that remains of the bustling military base is a broad Eagle Park meadow interlaced with abandoned roads and trails. Hemmed in by towering alpine walls, this site makes a favorable expanse for gentle touring. Skiers may choose between a variety of short tours or invent their own combinations to suit the needs of the group. The possibilities range from touring along the old road grades of the former barracks area to pushing farther into the higher drainages via moderate summer jeep trails. This is a great place to ski during the warm days of spring (you'll probably be skiing in shorts and T-shirts) and a pleasant introductory area with a good variety of trails.

Camp Hale is reached by driving on US 24 south from Minturn or north from Leadville. Eagle Park occupies a large flat section of the valley bottom, which is easily located.

Camp Hale has three possible trailheads: the southernmost near 9,280 feet, the primary trailhead at 9,250 feet and the northernmost at Pando at roughly 9,200 feet. For now, forget about the new Tenth Mountain Division trails and concentrate on these fine short tours.

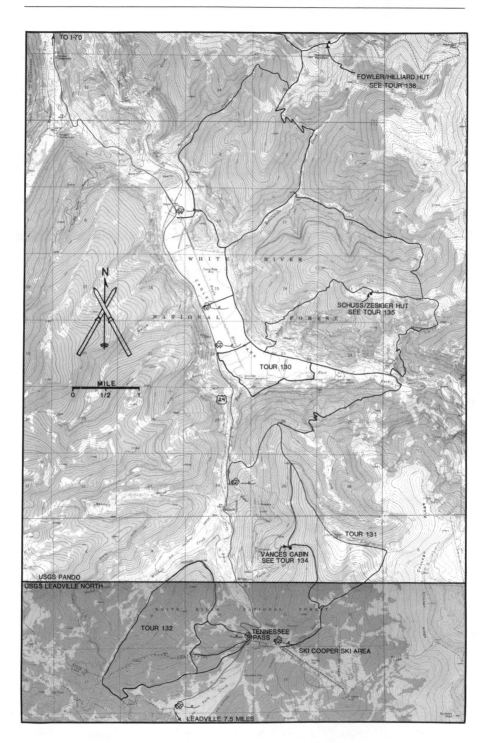

## East Fork Valley

The East Fork Trail leaves the southern trailhead, near the large pond, and follows a roadbed to the south. After 6 miles the trail passes a campground and veers east, crossing the South Fork of the Eagle River. Traversing near the edge of the steeper south slopes of Eagle Park, gentle skiing carries you several miles upstream along the East Fork of the Eagle River. Just past the 2-mile mark you'll cross a road. Follow it north to the East Fork road or cross it and extend the tour farther upstream to a point where the ski trail intercepts the East Fork road and the return downstream begins. As you ski back toward Camp Hale, the road contours slightly north. The parking area is reached by following a road back across the valley bottom.

## South Fork Road

A little over 2 miles south of the East Fork Valley Trailhead lies a small, plowed parking area on the east side of US 24. From here a road leads back to the north, traversing the mountain on a moderate course. At 1.3 miles leave the road as the route drops down the abandoned "B-slope." This was the practice incline where many aspiring mountain troops tasted their first downhill skiing (probably a bit of snow too!). At the bottom of this short run, it is simple to ski to the southern alternate trailhead at Camp Hale.

## Resolution Creek

This trail can be the most difficult of these tours, depending on how far you decide to push up Resolution Creek. Park at the main trailhead for Camp Hale and glide directly across Eagle Park to the east-northeast. At 0.5 miles the road intersects the East Fork road, which contours along the base of the higher cliffs. Turn left (north) and follow the road to the mouth of Resolution Creek. This spot is 1.2 miles from the trailhead and is the line of demarcation between the novice terrain and the slightly more difficult ascent up the drainage. The wide road leads 1.4 more miles upstream to the spot where Pearl Creek and Resolution Creek meet. This is where this route joins the higher Tenth Mountain Division trails.

*Shrine Mountain Inn, Vail Pass (tour 137), Brian Litz photo.*

# 131 TRAIL OF THE TENTH

> **DESCRIPTION: Winter ski tour, strenuous and scenic, fast descent, car shuttle recommended**
> **SKILL LEVEL: Advanced**
> **TIME: Full day**
> **DISTANCE: 6.5 miles one way**
> **ELEVATION CHANGE: 1,200 feet total gain/1,920 feet total loss**
> **STARTING ELEVATION: 10,540 feet**
> **AVALANCHE TERRAIN: None**
> **USGS 7.5 MINUTE MAPS: Leadville North, 1970, Pando, 1987-PR**
> **MAP: page 241**

Somewhat like a mini–Commando Run, this action-packed tour features breathtaking views of the Sawatch Range to the south and Mount of the Holy Cross directly to the west, steep climbing to Taylor Hill, spectacular glade skiing and finally a fast descent down a twisting trail to the Tennessee Pass road within its mere 6.5 miles. A graph of the elevation gain and drop on this tour would look like a pyramid, steeply accumulating all the elevation in one steady climb, while losing it with equal efficiency. The Trail of the Tenth deserves more attention from Front Range skiers, as it is one of the finest tours in the area.

This tour begins on the summit of Tennessee Pass and ends at an unmarked turnoff on the east side of US 24, 3 miles north from the summit of Tennessee Pass. A car shuttle is recommended but not essential. Leave the drop-off car at the small parking area 3.2 miles north of the summit of Tennessee Pass. Drive north from Leadville or south from I-70 and Minturn on US 24 to Tennessee Pass. When you reach the summit, park at the Ski Cooper ski area if it is open (weekends) or outside the gate if it is closed. Walk to the ski-touring center (a small trailer) and start skiing on the Burton Ditch roadbed, which leads off to the east-northeast.

Double-pole this road for several hundred yards until a trail forks north across the drainage. This turnoff is marked by a sign indicating "Tenth Mountain Trail." Begin climbing up the west (left) side of Piney Gulch on an obvious trail marked by trailblazes. The trail follows the contours of the main creekbed, moving in and out of thick stands of trees, allowing glimpses to the south of the Sawatch Range. The route climbs steadily into larger clearings before it bends north up a tributary of Piney Creek that follows the line of clearings. Direct your skis almost due north, tracing the meadows that reach all the way up to the saddle lying to the east of Taylor Hill. Although the last portion of this climb is fairly strenuous, the view from the high point on this tour is well worth the elevated respiratory rate!

Once you are on the Taylor Hill ridge, ski west through small openings in the dense trees. If you are unable to follow the exact path of the trailblazes, don't fret; simply follow the crest of the ridge as it heads gently west up to the actual summit of Taylor Hill (at 2.7 miles). From this vantage point a magnificent mountain panorama fills the horizon, a view relatively few skiers see. Push along the crest of the ridge heading northwest, staying on the ridge. The descent from this ridge is long and carries you through a forest of varying density. Choose the path of least resistance, continue down past the first roadbed that you encounter (4.2 miles) and eventually reach the second road at 4.9 miles, which you follow back to the Tennessee Pass road.

Beginning as a gentle climb around to the southwest, this mild-mannered road turns into a screaming and twisting downhill joyride. After you survive this stretch, a final short flat section delivers you onto the east edge of US 24. Car shuttle or walk 3 miles back to the top of the pass.

# 132 TENNESSEE PASS TRAIL SYSTEM

**DESCRIPTION: Winter ski tour, marked trails, rolling terrain, good for families and groups**
**SKILL LEVEL: Novice to intermediate**
**TIME: Optional, up to full day**
**DISTANCE: Optional, 2.3 miles or more**
**ELEVATION CHANGE: Optional, up to 500 feet total gain**
**STARTING ELEVATION: 10,424 feet**
**AVALANCHE TERRAIN: None**
**USGS 7.5 MINUTE MAP: Leadville North, 1970**
**MAP: page 241**

This trail system, located in the gently rolling terrain just west of Tennessee Pass, offers an outstanding array of novice and intermediate ski tours. Families and large groups will especially like the variety of choices available. Short loop trips, long loop trips, powder runs through scattered trees and several miles of moderate trail skiing are all accessible from the same starting point. The entire area is above 10,000 feet and surrounded by high peaks, so there is plenty of good snow all season.

The Leadville Forest Service Ranger District did an excellent job planning and marking all the trails. A sign in the parking area maps out the tours, with information on length and relative difficulty of each trail. The trail segments are organized into loop trips. The Powderhound Loop is a 2.5-mile course that heads west to the Continental Divide and then turns right for a moderate downhill run through scattered trees to the Old Railroad Run. The Treeline Loop takes the same trail to the Continental Divide but then drops south off the other side of the ridge to the Colorado Trail. The Mitchell Creek Loop makes a wide circle around the entire area, connecting the Colorado Trail with the Old Railroad Run. An extended loop around Lily Lake is possible from the intersection of the Colorado Trail with the north-south Wurtz Ditch road. This road and the Lily Lake Trail drop to the highway a few miles south of the top of the pass, making a car shuttle loop trip possible. The Old Railroad Run is a docile railroad grade descent off the north side of the pass into Mitchell Creek.

# 133 MOUNT ELBERT (14,431 FEET)

**DESCRIPTION: Spring ski-mountaineering descent, approach hike, highest point in Colorado**
**SKILL LEVEL: Advanced**
**TIME: Full day**
**DISTANCE: 8 miles round trip**
**ELEVATION CHANGE: 4,371 feet**
**STARTING ELEVATION: 10,060 feet**
**AVALANCHE TERRAIN: Mostly avalanche terrain; wait for spring consolidation**
**USGS 7.5 MINUTE MAP: Mount Elbert, 1979-PR**
**MAP: page 246**

If you're going to climb to the highest point in the state, why not bring your skis along and have a little fun on the way down? It is possible to ski either the western couloir or the Box Creek cirque on the northwest side of the mountain. The western couloir is a steep advanced descent from top to bottom, but unfortunately its snowpack melts out rather early in the season. The Box Creek cirque is a varied route that starts out moderately but gets steeper the farther down you go.

Although Mount Elbert can be climbed by several different routes, the northeast ridge is probably the easiest. From Malta, 3 miles west of Leadville on US 24, take Colo. 300 west for 1 mile, then south and southwest along Halfmoon Creek for 5 miles to Halfmoon Campground. Continue another mile past the campground to a small parking area where the Main Range Trail intersects the road. Hike south along the Main Range Trail up over a ridge. When the trail begins to drop into the Box Creek valley, you'll come to an obvious but unsigned fork. Go right here and proceed up through the trees to treeline. At treeline the trail continues up the northeast ridge to the summit, staying right of the Box Creek cirque. To ski the Box Creek cirque go straight east from the summit, aiming for the southwest corner of the cirque. Descend one of the steep chutes to the base of the cirque and then traverse back out onto the ridge and pick up the trail for the hike out.

If you plan to ski the western couloir, it is better to ascend the mountain from the west side so you can scout the descent route. From the Main Range Trail continue driving up the road 2 miles to South Halfmoon Creek. Hike (or four-wheel) south up the creek for another 2 miles to the base of the central descent couloir. Ascend the couloir or one of the spur ridges off to either side, noting the snow conditions for the descent. Since the snow does not last as long in the western couloirs as in the Box Creek cirque, you may find that the latter is your only option.

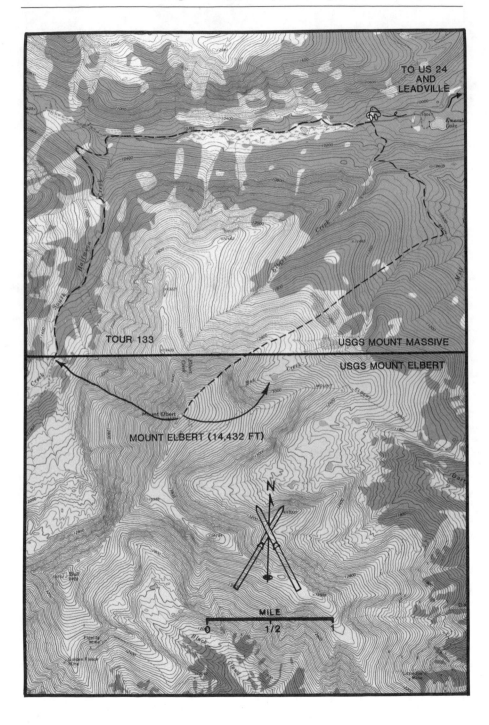

TO US 24
AND
LEADVILLE

TOUR 133

USGS MOUNT MASSIVE

USGS MOUNT ELBERT

MOUNT ELBERT (14,432 FT)

N

MILE

0          1/2          1

# 134 VANCE'S CABIN

Two access routes to Vance's Cabin are described. The Ski Cooper ski area access is the starting point for parties traveling south to north on the Tenth Mountain Trail. It is also the most widely used access for parties that do not continue on to the Schuss–Zesiger Hut. The second access route is from the Schuss–Zesiger Hut. It is normally used by parties traveling north to south who plan to visit all four of the TMTA huts between Vail Pass and Tennessee Pass.

Vance's Cabin is a cozy trilevel affair with all the amenities of a well-equipped ski-touring hut plus some extras, such as a sauna, refrigerator and gas stove. It has a marvelous view of the Holy Cross wilderness as well as Massive, Elbert and the peaks of the northern Sawatch. A renovated private cabin, it is loaned to the TMTA for winter use. It sleeps 16, with most of the bunks in the basement level and the balance in the upstairs loft. The bunks have good pads; all you need for a comfortable night's rest is a light sleeping bag, and the cabin is stocked with all the kitchen items you could ever want. Contact the Tenth Mountain Trail Association for reservations (see Appendix 4).

Skiing in the vicinity of the cabin is somewhat limited to the TMTA trails which traverse in from the north and south. Also, the small glade immediately adjacent to the cabin makes a good practice run. The Trail of the Tenth (tour 131), which starts from the Ski Cooper ski area, then climbs up onto the ridge above Vance's Cabin and finally drops back down to US 24, makes an excellent extended day trip.

## SKI COOPER TO VANCE'S CABIN

> **DESCRIPTION: First third on flat road; second third, steeper trail skiing; last third, level traverse through forest**
> **SKILL LEVEL: Intermediate**
> **TIME: One-third day**
> **DISTANCE: 3.1 miles**
> **ELEVATION CHANGE: 550 feet total gain**
> **STARTING ELEVATION: 10,430 feet**
> **AVALANCHE TERRAIN: Some avalanche terrain encountered; easily avoided**
> **USGS 7.5 MINUTE MAPS: Leadville North, 1970, Pando, 1987-PR**
> **MAP: page 241**

Vance's Cabin is one of the easier TMTA huts to reach. Located about 3 miles north of Ski Cooper, just off Tennessee Pass on US 24 between Leadville and Minturn, it can be reached in just a few short hours. As is normally the case with TMTA huts, the routes are somewhat sparingly marked by blue diamond trail markers. The normal route starts from the Nordic Center at the northeast end of the Ski Cooper parking lot. Permission must be obtained to leave a vehicle there overnight. There is also parking on the west side of the highway directly opposite the entrance to Ski Cooper.

From the Ski Cooper parking lot ski east on a cat-tracked road, part of the Nordic Center's Piney Loop Trail, which skirts around the left side of the ski area. After 0.6 miles turn left on the Nordic Center's Tenth Mountain Trail, which crosses the creek and heads northeast up a shallow draw. A short distance (approximately 0.3 miles) up the draw, the trail turns north and switchbacks steeply up an open hillside to the left. This is an easy turn to miss. If you find yourself skiing more than 0.5 miles up the draw, you probably have gone too far. After the switchbacks the trail ducks into the trees for good, climbing northeast, then switchbacking again northwest. Several hundred feet of elevation are gained before the trail levels out and contours north around the ridge. An open glade is reached at the end of this traverse which provides a short run straight down to Vance's Cabin.

## SCHUSS–ZESIGER HUT TO VANCE'S CABIN

**DESCRIPTION: Steep, fast, south-facing descent to valley floor, long gradual ascent through dense trees, mostly trail skiing**
**SKILL LEVEL: Advanced**
**TIME: Full day**
**DISTANCE: 8.6 miles**
**ELEVATION CHANGE: 1,560 feet total gain/2,235 feet total loss**
**STARTING ELEVATION: 11,660 feet**
**AVALANCHE TERRAIN: Route crosses avalanche slopes; prone to skier-triggered avalanches during high-hazard periods**
**USGS 7.5 MINUTE MAP: Pando, 1987-PR**
**MAP: page 241**

This is a long and difficult ski, especially with packs. If you have to break trail on the second half, plan to get a very early start or consider skiing out to Camp Hale instead.

From the Schuss–Zesiger Hut ski east along the ridge, dropping to a saddle at 11,400 feet where the trail branches. Take the right branch straight along the ridge over a small hump to a clearing. The descent from here to the valley floor is primarily on south-facing slopes. After sunny, warm days, when the snow surface melts and refreezes, skiing can be extremely difficult on the melt-freeze crust. If you are lucky to be there after a few inches of fresh powder, you'll be treated to an action-packed 2,200-foot schuss with lots of variety and loads of fun. About a third of the way down, you'll hit a jeep road which is part of the Colorado Trail. Much of the lower section of this road may completely melt out after a warm spring day.

Once you reach the valley floor ski east 0.25 miles on a wide road that runs the length of the valley. Keep an eye out for blue diamond trail markers which indicate where the trail takes off to the right and crosses the river. After crossing, begin a gradual traversing ascent southwest through the dense, north-facing forest. There are several short stretches of surprisingly steep trail in this section—climbing skins are recommended. One of the few landmarks, a meadow at Jones Gulch, is encountered 2.2 miles after crossing the river. It is skirted on its north side, then the trail continues its traversing ascent toward the nose of the long tree-covered skyline ridge that swoops down from the crest of Taylor Hill. Once at the ridge the trail turns left (southeast) and climbs several hundred feet to a road at 11,033 feet. Follow this road for nearly a mile to the small clearing that holds Vance's Cabin.

# 135 SCHUSS–ZESIGER HUT

The Schuss–Zesiger has one of the more breathtaking locations of all of Colorado's backcountry cabins. This handsome log shelter clings to the slopes high on the southwest side of a ridge running west from the Continental Divide. The panorama from the front deck is spectacular. To the south lie the Collegiate Peaks (see how many you can identify!) and to the west, the ripsaw massif of Mount of the Holy Cross. Skiing around the cabin is superb, with many acres of varied high-mountain terrain to explore. Accommodations are similar to the newer Tenth Mountain structures, with a large main floor with several large tables, comfortable couches opposite a wood-burning stove, a large kitchen equipped with both a wood-burning stove/oven and a gas stove, pots and pans, plates and utensils. The lighting is electric, powered by a set of photovoltaic cells mounted on the front of the building. Upstairs is a massive sleeping berth featuring two private bedrooms, several semiprivate cubbyholes, with enough thick foam pads to sleep 16. Attached to the rear of the structure is a sheltered wood-chopping alcove with a double outhouse forming the outer wall.

The routes to the Schuss–Zesiger Hut unfortunately are all quite demanding in terms of elevation gain. Whether your party is ascending from Resolution Creek or from the East Fork of the Eagle River, be prepared for a strenuous day. Contact the Tenth Mountain Trail Association for reservations (see Appendix 4).

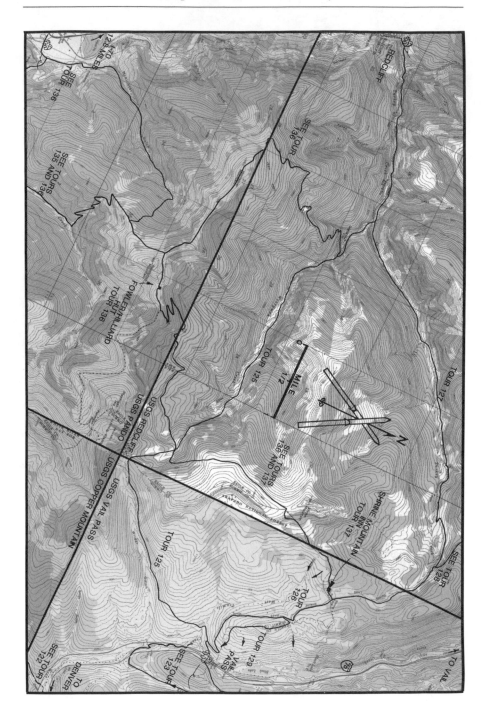

## FOWLER–HILLIARD HUT TO SCHUSS–ZESIGER HUT
## (FROM THE NORTH)

> **DESCRIPTION: Winter hut tour, long, strenuous route on backcountry trails and roads**
> **SKILL LEVEL: Advanced**
> **TIME: Full day**
> **DISTANCE: 7.8 miles one way**
> **ELEVATION CHANGE: 2,132 feet total gain/1,972 feet total loss**
> **STARTING ELEVATIONS: Fowler–Hilliard Hut: 11,500 feet**
> **AVALANCHE TERRAIN: Some avalanche terrain encountered; easily avoided**
> **USGS 7.5 MINUTE MAP: Pando, 1987-PR**
> **MAPS: pages 241, 250**

This route drops from the summit of Resolution Mountain into Resolution Creek, then regains all that elevation plus several hundred feet more. While most of the route follows well-marked trails, certain portions cover difficult terrain via an elusive path. From the Fowler–Hilliard Hut ski west into the obvious trough/drainage that cuts through the north half of Resolution Mountain. Cross a notch/pass, bypassing the trail intersection to Redcliff, and begin a short descent to the west before contouring south along the McAllister Gulch Trail. Traverse and descend along the ridgeline as trail markers guide you toward the steep drop into Resolution Creek (this section of the route is very scenic, so have your cameras ready). Leave the ridgeline at 1.6 miles where a small forested saddle is reached. Descending into this valley is the toughest part of the tour, with steep and demanding trail skiing. The trail markers can be difficult to follow.

Once you have reached Resolution Creek turn south and glide down to the intersection with Pearl Creek (at 9,678 feet, this is the lowest spot on this trail, roughly at the halfway mark). Cross Resolution Creek on a road, then turn sharply southeast and follow the Pearl Creek road for slightly more than 2 miles (crossing the north side of the creek en route). Cross Pearl Creek to the south and climb for 1.2 miles to a large and obvious saddle and the intersection with the Cataract Creek route. This relatively short ascent is strenuous (climbing skins are recommended) and the trail markers are somewhat hard to locate. From the saddle turn west (right) and ski along the beautiful ridge line, crossing over a small hill before a short descent brings you to the hut (about 0.6 miles).

# CAMP HALE TO SCHUSS–ZESIGER HUT
## (VIA RESOLUTION CREEK, FROM THE WEST-NORTHWEST)

**DESCRIPTION: Winter ski tour, long, moderately difficult hut approach, steady uphill climb**
**SKILL LEVEL: Advanced**
**TIME: Full day**
**DISTANCE: 6.6 miles**
**ELEVATION CHANGE: 2,410 feet total gain**
**STARTING ELEVATION: 9,250 feet**
**AVALANCHE TERRAIN: None**
**USGS 7.5 MINUTE MAP: Pando, 1987-PR**
**MAPS: pages 241, 250**

This approach route, while accumulating over 2,000 feet of elevation gain, is actually quite straightforward and easy to follow for the majority of the day. The trail begins on very gentle terrain, then climbs up Resolution Creek and on up Pearl Creek (see previous route). The most difficult stretch is where it leaves Pearl Creek and climbs to the saddle/ridge where the hut sits. Climbing skins are recommended for this portion of the route, especially if you are toting big packs. Moderate climbing and easy-to-follow roads characterize the balance of this tour.

Drive to the Camp Hale Trailhead located on US 24, 14.7 miles north from the intersection of US 24 and Colo. 91 at Leadville; or drive south 18.5 miles from the intersection of US 24 and I-70.

From the Camp Hale Trailhead, ski across Eagle Park to the northeast. At the far side, intercept the East Fork road and turn northwest (left). At 1.2 miles turn northeast and ski into the Resolution Creek drainage, following the Resolution road. At the junction with Pearl Creek, turn off the main Resolution road and head southeast, touring along the south side of Pearl Creek for just over 2 miles (crossing the creek en route). Cross the creek to the south and climb to the saddle/ridge where the hut sits. Once you reach the saddle, and the intersection with the Cataract Creek Trail, turn west (right) and follow the ridge for 0.6 miles to the hut. The ascent from Pearl Creek to the ridge is the toughest portion of the trip, as it climbs directly upward on a difficult backcountry trail.

## CAMP HALE TO SCHUSS–ZESIGER HUT
## (VIA RANCH CREEK, FROM THE WEST)

**DESCRIPTION: Winter ski tour, shortest route to the Schuss–Zesiger Hut, very steep**
**SKILL LEVEL: Advanced**
**TIME: Full day**
**DISTANCE: 4.7 miles one way**
**ELEVATION CHANGE: 2,410 feet total gain**
**STARTING ELEVATION: 9,250 feet**
**AVALANCHE TERRAIN: Some avalanche terrain encountered; easily avoided**
**USGS 7.5 MINUTE MAP: Pando, 1987-PR**
**MAPS: pages 241, 250**

For those skiers who seek the most direct route to this hut, this is the choice. Be prepared for a grueling climb, as the trail gains over 500 feet per mile and offers little respite during the final 3.2 miles. Climbing skins are recommended.

Drive to the Camp Hale Trailhead located on US 24, 14.7 miles north from the intersection of US 24 and Colo. 91 at Leadville; or drive south 18.5 miles from the intersection of US 24 and I-70. From the Camp Hale Trailhead ski to the east-northeast directly across Eagle Park. Cross the Eagle River (no bridge) at 0.2 miles and reach a road on the far side. Turn south (right) and ski along the road, contouring southeast until you reach the trail junction of the East Fork–Cataract Creek and the Ranch Creek routes. Turn left and ski north on the Ranch Creek jeep road. From here to the hut the tour climbs constantly northeast up Ranch Creek.

## CAMP HALE TO SCHUSS–ZESIGER HUT
## (VIA CATARACT CREEK, FROM THE WEST AND SOUTH)

**DESCRIPTION: Winter hut tour, gentle first half followed by a stiff 3.4-mile ascent to Schuss–Zesiger Hut**
**SKILL LEVEL: Intermediate to advanced**
**TIME: Full day**
**DISTANCE: 6.81 miles one way**
**ELEVATION CHANGE: 2,485 feet total gain**
**STARTING ELEVATION: 9,250 feet**
**AVALANCHE TERRAIN: Some avalanche terrain encountered; easily avoided**
**USGS 7.5 MINUTE MAP: Pando, 1987-PR**
**MAPS: pages 241, 250**

Cataract Creek is similar to the route in from Resolution Creek. The first half is very moderate, then it climbs more steeply the last few miles. This tour begins on level terrain until it turns up Cataract Creek and ascends a pretty valley to the ridge east of the hut. This 2.5-mile stretch is strenuous; climbing skins are recommended. Look for herds of elk, often lounging throughout the Cataract drainage.

Drive to the Camp Hale Trailhead located on US 24, 14.7 miles north from the intersection of US 24 and Colo. 91 at Leadville; or drive south 18.5 miles from the intersection of US 24 and I-70.

Leave the Camp Hale Trailhead and ski east-northeast directly across Eagle Park. Cross the Eagle River (no bridge) and intercept the East Fork road on the far east side. Turn right (south) and ski along the road as it contours east and up toward the head of the East Fork. Remain on the north side of the valley to the turnoff to Cataract Creek (and the Colorado Trail) at 3.5 miles (near the 9,580-foot level).

Head up the trail directly north for several hundred feet before turning east and climbing a steep jeep road that contours around a steep rock outcrop. Ski north along the creek, cross the creek, then climb along two switchbacks. Ski up and across a large clearing and swing east, following the drainage. Enter thicker forest cover and follow the trail (TMTA and Colorado Trail) markers until you break into a small clearing at 5.3 miles.

Turn sharply north again and ascend the steep tributary of Cataract Creek. Near the top of this climb this drainage bends east, in a large clearing. Leave the creek and climb more to the northwest to attain the top of the ridge. Head west along the crest of the ridge, passing the Pearl Creek turnoff on a prominent saddle en route, and continue 0.6 miles to the Schuss–Zesiger Hut. As you make the final ascent to the hut, look for the Fowler–Hilliard Hut directly north.

## VANCE'S CABIN TO SCHUSS–ZESIGER (FROM THE SOUTH)

**DESCRIPTION: Winter hut tour, long, physically demanding trail**
**SKILL LEVEL: Advanced**
**TIME: Full day (be prepared for a long one)**
**DISTANCE: 8.6 miles one way**
**ELEVATION CHANGE: 2,235 feet total gain/1,555 feet total loss**
**STARTING ELEVATION: 10,980 feet**
**AVALANCHE TERRAIN: Some avalanche terrain encountered; easily avoided**
**USGS 7.5 MINUTE MAP: Pando, 1987-PR**
**MAPS: pages 241, 250**

Skiing from Vance's Cabin to the Schuss–Zesiger Hut is one of the more deceptive sections of the TMTA route in this area. It has almost as much elevation gain as the other approaches to the hut but is longer. The grueling uphill section comes after many miles of rolling terrain with many short drops and climbs. Additionally, this trail spends more time in the woods, making route finding slightly more difficult.

From Vance's Cabin ski north along a road/trail until you reach the main road, which traverses in below you from the south. Continue north on the well-marked route along the crest of the ridge, descending continuously. At the 1.3-mile mark, the main road veers back to the southeast (this is close to where the Trail of the Tenth, tour 131, merges from the right). Leave the road and drop north along a fast and fun trail until you intercept a second road. Turn right (southeast) and descend into a small meadow/swamp which is prominently marked on the USGS 7.5 minute map (the Trail of the Tenth deviates and turns southwest at the intersection).

Leave the meadow and trace the small creek north on a very tricky descent down a steep and narrow trail (this section is thankfully short!) until more moderate terrain carries you east and finally down several small switchbacks. The final mile or so to the East Fork road is forest trail skiing and alternates between gentle glides and fun drops. When you reach the valley bottom follow the wide trail around to the northwest to the intersection with the Cataract Creek–Camp Hale routes.

Head up the trail directly north for several hundred feet before turning east and climbing a steep jeep road that contours around a steep rock outcrop. Ski north along the creek, cross the creek, then climb along two switchbacks. Ski up and across a large clearing and swing east, following the drainage. Enter thicker forest cover and follow the trail (TMTA and Colorado Trail) markers until you break into a small clearing at 5.3 miles.

Turn sharply north again and ascend the steep tributary of Cataract Creek. Near the top of this climb this drainage bends east, in a large clearing. Leave the creek and climb more to the northwest to attain the top of the ridge. Head west along the crest of the ridge, passing the Pearl Creek turnoff on a prominent saddle en route, and continue 0.6 miles to the Schuss–Zesiger Hut. As you make the final ascent to the hut, look for the Fowler–Hilliard Hut directly north.

# 136 FOWLER–HILLIARD HUT

The Fowler–Hilliard Hut is unmatched for its lofty position and 360-degree rugged alpine panorama. Situated only a few hundred feet below the summit of Resolution Mountain (11,905 feet), it holds a commanding position, high over valleys northeast of Camp Hale, where the historic Tenth Mountain Division trained for battle during World War II. The hut is a memorial to Ann Fowler and Ed Hilliard of Denver, who were killed in a mountaineering accident. It is owned and operated by the Tenth Mountain Trail Association (TMTA) (see Appendix 4 for reservation information).

For telemark enthusiasts, skiing in the immediate vicinity of the hut is superb. Most notable are the numerous sparsely timbered glades on the west side of Resolution Mountain. The hut itself is a spacious two-story building with enough bunk space for 16. The bunks have pads and the cabin is warm and tight—all you need for a comfortable night's rest is a sleeping bag. The hut is equipped with a solar lighting system with plenty of storage capacity, and it works like a charm. Heated by two wood stoves, a modern one and an antique that can also be used for cooking, the cabin can be toasty warm in a short period of time. There should be plenty of wood available—some may need to be split. There is also a small two-burner propane stove for cooking and plenty of dishes, pots, pans and eating utensils. Water must be obtained by melting snow.

The hut is extremely isolated and requires a long, difficult approach by any route. For this reason, it is not recommended as a destination for novice skiers.

## SHRINE MOUNTAIN INN TO FOWLER–HILLIARD HUT

> **DESCRIPTION: First half, spectacular but rugged backcountry touring over exposed ridge; second half, gradual ascent on logging road with several long switchbacks**
> **SKILL LEVEL: Advanced**
> **TIME: Full day**
> **DISTANCE: 6.8 miles**
> **ELEVATION CHANGE: 1,230 feet total gain/940 feet total loss**
> **STARTING ELEVATION: 11,209 feet**
> **AVALANCHE TERRAIN: Route crosses avalanche slopes; prone to skier-triggered avalanches during high-hazard periods**
> **USGS 7.5 MINUTE MAPS: Redcliff, 1987-PR, Pando, 1987-PR**
> **MAPS: pages 228, 250**

From the Shrine Mountain Inn ski southwest, following blue diamond trail markers through clearings and sparse timber. Begin a steep climb, heading for a saddle on the ridge just south (left) of Shrine Mountain. The blue diamond trail markers can be difficult to locate in this section. Shrine Mountain has some rock outcrops which serve as convenient landmarks for route finding. Break out of the trees just below a saddle that is immediately south of Shrine Mountain and proceed west over the exposed ridge. Traverse south, contouring on the west side of the ridge around a shoulder and drop a quick 700 feet through powder glades to Wearyman Creek. Cross Wearyman Creek, continuing down and west a short distance before proceeding south. The trail climbs a bit, then follows a logging road west a short distance. Continue west and south up through trees to another logging road. Turn right on this road and follow it on a long traverse west. Eventually, four long, tiring switchbacks take you to a fork in the saddle between Resolution Mountain and Ptarmigan Hill. Turn west (right) here and proceed 0.3 miles to the Fowler–Hilliard Hut, which sits in a saddle on the ridge just below the bald summit of Resolution Mountain.

## Schuss–Zesiger Hut to Fowler–Hilliard Hut

**DESCRIPTION: First half, big drop down steep trail and road; second half, steep grueling uphill, many switchbacks, climbing skins recommended**
**SKILL LEVEL: Advanced**
**TIME: Full day**
**DISTANCE: 7.8 miles**
**ELEVATION CHANGE: 1,970 feet total gain/2,130 feet total loss**
**STARTING ELEVATION: 11,660 feet**
**AVALANCHE TERRAIN: Route crosses avalanche slopes; prone to skier-triggered avalanches during high-hazard periods**
**USGS 7.5 MINUTE MAP: Pando, 1987-PR**
**MAPS: pages 228, 241, 250**

From the Schuss–Zesiger Hut ski east along the ridge crest 0.6 miles to a saddle and trail junction. Turn left and begin a long steep run that drops through the trees. About midway down, the trail makes a short jog to the east (right) before continuing a relentless drop into Pearl Creek. At Pearl Creek the grade lessens considerably. The trail crosses the creek and picks up a logging road on its north bank which continues west down the creek. After another 0.35 miles the road crosses to the south side of Pearl Creek and continues another 0.8 miles to Resolution Creek. Cross Resolution Creek and turn right on a good road. Proceed 1 mile up Resolution Creek, scanning for blue diamond trail markers which cut northwest (left) up a shallow draw. The trail now begins a grueling 1,000-foot climb with numerous switchbacks up the left side of this draw. Climbing skins are recommended for this section. When you finally reach a saddle, turn right and continue climbing up the ridge, gaining another 500 feet. Turn north (left) in the sparsely timbered glades below Resolution Mountain and diagonal up a short distance to a saddle on the ridge between Hornsilver Mountain and Resolution Mountain. Find a shallow trough that cuts down and east along the north flank of Resolution Mountain. This trough is known as "the Narrows." From here it is a short but sweet 0.5-mile run to the Fowler–Hilliard Hut, which sits on a saddle below the east ridge of Resolution Mountain, just above the base of the Narrows trough.

## Camp Hale to Fowler–Hilliard Hut

**DESCRIPTION: Marked backcountry trail skiing, considerable elevation gain, climbing skins recommended**
**SKILL LEVEL: Advanced**
**TIME: Full day**
**DISTANCE: 4.9 miles**
**ELEVATION CHANGE: 2,300 feet total gain**
**STARTING ELEVATION: 9,200 feet**
**AVALANCHE TERRAIN: Route crosses avalanche slopes; can be dangerous during high-hazard periods**
**USGS 7.5 MINUTE MAP: Pando, 1987-PR**
**MAPS: pages 228, 241, 250**

To reach the Fowler–Hilliard Hut this route takes the approach that the shortest distance between two points is a straight line. Over 2,300 feet are gained in a relatively short distance, 4.25 miles—that means a lot of uphill.

Start from Pando, located at the north end of Camp Hale between Leadville and Minturn on US 24. The normal parking area for Camp Hale is near the south end of the open valley. This route, however, climbs up McAllister Gulch, which is at the north end. A plowed turnout is near the old townsite of Pando, just south of where US 24 crosses the railroad tracks and approximately 1.5 miles north of the Camp Hale turnout. This is the recommended starting point.

Ski east on a road that heads directly across the flats and over the Eagle River. Then curve north and continue along the east side of the valley to the first right turn. Here a road climbs north out of the valley and curves up into McAllister Gulch. This is the route. Follow blue diamond trail markers up this road as it steadily climbs northeast up the right side of McAllister Gulch. After 2.6 miles the road makes a sharp right turn heading southeast for the right skyline ridge. Once at the ridge the road turns left and continues up the ridge to some open glades below Resolution Mountain. The route then diagonals north up to a saddle on the main ridge between Hornsilver Mountain and Resolution Mountain. From the saddle, find a shallow trough that cuts down and east along the north flank of Resolution Mountain. This trough is known as "the Narrows." From here it is a short but sweet 0.5 mile run to the Fowler–Hilliard Hut, which sits on a saddle below the east ridge of Resolution Mountain, just above the base of the Narrows trough.

## REDCLIFF TO FOWLER–HILLIARD HUT

> **DESCRIPTION: Long slog up logging road to treeline ridge, then east along ridge to hut**
> **SKILL LEVEL: Intermediate**
> **TIME: Full day**
> **DISTANCE: 9 miles**
> **ELEVATION CHANGE: 3,080 feet total gain/260 feet loss**
> **STARTING ELEVATION: 8,680 feet**
> **AVALANCHE TERRAIN: Some avalanche terrain encountered; easily avoided**
> **USGS 7.5 MINUTE MAPS: Redcliff, 1987-PR, Pando, 1987-PR**
> **MAPS: pages 228, 241, 250**

This route is not as steep as the other routes and does not require as much technical skiing ability, so many choose it as a descent route rather than the hair-raising plunge into Resolution Creek. It also has merit as an ascent route for those not equipped with climbing skins who are discouraged by the idea of skiing steep terrain with big packs. Even so, it cannot be recommended as a first choice for an ascent route because it is an extremely long, hard trail.

The route begins from Redcliff, an interesting little mining town a short distance up a side valley from US 24, which runs between Minturn (just west of Vail on I-70) and Tennessee Pass. Once at Redcliff park on a side street or in the lot by the marshall's office. Find the Shrine Pass road, which heads east from Redcliff up Turkey Creek. Ski this for 2.5 miles to a junction with the Wearyman Creek road. Turn right and follow this road 0.8 miles to the Hornsilver Mountain road at 9,300 feet. Turn right again and climb slowly but surely all the way up this road and then up Hornsilver Mountain, gaining an unbelievable 2,270 feet in the process. Descend east along the ridge, then climb and traverse southeast, heading for Resolution Mountain. At the saddle just west of Resolution Mountain, the route intersects with other routes coming up from McAllister Gulch and Resolution Creek. Find a trough, "the Narrows," which cuts east below the north side of Resolution Mountain. Quickly descend this and hop back up on the ridge, right, to the Fowler–Hilliard Hut, sitting in the saddle just east of Resolution Mountain.

## OTHER ROUTES TO THE FOWLER–HILLIARD HUT

There are two other alternate routes to the Fowler–Hilliard Hut. One starts from Camp Hale and goes up Resolution Creek to Pearl Creek, where it intersects the route from the Schuss–Zesiger Hut. This is a little longer (6.5 miles) than the route that starts from Camp Hale and follows McAllister Gulch but it may stand a better chance of having a trail broken.

The second route, which is not marked by blue diamond trail markers, starts

at Vail Pass and traverses southwest into Wilder Gulch. It then follows Wilder Gulch
to its end, where it climbs steeply to a saddle at Ptarmigan Pass just left of Ptarmigan
Peak. The ridge at Ptarmigan Pass is often corniced. From Ptarmigan Pass the route
drops 400 feet down the back (west) side and picks up a road that traverses west
around Ptarmigan Hill. This road is then followed on a level traverse to a saddle in
the trees east of Resolution Mountain, where it intersects the route from the Shrine
Mountain Inn.

# 137 SHRINE MOUNTAIN INN

The majestic Shrine Mountain Inn represents backcountry hut accommodations in the supreme. Inside this grand structure skiers are treated to private rooms
with real beds, a muscle-wilting sauna, running water and even a pot-bellied stove
complete with mica (muscovite) "glass" windows. The inn also features a large front
deck surrounded by exquisite spruce forests and awe-inspiring mountain vistas. The
terrain around the inn is perfect for exploration and the route in is moderate enough
for winter adventurers of all abilities. A night at the inn is an ideal jumping-off spot
for more adventurous escapades, such as the Tenth Mountain Division Trail to the
Fowler–Hilliard Hut, Commando Run or the Shrine Pass Tour. It is also a cozy, safe
hideaway for those searching for a romantic escape from civilization. The inn is
privately owned. Contact the Tenth Mountain Trail Association for reservations (see
Appendix 4).

## VAIL PASS TO SHRINE MOUNTAIN INN

**DESCRIPTION: Winter hut tour, easiest and shortest tour to any
TMTA hut, moderate and scenic trail**
**SKILL LEVEL: Novice to intermediate**
**TIME: Half to full day**
**DISTANCE: 3.5 miles one way**
**ELEVATION CHANGE: 1,000 feet total gain**
**STARTING ELEVATION: 10,580 feet**
**AVALANCHE TERRAIN: None**
**USGS 7.5 MINUTE MAP: Vail Pass, 1987-PR**
**MAPS: pages 223, 228, 250**

The shortest and easiest route to the Shrine Mountain Inn begins at the main
parking area (near the rest area) on Vail Pass. Follow the Shrine Pass Tour (tour 127)
for 2.4 miles until you reach the summit of Shrine Pass. Near the snow-covered
outhouse and summit road sign, turn left (southwest) and follow the normally well-
tracked trail that leads out of the large clearing and into the thick stands of trees. From

here the inn is only about 0.5 miles away. The trail follows an obvious roadbed that is easy to follow.

## FOWLER–HILLIARD HUT TO SHRINE MOUNTAIN INN

**DESCRIPTION: Winter hut tour, spectacular and challenging**
**SKILL LEVEL: Intermediate to advanced**
**TIME: Full day (be prepared for a very long day with heavy packs)**
**DISTANCE: 6.8 miles one way**
**ELEVATION CHANGE: 940 feet total gain/1,231 feet total loss**
**STARTING ELEVATION: 11,500 feet**
**AVALANCHE TERRAIN: Route crosses avalanche slopes; prone to skier-triggered avalanches during high-hazard periods**
**USGS 7.5 MINUTE MAPS: Redcliff, 1987-PR, Vail Pass, 1987-PR**
**MAPS: pages 223, 228, 250**

Skiing from the Fowler–Hilliard Hut to the Shrine Mountain Inn is a truly varied route, from wide roads through thick forests to exposed alpine (above treeline) passages. The trail is recommended for advanced skiers but it may be managed by strong intermediate-level skiers too. Get an early start as there is lots of climbing, exposed traverses and, if the weather is less than perfect, route finding may be difficult and time-consuming. In general, the trail is well marked with blue trail markers.

From the Fowler–Hilliard Hut ski east to the logging road which crosses the saddle from south to north. Turn left (north) and descend on the road through four large switchbacks until the primary road contours to the northeast, crossing to and following another small road down and into a large clearing in Wearyman Creek. This spot is roughly one-half the distance between the huts.

The next stretch begins by climbing along a faint road/clearing that ascends steeply north-northeast. Follow the trail markers as they contour up to the northwest through a faint bowl (near the 11,400-foot mark on the map) filled with clearings and trees. When you reach treeline, traverse along the west side of Shrine Mountain, staying between the 11,600-foot and 11,800-foot contour intervals. An altimeter is useful here. This is a beautiful portion of the trail, moving through small stands of trees often covered with snow and rime ice, with views to the west of Mount of the Holy Cross (14,005 feet). After 2.2 miles, ski up onto a small saddle situated southeast of Shrine Mountain. At 11,760 feet, this is the highest point on the Tenth Mountain Division Trail.

From the saddle descend east for several hundred feet, then turn sharply north and ski into the protection of the trees. Continue on a descending trail through alternating stump-filled burned areas and trees. Follow the trail markers for about 1.4 miles (from the saddle) to the inn.

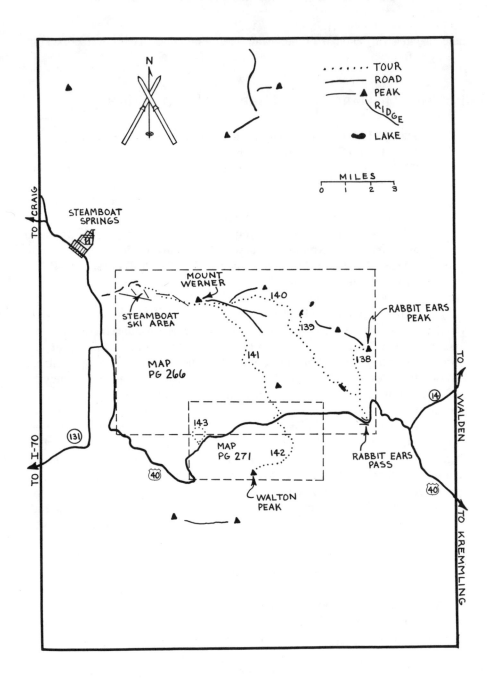

# CHAPTER TWELVE

# STEAMBOAT SPRINGS AND RABBIT EARS PASS

## INTRODUCTION

The Steamboat Springs–Rabbit Ears Pass area is the most isolated area for backcountry skiing covered by this book. Located in the "far north" of Colorado, the landscape here is dominated by vast rolling plateaus covered by thick stands of evergreens, quiet meadows and isolated glades. The countryside is ideal for all varieties of ski touring, from perfect novice trails to unmatched telemark terrain, and its atmosphere is entirely different from the Front Range and the area near Summit County and Vail. The combination of a consistently deep snowpack, frequent storms and western ranch-country charm has made this area a favored skiing mecca since the early 20th century.

Rabbit Ears Pass, where most of the tours in this chapter lie, towers east of the town of Steamboat Springs. The pass is not a simple mountain barrier but is actually a long plateau with minor summits on the eastern and western boundaries. Between these subtle high points is a vast oasis of moderate terrain and forested peaks. North of the eastern summit is historic Rabbit Ears Peak. Several miles west is the Hogan Park ski trail, a notable Colorado ski trail since the late 1940s. South of US 40 Walton Mountain features additional excellent trails and telemark skiing.

Every tour on this broad expanse crosses wide open meadows perfect for relaxing kick and glide. Advanced skiers can strike off toward steeper terrain and investigate clandestine powder caches while others ski around on the flats.

The town of Steamboat Springs possesses a true western ambience derived from a history of ranching. Contrasted with the younger, upstart Colorado resorts, this community exudes a warm friendly feeling and a relaxed lifestyle. Perhaps the only drawback to skiing this area is its distance from the Front Range communities. The drive from Denver can take from three to four hours, and if the weather is poor, the crossing of Rabbit Ears Pass can increase the travel time considerably. Skiing on Rabbit Ears Pass consequently requires a greater commitment of time. The minimum time necessary for a leisurely paced trip is probably a day and a half. Plan for a longer trip, so you'll have more time for logistics and exploration. This guide has highlighted the Rabbit Ears area but many more tours are possible, many originating closer to Steamboat Springs. Take some time to enjoy this outstanding Nordic area.

## HISTORY

Rabbit Ears Pass lies in Routt County and is part of the Park Range. Geologically these mountains are some of the oldest and hardest rock formations exposed on the North American continent. Spread across these mountains are dense forests interspersed with large meadows, marshes and lakes. Ute Indians, as well as a few Arapaho, Gros Ventre (pronounced "Grow Vaunt"), Sioux, Shoshone and Cheyenne, spent their summers in these mountains hunting the vast assortment of wildlife: buffalo, elk, mule deer, antelope, mountain lion, beaver, black and grizzly bear, moose, mink, muskrat, fox, wolf and bighorn sheep. The Yampa, the main river draining this area, was named after a plant found only in northwestern Colorado. The plant bears an underground tuber, similar to a sweet potato, that was a main food source for the Utes.

White people passed through this area in the 1830s when hunters and trappers found their way into northern Colorado. Even the perambulatory "Lord Gore" (see the Vail Pass chapter) visited Routt County, creating the first wagon road from Summit County in 1855. For several decades itinerant groups of mountain men passed through but no one created a permanent settlement until 1866, when gold prospectors, fueled by the discoveries to the south in Summit County, began to explore the mountains. Although gold was found near present-day Hahn's Peak, the veins (or lodes) were not as rich or extensive as their southern counterparts. It was agriculture, not mining, that became the focal point of Routt County's economy. Since the 1880s, cattle ranching and farming have remained highly productive. In addition, coal and uranium have played an important economic role.

Perhaps Routt County's greatest claim to fame is its pivotal role in the development of Colorado's downhill and cross-country skiing. Steamboat boasts some of the most consistent and deep snowfalls in the state. As in all mountain communities, skis were originally used for transportation. Carl Howelson, an immigrant stonemason from Norway and expert skier, journeyed west from Chicago to pursue his chosen career in Denver. An avid daredevil who had even logged time with Barnum and Bailey's circus, he built Nordic-style ski jumps in the Front Range and near Hot Sulphur Springs (the county seat of Grand County). Eventually he moved to Steamboat, where he could take advantage of the abundant snowfall and varied terrain. Howelson began jumping regularly on what was to become Howelson Hill, still in use as a Nordic-jumping training site. Howelson inspired the Winter Sports Carnival, held each winter and featuring women's and men's ski races, ski-joring (skiing while being pulled by a horse), novelty events and, of course, distance jumping. Steamboat's skiing tradition is as rich as any in the state and today the area is one of the finest ski destinations for all types of skiers.

# 138 RABBIT EARS PEAK

DESCRIPTION: Winter ski tour, classic, moderate trail
SKILL LEVEL: Intermediate*
TIME: Full day
DISTANCE: 9.3 miles round trip
ELEVATION CHANGE: 1,215 feet total gain
STARTING ELEVATION: 9,439 feet
AVALANCHE TERRAIN: Some avalanche terrain encountered; easily avoided
USGS 7.5 MINUTE MAP: Rabbit Ears Peak, 1956
MAP: page 266

*NOVICE HIGHLIGHT: The first part of this tour (to the old US 40 road), and the meadow near the highway, is a wonderful area for novice skiers.

If a skier had only one day to spend touring in the environs of Rabbit Ears Pass, this fine route would be our recommendation. A tour to the summit of Rabbit Ears Peak embodies all the ingredients for pleasurable backcountry skiing; the excellent snow, beautiful uncrowded scenery and moderate rolling terrain with hidden bowls and glades will satisfy skiers of all abilities. The peak's 10,654-foot summit, capped by distinctive twin towers of weathered granite, makes a beautiful spot for lunch on crisp cloudless days, while the lower protective forests provide ample area for novice skiers to play.

Keep in mind that the 1954 USGS 7.5 minute map is seriously out-of-date and does not show the position of modern US 40! Drive on US 40 to the east summit of Rabbit Ears Pass, marked by a Continental Divide highway sign and a small parking area. Remember that Rabbit Ears Pass is roughly three to four hours from the Denver metropolitan area, so if you start from there, a very early start is required.

From the parking area begin skiing north-northwest, crossing the east edge of a large meadow. Ski fairly close to the woods to the east. After approximately 0.4 miles cut into the forest and tour along an old roadbed, bypassing a road fork that heads off to the right. This road gradually climbs back up onto the Continental Divide and reaches the old US 40 roadbed after roughly 1.3 miles. A small meadow and an old stone monument mark this spot.

Re-enter the woods to the north and follow another old jeep road. Reach another fork after 0.25 miles. Turn right here and contour briefly east and then back north. Continue gradually climbing along the east slopes of the Continental Divide, skiing in and out of several large meadows, staying well above Grizzly Creek.

The road forks once again at the 2.5-mile mark. Ski to the right and head straight north, remaining west of the creekbed. The valley's head forces the trail to contour stiffly back southeast and the final ascent begins. Moderate climbing along

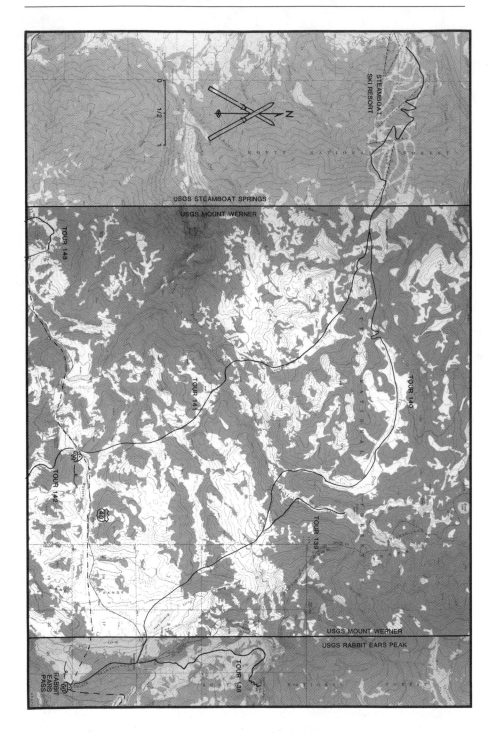

the road brings you to the summit. Many skiers simply follow a route of their own choosing for the last few miles and some cut directly across the large looping switchback in an attempt to shave off some mileage. Either way the view from the summit is great and the tour back to the cars is enjoyable.

# 139 FISHHOOK LAKE

**DESCRIPTION: Winter ski tour, remote backcountry trail**
**SKILL LEVEL: Intermediate**
**TIME: Full day**
**DISTANCE: 13.5 miles round trip**
**ELEVATION CHANGE: 840 feet total gain/400 feet total loss**
**STARTING ELEVATION: 9,440 feet**
**AVALANCHE TERRAIN: None**
**USGS 7.5 MINUTE MAPS: Rabbit Ears Peak, 1956, Mount Werner, 1956**
**MAP: page 266**

Essentially a short version of the Long Park Tour, this round-trip excursion takes you on a rolling, lightly forested course 6.7 miles into the remote Fishhook Creek drainage. This tour is a bit more challenging than the other intermediate-level tours in this area. The route finding is more complicated and if the weather turns foul, it can become extremely difficult.

The Rabbit Ears Pass area is a prime example of the problems encountered with out-of-date USGS topographic maps. The new highway is not shown on the USGS map; it is hand-drawn onto the maps in this book—keep this in mind. Drive on US 40 to the east summit of Rabbit Ears Pass, marked by a Continental Divide highway sign and a parking area. The drive takes roughly three to four hours to complete from Denver, depending on conditions.

The tour begins with easy skiing on a northerly heading that traces the Continental Divide via a snowmobile trail. Continue north until you reach the old Rabbit Ears Pass East Summit, marked by a stone marker. At this spot change course and follow the old roadbed to the northwest, aiming for flat, snow-covered Dumont Lake. Tour around the southwest corner of the lake and proceed northwest. The objective is to intercept the old roadbed that runs north, through "Base Campground" and down into Fishhook drainage. From the corner of the lake a 200-foot-plus climb up a moderate, sparsely vegetated grade will place you on this road, just under 3 miles from the parking area.

Fishhook drainage lies an additional 3 miles away to the north. Double-pole along the roadbed through majestic stands of conifer trees and cross the open head of a tributary of Fishhook Creek. After skiing through a large stand of trees roughly 1 mile past the point where you gained the roadbed, break out into a vast windswept clearing dotted with clumps of evergreen trees and snags. The roadbed now becomes more elusive, since it is buried under the drifted snows of the meadow. If you are unable to locate it, set a course following true north and skirt east (right) of a small knoll, passing through or around several islands of trees marked on the map. After you pass these trees head northwest, traversing and slightly dropping with the contours of the slopes to the east (right).

Try to locate the road where it turns west along the north edge of the large clearing. The road enters the forest 0.2 miles west of this point, then drops west into Fishhook Creek. Instead of following the road, it is quicker and more interesting to timber-bash 0.6 miles northwest from the edge of the clearing through the forest to Fishhook Creek. Turn right (north) at Fishhook Creek and proceed approximately 0.6 miles upstream to Fishhook Lake, the tour's final destination.

For the return trip, simply retrace your tracks back to Rabbit Ears Pass.

# 140 LONG PARK

**DESCRIPTION: Winter ski tour, usually an overnight tour through beautiful country, steep climb at finish to Mount Werner, car shuttle required**
**SKILL LEVEL: Intermediate**
**TIME: Full day or overnight**
**DISTANCE: 17.3 miles one way**
**ELEVATION CHANGE: 1,505 feet total gain/4,045 feet total loss**
**STARTING ELEVATION: 9,440 feet**
**AVALANCHE TERRAIN: Some avalanche terrain encountered; easily avoided**
**USGS 7.5 MINUTE MAPS: Rabbit Ears Peak, 1956, Mount Werner, 1956, Steamboat Springs, 1969**
**MAP: page 266**

Long Park is a wilderness experience that journeys from the summit of Rabbit Ears Pass to the base of the Steamboat Springs ski area. Except for the descent of the groomed ski runs on the final leg of the trip, this tour crosses primarily moderate rolling terrain through dense evergreen forests and open meadows. Long, serene stretches of double-poling broken only by the drop into Fishhook Creek and the climb to the summit of Mount Werner allow plenty of time to enjoy the pristine surroundings. The south slopes of Mount Werner offer some of the finest downhill glade skiing in this book, and can provide an entire afternoon of telemark skiing (if time and snow conditions permit). While it is possible for strong groups to cover this trip in a day, spending the night (placing a camp somewhere in Long Park) will ensure a more leisurely outing and a chance to ski some of Colorado's finest backcountry powder.

The Rabbit Ears Pass area is a prime example of the problems encountered with out-of-date USGS topographic maps. The new highway is not shown on the USGS map; it is hand-drawn onto the maps in this book—keep this in mind. Drive on US 40 to the east summit of Rabbit Ears Pass, marked by a Continental Divide highway sign and a parking area. The drive takes roughly three to four hours to complete from Denver, depending on conditions. It is also necessary to leave a car or pick-up person near the base of the ski area to allow for the return to the top of the pass.

The tour begins with easy skiing on a northerly heading which traces the Continental Divide via a snowmobile trail. Continue north until you reach the old Rabbit Ears Pass East Summit, marked by a stone marker. At this spot change course and follow the old roadbed to the northwest, aiming for flat snow-covered Dumont Lake. Tour around the southwest corner of the lake and proceed northwest. The objective is to intercept the old roadbed that runs north, through "Base Campground" and down into Fishhook drainage. From the corner of the lake a 200-foot-plus climb up a moderate, sparsely vegetated grade will place you on this road, just under 3 miles from the parking area.

Fishhook drainage lies an additional 3 miles away to the north. Double-pole along the roadbed through the majestic stands of conifer trees and cross the open head of a tributary of Fishhook Creek. After skiing through a large stand of trees roughly 1 mile past the point where you gained the roadbed, break out into a vast windswept clearing dotted with clumps of evergreen trees and snags. The roadbed now becomes more elusive, since it is buried under the drifted snows of the meadow. If you are unable to locate it, set a course following true north and skirt east (right) of a small knoll, passing through or around several islands of trees marked on the map. After you pass these trees head northwest, traversing and slightly dropping with the contours of the slopes to the east (right). Try to locate the road where it enters the forest on the north side of the large clearing and follow the road as it drops into Fishhook Creek or ski straight down enjoyable timbered slopes.

From the bottom of Fishhook Creek it is necessary to attain the Long Creek drainage, which leads you to the crescent-shaped Long Park. The quickest route follows a rising traverse to the northwest, beginning directly from the point where the road dropped to the creek. Contour into Long Creek and turn upstream, skiing along the main creekbed. Eventually you will reach the narrow beginning of Long Park. The main meadow is just around a noticeable "dogleg" in the creek, which bends east (right). Long Park is nearly 4 miles in length and virtually flat. Rapid progress is made through this beautiful spot. You'll find a wide choice of fine campsites throughout its length.

The tour continues at the very end of the park, where trees begin to choke off the valley bottom and meadow skiing gives way to strenuous climbing onto the ridge, which stretches east from the summit of Mount Werner. The difficulty of this ascent depends on the exact route chosen; the easiest path leaves the southwest corner of the park. As you climb, the views north and south open up, revealing rolling forests to the north and Hogan Park immediately to the south. From here to the summit of Mount Werner (marked by radio towers), it is a straight shot over and around several small forested knobs protruding from the crest of the ridge. On the southeast side of Point

10,452, there are many superb slopes to ski and the descent off the west side of Point 10,447 is equally fine. These slopes are generally safe, but always assess potential avalanche danger. As you approach the back side of Mount Werner and the top of the ski area, take care in route selection as there are several potentially dangerous avalanche-prone slopes lying to the north. A relatively safe line traverses along the base of these as you ski west toward the top of the ski area. Advanced skiers will find many challenging downhill runs in this area.

For the final 3,000-foot descent of the ski area, the possibilities are many, ranging from cat tracks to difficult "bump runs." Use a ski-area map to help in selecting a trail to the bottom.

# 141 Hogan Park

DESCRIPTION: Winter ski tour, strenuous but well-marked passage, classic and popular, route ends at base of ski area, car shuttle required
SKILL LEVEL: Advanced
TIME: Full day +
DISTANCE: 12.7 miles one way
ELEVATION CHANGE: 1,180 total gain/3,740 total loss
STARTING ELEVATION: 9,560 feet
AVALANCHE TERRAIN: Some avalanche terrain encountered; easily avoided
USGS 7.5 MINUTE MAPS: Mount Werner, 1956, Steamboat Springs, 1969
MAPS: pages 266, 271

The Hogan Park Trail is a Colorado classic. Like the Seven Mile Run on Berthoud Pass, this tour has remained a popular winter excursion since the days before nylon and plastic, and of course before Gore-Tex, hydrophobic polypropylene and Kevlar! Linking Rabbit Ears Pass to the town of Steamboat Springs, the route traverses mostly moderate backcountry terrain. It is normally tracked and is flagged with ski trail markers. Today most people make this crossing in a day, although a few skiers (the smart ones) spend the night out. This allows them the experience of sleeping out in the winter environment and provides more time to telemark in the powder snow on the southeast flanks of Mount Werner. Bear in mind that the most physically taxing leg of the tour comes near the end of the day, when the trail ascends Mount Werner and drops to the base of the Steamboat Springs ski area via the groomed downhill runs. If you ski the Hogan Park Trail in one day, get an early start so that everyone in your group can enjoy the trip.

Drive on US 40 to the Hogan Park Trail parking area, roughly halfway between the east and west summits of Rabbit Ears Pass (approximately 3.8 miles each way).

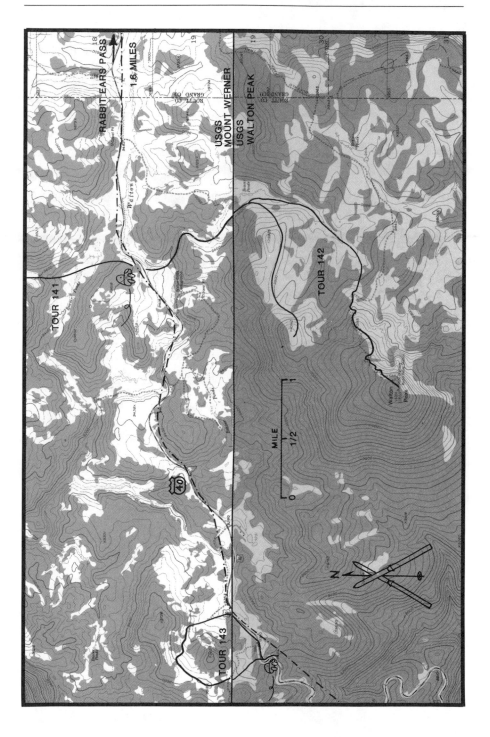

After crossing the highway to the north side, begin skiing northeast on the roadbed of old US 40. After several hundred feet the old road curves directly east; at this point the trail leaves the road, striking off into the backcountry to the northwest. Cross a snow-covered meadow (beaver ponds at 9,458 feet) and aim for the drainage to the north, where the route climbs along the open west side of the creek. Pass over a subtle ridge/saddle and begin a moderate descent into the forest to the north. From here the terrain levels out considerably as you cross a series of parks while following the tributary of Fishhook Creek northwest into the main Fishhook Creek. Telemark and/or snowplow directly into the drainage.

The next section of this tour begins with a moderate climb to the west-northwest, away from Fishhook Creek, and then crosses between two small forested points (9,505 feet and 9,370 feet). Veer north and begin the long and gradually inclined stretch through intermittent evergreen trees, skiing along the west edge of Hogan Creek. After about 4.5 miles, you'll reach Hogan Park. Like Long Park to the northeast, this is a beautiful and serene spot that permits easy gliding. A noticeable bend to the west near the 6-mile mark (near "Hogan" on the topographic map) signals the start of the ascent to Mount Werner.

Ski out from the northwest perimeter of Hogan Park and ascend to the northwest, following a series of trail markers across the upper reaches of the Storm King Creek drainage. For 2 miles this climb continues until you reach the small saddle on Mount Werner's southwest shoulder. This airy perch is the top of the Steamboat Springs ski area and is the high point of the tour (10,340 feet). It is a good resting spot before the final descent to the base of the mountain begins. Be aware of many small avalanche slopes, which lie on the southern slope of Mount Werner.

There are obviously a multitude of groomed runs to choose from for the ski down. Consult a ski-area map for all the options. For those skiers seeking the easiest route to the bottom previous guides have recommended Buddy's Run to the top of Four Points Lift via Four Points Cutoff, Rainbow to Rainbow Saddle, Park Lane to Central Park, then Why Not Road and finally Right-O-Way to the base area.

# 142 WALTON PEAK AND WALTON MOUNTAIN

**DESCRIPTION: Winter ski tour, several easy to moderately strenuous routes, optional telemarking**
**SKILL LEVEL: Novice to intermediate**
**TIME: Full day**
**DISTANCE: 6 miles round trip to northern sub-summit**
              **8.4 miles round trip to main southern summit**
**ELEVATION CHANGE: 630 feet total gain to northern sub-summit**
                   **1,049 feet gain to main southern summit**
**STARTING ELEVATION: 9,560 feet**
**AVALANCHE TERRAIN: Some avalanche terrain encountered; easily avoided**
**USGS 7.5 MINUTE MAPS: Mount Werner, 1956, Walton Peak, 1956**
**MAPS: pages 266, 271**

Like all tours on the broad summit plateau of Rabbit Ears Pass, a ski ascent of Walton Mountain provides access to beautiful glade skiing and first-rate snow. Walton Mountain (Point 10,142), the lower northern sub-summit of Walton Peak (10,559 feet), is more often and more easily reached than Walton Peak. This tour differs from the other classic Rabbit Ears routes because it lies south of US 40 and ascends the northeast aspect of this subalpine protuberance. Novices as well as advanced "freeheelers" can indulge in a little mirth and merriment crashing into the deep powder snow always found in the trees scattered over this mountain. Cross-country skiers with additional endurance can top off the day with lunch on the summit of Walton Peak and treat themselves to one of the best views of northern Colorado found in the Steamboat-Rabbit Ears area.

The tour begins across the road to the south from the Hogan Park Trail. Drive on US 40 to the Hogan Park Trail parking area, almost exactly halfway between the west and east summits of the pass (roughly 3.8 miles each way).

From the parking area head south, ascending a small ridge. Traverse along the top, then drop into the Walton Creek drainage. After crossing the snow-covered creek, swing southeast and follow the east-southeast fork of the creek. This gradual ascending traverse contours above the drainage to the west, entering an open park or meadow near the 0.5-mile mark. Continue, tracing the main branch of the creek on an undulating course heading roughly southeast; bypass a smaller side tributary that splits off to the south at 1 mile.

Find a faint roadbed several hundred yards farther (near the 9,600-foot mark) which traverses gradually upward to the south. When you reach the southeast ridge of Point 9,925, the trail contours sharply around to the west and traverses westward toward the small sub-summit known as Walton Mountain (Point 10,142 feet). From the summit of Walton Mountain the final 200-foot climb of Walton Peak begins with a jog south at the west edge of the small saddle between points 9,925 and 10,142 (Walton Mountain) that leads up the summit of the latter via the south slopes.

Advanced skiers may climb the higher Walton Peak (10,559 feet) by deviating from the Walton Mountain Trail near the 1.5-mile mark (or the 9,600-foot mark). From this point it is easy to traverse into Walton Creek and double-pole south and west over gentle, open terrain. Follow the natural route through the park and contour west, skiing through a passage cut between a group of trees. The final ascent begins at this point as the trail gains a power-line route leading right up to the summit of the mountain.

Returning from either of these destinations, skiers will be treated to a variety of challenging downhill runs. If the snow is fairly new, any route is superb.

# 143 WEST SUMMIT LOOP

**DESCRIPTION: Winter ski tour, novice's special**
**SKILL LEVEL: Novice**
**TIME: Quarter day**
**DISTANCE: 3.5 miles one way**
**ELEVATION CHANGE: 280 feet total gain**
**STARTING ELEVATION: 9,400 feet**
**AVALANCHE TERRAIN: None**
**USGS 7.5 MINUTE MAP: Mount Werner, 1956**
**MAPS: pages 266, 271**

O.K. beginners! If you are enthusiastic for a fun romp that includes all of the prerequisites of pleasant ski touring, then this route is for you. The West Summit Loop is great for those with limited time or a taste for compelling panoramas with minimal exertion. The loop begins on the west summit of Rabbit Ears Pass, circumnavigates to the north, scales a small thinly wooded hill and returns to the flats via an exciting drop down a south-facing bowl. This outing is one of the great novice tours in this book.

Drive on US 40 to the plowed parking area on the west summit of Rabbit Ears Pass. The tour heads due north from the parking area, entering an opening in the trees. Within several hundred feet you'll reach the old US 40 roadbed. Double-pole along the road, descending to a large, quiet meadow. Swing slightly northwest and climb gradually toward the aspen trees, that cover the northern corner of the meadow. When you reach the trees, you will have gained a small saddle. To the northeast (right), you'll see a gentle ridge covered with trees and small clearings. Continue the ascent in this direction by contouring more sharply to the northeast and following the ridge line by skiing through the open area on its top. Near the 1-mile mark you'll reach the imperceptible summit marked 9,618 feet on the USGS 7.5 minute map.

Ski along the ridge and follow the natural descent down the southeast-facing bowl. The wide open slopes funnel into a narrow passage. Telemark or snowplow down until you reach the flat area. Cross the flat snowfield, aiming for US 40. As you approach the highway, head southwest once more and ski toward the parking area via the old US 40 roadbed.

*Enjoying the winter sun on Rabbit Ears Pass, Brian Litz photo.*

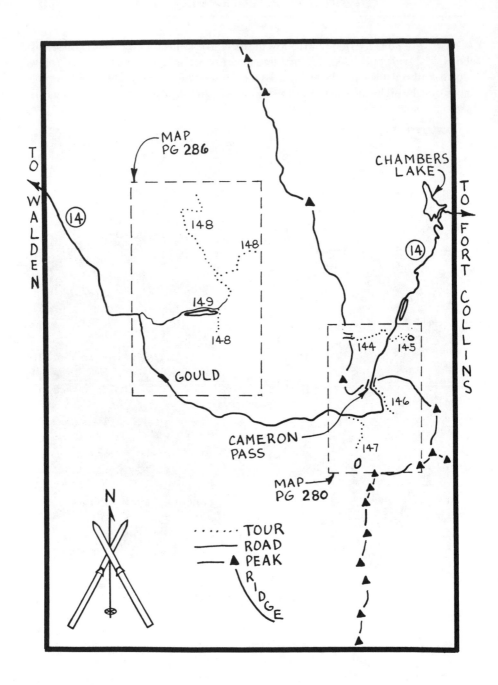

MAP
PG 286

TO WALDEN

14

148
148
149
148

GOULD

CHAMBERS LAKE

TO FORT COLLINS

14

144    145

146

CAMERON PASS

147

0

MAP
PG 280

N

TOUR
ROAD
PEAK

RIDGE

# CHAPTER THIRTEEN

# CAMERON PASS

## INTRODUCTION

Cameron Pass is located some 65 miles west of Fort Collins on Colo. 14. It divides the Medicine Bow range on the north from the Continental Divide on the south. Its apex is 10,285 feet above sea level, and it is flanked by peaks 11,000 to 12,000 feet high. The broad, high valley of North Park lies to the northwest, Rocky Mountain National Park lies to the south, and the headwaters of the Cache la Poudre River lie to the east.

It was not until 1978 that the Colorado Department of Highways decided to pave the road and keep Cameron Pass open year-round. Since then, backcountry ski touring has become quite popular in this area, particularly the trails near the summit of the pass and on the west side in the Colorado State Forest. A variety of ski-touring terrain is accessible. Advanced skiers will want to try the Montgomery Pass and Lake Agnes trails, steep, challenging runs with good potential for powder telemarking in the high bowls. Intermediate skiers will enjoy the Zimmerman Lake Trail, one of the nicest ski tours in northern Colorado. Novice skiers will find a very scenic and almost perfectly level trail by following the Michigan Ditch Tour. Everyone will want to experience an overnight stay in one of the rustic cabins or unique "yurt" shelters in the Colorado State Forest.

## HISTORY

Journeying today with ease along what is sometimes called the "one-gear" highway up Poudre Canyon to Cameron Pass, it is difficult to imagine what it was like when the first frontiersmen and trappers ventured into this region. The first recorded visit was in 1836, when a late fall blizzard caught a large party of French trappers. Fighting their way across the unknown frontier, they entered the canyon and, in order to lighten their loads, cached their provisions and supplies. The following spring, another party unearthed these treasures and found among them 300 pounds of black powder. The canyon thus became known as the Cache la Poudre or "Hiding Place of the Powder."

The Cache la Poudre was the hunting ground of both Indians and trappers. Through its lofty, rocky citadels and sparkling rivers and streams roamed the fur-bearing animals the trappers were seeking. Many of the men who hunted in this region were almost as wild as their prey. To enter the canyon during those early years was to run the gauntlet of a thousand dangers. Perhaps the Indians would steal down from the headwaters of the Poudre, with their bows of ash, which had already given a name to the Medicine Bow Mountains to the north; or it might be that a suspicious trapper would not like the looks of the hapless stranger. The canyon was also an ideal hideout for cattle rustlers, renegades and other outlaws from justice.

Perilous as these early days were, the Cache la Poudre Canyon stirred the romantic souls and adventurous spirits of such great men as Kit Carson, who scouted this region in 1849 and 1850. Cameron Pass was named for General R. A. Cameron, president of the Fort Collins settlement and an associate of N. C. Meeker in the Greeley settlement during the late 1860s and 1870s. In the fall of 1858 Robert Chambers, a gentleman from Iowa, discovered and gave his name to Chambers Lake, located a few miles below Cameron Pass. Chambers was camped on the shore of the lake while he hunted, trapped and fished. When his powder ran short, he sent his son and only companion down the canyon in search of more ammunition and provisions. Soon after the boy embarked on his mission, Chambers became aware that he was not alone. All about, he could hear the stealthy approach of Indians and he knew that he was in big trouble. He fought bravely against their attack, but the odds were hopelessly against him. When his son returned, he found his father murdered and scalped, the story of the battle in all its gruesome detail strewn about the shores of the lake.

In 1884, John Zimmerman came to Colorado from Switzerland to seek his fortune as a frontiersman, hunter, guide and miner. To him the Cache la Poudre Canyon and Cameron Pass were like discovering his own native Alps in the new world. Building the first hotel in the canyon, he established Zimmermans Place, 30 miles west of the town of La Porte. After his death his daughters carried on the tradition, adding on to the hotel and operating it for many years. Lake Agnes, located high above the west side of Cameron Pass, is named after one of the Zimmerman daughters and Zimmerman Lake is named after their pioneer father.

# 144 Montgomery Pass

**DESCRIPTION: Winter ski tour, steep narrow jeep trail**
**SKILL LEVEL: Advanced**
**TIME: Half day**
**DISTANCE: 3.5 miles round trip**
**ELEVATION CHANGE: 1,000 feet total gain**
**STARTING ELEVATION: 10,020 feet**
**AVALANCHE TERRAIN: Some avalanche terrain encountered; easily avoided**
**USGS 7.5 MINUTE MAP: Clark Peak, 1977-PR**
**MAP: page 280**

This tour packs loads of fun and adventure into a relatively short half-day trip. It follows a narrow jeep trail to an 11,000-foot pass located north of Cameron Pass. The trail takes a fairly direct route to the pass, gaining elevation quickly and steadily. There are some nice telemark glades near treeline, just below the pass. The return trip down the trail is fast and furious.

From Fort Collins, drive approximately 10 miles northwest on US 287 to Ted's Place. Turn left (west) on Colo. 14 and proceed approximately 50 miles up seemingly endless Poudre Canyon to Chambers Lake. Continue past Chambers Lake approximately 5.6 miles to the Zimmerman Lake parking area. This is on the left (east) side of the highway, 0.7 miles beyond Joe Wright Reservoir and 1.7 miles below the summit of Cameron Pass.

The trailhead is located on the west side of Colo. 14, opposite the Zimmerman Lake parking area. There is a trailhead marker at the lower (northeast) end of the lot. From the trailhead marker cross the road and begin skiing right and upward a short distance into the trees. Then traverse north, staying parallel to the highway, on a narrow unmarked path. This path intersects the Montgomery Pass jeep trail a few hundred yards down and just above the highway. It is often easier to simply ski next to the highway and then cut up to the jeep trail instead of following the path.

The jeep trail is occasionally marked with blue diamond trail markers. It climbs very steeply for the first half mile, cutting a narrow undulating swath directly up the hillside parallel to the creek. Pass an old cabin at the 1.2-mile point. Just beyond the cabin, bend right and traverse approximately 0.2 miles northwest to treeline. The windswept saddle of Montgomery Pass lies another 0.2 miles to the west. This section (all above treeline) is exposed to strong winds and may be prone to avalanches during high-hazard periods.

There are some wonderful glades near treeline that are just right for practicing telemark turns. The return trip simply travels back down the jeep trail to the highway—a fast, furious descent that requires excellent control.

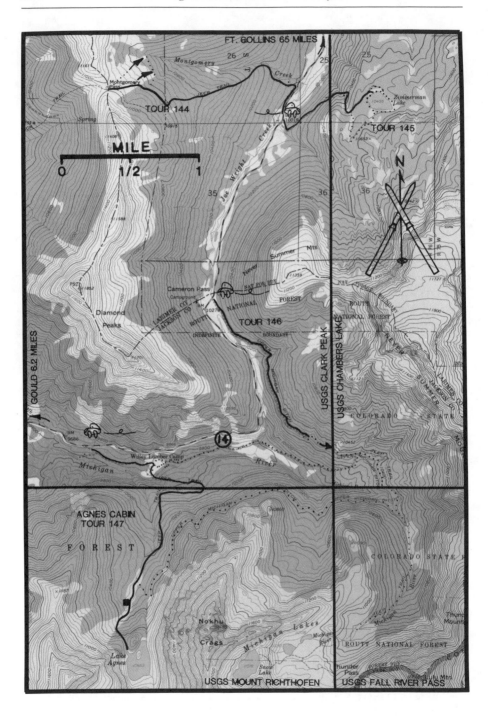

# 145 ZIMMERMAN LAKE

**DESCRIPTION: Winter ski tour, steady but moderate climb on narrow jeep trail**
**SKILL LEVEL: Intermediate**
**TIME: Half day**
**DISTANCE: 2.2. miles round trip**
**ELEVATION CHANGE: 475 feet total gain**
**STARTING ELEVATION: 10,020 feet**
**AVALANCHE TERRAIN: None**
**USGS 7.5 MINUTE MAPS: Clark Peak, 1977-PR, Chambers Lake, 1977-PR**
**MAP: page 280**

This is perhaps the best ski tour in the area. A nicely graded jeep trail with consistently good snow leads uphill through thick lodgepole forest to an idyllic lake setting. The tour is quite short but there is an alternate loop around the lake, then through adjacent meadows and forest that extends the tour another half mile. This alternate loop is highly recommended unless snowcover is inadequate (a rare occurrence, even in November).

From Fort Collins, drive approximately 10 miles northwest on US 287 to Ted's Place. Turn left (west) on Colo. 14 and proceed approximately 50 miles up seemingly endless Poudre Canyon to Chambers Lake. Continue past Chambers Lake approximately 5.6 miles to the Zimmerman Lake parking area. This is on the left (east) side of the highway, 0.7 miles beyond Joe Wright Reservoir and 1.7 miles below the summit of Cameron Pass.

From the upper (south) end of the parking area, ski southeast into the trees, looking for blue diamond trail markers. The tour follows a jeep trail that climbs directly east a short distance, then diagonals left (northeast), cutting across the hillside through dense lodgepole forest. After 0.4 miles of steady uphill grade, the road makes a wide hairpin turn east, followed by a more gradual climb through scattered trees. Bend left (northeast) again, cutting across a shallow drainage. Just before the drainage, there is a sign indicating the loop trail (an alternate route) and blue diamond trail markers cutting up and right through intermittent trees and open meadows. Although it can be skied in either direction, the loop trail is best when started at Zimmerman Lake and completed here at the shallow drainage.

To continue on the normal route, follow the jeep trail northeast another 0.2 miles to Zimmerman Lake. At Zimmerman Lake you will be rewarded with nice views of the high ridges that surround the area. If you wish to follow the loop trail, it circles counterclockwise around the lake, then cuts southwest, following blue diamond trail markers through an open area. It then traverses a short distance south to a sharp right turn. From there the trail drops into the previously mentioned shallow drainage and continues down this to the jeep road.

If you do not wish to ski the loop trail, simply return back down the jeep trail. There is a fun little detour about a third of the way down that shortcuts the sharp hairpin turn. Below this the trail has no sharp curves, so you can pick up speed and let your momentum carry you out into the parking lot.

# 146 UPPER MICHIGAN DITCH

DESCRIPTION: Winter ski tour, nearly level road, scenic views
SKILL LEVEL: Novice*
TIME: Optional, half day or more
DISTANCE: Optional, 2.6 miles round trip as described
ELEVATION CHANGE: 40 feet total gain
STARTING ELEVATION: 10,260 feet
AVALANCHE TERRAIN: Some avalanche terrain encountered; easily avoided
USGS 7.5 MINUTE MAP: Clark Peak, 1977-PR
MAP: page 280

*ADVANCED HIGHLIGHT: It is possible to ski all the way around into the upper Michigan River drainage, then drop down a jeep trail parallel to the river and come out at the Lake Agnes Trailhead (tour 147). This route requires a car shuttle to get back to the summit of Cameron Pass.

This tour follows the nearly level Michigan Ditch road as it traverses southeast from the summit of Cameron Pass into the upper reaches of the Michigan River drainage. The level gradient, scenic views and consistently good snowcover make this an excellent choice for novice skiers. Advanced and intermediate skiers also enjoy this area, taking advantage of the normally well-tracked road to improve on their skating and diagonal stride techniques. The length of the tour is somewhat arbitrary. It can be extended for several miles beyond what is described here by following the continuation of Michigan Ditch as far as desired. (Michigan Ditch is an aqueduct used to divert water from the Western Slope into the Cache la Poudre River.)

From Fort Collins, drive approximately 10 miles northwest on US 287 to Ted's Place. Turn left (west) on Colo. 14 and proceed approximately 57 miles up seemingly endless Poudre Canyon to the summit of Cameron Pass. Park in the well-marked parking area on the right (northwest) side of the highway. Cross over to the opposite side of the highway and begin skiing on the level Michigan Ditch road. This road traverses southeast along a densely timbered hillside. Cross a shallow drainage at the 0.6-mile point. The ditch road continues from here, slowly bending left around the corner into the upper Michigan River drainage. At the 1.3-mile point, you will encounter a cluster of old buildings and cabins built during construction of the

Michigan Ditch aqueduct. Although the ditch continues for several miles beyond this point, the buildings make a convenient stopping point for novice tourers.

The return trip simply glides back to Cameron Pass along the same route.

# 147 AGNES CABIN

**DESCRIPTION: Winter ski tour to rustic backcountry cabin**
**SKILL LEVEL: Advanced**
**TIME: Half day to cabin**
**DISTANCE: 2.6 miles one way to cabin**
**ELEVATION CHANGE: 660 feet total gain**
**STARTING ELEVATION: 9,700 feet**
**AVALANCHE TERRAIN: Some avalanche terrain encountered; easily avoided**
**USGS 7.5 MINUTE MAPS: Clark Peak, 1977-PR, Mount Richthofen, 1977-PR**
**MAP: page 280**

This is a charming little cabin, perched in a steep-sided valley, high above the west side of Cameron Pass. The setting is splendid. Jagged peaks rise precipitously to the east and south. Lake Agnes lies a short distance farther up valley, nestled in a spectacular cirque. Sparse trees dot the landscape. And, in the middle of this idyllic setting, a tiny rustic cabin sits all by itself, offering warmth and solitude to adventurous backcountry travelers.

The ski tour in is quite steep; thankfully, it is also reasonably short. Most advanced skiers can make the trip in half a day, even with full packs. Intermediate skiers should plan a little more time. Climbing skins are recommended but not essential.

Day touring in the vicinity of the cabin is superb, although somewhat limited. There are excellent glades for short telemark runs both above and below the cabin. A short trip up to Lake Agnes makes a fine destination. It is also possible to ski east along the Michigan Ditch aqueduct, but this cuts across several large avalanche paths before reaching more moderate terrain and, therefore, is not recommended.

Agnes Cabin is a fixed-up, one-room settlers' cabin with very few amenities. There are bunk beds with mattresses that sleep six, but you must bring your own sleeping bags. There is a wood stove for heat, but you must bring a camp stove and utensils for cooking. There is a supply of wood (outside in the woodshed), but you must bring an axe or hatchet to split it.

The trailhead is located on the west side of Cameron Pass, 2.4 miles below the summit. From Fort Collins, drive approximately 10 miles northwest on US 287 to Ted's Place. Turn left (west) on Colo. 14 and proceed 57 miles up seemingly endless Poudre Canyon to Cameron Pass. From the summit of Cameron Pass, continue approximately 2.4 miles down the back (west) side to a marked turnoff (left) for Lake Agnes. Park as far off the highway as possible, and ski east down the snowcovered access road 0.5 miles to the entrance sign for the Colorado State Forest. A valid Colorado State Parks Pass is required to enter the Colorado State Forest, even in winter. Self-service passes are available at park entrances. Annual park passes are available at the park office, located just off the access road to North Michigan Reservoir. From the entrance sign, turn right up a jeep trail (marked to Lake Agnes). Cross the creek and begin climbing southeast. Immediately after rounding a corner 0.2 miles up, bear right at an obvious fork (the left fork leads to a dead end at a summer campground). The jeep trail then turns southwest and continues climbing into Agnes Gulch. The trees begin to thin out as the trail curves south parallel to Agnes Creek. The cabin lies another 0.6 miles up the creek at the south end of a clearing.

The cabin is managed by the Colorado Division of Parks and Recreation. It is available to rent on a reservation basis year-round. Reservations are handled by Mistix Corp. They can be made by mail up to 150 days in advance (send to Mistix Corp., P.O. Box 315, 10065 East Harvard, Denver, CO 80231) or by phone up to 120 days in advance (in Denver 671-4500 or 1-800-365-CAMP). Major credit cards are accepted. The cabins must be left clean and tidy and must be vacated by noon on the last day of occupancy.

# 148 NEVER SUMMER NORDIC YURTS

**DESCRIPTION: Winter ski tours to three backcountry "yurts"**
**SKILL LEVEL: Grass Creek Yurt, Novice**
          **Ruby Jewel Yurt, Intermediate**
          **North Fork Canadian Yurt, Intermediate**
**TIME: Quarter day to Grass Creek Yurt**
       **Three-quarters day to Ruby Jewel Yurt**
       **Full day to North Fork Canadian Yurt**
**DISTANCE: Grass Creek Yurt, 0.6 miles**
           **Ruby Jewel Yurt, 3.2 miles**
           **North Fork Canadian Yurt, 5.6 miles**
**ELEVATION CHANGE: Grass Creek Yurt, 120 feet**
                   **Ruby Jewel Yurt, 670 feet**
                   **North Fork Canadian Yurt, 600 feet**
**STARTING ELEVATION: 8,950 feet**
**AVALANCHE TERRAIN: None**
**USGS 7.5 MINUTE MAPS: Clark Peak, 1977-PR, Gould, 1955**
**MAP: page 286**

This is a system of three *yurts* located in the backcountry of Colorado State Forest on the west side of Cameron Pass. Yurts offer the ski-touring enthusiast a very pleasant and unique way to experience the finest in backcountry solitude, surrounded by beautiful mountain scenery. All of the yurts are situated well below treeline, within reasonable skiing distance of the trailhead and of each other. The approach routes are all via very moderate roads and trails, making the yurts accessible to groups and individuals of all abilities.

A yurt is a unique, hutlike shelter constructed primarily of canvas over a sturdy timber frame. A large wooden deck, built well off the ground, serves as both the floor of the yurt and as an outdoor sun deck. Plexiglass skylight and windows allow ample sunlight to filter in. Each yurt sleeps up to six. Mattresses are provided, but sleeping bags must be carried in as well as food, clothing and other items for an overnight trip (see Appendix 2 for a suggested equipment list). Each yurt is equipped with a wood-burning stove, propane cookstove, lantern, pots, pans and dishes. The yurts are available to rent on a reservation basis. To reserve a yurt, contact Never Summer Nordic, P.O. Box 1254, Fort Collins, CO 80522 (303-484-3903).

Approach the yurts from the North Michigan Reservoir access to the Colorado State Forest just north of Gould. To get there from Fort Collins, drive approximately 10 miles northwest on US 287 to Ted's Place. Turn left on Colo. 14 and proceed 65 miles up Poudre Canyon and over Cameron Pass to Gould. Approximately 2.1 miles beyond Gould, look for a KOA Campground on the right side of the road. Turn right, then immediately left and proceed to the entrance for the Colorado State Forest. A valid Colorado State Parks Pass is required to enter. Self-service passes are available at park entrances. Annual park passes are available at the park office, located just off the access road to North Michigan Reservoir. Once past the entrance, bear right and continue 1 mile to another fork. Bear left here (the right fork generally is not plowed) and proceed 1.5 miles to the north side of North Michigan Reservoir. Approach Grass Creek Yurt from the east end of North Michigan Reservoir. Ruby Jewel Yurt and North Fork Canadian Yurt are usually approached from a turnoff 0.5 miles east of North Michigan Reservoir. This turnoff is marked by a sign indicating "cirques and lakes" to the left, Bochman Lumber Camp and Montgomery Pass to the right. Access may vary from year to year or month to month, depending on lumber industry activity in the area. Some years the access road north from this turnoff may be plowed, allowing a much shorter approach to Ruby Jewel and North Fork Canadian yurts.

Grass Creek Yurt, located less than a mile from the trailhead, is the easiest to reach. It sits on the western edge of a large meadow, a short distance southeast of North Michigan Reservoir. Ski around the east end of the reservoir, then head due south across an open meadow, aiming for its west edge, approximately 0.5 miles south. Grass Creek Yurt is tucked in next to the trees on the west edge of this open meadow.

Several nice day tours emanate from Grass Creek Yurt, including the continuation of Grass Creek itself, a very enjoyable intermediate trail. Other possibilities include Bull Mountain, a steep jeep trail heading north from a trailhead on the north side of North Michigan Reservoir, and Montgomery Pass, a long challenging trail that climbs up toward the crest of the Never Summer Range.

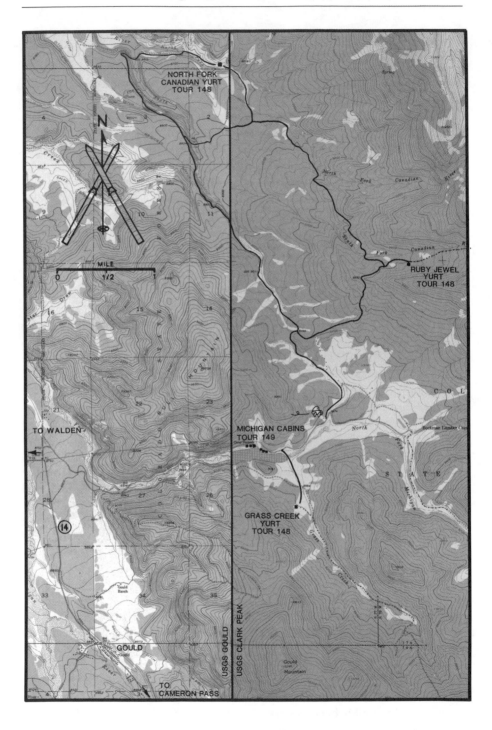

NORTH FORK
CANADIAN YURT
TOUR 148

N

RUBY JEWEL
YURT
TOUR 148

MILE
0      1/2      1

TO WALDEN

MICHIGAN CABINS
TOUR 149

14

GRASS CREEK
YURT
TOUR 148

USGS GOULD

USGS CLARK PEAK

Gould
Mountain

GOULD

TO
CAMERON PASS

Ruby Jewel Yurt requires a bit more uphill climbing than the other yurts. It is located partway up a steep drainage, the South Fork of the North Canadian River, which descends from Jewel Lake, high in the Never Summer Range. Unlike the other yurts, it is surrounded by dense forest, creating a feeling of solitude and isolation. Day touring around Ruby Jewel Yurt is somewhat limited to an advanced but highly recommended excursion into the high bowls below Jewel Lake.

To reach Ruby Jewel Yurt from the previously mentioned turnoff 0.5 miles east of North Michigan Reservoir, ski north on the road marked to "cirques and lakes" for 1.2 miles to a clearly marked turnoff for Ruby Jewel Yurt. An alternate shortcut branches off right through a meadow 0.5 miles past the start. From the turnoff on the normal route, ski east on a narrow jeep trail that soon begins to climb steeply through the forest. The alternate route intersects this jeep trail from the south, approximately 0.2 miles up. Another fork is encountered 0.7 miles farther. Bear right here, following orange-and-blue diamond trail markers up a steep hill. The trail levels out, then forks. The left fork is an alternate route to North Fork Canadian Yurt and is marked as such. Proceed up the right fork another 0.2 miles to Ruby Jewel Yurt.

North Fork Canadian Yurt is the most isolated of the three. It is located on a hillside overlooking a large open meadow and has a magnificent view of the Never Summer Range. If you plan to ski into North Fork Canadian Yurt from the trailhead in a day, be sure to get an early start—it is a long, somewhat tedious ski. Most people prefer to combine North Fork Canadian Yurt with Ruby Jewel Yurt to make a more enjoyable multiday trip.

To reach North Fork Canadian Yurt from the previously mentioned turnoff 0.5 miles east of North Michigan Reservoir, ski north on the left fork road marked to "cirques and lakes." After 1.2 miles, pass the turnoff to Ruby Jewel Yurt and begin a gradual descent into the Canadian River drainage. Stay on this main road for another 2.5 miles. At this point a narrow jeep trail switchbacks east, leading across the river. This trail is marked with orange-and-blue diamond trail markers. Ski east 0.7 miles on this trail to a fork where the alternate route from Ruby Jewel Yurt comes in. Turn left here and proceed 0.6 miles north along the creek, then cross an open meadow to North Fork Canadian Yurt.

# 149 MICHIGAN CABINS

**DESCRIPTION: Six rustic cabins in the Colorado State Forest, normally accessible by car, numerous day-tour possibilities**
**SKILL LEVEL: Novice to advanced**
**TIME: Overnight with optional-length day tours**
**DISTANCE: Optional-length day tours, cabins normally accessible by car**
**ELEVATION CHANGE: Day tours up to 2,000 feet total gain**
**STARTING ELEVATION: 8,940 feet**
**AVALANCHE TERRAIN: None**
**USGS 7.5 MINUTE MAPS: Clark Peak, 1977-PR, Gould, 1955**
**MAP: page 286**

If spending the night in an old rustic cabin sounds appealing but having to ski with a backpack does not, try the Michigan Cabins. These cabins are located in the Colorado State Forest on the north shore of Michigan Reservoir and are normally accessible by car throughout the year. There are six cabins in all. Cabins 1 and 2 are ideal for large groups, sleeping up to 15 people each. Cabins 3 through 6 sleep up to six each. Each cabin has a wood stove for heat, but you must bring a camp stove for cooking. The cabins are stocked with a supply of cut wood, but you must bring an axe or hatchet to split it. There are bunk beds with mattresses, but you must bring your own sleeping bags. There is no electricity or running water. There are no lanterns, candles or eating utensils. Cabins 1, 2 and 3 are nestled in the trees and have a warmer, more rustic appeal than cabins 4, 5 and 6, which sit out in the open.

There are a number of good day ski tours in the area. Intermediate and advanced skiers will enjoy Bull Mountain, Montgomery Pass or the trail to Jewel Lake. Novice and intermediate skiers will enjoy Grass Creek or simply skiing farther along the main road.

To reach the cabins from Fort Collins, drive approximately 10 miles northwest on US 287 to Ted's Place. Turn left on Colo. 14 and proceed 65 miles up Poudre Canyon and over Cameron Pass to Gould. Approximately 2.1 miles beyond Gould, look for a KOA Campground on the right side of the road. Turn right, then immediately left and proceed to the entrance for the Colorado State Forest. A valid Colorado State Parks Pass is required to enter. Self-service passes are available at park entrances. Annual park passes are available at the park office, located just off the access road to North Michigan Reservoir. Once past the entrance, bear right and continue 1 mile to another fork. Bear left here (the right fork generally is not plowed) and proceed 1.5 miles to the north side of North Michigan Reservoir, where the cabins are located. The access road may be closed for short periods of time during heavy snowstorms.

The cabins are managed by the Colorado Division of Parks and Recreation. They are available to rent on a reservation basis year-round. Reservations are handled by Mistix Corp. They can be made by mail up to 150 days in advance (send to Mistix Corp., P.O. Box 315, 10065 East Harvard, Denver, CO 80231) or by phone up to 120 days in advance (in Denver 671-4500 or 1-800-365-CAMP). Major credit cards are accepted. The cabins must be left clean and tidy and must be vacated by noon on the last day of occupancy.

*Trail skiing on Cameron Pass, Brian Litz photo.*

# APPENDIX ONE

## Tour Summary Table

Tours are first grouped according to type; then, within each group, they are ranked according to overall difficulty. The overall difficulty ranking takes into account not only skill level, but many other pertinent factors, including distance, time, elevation gain, avalanche terrain, route-finding difficulty, exposure to weather and remoteness of location.

\+ indicates recommended route
(*) indicates highlight

| No. | Tour Name | Type | Skill Level | Location |
|---|---|---|---|---|
| 20 + | Brainard Lake Road | Road | Nov | Brainard |
| 146 | Upper Michigan Ditch | Road | Nov | Cameron Pass |
| 99 + | Sally Barber Mine | Road | Nov | Breckenridge |
| 30 | Left Hand Reservoir | Road | Nov | Brainard |
| 76 | Naylor Lake | Road | Nov | Guanella Pass |
| 73 | Squaw Pass Trail | Road | Nov | Mt Evans |
| 98 | French Gulch & Little French Gulch | Road | Nov(*Int) | Breckenridge |
| 104 | Indiana Creek | Road | Nov | Breckenridge |
| 72 | Shipler Park and Lulu City | Road | Nov | Grand Lake |
| 45 | Fall River Reservoir | Road | Nov | St Mary's |
| 97 | Keystone Gulch | Road | Nov | Keystone |
| 32 | Fourth of July Road | Road | Nov | Eldora |
| 91 + | Peru Creek | Road | Nov(*Int) | Montezuma |
| 44 + | Jenny Lind Gulch | Road | Nov/Int | East Portal |
| 49 + | Jones Pass | Road | Nov/Int | Berthoud |
| 120 + | Mayflower Gulch | Road | Int | Copper Mtn |
| 103 + | Boreas Pass | Road | Nov | Breckenridge |
| 64 | Crooked Creek | Road | Nov | Fraser |
| 105 | Pennsylvania Creek | Road | Nov/Int | Breckenridge |
| 17 | Middle St. Vrain | Road/Trail | Nov(*Int) | Brainard |
| 43 | Mammoth Gulch | Road | Nov/Int | East Portal |
| 59 | West St. Louis Creek | Road | Nov | Fraser |
| 75 | Waldorf Road | Road | Nov | Guanella Pass |
| 115 | McCullough Gulch | Road | Int(*Nov) | Breckenridge |
| 57 | Jim Creek | Road | Int(*Nov) | Winter Park |
| 127 + | Shrine Pass Road | Road | Int(*Nov) | Vail Pass |
| 92 + | Webster Pass | Road | Nov/Int | Montezuma |
| 93 + | Deer Creek | Road | Nov/Int | Montezuma |
| 145 + | Zimmerman Lake | Road | Int | Cameron Pass |

| No. | Tour Name | Type | Skill Level | Location |
|---|---|---|---|---|
| 80 | Stevens Gulch and Grizzly Gulch | Road | Int(*Nov) | Off I-70 |
| 119 | North Tenmile Creek | Road | Int | Frisco |
| 47 | Bard Creek | Road | Int | Empire |
| 63 | Tipperary Creek | Road | Int(*Nov) | Fraser |
| 62 + | Morse Mountain Loop | Road | Int(*Nov) | Fraser |
| 70 | Kawuneeche Valley Loop | Trail | Nov | Grand Lake |
| 12 | Sprague Lake | Trail | Nov | RMNP |
| 18 | Coney Flats Trail | Trail | Nov | Brainard |
| 106 | The Flume | Trail | Nov(*Int) | Breckenridge |
| 79 | Geneva Creek | Trail | Nov | Guanella Pass |
| 130 | Camp Hale Trail System | Trail | Nov/Int | Tennessee Pass |
| 11 | Glacier Creek | Trail | Nov | RMNP |
| 7 | Emerald Lake | Trail | Nov/Int | RMNP |
| 67 + | Tonahutu Creek | Trail | Nov | Grand Lake |
| 132 + | Tennessee Pass Trail System | Trail | Nov/Int | Tennessee Pass |
| 58 + | Winter Park Trail System | Trail | Nov/Int | Fraser |
| 66 | East Inlet | Trail | Int | Grand Lake |
| 21 + | CMC Trails (South and North) | Trail | Nov/Int | Brainard |
| 19 | South St. Vrain Trail | Trail | Int | Brainard |
| 29 | Little Raven Trail | Trail | Int | Brainard |
| 94 + | Sts. John and Wild Irishman Mine | Tr/Rd/Tele | Int(*Nov/Ad) | Montezuma |
| 114 + | Spruce Creek Loop | Trail | Int(*Nov) | Breckenridge |
| 121 | Guller Creek | Trial | Nov/Int | Copper Mtn |
| 122 | Stafford Creek | Trail | Nov(*Int) | Copper Mtn |
| 117 | South Willow Creek | Trail | Int | Dillon |
| 68 | Green Mountain Trail | Trail | Int | Grand Lake |
| 65 | Arapaho Creek | Trail | Int | Grand Lake |
| 48 + | Butler Gulch | Trail/Tele | Int(*Adv) | Berthoud |
| 116 + | Breckenridge to Frisco | Trail | Int | Breckenridge |
| 31 + | Sourdough Trail | Trail | Int(*Nov) | Brainard |
| 36 | Lost Lake | Trail | Int | Eldora |
| 3 | Bear Lake to Hallowell Park | Trail | Int | RMNP |
| 26 | Long Lake and Isabelle Lake | Trail | Int(*Nov) | Brainard |
| 96 | Hunkidori Mine | Trail | Int(*Nov) | Montezuma |
| 38 + | Jenny Creek | Trail | Int/Adv | Eldora |
| 22 | Mitchell Lake and Blue Lake | Trail | Int | Brainard |
| 16 | Meadow Mountain Bowl | Trail/Tele | Int(*Adv) | RMNP |
| 13 | Longs Peak Trail | Trial | Adv(*Int) | RMNP |
| 8 | Loch Vale | Trail | Int/Adv | RMNP |
| 14 | Wild Basin | Trail | Adv(*Nov) | RMNP |
| 144 | Montgomery Pass | Trail | Adv | Cameron Pass |
| 69 | Onahu Creek | Trail | Adv | Grand Lake |
| 10 + | Glacier Gorge to Black Lake | Trail | Int/Adv | RMNP |
| 35 + | King Lake | Trail | Int/Adv | Eldora |
| 15 | Finch Lake and Pear Reservoir | Trail | Adv | RMNP |
| 2 + | Lake Helene and Odessa Lake | Trail | Adv(*Int) | RMNP |
| 128 + | Commando Run | Tr/Off Tr | Adv | Vail Pass |
| 149 | Michigan Cabins | Hut | Nov/Adv | Cameron Pass |
| 137 + | Shrine Mountain Inn | Hut | Nov/Adv | Vail Pass |
| 148 | Never Summer Nordic Yurts | Hut | Nov/Adv | Cameron Pass |

| No. | Tour Name | Type | Skill Level | Location |
|---|---|---|---|---|
| 40 | Tennessee Mountain Cabin | Hut | Int | Eldora |
| 54 | Second Creek | Hut | Int(*Adv) | Berthoud |
| 56 | First Creek | Hut | Int | Berthoud |
| 134 + | Vance's Cabin | Hut | Int | Tennessee Pass |
| 147 | Agnes Cabin | Hut | Adv | Cameron Pass |
| 37 | Guinn Mountain (Arestua Hut) | Hut | Adv | Eldora |
| 135 + | Schuss–Zesiger Hut | Hut | Adv | Vail/Tennessee |
| 136 + | Fowler–Hilliard Hut | Hut | Adv | Vail/Tennessee |
| 126 | Shrine Bowl | Off Tr/Tele | Nov/Int | Vail Pass |
| 143 | West Summit Loop | Off Trail | Nov | Rabbit Ears |
| 129 + | Black Lakes Ridge | Off Tr/Tele | Nov(*Adv) | Vail Pass |
| 123 + | Corral Creek | Off Tr/Tele | Nov/Adv | Vail Pass |
| 142 | Walton Peak and Walton Mountain | Off Trail | Nov/Int | Rabbit Ears |
| 53 | Current Creek | Off Tr/Tele | Int(*Adv) | Berthoud |
| 52 + | Seven Mile Run | Off Trail | Adv | Berthoud |
| 102 + | Bald Mountain—"Baldy Bowl" | Off Tr/Tele | Int(*Adv) | Breckenridge |
| 83 | Herman Gulch | Off Trail | Int | Off I-70 |
| 78 | Scott Gomer Creek | Off Trail | Int(*Nov) | Guanella Pass |
| 41 | Forest Lakes | Off Trail | Int(*Nov) | East Portal |
| 42 + | Heart Lake and Rogers Pass Lake | Off Trail | Adv(*Nov) | East Portal |
| 86 | Tundra Run | Off Trail | Int/Adv | Loveland Pass |
| 131 + | Trail of the Tenth | Off Trail | Adv/Int | Tennessee Pass |
| 138 + | Rabbit Ears Peak | Off Tr/Tele | Int | Rabbit Ears |
| 55 | Second Creek to Winter Park | Off Trail | Adv/Int | Berthoud |
| 71 | Baker Gulch | Off Trail | Int(*Adv) | Grand Lake |
| 34 | Woodland Lake | Off Trail | Adv | Eldora |
| 125 + | Wilder Gulch to Wearyman Creek | Off Tr/Road | Adv(*Int) | Vail Pass |
| 141 + | Hogan Park | Off Trail | Int/Adv | Rabbit Ears |
| 50 | Jones Pass to Winter Park | Off Tr/Road | Int | Berthoud |
| 107 + | Beaver Ridge | Off Trail | Adv | Breckenridge |
| 139 | Fishhook Lake | Off Trail | Adv | Rabbit Ears |
| 33 | Devil's Thumb Lake | Off Trail | Int | Eldora |
| 95 | Montezuma to Breckenridge | Off Trail | Adv | Mont/Breck |
| 61 + | Bottle Peak Loop | Off Trail | Adv | Fraser |
| 124 | Vail Pass to Frisco | Off Trail | Adv | Vail Pass |
| 140 + | Long Park | Off Trail | Adv | Rabbit Ears |
| 39 | Rollins Pass | Off Trail | Adv | Eldora |
| 85 + | Loveland Pass Runs | Spring/W | Int/Adv | Loveland Pass |
| 108 | Northstar Mountain (13,350') | Spring/W | Int/Adv | Hoosier Pass |
| 9 | Andrews Glacier | Spring | Adv/Int | RMNP |
| 5 | Flattop Mountain Snowfields | Spring | Int(*Adv) | RMNP |
| 23 | Mount Audubon (13,223') | Spring | Int | Brainard |
| 27 | Pawnee Peak (12,860') | Spring | Adv(*Int) | Brainard |
| 46 + | James Peak (13,294') | Spring | Adv(*Int) | St Mary's |
| 100 | Mount Guyot (13,370') | Spring | Adv | Breckenridge |
| 77 | Squaretop Mountain (13,794') | Spring | Adv | Guanella Pass |
| 4 | Ptarmigan Point Snowfields | Spring | Adv | RMNP |
| 109 | Fletcher Mountain (13,951') | Spring | Adv | Breckenridge |
| 111 + | Quandary Peak—East Ridge (14,264') | Spring | Int/Adv | Hoosier Pass |

| No. | Tour Name | Type | Skill Level | Location |
|-----|-----------|------|-------------|----------|
| 87 | Grizzly Bowl | Spring | Adv | Loveland Pass |
| 81 | Grays and Torreys Peaks (14,270' & 14,267') | Spring | Adv | Off I-70 |
| 133 | Mount Elbert (14,431') | Spring | Adv | Leadville |
| 113 + | Crystal Peak (13,852') | Spring | Adv | Breckenridge |
| 101 + | Bald Mountain–"Baldy Chutes" (13,684') | Spring | Adv | Breckenridge |
| 84 | Hagar Mountain (13,195') | Spring | Adv | Off I-70 |
| 88 + | Dave's Wave | Spring | Adv | Loveland Pass |
| 60 | Byers Peak (12,804') | Spring | Adv | Fraser |
| 89 | Grizzly Peak (13,427') | Spring | Adv | Loveland Pass |
| 24 | Paiute Peak (13,088') | Spring | Adv(*Int) | Brainard |
| 25 + | Mount Toll (12,979') | Spring | Adv(*Int) | Brainard |
| 112 | Pacific Peak (13,950') | Spring | Adv | Breckenridge |
| 74 | Mount Evans (14,264') | Spring | Adv+ | Mt Evans |
| 1 + | Sundance Bowl | Spring | Adv+ | RMNP |
| 6 + | Tyndall Glacier | Spring | Adv+ | RMNP |
| 51 | Skyline Traverse | Spring | Adv | Berthoud |
| 90 | Loveland Pass Grays Pk Trav | Spring | Adv | Loveland Pass |
| 28 | Apache Peak (13,441') | Spring | Adv+(*Int) | Brainard |
| 110 + | Quandary Peak—S. Couloir (14,264') | Spring | Adv+ | Hoosier Pass |
| 82 + | Torreys Peak—N. Couloir (14,267') | Spring | Adv+ | Off I-70 |
| 118 + | Buffalo Mountain—N. Couloir (12,777') | Spring | Adv+ | Dillon |

# APPENDIX TWO

## SUGGESTED EQUIPMENT

### EQUIPMENT

skis/poles/boots
day pack (or large pack for
    overnight tours)
climbing skins
wax kit
headlamp
maps
compass
altimeter
shovel
probe pole

avalanche transceiver
ensolite pad/foam pad
bivouac sack
ground cloth
stove
sunglasses and goggles
sunscreen
first aid kit
water bottle
sleeping bag for overnighters

### CLOTHING

insulated parka/vest
windbreaker/mountain parka
windpants
knickers/pants
sweater
shirts

socks plus extras
long underwear tops and bottoms
mittens or gloves, overmitts, liners,
    with extras
hat, balaclava, scarf
gaiters or supergaiters
insulated booties or moccasins for cabins

### SURVIVAL/REPAIR KIT

space blanket
hot packs
mirror
candles
lighters plus waterproof matches
alpine cord
knife
spare binding bails and cables
spare baskets
diaper pins
high-energy snacks

duct tape
razor blades
screws
ski tips
steel wool
glue stick
sewing materials
wire
webbing
stove parts
paper and pens/pencils

# APPENDIX THREE

## EMERGENCY INFORMATION

As a first resort for any emergency, dial 911. Other specific emergency numbers are listed below.

| | |
|---|---|
| Allenspark (sheriff) | (303) 747-2538 |
| Bailey (sheriff) | (303) 838-HELP |
| Clear Creek County (sheriff) | (303) 571-5631 |
| Empire (sheriff) | (303) 569-3232 |
| Fraser (sheriff) | (303) 726-5666 |
| Georgetown (sheriff) | (303) 569-3232 |
| Gilpin County (sheriff) | (303) 572-0750 or 258-3956 |
| Grand Lake (sheriff) | (303) 627-8244 |
| Idaho Springs (sheriff) | (303) 569-3232 |

All other locations: dial 911

# APPENDIX FOUR

## NONEMERGENCY TRIP INFORMATION

### AVALANCHE INFORMATION

The Colorado Avalanche Information Center provides current information on mountain weather and avalanche conditions for all the Colorado mountains. The recordings are updated twice a day, seven days a week, and are accessible 24 hours per day from November into April.

| | |
|---|---|
| Colorado Avalanche Information Center | (303) 371-1080 |
| Denver/Boulder (recorded message) | (303) 236-9435 |
| Fort Collins (recorded message) | (303) 482-0457 |
| Colorado Springs (recorded message) | (303) 520-0020 |
| Dillon (recorded message) | (303) 468-5434 |
| Minturn/Vail/Leadville (recorded message) | (303) 827-5687 |

### AVALANCHE EDUCATION (IN COLORADO)

American Avalanche Institute     (307) 733-3315
P.O. Box 308
Wilson, WY 83014

International Alpine School—     (303) 494-4904
   Boulder Mountain Guides
San Juan Avalanche Seminar
P.O. Box 3037
Eldorado Springs, CO 80025

Colorado Outward Bound     (303) 837-0880
945 Pennsylvania St.
Denver, CO 80203

Summit County Search & Rescue
P.O. Box 1794
Breckenridge, CO 80424

Silverton Avalanche School
San Juan Mountain Search and Rescue
Silverton, CO 81433

In addition, some mountaineering stores, ski areas and parks and recreation departments offer short avalanche awareness courses.

## ROAD AND WEATHER CONDITIONS

National Weather Service               (303) 398-3964
Colorado Highway Patrol                (303) 639-1234
Mountain Roads                         (303) 639-1111
Boulder County Highway Dept.           (303) 441-3962

## SKI CONDITIONS

Cross-Country Ski Reports              (303) 573-SNOW
Colorado Ski Country Snow Report       (303) 837-9907

## MAPS

National Cartographic Information Center   (303) 236-5829
United States Geological Survey
507 National Center
Reston, VA 22092

United States Geological Survey        (303) 236-7477
Denver Federal Center
Lakewood, CO 80225

## MOUNTAIN CLUBS AND HUTS

Tenth Mountain Trail Association
    (TMTA) Reservations                (303) 925-5775
1280 Ute Avenue
Aspen, CO 81612

Colorado Mountain Club (Denver Group)  (303) 922-8315
2530 W. Alameda Ave.
Denver, CO 80219

Colorado Mountain Club (Boulder Group)  (303) 449-1135
1107 12th St.
Boulder, CO 80302

Colorado Mountain Club                      (303) 586-9411
    (Enos Mills Group—Estes Park)          (303) 586-3757

Never Summer Nordic (yurts)                 (303) 484-3903
P.O. Box 1254
Fort Collins, CO 80522

## FOREST SERVICE INFORMATION

Federal Center                              (303) 236-9431
Arapaho & Roosevelt National Forests        (303) 224-1274
    (Fort Collins)
Boulder                                     (303) 444-6001
Idaho Springs                               (303) 893-1474
Granby                                      (303) 887-3331
Silverthorne                                (303) 468-5400
Holy Cross                                  (303) 827-5715
Steamboat Springs                           (303) 879-1722

# APPENDIX FIVE

## CROSS-COUNTRY TOURING CENTERS

With recent innovations in equipment and techniques, cross-country skiing has become a distinct and separate sport from backcountry skiing. Cross-country skiing is characterized by set, groomed trails, comparatively moderate terrain, skating, gliding and double-poling techniques, competition, track fees, thin, light skis for maximum speed and sleek, stretchy outfits. Backcountry skiing has untracked glades, warm, functional clothing, versatile equipment, challenging terrain, freedom, adventure, telemark, parallel and classic diagonal techniques and occasional avalanche danger. The choice, or both options, is yours.

Touring centers provide perhaps the best novice introduction to both cross-country and backcountry skiing. Rental equipment and lessons are easily accessible and groomed trails allow carefree, no-hassle skiing, especially on days when avalanche hazard is a problem.

The following is a list of cross-country touring centers with maintained and groomed trails.

C Lazy U Ranch (located near Granby) (303) 887-3344
Copper Mountain Trak Cross-Country Center (303) 968-2882 ext. 6342, or (800) 458-8386
Devil's Thumb (located near Fraser and Winter Park) (303) 726-8231 or (303) 726-5564
Eldora Nordic Center (303) (located near Boulder) 258-7082 or (303) 440-8700
Frisco Nordic Trail System (303) 668-0866
Grand Lake Golf Course Touring Center (303) 627-3402
Great Divide Nordic Center (Breckenridge) (303) 453-6855
Idlewild (located near Winter Park) (303) 726-5564 or (303) 887-2806
Keystone Ski Touring Center (303) 468-4275
Latigo Ranch (located near Kremmling) (303) 724-3596 or (800) 227-9655
Peaceful Valley (located near Ward) (303) 440-9632
Ski Cooper Nordic Center (303) 486-3684
Silver Creek Nordic Center (located near Winter Park) (303) 887-3384
Snow Mountain Nordic Center (located near Fraser and Winter Park) (303) 887-2152
Steamboat Touring Center (303) 879-8180 or 879-0517
The Home Ranch Resort (located near Steamboat Springs) (800) 223-7094
Vail Cross-Country Ski Center (303) 476-5601
Vista Verde Guest and Ski Touring Ranch (located near Steamboat Springs) (303) 879-3858 or (800) 526-7433

# SUGGESTED READING

## AVALANCHE, WEATHER AND GEOLOGICAL INFORMATION

Armstrong, Betsy, and Knox Williams. *The Avalanche Book*. Golden: Fulcrum, 1986.

Chronic, John. *Roadside Geology of Colorado*. Missoula: Mountain Press Publishing Company, 1980.

Daffern, Tony. *Avalanche Safety for Climbers and Skiers*. Seattle: Cloud Cap Press, 1983.

Keen, Richard. *Skywatch: The Western Weather Guide*. Golden: Fulcrum, 1987.

LaChapelle, Edward R. *The ABC's of Avalanche Safety*. 2nd ed. Seattle: The Mountaineers, 1985.

Mutel, Cornelia Fleischer, and John Emerick. *Grassland to Glacier*. Boulder: Johnson Books, 1984.

## GENERAL SKIING INFORMATION AND INSTRUCTION

Barnett, Steve. *Crosscountry Downhill*. 3rd ed. Chester: Globe Pequot Press, 1987.

Bein, Vic. *Mountain Skiing*. Seattle: The Mountaineers, 1982.

Cliff, Peter. *Ski Mountaineering*. Seattle: Pacific Search Press, 1987.

Gillette, Edward F., and John Dotsal. *Cross Country Skiing*. 3rd ed. Seattle: The Mountaineers, 1988.

Kals, W.S. *Land Navigation Handbook: The Sierra Club Guide to Map and Compass*. San Francisco: Sierra Club Books, 1983.

Masia, Seth. *Ski Maintenance and Repair*. Chicago: Contemporary Books, Inc., 1987.

Parker, Paul. *Freeheel Skiing: The Secrets of Telemark and Parallel Skiing—in All Conditions*. Chelsea: Chelsea Green Publishing Company, 1988.

Peters, Ed, ed. *Mountaineering: The Freedom of the Hills*. Seattle: The Mountaineers, 1982.

Tejada-Flores, Lito. *Backcountry Skiing: The Sierra Club Guide to Skiing off the Beaten Tracks*. San Francisco: Sierra Club Books, 1981.

## ROUTE INFORMATION

Borneman, Walter, and Lyndon J. Lampert. *A Climbing Guide to Colorado's Fourteeners*. 2nd ed. Boulder: Pruett Publishing Company, 1988.

Ormes, Robert. *Guide to the Colorado Mountains*. 8th ed. Colorado Springs: Robert M. Ormes, 1986.

# AFTERWORD

The Colorado Mountain Club (CMC), founded in 1912, is pleased to endorse this publication, which complements the club's purpose and mission: "To unite the energy, interest and knowledge of students, explorers and lovers of the mountains of Colorado." The CMC is organized into 15 chapters with 7,000 members throughout the state. Members conduct more than 1,800 events annually in Colorado and other areas of the United States as well as overseas. These include hiking, backpacking, technical climbing, skiing, snowshoeing, canoeing and rafting, horse and bicycle trips, and trail building. The CMC offers many instructional courses and is a leading organization in conservation and environmental matters. Prospective members are encouraged to learn more about the club by contacting the CMC State Office at 2530 West Alameda Avenue, Denver, CO 80219; telephone (303) 922-8315.

# NOTES

# NOTES